IRIS

THE GARDENER'S HANDBOOK: A SERIES OF USEFUL BOOKS—VOLUME 2
DR. JOHN PHILIP BAUMGARDT, GENERAL EDITOR

Fritz Köhlein

Translated by
Mollie Comerford Peters

John Philip Baumgardt
Technical Editor

TIMBER PRESS
Portland, Oregon

Library of Congress Cataloging-in-Publication Data

Köhlein, Fritz.
    Iris.

    (The Gardener's handbook ; v. 2)
    Translation of: Iris.
    Bibliography: p.
    Includes index.
    1. Iris (Plant) I. Title. II. Series: Gardener's
handbook (Portland, Or.) ; v. 2.
SB413.I8K65 1987   635.9'3424   87-26724
ISBN 0-88192-049-5

German edition published 1981 by Eugen Ulmer GmbH & Co.
Wollgrasweg 41, 7000 Stuttgart 70 (Hohenheim), W. Germany

Translation © 1987 by Timber Press
2nd Printing 1989

ISBN 0-88192-049-5

Printed in Hong Kong

Timber Press
9999 S.W. Wilshire
Portland, Oregon 97225

Drawings by Marlene Gemke

Contents

6

Preface

I cannot deny that a lot of time has passed and not a few hurdles had to be overcome before this book was completed. It is with great relief that I come to write this preface, as the conclusion of this long and difficult task.

I am very grateful to the many people who have helped me. I would particularly like to thank Mr. Peter Werckmeister, one of the most knowledgeable growers of Iris, for his willingness to write the section of the book on hybridizing. He did not, unfortunately, live to see the completion of the book. I am also grateful to Hermann and Martel Hald, President and Director respectively of the Gesellschaft der Staudenfreunde, formerly the Deutsch-Iris-und Lilien-Gesellschaft. As an unknown amateur gardener I found such a friendly reception there that before long I became an iris enthusiast.

In gathering the material for this book, I received willing help from many different sources: from Frau Helene von Stein-Zeppelin of Laufen/Baden, whose life has been very closely connected with the iris; also from Dr. Tamberg of Berlin, Prof. Franz Kurzmann from Baden near Vienna, Herr Mathes of Gladbeck, Bruno Muller of Frankfurt a. M., and from many other iris lovers.

As always, I am grateful to my publisher Roland Ulmer, who kindly encouraged my plans and did such a beautiful job of bringing out this latest book. The working relationship I had with the men and women in that house can only be described as amicable.

As with my other books, my wife Annemarie gave her energetic assistance in its preparation, as did my sons Norbert and Gerald. I thank each of them.

The result is a gardening book about Iris, albeit botanically grounded. Differing usages and interpretations by horticulturists and botanists lead to disagreements, especially in regard to systematics and nomenclature. One cannot please everyone, neither the botanists nor the gardeners. However, this is not, perhaps, a really critical thing. I believe everyone will be able to find their way about with the use of the extensive index at the back of the book.

This work differs fundamentally from books previously published. The breeding of Iris is in great flux so any book dealing primarily with varieties of Tall Bearded Iris and the other extensively cultivated groups will be quickly outdated. For this reason, I have tried to present an overall view of this enormous field as well as clarify certain relationships so that the book would be useful for years to come. The leading hybrids and hybridizers change every year, but can be found in current catalogues from iris nurseries. In the fourth section, iris fanciers will find a wealth of information about iris varieties in tabular form.

In both writing and organizing this book, I tried to make it a help and joy to all those interested in Iris, for the botanist and the amateur gardener, the hybridizer or the landscape architect. The incomparable iris creates friendships all over the world. May this book contribute to cementing such friendships and to forming a few new ones.

Bindlach, Summer 1981   Fritz Köhlein

Dr. Peter Werckmeister

It is my privilege at this point to acknowl-
edge my co-author, Dr. Peter Werckmeister. Very few people have been so
associated with the iris as he has been on
all levels. He was first a scientist working
with many plant genera, though the iris
always remained his prime interest. His
principal contributions were in the fields
of germination, physiology, embryo culture, breeding and genetic questions of
iris, with an emphasis on species and section hybrids, analyses of blossom pigmentation, and tissue culture. A closely
related interest was the hybridizing of new
iris cultivars, often referred to in his
book.

He was a founding member of the
Deutsch Iris-Gesellschaft, which later
developed into the larger Gesellschaft der
Staudenfreunde. They published his *Catalogus Iridis,* which today serves as the basis
for work in the field of Iris the world over.
His publications, lectures and work as a
judge in iris competitions made him a true
pioneer leading the field.

Yet with all these activities, he always
found time to help those seriously interested in the study of iris. His contribution
to this book speaks for itself. The name of
Dr. Peter Werckmeister will always remain
synonymous with the genus *Iris.*

General Information

Iris the World Over

Iris are among the most fascinating of all plants, both in the wild and in the garden. Having appeared very early in the cloister gardens of Central Europe as "sword-lilies" or "flags", they are now grown the world over as favored ornamental plants. The description "orchids of the north" is no exaggeration for the enchanting, multicolored hybrids of the present day.

Though today in world-wide garden distribution, the genus *Iris* is in nature a plant of the Northern Hemisphere, and primarily the temperate zone. More than 200 species are known, plus many subspecies and varieties, natural hybrids and cultivars.

This large genus belongs to the plant family *Iridaceae,* with representative genera and species indigenous to every continent. Many of these are familiar to us as garden plants, such as the genus *Crocus,* which is native to the region around the Mediterranean Sea, or the Blackberry-lily, *Belamcanda,* which grows natively in China. But the members of this plant family are especially numerous in the Southern Hemisphere. Most familiar of all is the *Gladiolus,* one of the most popular cut flowers and a native of South Africa; *Ixia, Freesia* and *Sparaxis,* too, come from areas south of the equator.

But closer relatives of the iris that grow in the Southern Hemisphere are the genera *Dietes* and *Morea.* These are not widespread in Europe and North America because, in most cases, they are not hardy. They do, however, make ideal plants for cold frames and greenhouses. In the last century, these plants were frequently described as irises, which often led to mistakes and confusion.

In every respect iris show an enormous range of variations, and not just in the diverse color and form of their blossoms. Even the parts below the ground which are not visible vary greatly. Thus there are species with dense rootstocks, with rhizomes having tuberous, compressed roots that send out stolons, similar to *Dahlia* and *Hemerocallis.* Some have bulbs with thick, fleshy roots, and others tiny bulblets. The latter, the so-called Bulb Iris, were split off not very long ago and placed in their own genera, at least by some taxonomists.

There is also a tremendous variety in habitat requirements of iris. Germany's native Yellow Swamp Iris (*Iris pseudacorus*) usually grows in water, though it also grows in dry soils. The East Asian species, *Iris laevigata,* prospers only in swamps and marshes. On the other hand, there is the Oncocyclus Iris from the southern Near East, where summers are extremely dry. It will grow in the garden under similar conditions—too much summer moisture spells its death. Between these extremes lie all variations.

Of course, iris species are not equally distributed throughout the Northern Hemisphere. In some places only one species grows, elsewhere the habitats of several species overlap. In such a region, individual species may be separated by thousands of kilometers. On the other

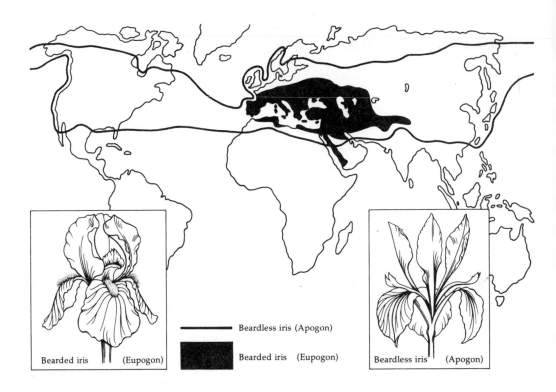

Bearded iris   (Eupogon)

———— Beardless iris (Apogon)

◼ Bearded iris   (Eupogon)

Beardless iris   (Apogon)

hand, there are those that are endemic, that is, occurring only in a very limited range, perhaps found only on a single mountain. In this book the reader will come across frequent references to individual species that occur naturally. If the particular climatic conditions can be duplicated in the garden, these naturally occurring species can be successfully grown far from their native habitat. Close attention to habitat and climate is the key to success. Actually any iris will grow in the garden, however sometimes only with the expenditure of much care and technical manipulations. Even then the result may not be a vigorous, hardy plant. The widespread occurrence of Beardless Iris (Apogon Iris) is particularly striking when the areas of natural distribution are observed more closely. In contrast to this, the wild forms and parent species of the

Tall Bearded Iris, the most popular garden iris, occur in a more limited region, from southern Europe and Southeast Asia, east to Kashmir, and south to the Arabian Peninsula. To be more precise, the Tall Bearded Iris is a cross between the hardiest species from Central Europe and the large-blossomed Near Eastern species. The species which have contributed to the formation of the beautiful Dwarf Iris occur in southern France, Austria, northern Italy, in the Balkans and in southern Russia. The genus *Xiphium* (Tall Bulb Iris) is indigenous to Spain, Portugal, Sicily and North Africa. The genus *Iridodictyum* (Dwarf Bulb Iris) grows further east, on the eastern shores of the Mediterranean and northeastward to the southern Soviet Union. Another Beardless Iris, the Spuria Iris, is a native to Central Europe and Southwest Asia. The Crested Iris, also

10

known as Evansia Iris, on the other hand, come from East Asia and the southeastern United States.

The triumphal procession of the iris through the gardens of the world only occurred in this century, the result of many advances in breeding. These were followed closely by the formal coming together of Iris enthusiasts, and by 1920 the A.I.S. (American Iris Society) had been founded in the U.S.A. Similar societies were also established in England, France, Germany, Italy, New Zealand, Switzerland, in South Africa and in Denmark.

A more peaceful invasion cannot be imagined; the multicolored ribbon encompasses the world, reminding us of the rainbow from the old saga, upon which the messenger of the gods, Iris, walked down to earth to bring man the message of peace.

For Beginners

Leaving aside the few non-hardy exceptions, iris belong to the group of blossoming, winter-hardy herbaceous plants. The popular, perennial hybrids of our gardens, and in many cases the wild-growing species too, have great ornamental value. The old names, "Flag" or "Sword-lily", are being superseded by the designation Iris.

Non-gardeners often associate the name *iris* only with the Dutch Iris (Hollandica hybrid Iris) found in florist shops, where they are sold in all seasons as "year-round iris", and whose popularity has increased in recent years. Even people who do garden sometimes think of iris or "flags" only as the Tall Bearded Iris still referred to in older gardening books. The old varieties go back to medieval hybrids which are, as geneticists call them, diploid. These robust iris, with their thick tangle of rhizomes, can be found in many gardens. They are pest and disease resistant, perennial, vigorous, and, one could even say, hard to kill.

By cross-breeding these with Near Eastern species, breeders have been able to create Bearded Iris with doubled pairs of chromosomes ("tetraploids"). These were intensively cross-bred and have, in turn, resulted in our modern, enchanting Tall Bearded Iris, officially known as Iris Barbarta-Elatior. It is unfortunate that, with this increase in beauty and elegance, vigor and hardiness have been decreased. This is partly due to the interbreeding of less hardy Near Eastern species and partly because, in the past, much of the work of breeding was done in climatically milder parts of the U.S. This means that today more care has to be taken regarding their location, soil requirements, etc.

Even 50 years ago Dwarf Iris were offered for sale through catalogues, incorrectly called "Iris pumila", even though hybrids were undoubtedly involved. Here too, a great assortment was created to enrich our gardens by breeders in Austria, Germany, England and especially in the United States.

Eventually Short Bearded Iris were crossed with Tall Bearded Iris to create medium-sized plants called Intermedia, or simply Median.

They say of iris that they have a relatively short blooming period, which in comparison to other blooming plants is true; on the other hand, very few other plants have blossoms that compare in beauty to that of the iris. Real iris lovers can, however, have iris blooming all year long and even the average gardener can enjoy masses of blooming iris in the garden for 15 weeks of the year—"from Carnival to the last song of the thrush in July," as Karl Foerster, who was a great authority on Iris, put it.

The Small Bulbous Iris are in bloom in

early spring. These are for sale in the fall, along with Tulips and Narcissus, very inexpensive, and requiring only minimal care. But here something must be said about Europe's Grass Iris, which grows in many gardens and is incorrectly called "Siberian Iris" (*Iris sibirica*). Its soil requirements are almost opposite to those of the Tall Bearded Iris. Native to damp meadows and lake shores, it needs somewhat damper conditions in the garden, too. Out of this same Central European treasure chest, breeding diligence and persistence have produced gorgeous species that can hardly be identified as *Iris sibirica* any more. From their small, narrow falls, large, broad horizontally held falls were created and their iridescence was increased as well.

These tips for novice Iris growers would not be complete without reference to another native European wild iris. Right now when water and marsh gardens are so popular, the Swamp Iris should not be overlooked. The Yellow Flag (*Iris pseudacorus*) grows wild in water and swampy areas, but does well in any normal, tolerably damp, garden soil.

The above mentioned Iris groups are the most important for the beginner to know about. They are, however, only a fraction of the many species and subspecies available to the iris specialist. Plants are classified into specific, systematically arranged units. Iris form the genus *Iris*. As dozens of species belong to this genus, they are, like many other comprehensive genera, divided and classified according to common characteristics. Such systematics often strike the beginner as incomprehensible, but it's like any other system of division, except the individual groups of this heirarchical classification have botanical names.

The beginner is also confronted with the botanical names of individual species. Unfortunately, this is a necessary evil. At a more advanced level, those interested in Iris realize that these botanical names are a great help in communicating, especially where different languages are involved. In Japan *Iris laevigata*, Rabbitear Iris, is the same as in the rest of the world. Moreover, many iris species have no common names whatsoever.

Much to many people's regret, some iris species have more than one botanical name, of which only one is correct, the others being synonymous designations. The beginner can be comforted in the fact that even specialists don't always know exactly which name is the right one. This complicated nomenclature (naming) is a science in itself. The comprehensive index to this book may help the beginner make his way through the labyrinth of names. If his interest in iris increases beyond the norm, he should familiarize himself with some of the more unusual iris species and their hybrids. Although an enormous number of iris are available on the market, there are still many that are very hard to come by; sometimes it is even impossible to get a desired species. This is not necessarily bad. Even stamp collecting would lose much of its appeal if every stamp could be purchased on the nearest street corner.

Many Iris species and cultivars not available in nurseries can be propagated from seed. The best way to get genuine seed is through the various seed exchange programs of iris societies (e.g. The American Iris Society and similar national organizations). Every year members receive extensive lists of seeds available, some very valuable. Sometimes botanical gardens can be helpful in obtaining rare seed. Working with iris is fascinating. Any gardener who hasn't tried it can only be

Iris in cultural history

Lily (=iris) of the Bourbons

Stylized iris from Minoan times

Contemporary iris depiction

marily for medicinal purposes. They were used against snake bite, as a remedy for stomach and intestinal ailments, and were even thought to have a palliative effect on mild coughs. Then, as sometimes even now, a piece of dried rhizome was put into a baby's mouth to alleviate teething pains.

In early times, iris were also gathered, and sometimes even cultivated, for their fragrance. In ancient Greece whole fields were planted with them. Expensive scented salves and other fragrant beauty products were made from the dried rhizomes. Small pieces of rhizome were also treated in various ways, dyed, and thrown into the embers of the fire so that a

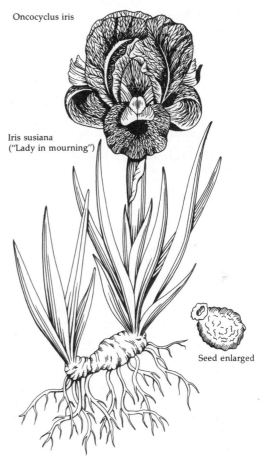

Oncocyclus iris

Iris susiana ("Lady in mourning")

Seed enlarged

encouraged to explore this wonderful world.

History of Small Iris Culture

Even in antiquity people were attracted to these fascinating plants, and particularly so in the regions around the Mediterranean Sea. The pharaohs of ancient Egypt were supposed to have cultivated *Iris susiana* or a similar species in their gardens. Iris also occurred on the island of Crete during the Minoan period, 2000 years before Christ. These beautiful plants with multicolored blossoms were given the name of the rainbow goddess, Iris, at the time of Theophrastes. The plant later called *Iris germanica* was known in Greece in classical times, and many dwarf iris species still grow wild there today.

Historically, the first reason people brought iris into their dwellings was not for their enchanting blossoms, but pri-

nen hoch treibet/tragen Blumen/so vber-
auß schön vnd hoch Königsfarb/fast wie
die Margaranten- oder Granatenblü-
he/doch ohne Geruch / vnnd weiln diese
zwo Plantê sehr hart fortzubringen/wañ
man auch gleich grosse Mühe vnd Fleiß
daran legt / hab ich mich derselben nie
groß geachtet.

Iris Susiana , schwartze Lilien oder J-
ris.

   Diese ist der schönsten vnnd realisten
Blumen eine auß allen / die da seyn mö-
gen/*ratione* jhrer Grösse/schönen / glei-
chen/wol *ordinirten* Blättern / durchge-
zognen Adern vnnd hoher Farb / die sich
auff liechtbraun/wie Silber gläntzend /
begibt/die vntenaußgewachsenen / vber-
worffnen Blätter aber kohlschwartz er-
scheinen.

   Ich habe zu Straßburg diese Lilien
vber Winter im Land stehen lassen / fleis-
sig zugedeckt/vnd auff den Früling Blüh
davon bekommen / so aber selten beschicht.

So man sie derowegen in etwas kal-
ten Landen fortbringen will / geschicht
die *transplantatio* folgender Gestalt :
man bekombt alsbald im Früling von
der Wurtzen ein Stuck / so etwan ein o-
der zwey Augen hat/ das aber abgebrochê
vnd nicht geschnitten werden muß / dann
es keine Waffen leidet/nimbt hernach ein
Erden/die zimlich mit gelben Leimen ver-
menget/ oder nimbt gemeine Erden von
einem Acker / mischet gelben Leim / klein
zerstossen / daß eines so viel als deß an-
dern/ darunter/ thut es in einen Scherben / vnnd setzet die Wurtzel drey zwerch-
finger tieff darein/vnd machet oben / mit
derselben Erden/den Scherben gar voll/
begeust es in der Wochen zweymal/ jedes
ein wenig/vnd ist gut/daß / ehe man die
Wurtzen setzet/vmb dieselbe/etwan eines
Fingers dick / pur lauter / feuchter Leim
gedruckt werde / dann derselbe sehr belie-
big solcher gestalt treibt sie den Sommer
durch schönes Kraut / setzet auch bey der
Wurtzen zu: Wann es nun anhcben will

Aus dem »Blumengarten« von Georgen Viescher, Nürnberg 1645

pleasant aroma filled the room. The Romans spiced their wine with them. And their mosaic floors were adorned with representations of Iris. Today we still use orris root, a violet-scented preparation of *Iris florentina* or *I. pallida* rhizomes.

At the time of Christ, iris—in this period we mean only Bearded Iris—grew all around the Mediterranean Sea and were cultivated in Egypt. Here, as in Rome, masses of flowers were used as decorations at extravagant banquets. Fresh blossoms were also said to have been added to wine.

As with other horticultural refinements and activities, little mention is made of the Iris for several centuries after the fall of the Roman Empire.

Around 840, Abbot Walahfried Strabo of Reichenau described the iris in his famous garden book *Hortulus,* and iris were being grown at this time in the monastery gardens of St. Gallen. Charlemagne recommended them to the administrators of the estates under his jurisdiction. An exact description exists from the 13th century by an Arabian physician Ibn-el-Beithar, who gives considerable praise

kalt zu werden/setzt man solche Scherben etwan Nachts in ein Kammer vnd deß Tages/wann der Reiffen fürüber/wider herauß/so lang/biß man sie gar in Keller setzen muß/da sie dann an ein solch Ort zu stellen/an welchem sie nahe bey der Thür/auff daß/wann man die Thür auffthut/sie frischen Lufft empfangen/vnd doch nit gefrieren möge/dann wann sie gar zu verdumpffen stehet / so wird das Kraut schwach vnd gelb. So bald nun der Winter fürüber/längst vmb den halben Febr. macht man im Garten in ein Land ein groß Loch in die Erden / also daß der Scherben/darinn die Lilien stehet/könne hineingesetzt werden/vnd bringet/wie oben gemeldet/mit Leim gemischte Erden darzu/schneidet mit einer Sege den Boden vom Scherben sittiglich hinweg/zerschlägt hernach auch auff den Seiten denselben ein wenig/daß er sich spaltet/setzet also solchen Scherben in die Gruben/da am Boden zuvor gemischte Erden einer zwerchen Hand dick geleget ist/füllet

auch neben her mit solcher Erden das Loch vest vnnd gantz auß / alsdann die Scherben gemach herauß gezogen / so treibet hernach solche Wurtzel selbigen Jahrs gewisse Blumen / welches sonst nit leichtlich beschicht. Wie aber oben gedacht/so muß man zusehen/daß das Graß oder Schoß/welches vorgehendes Jahr getrieben vnnd grün in den Keller kommen ist/fein grün erhalten vnd nicht gelb werde/hernach abfaule / dann sonsten muß die Wurtzel erst newes Kraut vnnd Schoß treiben/darmit verzehret sie jhre Krafft vnnd vergehet die natürliche Zeit/darinnen sie blühen solle.

Majorana hyemalis, Winter Majoran/ dieser gehöret in den Keller / weiln er nit Samen trägt/wird er / wie der Roßmarin / von Zweigelein fortgebracht.

Myrtus lati- & angustifolia, Myrten oder Myrtillen mit breiten vnnd schmalen Blättern.

Ruscus, Maußdorn.

Hyssopus montana, Klosterisop.

---

to the many positive properties of the Iris along with other herbal remedies.

By the Middle Ages, the inventory of iris in palace and castle gardens was extensive. The book *Hortus Eystettensis* (The Garden of Eichstatt) offers a good example. Although a bit of imagination has to be used with some of the illustrations in this famous book to figure out the right species from its picture and name, *Iris chamaeiris, I. sibirica, I. florentina, I. illyrica, I. susiana, I. germanica* types, *I. biflora, I. variegata, I. pseudacorus, I. foetidissima, I. anglica* (syn. *Xiphium latifolium*) and *I. hispanica* (syn. *Xiphium vulgare*) were already certainly being cultivated.

To this period, painters had only been interested in religious subjects. Now they discovered the flower and bouquets. Many artists, especially in Germany and Holland, began using iris in their paintings, sometimes as the subject matter, sometimes in the border; frequently they were combined in still-life paintings with other flowers having a completely different blooming period. But that was no doubt a part of artistic freedom, even then. A few are worth noting. The oldest record is a painting by Hugo van der Goes (ca. 1435–1482) depicting *Iris florentina* and a dark violet-blue *I. germanica* together with *Lilium* × *hollandicum* on an altarpiece. In a picture by Jan Brueghel the Elder (1568–1625), depicting a clay vase filled with a voluminous mixed bouquet, we can recognize as its centerpiece, next to a Madonna Lily, an indeterminate bluish iris. In a floral still life by Peter Binoit (1590–1632) painted in 1611, there is no doubt as to the species in the bouquet. They are *I. florentina* and *Xiphium latifolium* (*I. anglica*). In another painting by Jan Brueghel the Elder, *I. variegata* and *I. susiana* can be seen. Other pictures depict *I. sibirica* and *I. pseudacorus.* It is interesting to note the marked diversity of color which existed even then in *I. germanica.*

It is reported that in 1599 in England a man by the name of John Gerard had "bred" 16 different Iris in his garden. No cross-breeding was taking place at that time, of course, but where different species grew next to each other, natural hybrids occurred. If several species were planted together in a garden, new seedlings undoubtedly sprang up with new colors and patterns.

In 1645, one of the first practical gardening books, *Blumengarten* by Georgen Viescher of Nurnberg, was published. In it *Iris susiana* is the focal point of iris culture. This book is still of interest today (see pages 14–15).

But to return to art, iris were being pictorially represented not only in Europe, but in China and Japan as well. Japanese lacquer work is well known; however, it is not well known that the "Flags" represented in it were always *Iris kaempferi.* In the 18th century in Europe, very little was happening with iris, nor with other garden plants.

Iris were also used as floral emblems, even if quite stylized. Dante wrote that the ancient coat-of-arms of Florence was a white Iris on a red background. The "lily" of the Bourbons was not a lily at all, but an iris. In the Palace of Versailles, the iris is more frequently seen in the form of sculpture. Fine tapestries also showed both naturalistic and stylized irises. When painting on porcelain was in its heyday, the

Tall and short bearded iris.

Above: Display gardens give many garden owners their first impression of how to use iris. effectively in the garden. This is not always easy and combining them with other plants takes a bit of knack.
Below: The blooming period of many azaleas often coincides with dwarf iris varieties. But they have different requirements, azaleas prefer semi-shade and an acid soil, while dwarf iris like lime and full sun. However, with a little skill they can be beautifully combined, as the photograph with the dwarf iris 'Tonya' demonstrates.

lovely orchid-like blossoms of the iris were often used as models. During the Bieder-meyer period, a more mundane use for iris became the fashion. Lavender sprigs and dried iris rhizomes were slipped between layers of clean laundry in the closet to lend a fine and delicate fragrance to the cloth. During the Jugendstil period, and up to the First World War, iris were a very popular motif, especially in the wrought-iron work so much used at that time. Obviously modern painters have also made frequent use of the iris. A stamp from Paraguay, for instance, depicts a bouquet of "Sword Flags" by Vincent van Gogh.

This brings us to a special field. Among the millions of stamp collectors, more and more concentrate on a particular subject. Flower stamps are particularly popular, not a few of which depict various species of iris. It is even possible to make a small collection of a particular species. Really delightful ones are: *I. kaempferi* on a stamp from Ras al Khaima (Saudi Arabia), *I. mesopotamica* (Lebanon), *I. germanica* (San Marino), *I. cretensis* (Greece), *I. florentina* (Italy), *I. bungei* (Mongolia), *I. kaempferi* (U.S.S.R.), *I. sibirica* (Bulgaria), *I. pseuda-corus* (Czechoslovakia), *I. pumila*

(Romania), *I. hungarica* and *I. germanica* (Hungary), *I. sibirica* and *I. barbata* (Poland), *I. brandzae* (Romania) and *I. tingitana* on a stamp from Morocco. There are also *I. unguicularis* (Lebanon), *I. spuria* (Denmark), Iris-Hollandica hybrids (Afghanistan), *I. mariae, I. lortetii, I. haynei* and *I. nazarena* (Israel). The bulbous Iris (*Xiphium latifolium*) is found on a stamp from Andorra. *I. sisyrinchium*, also known as *Gynandriris sisyrinchium*, is on a stamp from Gibraltar, and the southern repre-sentative of the Iris, *Dietes grandiflora*, on one from South Africa. This is only a small sampling of the variety that exists. Almost all are small works of modern art, for behind the creation of any stamp lies the work of a painter or graphic artist.

Tourists will also come into contact with the history of iris culture, as many old structures bear iris motifs. Two are note-worthy. The iris in the Minoan culture has already been mentioned. But travelers to Crete will undoubtedly visit the Palace of Knosses, in which frescoes of iris, as well as lilies, were to be found. They can now be seen in the Museum of Heraklion. The pic-ture postcards call them all lilies, but they are probably stylized iris. These frescoes

Bearded iris varieties, tall and short.

Above: 'Path of Gold' is a relatively old dwarf iris cultivar that still maintains its value in the garden. It grows beautifully, especially along walls and rocks, shown in this photo among phlox.
Below left: 'Aprikosenprinzess', a German cul-tivar, is now one of the old veterans, but it can hold its own against any of the modern cultivars in flower production. Such older varieties should

be used as a mass of color in the background rather than for close-up viewing. Lupines, which bloom at the same time, make good companion plants.
Below right: The dwarf iris 'Stockhom' is a more recent cultivar that is highly recommended and will tolerate a damper, cooler location. Its real place is in the rock garden, as here among aubretia, alyssum and primroses.

were done during the Older Palace Period, which lasted from 2000–1700 B.C.

Dating from a much later period are the iris on the Taj Mahal in Agra, India. Shah Jahan had this world-famous structure erected after the death of his favorite wife in 1631. The rooms are decorated with stone inlay work. Among the motifs is *I. susiana*, called *I. chalcedonica* in the Middle Ages and also known as Lady in Mourning. The visitor cannot help but be filled with awe and respect by such works.

Before any significant breeding began, iris were gradually brought from the gardens of castles and monasteries into the gardens of landed noblemen and burghers. At the same time, therefore, they began to be bought and sold. *I. persica*, *I. susiana* and a dwarf iris were already being offered for sale in a catalogue by William Lucas, which appeared about 1677. The firm of Telford of Yorkshire, England, offered 25 different *English Bulbous Iris* (*Xiphium latifolium*) for sale as early as 1775, compared to which today's selection appears paltry. Along with *Iris florentina*, *I. susiana*, *I. persica* (syn. *Juno persica*) and *Gynandriris*, various species of "Spanish Iris" were also available. In addition, *I. sibirica* could be obtained through the catalogue of Flanagan and Nutting of London.

Manifestly the iris was an early, popular garden plant and was used as an ornamental motif. This remains so today. Iris motifs, whether naturalistic or stylized, can be found on everything from matchbook covers and curtains to silk scarves and calendars.

Contemporary artists have also made use of the iris. Notable among such works are the hand-colored engravings of K. H. Muller-Kollges of Oberschleichach in *Der Irisgarten*, a book of plates, which is constantly being added to.

This has been only a brief look at the history of iris in culture. The reader wishing to know more should search the literature and, while travelling seek the historical evidence still extant. There is much of interest to be learned in such pursuits.

The question then arises: when did the first conscious breeding of Sword Flags begin? It was around the beginning of the 19th century, the time when the iris began making its widespread appearance in the garden. More will be said of this in the following section.

A Look at the History of Cultivation

From Hybrid Sword Flags of the Middle Ages to the Modern Iris-Barbara-Eliator Hybrids

The secret of the origins of *Iris germanica* will probably never be fully explained. It is likely, however, that a hybrid, rather than a pure species, was involved. But just what species were used, *I. pallida*, *I. variegata*, *I. aphylla* or even Near Eastern diploids, is uncertain.

Many of these medieval hybrids, which later received species names, go back, in all probability, to a cross between *I. pallida* and *I. variegata*. Or were individual specimens brought from the Near East already as hybrids? No other plant is quite so well adapted to being dispersed by merchants and soldiers. A dormant rhizome could have travelled for weeks by camel caravan, or a crusader might have brought one back with him from the Near East. Planted in reasonably moist soil, a rhizome would soon leaf out again.

In any case, it is certain that the origins of this Sword Flag were not in Germany, as its name *Iris germanica*, given to it by Linnaeus in 1750, implies.

We know that a large number of the early specimens appeared further south, mainly in the regions where the natural incidence of *I. pallida* and *I. variegata* overlap. Thus such forms can be found on Lake Como (*I. kochii*) and in the southern Tyrol. Naturally, *I. germanica* types also grow wild further north, but they are probably volunteers from gardens. This surmise is also supported by their increased incidence around castles and palaces. Natural hybrids from regions where boundaries overlapped, as well as pure species, were taken and planted in gardens where further hybrids arose spontaneously because iris cross-breed so readily. Of these, the most robust specimens would become the first "garden escapees".

Generally speaking, the diploid *I. germanica* has to be regarded as an undefinably genetic conglomerate. The multiplicity of its forms and color variants increased. More than 350 years ago, Carolus Clusius had already described 28 different *I. germanica* types. He talked about culture from seed and other color variants derived from this practice. Of course, he was only referring to seed that had derived from insect pollination. An even more complete description was given a little later by Francois von Rawelingen in Dodanaeus's *Herbarium*. He described 19 different standards, 18 different falls, and 74 other variations in 9 other parts of the flower, stalk and rhizome. From this we can infer that an abundance of distinguishable iris were already extant. Many of them received botanical names, which led to confusion later on. But many of the old designations have remained of which examples exist today (*amoena, neglecta, plicata, squalens, sambucina*); at one time these descriptive terms were used as species names for various hybrid color patterns of *I. pallida*.

Up to the beginning of the 19th century, things were more or less left to chance. Then the second phase of Iris development began. Intensive and directed efforts were made to breed Iris from seed and to single out the best varieties. From 1800 to 1820, E. von Berg of Neukirchen (Mecklenburg-Strelitz) made important contributions. But the first center of iris breeding was in France, also in the early 19th century. De Bure had by 1830 several hundred varieties. As basic species and forms for his crossings he used, among others, *Iris pallida* variants which he refers to as "*I. plicata*", "*I. squalens*", "*I. sambucina*", and "*I. variegata*". His notes, which he published in 1837, are still available today. The chief royal gardener, H. A. Jacques, took over these varieties and used them for breeding and trading. (The cultivar 'Aura', which he bred, was for a long time considered one of the best yellow iris.) From the 1820's to the 1840's Jacques was one of France's most famous gardeners.

These iris drew the attention of Lemoine, of Paris-Belleville, from whom we have so many other hybrids (lilacs, peonies, etc.). He bred Jacques' Iris further and introduced almost a hundred cultivars in 1840, of which 'Mme Chereau', a *plicata*, was still on the market 80 years later and was photographed in an English garden as late as 1948. Among his seedlings was a dark purple iris, which he named after the man who had awakened in him the love of iris, 'Jacquesina'. This was a significant cultivar for many years.

Lemoine also published catalogues that were widely known. Through these, Louis Van Houtte in Gent, the brothers Verdier in Paris, and John Salter in England received bulbs and used Lemoine's cultivars as the basis for further breeding. After 1870, Peter Barr, Robert Parker, and Thomas Ware were making names for themselves in England and, somewhat later, around 1890, Amos Perry and George Reuthe. From 1865 on, the French firm of Vilmorin, Andrieux et Cie., was active in the business of iris breeding. Beginning about 1870, blossoms were hand-pollinated and systematically bred. This breeding program was still being undertaken with *Iris pallida* forms such as "*I. variegata*", "*I. amoena*", "*I. neglecta*", "*I. plicata*" and "*I. squalens*". In Barr's catalogue, hybrids were listed according to these divisions.

At this time German iris breeding resurfaced undertaken by the company of Goos & Koenemann. In 1885, after working for many years in well-known European nurseries, Max Joseph Goos purchased a small nursery in Niederwalluf am Rhein. In 1887, his friend August Koenemann became his partner and with that the later world-famous firm of Goos & Koenemann was founded. By the time August Koenemann died in 1910, the nursery grounds had grown to approximately 79 acres (32 hectares). The business was later run by Goos' son, Dr. Hermann Goos, after whose death in 1933 it was taken over by their chief horticulturalist Friedrich Buchner. This well known company existed up to World War II, but was not rebuilt after being destroyed.

Only 2 years after the company was founded, the Tall Bearded Iris 'Trautlieb' and various Dwarf Iris were introduced. Other Tall Bearded Iris hybrids continued to make their appearance, most of which took their names from old Germanic sagas or had some reference to the nearby Rhine River. In 1952, more than 40 varieties hybridized by the firm of Goos & Koenemann, were still being carried in a Germany nursery catalogue.

But to return to the beginning of the century, breeding of iris was also beginning to take place in the United States. It started with H. Farr, who imported all of Barr's varieties as basic material. Besides Farr, the Rev. C. S. Harrison was also breeding iris. He was later to influence the Sass brothers, who achieved great success in the field. Farr introduced his first varieties in 1909. Work was also being done in California, primarily by William Mohr, who introduced genes from species other than *I. pallida* into his crosses, and by S. B. Mitchell. Farr also imported German cultivars from Goos & Koenemann for interbreeding, e.g. 'Iriskönig', 'Loreley', 'Rheinnixe', and 'Frithjof'. He also imported many varieties from the English firm of W. J. Caparne.

The third phase in the history of Bearded Iris breeding began with the development of tetraploids. At the turn of the century, Sir Michael Foster received from missionaries various tetraploid hybrids from Asia Minor and the Near East: *Iris cypriana, I. mesopotamica, I. trojana* and the form *Iris* 'Amas'. He crossed them with existing forms and got, for example, from *I. cypriana* × *I. pallida* the cultivars 'Lady Foster', 'Caterina' and 'Shelford Chieftain'. Several American breeders based their work on 'Caterina'. After Sir Michael Foster's death, Robert Wallace introduced other cultivars, some of which had 50 or even 51 chromosomes. Vilmorin, Andrieux et Cie. also introduced similar cultivars in 1910, of which *I.* 'Alcazar', *I.* 'Orientflamme' and *I.* 'Tamerlan' are especially well known. The latter two were crosses between *I. macrantha* and *I. cypriana*.

Just before World War I, these large-blossomed cultivars reached America, where they were intensively interbred. The famous cultivars 'Queen Caterina', 'Lent A. Williamson' and 'Morning Splendor' resulted from this work.

Pentaploid varieties were also introduced, but they had little significance in the breeding world, as they were for the most part sterile. Even the War could not halt the work of hybridizing. W. R. Dykes, Sir Arthur Hort, and A. J. Bliss kept on working with this group of iris. In 1917, Bliss brought out his famous 'Dominion' (from 'Cordelia' × Iris macrantha). Since 'Cordelia' was a diploid, the cross with the tetraploid I. macrantha should have resulted in a triploid. But the tetraploid pollen combined with an unreduced egg cell of 'Cordelia', resulting in the tetraploid 'Dominion'. A similar thing happened when breeder Clara Rees crossed the diploid I. 'Thais' with the tetraploid iris I. 'Purissima' to produce I. 'Snow Flurry'. The latter has become one of the most important varieties for cross-breeding. An enormous number of today's iris have 'Snow Flurry' as one of their antecedents. From then on, iris breeding in the U.S. was on the upswing. In 1920, the American Iris Society was founded. Many of these hybridizers are still highly regarded today: Cook, Craig, Gibson, Fay, Plough, Muhlestein, Salbach, Tomkins and the Schreiner brothers, among others.

A French breeder working in the first half of this century did work which should not be forgotten: Cayeux. His frequently somber-colored cultivars have long since disappeared completely, but I still remember clearly a brilliant, golden-yellow diploid. It was one of the first Sword Flags in my own garden. It was called I. 'Pluie d'Or' and had an orange-colored beard that added a touch of brightness to the garden.

Just before World War II, Dr. Alexander Steffen was working with iris in Germany. He was a close friend of the Sass brothers in the United States. His cultivars can still be seen when thumbing through garden catalogues: I. 'Goldfackel', I. 'Grosse Zitrone', I. 'Pascha', I. 'Sankt Andreas', I. 'Schneeferner', I. 'Veilchenkonig', I. 'Weisses Segel', I. 'Hochspannung' and others, even if they have now been surpassed. Since 1930, Werner Dorn, who has an iris nursery in Aachen, has also been working with American Iris.

During the War and for a period afterwards, no one in Europe could consider breeding iris, since every square foot of ground was devoted to raising edible crops. But this was not so in the United States. The lead the U.S. breeders enjoyed was only increased by their ability to work almost without interruption through the war years and the post-war period.

The "pinks" were a completely new color line. I. 'Sea Shell' and I. 'Spindrift' opened this round. This new range of colors went from pure pink through shades of apricot to something approaching orange. Their creator was a man named Loomis. The red beards of these varieties have only increased their beauty. Cook's Progenita line, which came from the many new Amoena forms, took this color a step further.

As the post-war economy slowly recovered, people the world over could once again turn their thoughts to the beauties and ideals of this world. Iris fanciers and breeders joined in this revival. New iris societies were created and old ones reactivated. In addition to the American Iris Society (A.I.S.), which was founded in 1920, there was also the British Iris Society (B.I.S.), which had been active since 1922. Similar iris societies were established in the 1950s in New Zealand, Australia, France, Japan, South Africa,

Italy, Denmark and Switzerland. In Germany, gardeners, breeders and nurserymen joined together to form the "Deutsche Iris-Gesellschaft" in 1950 which changed into the "Deutsche Iris- und Lilien-Gesellschaft" in 1960. Today this active group is called the "Gesellschaft der Staudenfreunde", giving itself an even broader base.

After the war, German breeders were presented with an awesome task. Unfortunately, a large number of the American cultivars were unsuitable for growing in Germany because they had largely been bred and selected for warmer summer climates. Thus, many of these fine cultivars were suitable for wine-growing regions, but failed completely in areas with cool, wet summers. Werner Dorn from Aachen used *Iris croatica* as a breeding partner to produce hardier cultivars. Frau von Stein-Zeppelin first worked with diploids and later introduced seedlings under the name 'Zeppelin Auslese Rosa' (Zeppelin Select Pinks), which had attractive shades and were hardy. The greatest successes were achieved by Dr. Peter Werckmeister of Geisenheim and von Martin of Homburg am Main and Berchtesgaden. Their hybrids won international recognition and medals (Florence and Vienna). Of all the Werckmeister cultivars, 'Rosenquarz' became by far the best known. Others worth mentioning are *I.* 'Hermann Hesse', *I.* 'Goldene Acht', and *I.* 'Segelfalter'. Of Martin's cultivars should be made of: *I.* 'Fuchsjagd', *I.* 'Markgrafin Margarete von Kirchbach', *I.* 'Antiker Goldschmuck', *I.* 'Omas Sommerkleid', *I.* 'Krönungsmantel', *I.* 'Karin von Hugo,' and *I.* 'Hephaistos'.

No one of the younger generation should say what's all the fuss about. There are a lot better and more beautiful cultivars today! Without the often arduous groundwork of the breeders preceding them, today's hybrids would not have been possible. It also has to be looked at in relative terms: at that time, those varieties were as markedly more attractive relative to their predecessors as are the newest cultivars relative to the cultivars of the 1950's.

Breeders have recently been at work in countries where there is no tradition of iris breeding, particularly Dr. Milan Blazek in Czechoslovakia. In the Soviet Union there are new developments too, as illustrations on stamps show.

The breeding of Tall Bearded Iris proceeds apace, although some might have thought their limits had been reached. In my opinion, though, there is still much to be done. Only when the fascinating, modern Iris Barbata-Elatior group has attained the hardiness and vigor of the old diploids, can we speak of having reached a specific limit. But who knows? Perhaps in the process of getting there, totally new possibilities and prospects will arise which will give another new impetus to iris breeders.

The reader may rightly ask: what cultivars shall I plant? The purpose of this book is to inform the reader about long term developments. Hardly any area is in greater flux than the breeding of Iris Barbata-Elatior hybrids. Today's best cultivars will be surpassed in a few years and forgotten. Therefore, this book consciously refrains from burdening the main text with long lists of cultivars. Nonetheless, the reader should acquaint himself with the standard and some of the latest fine cultivars. Such recommendations appear at the back of the book in table form.

Median Iris and Similar Cultivars

Soon after the first Dwarf Iris hybrids appeared, the firm of Goos & Koenemann brought out the first "Interregnas". These are medium-sized iris that come from crosses between Dwarf Iris and Tall Bearded Iris. Even their blooming period lies somewhere between their parent cultivars which ensures a continuous blossoming of bearded iris. Among the best known cultivars of Goos & Koenemann are I. 'Walhalla', I. 'Halfdan', I. 'Ingeborg', I. 'Helga', I. 'Frithjof' and I. 'Gerda'. All of them have a chromosome count of 2n = 44. According to data then available, *Iris germanica* was crossed with *I. pumila*. What type or what variety of *I. germanica* is unknown. What we do know is that it was the hybrid form of *I. pumila*, known then under this name, and not the wild species. Shortly thereafter, the name Interregnas was changed to Intermedias, and today we speak of Median Iris or officially of Iris Barbata Median hybrids. American literature uses three epithets interchangeably for these: Median, Intermediate, and Table Iris. The British are beginning to use the same three terms.

For some time early in their development, this group stood on the sidelines of iris cultivation. Again, it was breeders in the U.S. who took a keen interest in them. They formed a separate Median Iris Society with the extremely active breeder Mrs. Bee Warburton. Because of the American division of bearded iris according to height, Median Iris are strictly defined: from 15–28" (41–70 cm). They are further characterized by their blooming period, which lies between the Dwarf Iris and the Tall Bearded Iris.

Old cultivars which appeared in catalogues over a long period should be briefly mentioned: I. 'Golden Bow', I. 'Sangreal', I. 'Snow Maiden', I. 'Red Orchid' and I. 'Autumn King'. Hertha van Nes, a German breeder, produced some very popular cultivars after the war, for example, I. 'Schwansee', I. 'Hilmteich', I. 'Jerry Rubin' and I. 'Gletscherspalte'. In international Dwarf Iris competition, a few German and Austrian breeders also achieved recognition, such as Werckmeister with I. 'Libellula', H. Hald with I. 'Intermezzo', E. Berlin with I. 'Valeska' and I. 'Ottonel', L. Denkewitz with I. 'Frechdachs' and I. 'Kolksee', F. Kurzmann with I. 'Donauweise' and S. Ziepke with 'Morgendammerung'.

There are two other groups of Iris developed in the U.S., which deserve a wider audience. The first is the Border Iris (Border Bearded). They might actually be called Tall Bearded Iris with shortened stems. Their height corresponds to that of the Median Iris, between 15–28" (41–70 cm). The size of their blossom is approximately that of the old diploid Bearded Iris cultivars, 4–5" (10–13 cm) in diameter. Their stems have to be strong and upright and the leaves shorter than the Tall Bearded Iris. For a long time these lower-growing types were not really appreciated, but now they have become very popular because they are particularly vigorous. Landscape gardeners have found them useful since they require less care than the Tall Bearded Iris.

The second group are the Cut Iris (Miniature Tall Bearded), which have also become known as Table Iris, because they were originally used as table decorations. Here too, the height division is the same (15–28" or 41–70 cm). Miniature Tall Bearded Iris are borne on thinner, more flexible stalks. The blossoms are smaller and should not, taking height and width together, exceed 6" (15 cm). Most of the hybrids bred along these lines were accidental. In America these are included with the Median Iris.

Let one thing be said. It is not always easy for the breeder to control his product exactly, especially when the size of a plant's blossom or its height lies near the border of another group. One handful of fertilizer may push a plant into another category.

History of Dwarf Iris Cultivation

It is possible that, in the past, one or another Dwarf Iris, whether pure species or natural hybrid, was grown in the garden. The actual beginnings of Dwarf Iris breeding are not so far behind us. Their cradle was in Germany at the Goos & Koenemann wholesale nursery in Niederwalluf. Unfortunately, the notes on the original breeding stock no longer exist, but we assume that *Iris chamaeiris* and *I. pumila* were involved.

In 1889, the cultivars *I.* 'Cyanea', *I.* 'Excelsa', *I.* 'Florida', *I.* 'Citrea' and *I.* 'Formosa', some of which are still common today, were introduced. These were followed in 1906 by *I.* 'Compacta', *I.* 'Floribunda' and *I.* 'Schneekuppe'. For decades these Dwarf Iris were sold under the incorrect name of "*Iris pumila*", even though this name correctly applies only to the species *Iris pumila* from the Balkans.

The cultivars *I.* 'Bouquet' and *I.* 'Sapphire' were brought out by the Caparne firm in England. A few more German hybrids from Junge in Hameln and from Kayser & Seibert in Rossdorf appeared at long intervals. There were also the cultivars *I.* 'Azurea' and *I.* 'Coerulea', apparent natural hybrids between *I. chaemeiris* and *I. pumila,* and the cultivars 'Fairy' (van Tubergen), 'Marocain' and 'Negus' (Milet, France). However, the total figure remained at about 3 dozen, all quite similar types.

Then for almost half a century, even in Germany, Dwarf Iris breeding "fell into a deep sleep". The European Dwarf Iris, especially German cultivars, were imported into the U.S. early in the 20th century. The breeders there immediately recognized the value of these lovely early bloomers. Above all, they wanted to breed more beautiful forms, purer colors and create a larger selection. However, since only the *I. chamaeiris* hybrids were available at the start, these early attempts were not destined to succeed. Around 1935, the course of this breeding was to receive an impetus in the person of Paul Cook. His cultivars 'Tampa' and 'Keepsake' were very popular, but they were crosses with *Iris arenaria*, the Sand Iris. A major step forward in the whole picture of Dwarf Iris breeding in the U.S.A. was found in getting away from *I. chamaeiris* as a breeding parent. H. M. Mill later carried on the work of Paul Cook.

Only when plants from seeds of the authentic southeastern European *Iris pumila* were available, was the spell broken. Breeding of Dwarf Iris began on a broader basis in the U.S. right after the Second World War. Paul Cook, and even moreso Walter Welch, created completely new types by crossing existing cultivars with species, primarily *I. pumila*.

Rapidly and with firm direction, iris in brilliant shades, with new patterns and types of blossoms appeared. The Austrian teacher and iris collector, Rudolf Hanselmayer, played a significant role in this American success story. He sent breeders in the U.S. many southeastern European and Austrian wild iris forms, and also some from around the Black Sea. In the 50's, the American botanist Fitz Randolf travelled through large areas of southeastern Europe, systematically collecting iris in their natural habitat, thus making further interesting foundation material available.

Most of the small iris from the U.S. on today's market are crosses between modern Tall Bearded Iris (TB) and forms of *Iris pumila* or advanced crossings of TB × *pumila* seedlings. Noteworthy is *I.* 'Lenna M', the first salmon-pink small iris by Earl Roberts.

After World War II, the interest in Dwarf Iris increased in Germany and Austria, along with the general interest in Iris cultivation. Frau Hertha van Nes was a very successful breeder, and many of her cultivars are common in gardens: *I.* 'Adria', *I.* 'Dunkler Tiger', *I.* 'Frühlingserwachen', *I.* 'Gräfin Clementine', *I.* 'Goldhammer', *I.* 'Mitternacht', *I.* 'Purpurmeer', *I.* 'Ragusa', *I.* 'Radegund', *I.* 'Rosenknospe', *I.* 'Rosenmund' and many others. In Graz, Rudolf Hanselmayer was also breeding some interesting cultivars (*I.* 'Laurin', *I.* 'Goldhaube', *I.* 'Eisdom', etc.). Werckmeister, too, created some vigorous cultivars (*I.* 'Gelbgrünchen', *I.* 'Quietschgelb', etc.), although his primary interest lay with Iris Barbata-Elaitor and Regeliocyclus Iris. Ekkard Berlin, a landscape architect from Biberach/Riss, took an early interest in Dwarf Iris and made several trips to Hungary, Rumania and Czechoslovakia to collect *Iris pumila* forms from their natural habitats. Exceptionally beautiful and resistant cultivars could be achieved by sowing and breeding on a large scale in the field (*I.* 'Allotria', *I.* 'Bonbonniere', *I.* 'Hallo', *I.* 'Bembes', *I.* 'Toskaner Prinz' and 'Blauburgund'). Siegfried Ziepke from Bensheim bred several cultivars, outstanding for their vigor (*I.* 'Pirola', *I.* 'Weisser Dreispitz' and especially *I.* 'Sonnenprinz'). For some time now Lothar Denkewitz has been successfully breeding Dwarf Iris (*I.* 'Alsterquelle', *I.* 'Karin', *I.* 'Karamell'). Fine cultivars were created by Hermann Hald (*I.* 'Träumerei', *I.* 'Ouvertüre') and Erich Zelina in Austria ('Wiener Traumnacht').

And there are undoubtedly many other people in Central Europe today breeding Dwarf Iris. In my own garden I developed a series of new iris that were resistant to late frosts as they came into blossom. Many new iris originated in Great Britain, where Mr. Taylor was particularly successful.

Now as before, the U.S.A. is introducing most of the new Dwarf Iris hybrids. All the successful breeders cannot be mentioned. Earl R. Roberts of Indianapolis, Indiana, certainly belongs high on the list, as well as Schreiner's Gardens, and Bee Warburton of Westboro, Connecticut. Those who have had the pleasure of meeting this successful iris breeder, will not easily forget her. She is the President of the Dwarf Iris Society and well known as the author of a book on iris.

Dwarf Iris breeding receives a great deal of impetus from the International Dwarf Iris competition in Vienna. This competition is inseparable from the work of Prof. Franz Kurzmann. These activities are discussed in the section on Iris Gardens, Competitions and Awards at the end of the first section.

Planting Iris

Planting Bearded Iris

A widespread misconception is that Bearded Iris are completely problem-free and will grow anywhere. This might have been true for some of the old diploids or for the pale yellow "Sword Flag" of peasant gardens (*Iris flavescens*), but is not true of the new tetraploid varieties.

Anyone who gardens wants beautiful plants in his garden and none that are stunted. Bearded Iris come from the steppe and, therefore, must be planted in as sunny a location as possible. Gentle, south-facing slopes and beds on the south side of the house or along a wall are ideal. Other plants should not be allowed to encroach on them. If they are planted between giant delphinium, for example, not much should be expected of them. Particularly some of the magnificent new hybrids from the U.S.A., and specifically those from temperate zones, will thrive only in sunnier climates. For those who live in cool summer climates and want to plant some of the newer iris, particular attention has to be paid to the correct location so that not a ray of sunshine is lost.

Preparation of the soil, especially in the less favorable climatic regions, should also be done exactingly. Iris rhizomes require a loose soil and will not tolerate any standing water. If garden soil is light, little effort will be needed, but the heavier the soil the more thoroughly the bed must be prepared. It should be loosened to about the depth of a spade's blade. Add coarse river sand or gravelly sand to clay soils, as well as a little coarse, brown peat. The soil pH should be slightly alkaline or at least neutral. Lime (ground carbonate of lime) is very cheap and will neutralize slightly acid soils, as will larger additions of peat.

The addition of compost is often recommended, an excellent practice if the compost is weed-free. But who has weed-free compost? It is best to mix nutrients directly into the soil in the form of an organic fertilizer with a high content of phosphorous and potash, such as blood meal, horn meal, or bone meal, Peruvian guano, and the like. Incorporate all this thorough-

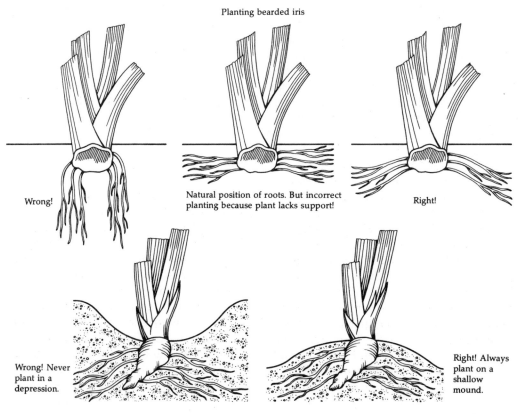

Planting bearded iris

Wrong!

Natural position of roots. But incorrect planting because plant lacks support!

Right!

Wrong! Never plant in a depression.

Right! Always plant on a shallow mound.

28

ly with a cultivator. Once the tilled and amended soil is loose and weed-free, the bed should be leveled with a rake. If larger areas are being planted, it is wise to set in a few stepping stones to facilitate later maintenance. These, of course, should be laid in sand so that even at the edge of the stones water will drain away quickly.

Today more and more cities no longer bury or burn their accumulated garbage and sewage, but are switching to processing or composting it. Such urban compost, has proved to be a good fertilizer for Bearded Iris.

There are a whole series of amendments which can be mixed with the soil to make it loose and well aerated. Fine, crumbled volcanic slag has proved to be excellent. So has crumbled, heat expanded clay (calcined clay), but do not use the clay pellets used in hydroculture. Styrofoam pellets loosen and warm up the soil quickly, but for aesthetic reasons they should not be used in the topmost layer. In very light soils, in which nutrients leach down to the lower strata quickly, the use of ground bentonite is recommended. It binds the soil particles and creates a slightly alkaline pH.

There are differing opinions on the correct method of planting iris. A rhizome simply stuck in well prepared earth won't die immediately, but here as with most things, careful and competent work pays off: the plant will grow more quickly and steadily. So in my opinion, the traditional methods are still the best and carry the least risk.

Dig a shallow hole and set the rhizome on a slightly raised mound in the center; spread the roots to either side, covering them with earth firmly pressed down. The roots should not hang down vertically as we normally see them; this inevitably leads to retarded growth with iris. On the other hand, the roots shouldn't lie flat, otherwise the plant has too little support and the first cat that comes wandering through will knock over the trimmed fan of leaves, uprooting the plant. The roots should not be pruned (an overly long or damaged root should, of course, be removed). The top of the rhizome should protrude just slightly above the soil line! Only if the soil is very light do newly set iris plants need to be thoroughly watered in; though summer plantings, during hot weather, benefit from one good soaking.

The correct planting time presents a small problem. Iris can be safely transplanted anytime. The question here is, what is the *best* time for planting. The new adventitious roots can be recognized as greenish-yellow protrusions beneath the fan, even when the plant is blooming. Almost immediately after the plant flowers, these new roots start to grow. This is a good time to divide and transplant iris. The old roots should not be removed, since they will support the plant until the new roots take over this function. In any case, plants should not be shipped at this time. This should be done no earlier than the end of July or beginning of August, when the adventitious roots are fully formed. Planting should be completed by October, much earlier where winter soil heaving is a problem. In the fall more small roots are usually forming and the iris goes into the winter well-anchored. If iris are planted too late, there is a risk of their being heaved out of the ground by winter frosts. Iris can also be planted in the spring, but blossom quality will suffer.

If a small cold frame is available, valuable new plants or very rare varieties should be precultivated in pots or containers. It is surprising just how quickly their roots fill these pots. They may then be set out with rootballs intact.

Because iris rhizomes have shallow root systems, do not hoe between clumps. Weeding should be done by hand, "the five-fingered spade," as Karl Foerster expressed it. If weeds are allowed to grow between rhizomes, it should come as no surprise to the gardener that rhizome rot soon appears, because the rhizomes simply can't mature properly.

A planting of Bearded Iris should look orderly and cared for, even after it has bloomed. If one does not plan to collect seeds for breeding, remove the flower stalk immediately after the last blossom has wilted. This is done by simply jerking it out. Frequently the leaves soon become

tilizers, such as horn meal, bone meal, or Peruvian guano, are best. Sterilized compost can also be mixed in with any of them and the mixture sprinkled between the rhizomes every spring. Completely rotted cattle manure is also good, just as it comes from the bag. Or it can, of course, be mixed with a commercial sewage compost. Apply fertilizer after the blooming period. Care should be exercised in using mineral fertilizers because the high nitrogen content commonly incorporated in these upsets the soluble nutrient balance of the soil and the plants become too succulent and susceptible to disease. Shortly before winter sets in, I always sprinkle some basic

Planting bearded iris after division

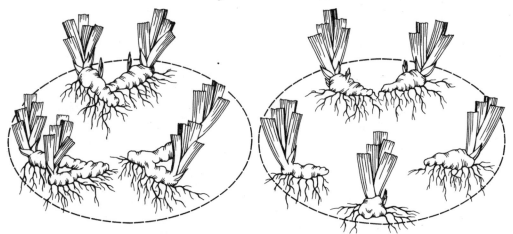

Double-fanned rhizomes in groups of three   Single-fanned rhizomes in groups of five

flecked with brown spots and some of the leaves wither. This is symptomatic of disease; preventative spraying can be done (see Iris Diseases). Established plantings (as well as newly set beds) ought to be tidied—weeded, faded leaves removed—two or three times prior to first frost. All dried foliage should be removed and brown-flecked leaf tips trimmed off.

The sumptuous Tall Bearded Iris cannot survive without fertilizer. Organic fer-

slag on the rhizomes. This addition of alkaline phosphate encourages the formation of blossoms and at the same time disinfects heavy soils, where rhizome rot starts easily. As a rule, light soils can take more fertilizer than heavy ones because nutrients leach away more quickly in porous soil.

A question often asked is how far apart should the rhizomes be planted? There is no single answer to this. Whether the ideal distance can be kept or not, usually depends on the space available. Those with a small garden will undoubtedly plant more closely in order to grow as many different varieties as possible, even if it means more work later. But 15–24" (40–60 cm) could be used as a general guide. It also depends on whether only one of a variety or several will be planted. Larger clumps will form more rapidly if 3 fans or 3 rhizomes with double fans are planted in a circle. Five fans in a circle will form clumps even more rapidly. In the latter case, these groupings usually will have to be thinned, or lifted and replanted after 3 years. Otherwise, thinning must only be done about every 5 years.

A word about rejuvenating old clumps is necessary. It is ideal if the old soil can be exchanged before being replanted. (Bearded Iris roots are not deep, so a layer of 6" (15 cm) should be sufficient.) At the minimum, the soil should be thoroughly turned and enriched with amendments and nutrients. The interval between transplanting can be extended somewhat by spading out the old center of the clump, thereby allowing the newer rhizomes to get some air again.

Though Bearded Iris are completely winter hardy, the rhizomes, which lie partly above ground, can be cracked by severe frosts, providing an easy entry for bacteria. This doesn't often happen, but a light sprinkling of sand covering the rhizomes will help. Any brown foliage and dead leaves that have blown into the clumps should be removed before winter sets in.

The same care and planting rules I have presented here, generally apply to Dwarf Iris, too, especially with regard to the requirement of sun, which if anything is even greater. It is especially important with the small irises, to guard against over-use of mineral or organic fertilizers with a high nitrogen content. On the other hand it is incorrect to assume, at least for hybrids, that they can get along without any care or fertilization. Really beautiful, profusely blooming, long-lasting Dwarf Iris can only be grown if something is done for them. Even if they don't quickly exhaust the soil (and this rate, by the way, is different for every variety), nutrients must be replaced from time to time, depending on the type and original fertility of the soil. Before Dwarf Iris bloom, a weak solution of a complete fertilizer may be applied as a drench.

A big mistake people make when they plant Dwarf Iris, is not giving enough attention to what is planted with them. The most important thing is to keep the iris clumps free of encroachment by neighboring plants. Cushion plants that spread rampantly and tall plants which throw shade should be kept at a distance. Single iris plants are more likely to be overrun by other nearby plants, so it is better to use large groupings of several iris varieties, then only the outer plants run the risk of being invaded. Vigorous plants can be used near iris, but they should not be allowed to come closer than 4" (10 cm), otherwise it becomes too much work to keep them back. *Campanula, Gentiana, Achillea,* dwarf *Artemisia, Thymus, Sempervivum* and slow-growing Sedums are suitable companion plants. Small, spring-blooming bulbs, such as *Crocus, Eranthis,* and *Galanthus,* are attractive in the foreground. But avoid *Muscari;* unfortunately, the foliage of the latter looks droopy just when the Dwarf Iris are in bloom.

A word to the wise about watering. The watering can should only be used on Tall Bearded and Median Iris when applying liquid fertilizer, otherwise neither it nor the hose have any business near them! Bearded Iris hold an ample supply of moisture and nutrients in their rhizomes. Even rhizomes which have been carried around in a suitcase for weeks, willingly begin growing again. Of course, gardeners in arid climates will need to irrigate their iris beds during prolonged summer droughts.

Planting Beardless Iris

Apogon Iris vary greatly in their requirements, but these can be looked up for each particular species. With few exceptions, however, they all have two requirements in common. They like a somewhat damp soil which is slightly acid to neutral. But as they say, no rule is without an exception. The winter-blooming iris of the series Unguicularis grow best in a slightly alkaline soil. All the other Apogon Iris are at their best in a soil with a pH of 6.5–6.9. Among these there are several which will tolerate a little lime, and others, lime-intolerant, that are extremely sensitive (*Iris verna, I. prismatica, I. gracilipes* and others in the series Californicae). The hardy, moisture-loving Apogon Iris are described in the section "Iris in the Water Garden"; all the others prefer moisture in the soil during the growing season. As long as wild forms are being used, most species show to best advantage in a natural setting, or in front of shrubs or conifers.

A common error is planting these Beardless Iris exactly like Bearded Iris rhizomes, with their tops showing above the soil line. This is absolutely incorrect and many Iris become stunted because of it. Spuria Iris are particularly sensitive to planting depth. About an inch of soil over the rhizomes is just right. After being planted, they should be well watered in, even if the soil is heavy. For most of these species, a sandy-clay soil with a high humus content is ideal. Tall Spuria Iris

grow best in clay soil, rich in nutrients. Further particulars can be found in the descriptions of individual species.

Planting Bulbous Iris

Like the Bearded Iris, all members of the genera *Iridodictyum, Xiphium* and *Juno* grow best in slightly alkaline soil. Moreover, the soil should be as porous as possible, well drained, drying on the surface quickly following each rain. The one exception is the English Iris (*Xiphium latifolium*), which requires quite a lot of moisture.

The ideal place to plant any of the small Bulbous Iris is in a rock garden, which should, of course, be in as sunny a location as possible. Depth of planting depends on the size of the bulb. The old planting rule is still applicable: about three times as deep as the bulb is tall.

Field mice and voles are, unfortunately, eager eaters of these little treasures. The best way to protect special rarities—which one would not want to lose in any case—is to make little baskets out of finely meshed chicken wire or hardware cloth, put the bulb in the basket and plant the whole thing. This will prevent rodents from gnawing their way to these precious morsels. Sprinkling the bulbs with red lead will also help temporarily, that is, for the first year after blooming. I repeat: *sprinkling*. There have been those who have diluted red lead with linseed oil and painted the bulbs with a brush before planting!

Small Bulbous Iris look especially attractive when planted in a natural setting, and contrariwise, somewhat ridiculous when arranged like soldiers standing in a row. An old gardener's trick has proven itself time and again. Take a handful of bulbs and make a fist. With the other hand, strike it from beneath, at the same

Iris for cold house culture (in winter +5 to +12 degrees C)

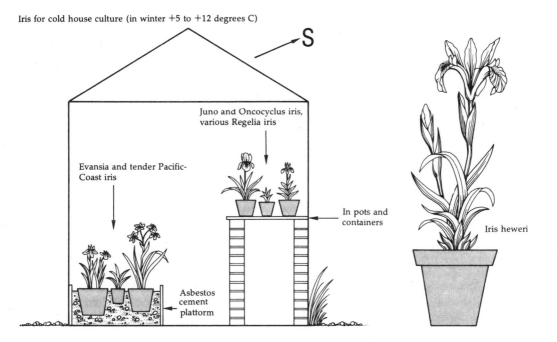

S

Juno and Oncocyclus iris, various Regelia iris

Evansia and tender Pacific-Coast iris

In pots and containers

Asbestos cement plattorm

Iris heweri

moment opening the hand to let the little bulbs go. Wherever they land, they are planted. The best place to plant them is as close to the house as possible. Then, when they start blooming in February, they can be viewed without having to wade through the mud.

The little Bulbous Iris species and cultivars are also suitable, of course, for planting in pots and bowls. Very rarely, especially in damp places, they will get Black Spot. If this happens, there is no way to save them and they must simply be thrown away.

Tall Bulbous Iris ("Spanish Iris", "Dutch Iris") make elegant cut flowers and can, therefore, be planted in a cut flower bed where the soil has been well worked. The bulbs are so inexpensive that it is best to throw them away after they have been cut, as they may not bloom the following year unless growing conditions are nearly perfect.

The All-purpose Iris

Iris Blossoms Year-round

One often hears I don't like iris because they don't bloom long enough! This may be true if we only take the individual blossom into consideration. But as Karl Foerster said: A concert is shorter still. So we should not look at the thing so one-sidedly, but rather think about how the blooming periods of the various iris groups relate to one another, and use this knowledge in planning a garden.

There are Tall Bearded Iris cultivars with blooming periods which significantly extend the normal season for this group. Another way of having flowers longer is to plant both early- and late-blooming varieties. The next step would be to combine Nana, Median and Elatior cultivars. The first Dwarf Iris blossoms usually appear in the last weeks of April.

Iris pseudacorus

These are replaced by the Media Iris, which merge into the blooming period of the Tall Bearded Iris. These flowers last well into the first week of June.

If iris from other sections are also planted, one can really speak of having iris the year-round. When the weather is favorable, the colorful, stippled dwarf Bulbous Iris *Iridodictyum histrio* var. *aintabensis* (in catalogues under Iris) will bloom in February. All through March and into late April, other small Bulbous Iris and Bulbous Iris hybrids follow one after the other. In mid-April the sequence is carried on by the tiny Pogon Iris. In some years there may be a short interlude of 8–14 days when no iris are in bloom. The lower-growing Bearded Iris start with *Iris pumila,* *I. pumila* var. *rozaliae* and with *I. attica.*

Iris for damp and dry garden situations.

Above: A symphony of color in late spring. The blooming period of grass iris (Iris sibirica) coincides with Japanese primroses (Primula japonica). Both need damp, slightly marshy sites to develop their full beauty, though Siberian iris thrive in average garden beds.
Below: Group of modern dwarf iris. It is true that each blossom lasts only for a relatively short time, but does this mean we should do without these charming dwarfs? Their palette of colors is more and more extensive. Easily identifiable in this picture are: 'Three Smokes' (center left), 'Lady' (above center, light blue) , 'Tonya' (above right), 'Gingerbread Man' (center, brown), 'Parinita' (center left, yellow with brown spot), 'Pink Amber' (below right).

Iris from other sections are, of course, also in bloom at the same time the various Bearded Iris are blooming. In mid-May the first *Iris sibirica, I. ensata,* various dwarf Spurias, *I. setosa* forms and Evansia Iris come into flower. June brings the greatest number of blooming iris species. We can't possibly name them all here, but they are listed in the descriptions of species iris.

Still blooming in July, at least in cooler climates, are the hybrids of the tall Spuria Iris, various Louisiana Iris and, of course, the lovely *Iris kaempferi* hybrids, which may continue to send up new stalks late into August. *I. laevigata* is also blooming again. *I. dichotoma,* a collector's plant that often only lasts for 2 years, is likewise blooming in July and August.

If prepared Dutch Iris have been purchased during spring bulb sales, kept cool (not cold), and planted late, they will be ready to cut in September. Prepared year-round iris are available to gardeners from the neighborhood greenhouse. In September and October some iris bloom again; I don't want to mention any particular variety because they are not that reliable, except for the remontant Bearded Iris cultivars. Every year a different species may surprise you. In my own garden, *Iris alberti* and *I. illyrica* reblossomed last year. In the U.S.A. breeders are working just to hybridize Tall Bearded Iris that bloom a second time; these are listed as "remontant" or "fall blooming" in catalogues.

In October *I. foetidissima* offers us, not blossoms, but a lovely ornament in the form of burst seed capsules brimming with striking red-orange seeds.

Beginning in November, owners of cold frames or those who employ pot culture can enjoy iris in bloom. From November into February, the species and varieties of winter iris (*Iris unguicularis*) blossom. I have tried growing them in pots, but it is a bit more trouble. Both *I. unguicularis,* a plant from the sparse oak forests of Algeria, and *I. lazica* from the Caucasus, have blossomed beautifully in a sunny basement window. In mild climates these bloom nicely outdoors, even through the snow. The link to the beginning of the new season is made by *Iridodictyum vartanii* 'Alba', which comes from Israel and is not too hardy. It is inexpensive, is cultivated in pots and blooms in December and January.

Many gardeners take their vacations in winter because they enjoy their gardens so much at other times of the year. On their travels they will unexpectedly run into occasional iris blooming. In the parks and gardens of the Mediterranean countries, *Iris unguicularis* is in bloom (as it is in England and Ireland) and *Juno alata* is blooming in the wild. Along the slopes of

Bearded iris plantings.

Above: Iris planting laid out naturally in the Botanical Gardens of Hof/S. am Theresienstein. In displays such as this, older cultivars are often more effective than modern tall bearded iris cultivars which are more rigid, suited to a stricter landscape architecture style.
Below: These tall bearded iris plants in the author's garden were not planted. They established themselves as seedlings between the dwarf iris. There are always usable seedlings among self-sown seed. The lily pond in the background is planted with Iris sibirica.

the Grand Canaries in February, one can see blooming *I. albicans* that have gone wild. On Crete and Rhodes it is *I. cretensis* (syn. *I. cretica*), in Lebanon, *Juno palaestina* and *Iridodictyum histrio*.

Iris flowers all year long. Blossoms can be had, as we have seen, if one absolutely wants it and is willing to do the work. But most of us really don't want that many iris. Variety is the spice of life, in gardens as well as with all other aspects. A person can be more than pleased and happy if he manages to have blooming iris in his garden for 5–6 months. Only the most rabid iris fanciers would aspire to more.

Iris in the Water Garden

Many non-gardeners automatically associate iris with water. Perhaps the sword-shaped leaves remind them of reeds and cattails and, from there, of ponds and river banks. Should one of these laymen, through unforeseen circumstances, such as buying a house, suddenly find himself becoming a "gardener", it often ends up a disaster. Tall Bearded Iris are stuck in damp, swampy soil and the outcome is that an often expensive rhizome becomes stunted and rots away. Because "the Iris"— and around the world, with the possible exception of Japan, this implies the Tall Bearded Iris—is and remains a flower from the sunny, well-drained steppes.

However that may be, many gardeners sooner or later express their wish for a water garden, whether only a small swamp-like area in the rock garden, or a large pond with water plants. So they inevitably become acquainted with some of the moisture-loving Iris species and hybrids.

Throughout the Northern Hemisphere, there are many wild Iris species that thrive in damp soils, along banks of lakes and rivers. Two of these can even stand in water constantly: *Iris laevigata* from the Far East and *I. pseudacorus*, our native Yellow Flag, which has in recent years taken over almost all the areas compatible to it in the Northern Hemisphere. Wherever it was not native, for instance in North America, it has become established in favorable sites such as ditches, as an uncultivated volunteer. Like all moisture-loving plants, water garden Iris are very vigorous and have few requirements. One exception is *Iris kaempferi*, the magnificent Japanese Iris, which will not grow where lime is in the soil. Various other species, too, take a slightly acid soil. *Iris setosa*, which occurs in the icy bogs of Siberia, the northern islands of Japan, Alaska and the Canadian lakes, is prone to chlorosis; in the case of the dwarf form from North America, this can even lead to the plant's death. Otherwise water garden iris are all healthy growers, so healthy in fact, that some of them have to be spaded back. Either that, or a collar has to be put around the whole plant to stop it from growing so rampantly. This is particularly advisable in the case of *Iris pseudacorus* forms, *I. versicolor*, *I. versicolor* var. *kermesain*, and *I. sibirica* (various varieties), which become rank in damp, rich soil along banks. All moisture-loving Iris have one thing in common: they grow best in full sun. Even a partially shaded place sharply decreases the blooming ability of *I. kaempferi* varieties.

a) True Aquatic Iris

The only iris that really always grows best when standing in water, or at least in water-saturated soil that never dries out, is *Iris laevigata*. This requirement can be somewhat modified for the hybrids between *I. laevigata* and *I. kaempferi*. The following forms and cultivars are particularly valuable:

I. laevigata 'Alba', pure white, a natural form

I. laevigata 'Monstrosa', a curious form

I. laevigata 'Variegata', during the entire growing season the foliage is striped with white; blossom bluish purple like the typical species or sometimes a little paler These Iris achieve their best development in water up to 8" (20 cm) deep.

b) Iris for Both Wet and Dry Areas

This is, of course, *Iris pseudacorus*, by nature a true swamp and aquatic plant. It grows in even deeper water than *I. laevigata*, developing best when planted 13–15" (35–40 cm) deep. Yet it will still survive in dry, parched soils. I first became acquainted with Iris through *I. pseudacorus*. My grandfather had brought some of these yellow Iris from a boggy pond at the edge of the city and planted them in a clay tub resting on a sandstone base. Usually nobody remembered to water them, so they were frequently quite parched. The foliage was naturally somewhat stunted, but the plants nonetheless blossomed profusely. This notwithstanding, *I. pseudacorus* is and remains a swamp and aquatic plant and only there do they develop completely. All forms and varieties are useful. The tetraploid hybrids of Eckard Berlin from Biberach are especially ornamental.

c) Iris for Damp Soils

Both *I. versicolor* and *I. versicolor* var. *kermesina* are almost as moisture insensitive as *I. pseudacorus*. However, they will only tolerate a water level which remains constant. Ideally they grow in a damp soil, though they will do reasonably well in drier situations. The pale violet forms are usually not very striking, so the forms with darker tones, as well as *I. versicolor* var. *kermesina*, with its beautiful reddish blossoms, are usually planted. Lovely pink forms and white ones with blue veins have recently been developed.

A species already mentioned, *I. setosa*, is commonly used in plantings near water. But only the taller, larger-blossomed forms are recommended. The dwarf forms only show to advantage in a rock garden.

I. virginica, and the more attractive, easier to grow *I. virginica* var. *shrevei*, also belong to this group, although it is not absolutely necessary to have them in the water garden as there are choicer Iris.

Another moisture-loving iris that does well is *I. sibirica*. None of this species, even the latest hybrids, has been so overbred that it can't be planted on the wet banks of a naturally arranged pool or bog. *I. sibirica* grows in normal garden soils as well as in damper situations. But it will get almost twice as big in the wetter location, which shows that it really does respond to a site resembling its natural habitat. But *I. sibirica* can also stand extreme wetness. I noticed this when I gave an acquaintance some seedlings. He planted them in a basin with their roots covered by 2–4" (5–10 cm) of water—and they did well. The most important cultivars are listed in the section on *I. sibirica* hybrids.

The spectacular Japanese iris, *I. kaempferi*, also belongs here. The opinion still prevails that *I. kaempferi*, like *I. laevigata*, belongs in water. Yet by nature it is a meadow plant. Japanese gardeners themselves have been partially responsible for this misunderstanding because, for aesthetic reasons, they flood *I. kaempferi* when it is in bloom; which this iris readily accepts, provided the site is drained through most of the year. There seems to be no agreement about its ideal habitat. Dr. Hirao (Japan), one of the greatest experts on this iris, advocates a normal soil; he even practices pot culture. For me *I.*

kaempferi cultivars grow best in the raised corner of my lily pond that is not covered by water. Since they are sensitive to lime, I lean toward the view that the more acid the soil, the drier conditions can be for *I. kaempferi*. Refer to the section on *Iris kaempferi* hybrids for more detailed information.

The following Iris succeed in damp soils and therefore are particularly well suited to damper sections along banks:

I. sanguinea
I. delavayi
I. chrysographes
I. clarkei
I. forrestii
I. wilsonii
I. bulleyana
Iris 'Charm of Finches' (a form of *I. bulleyana*)
All hybrids of the Chrysographes group
I. longipetala
I. missouriensis
I. fulva
I. brevicaulis
I. × fulvala (*I. fulva × I. brevicaulis*)
Iris 'Gerald Darby' (also suitable for growing in water)
The beautiful new cultivars of the Louisiana hybrids also belong here, though they are not hardy in colder climates. However, there may be one or two cultivars among them that will do well in warmer regions, despite the origins of many of the parent plants in the warm Mississippi Delta; but they should be given a try.

Iris for the container marsh garden
Iris fulva
Iris kaempferi (of gardens)
Iris laevigata
Iris pseudacorus
Iris sibirica

40

Tall Bearded Iris should also be considered for planting around the edge of a pond. The plants themselves don't have to come into direct contact with the wetness, and the heat retained by the stones along the edge will help them thrive. I can't think of anything in the way of form or aesthetics that would argue against using them in such an arrangement.

But back to the moisture-loving iris species and varieties. A bed along the banks of a pond should not be made too narrow; 2–3 ft wide would be minimum for an effective planting. If the garden soil is the usual sandy clay, an adequate amount of well-composted leaves or peat should be added to the planting soil, and well-rotted cattle manure or blood and bone meal serve as fertilizers. Sandier soils require more loam, clay soils an addition of coarse river sand. After that a little acidic, mineral fertilizer can be added from time to time.

Companion plants are important. Water lilies in the water itself, of course. Varieties that do well in relatively shallow water should be used, otherwise the sides of the pond have to be too steep. The following cultivars are both beautiful and vigorous:

Nymphaea 'Laydekeri Purpurata' grows in 6–8" (15–20 cm) of water
Nymphaea 'Marliacea Chromatella' grows in 9–11½" (25–30 cm) of water
Cattails (*Typha*) should be limited to dwarf species, if the iris are to remain the focal point of the planting. Mare's-tail (*Hippuris vulgaris*), Blue Bog-rush (*Juncus glaucus*) and Zebra Bulrush (*Scirpus tabernaemontani* 'Zebrinus') are good if the water is not too deep. There are many other fine companion plants; for further information refer to books on water plants (e.g. Karl Wachter, *The Water Garden,* Frances Perry, several water garden books).

I like to plant various species of Sweet Flag (Acorus) in with moisture-loving iris. Though their blossom is not particularly striking, the shape of their foliage goes well with iris. The variegated forms add a nice ornamental touch to marsh and water ponds. The following are available for combining with iris:

Acorus calamus	24–35" (60–90 cm)
Acorus calamus 'Variegatus'	24–28" (60–80 cm)
Acorus gramineus	8–12" (20–30 cm)
Acorus gramineus 'Aureovariegatus'	8–12" (20–30 cm)
Acorus gramineus 'Pusillus'	2–4" (5–10 cm)

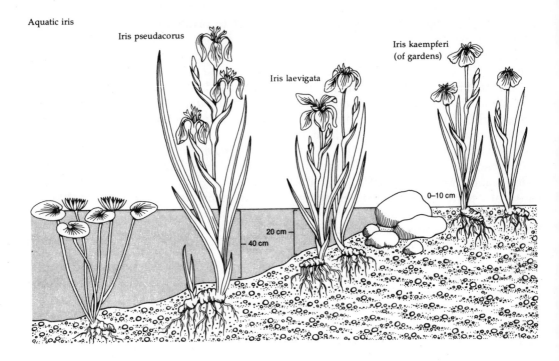

Aquatic iris

Iris pseudacorus

Iris laevigata

Iris kaempferi
(of gardens)

0–10 cm

20 cm

40 cm

One can really wallow in colors when it comes to bedding plants that go well with iris in a marsh or pond. It is unfortunate that they do not all bloom at the same time; the double yellow and the white Marsh Marigolds (*Caltha palustris* 'Plena' and *Caltha palustris* 'Alba'), the Rose Primroses (*Primula rosea*) with their lovely rose-pinks, the sky-blue Forget-Me-Nots (*Myosotis palustris* 'Thüringen') and the "queen of the swamp", the Amber Primrose (*Primula helodoxa*). There are many other flowers to plant with iris, but this should suffice for now.

Then there are all the companion plants that do well in damp soils, such as plantings along banks. The whole painter's palette of astilbes, Globe Flowers (*Trollius*) from ivory-yellow to orange-red, Candelabra Primroses in all shades, *Ligularia, Peltiphyllum,* etc. *Hemerocallis* can also be used in areas that are not too wet.

A word about fountains and statuary. Iris that grow directly in water are not as sensitive to moving water as, say, water-lilies, but they should not stand right in a moving stream either. There is no place in the landscape that can produce such enchanting scenes as a water garden, of whatever kind. The use of lighting will increase this effect still more. Illuminated by night, the blossoms of *Iris kaempferi* create a fanciful impression of geishas and Japanese temples.

The well-known iris specialist, Angela Marchant, published a selection of plants for a small, natural pond in 1968, which I thought was so good that it bears repeating here.

For planting in the water:
I. laevigata, all forms
I. pseudacorus var. *bastardii*
Iris 'Gerald Darby'

For the banks:

I. kaempferi 'Variegata'
I. sanguinea 'Snow Queen'
I. chrysographes 'Black Form'
I. chrysographes 'Rubellum'
I. forrestii
I. setosa var. *tricuspis* or
I. setosa var. *hondoensis*
I. setosa var. *canadensis*
I. longipetala

Natural plantings are enjoying a greater and greater popularity, and this applies to water gardens, too. Thus, more and more artificial "springs", using porous rock similar to that found in natural springs, are being used. A continuous water supply is not necessary. A hole is drilled through a granite boulder or a similar "found" stone, and an electric recirculating pump is installed from beneath. Water is held in a container underneath the "spring" stone, the container being made out of an asbestos-reinforced polyester material or strong polyethylene (e.g. mason's mixing trough would serve). This is covered with galvanized grating, which in turn is covered with more natural pebbles, gravel, or similar stone. The pump is regulated so that the water gently bubbles out, runs over the rocks and returns out of sight again into the pond. Only the water lost through evaporation has occasionally to be replaced. This is easily done with a hose or watering can; or a permanent water supply can be installed. Do-it-yourselfers can regulate the supply of water automatically by installing a float in the storage tank.

These natural-looking "oases" will enhance the appearance of almost any setting: at the edge of the obligatory lawn, in front of a shrubbery, between rhododendrons and conifers, next to a rock garden, and in similar intimate sites. Evaporation caused by the water bubbling over the rocks and from the pond water itself raises the humidity in the immediate area, as does the moisture content of the surrounding soil. So any of the Iris recommended for a damp embankment can be planted here and they will not only thrive, but will be stylistically pleasing as well. Medium-sized iris look best next to taller-growing varieties. The new dwarf Siberians, such as *I.* 'Weisschen' and *I.* 'Cambrita', bred by Dr. Tamberg, are especially good in this kind of setting.

The opportunity to combine early-blooming hemerocallis varieties with iris, such as *Hemerocallis minor* and *H. dumortieri*, should not be passed up. *Hosta* varieties, with their broad crowns of foliage, also go well with vertical-growing Grass Iris at these "springs". Since these groupings are supposed to look as natural as possible, forms with variegated leaves should not be used. Because of the wetness of the soil, plants can tolerate more sun than usual. This also applies to ferns, so some of the prettier ones can be used. Ornamental grasses and Candelabra Primroses complete the picture. There should be not limits to what imagination can do. The following plants can also be combined: *Trollius, Polygonum carneum, Polygonum bistorta* 'Superbum', *Caltha palustris* (double-yellow and white), *Myosotis palustris, Lysimachia nummularia* (yellow-leafed form), *Lythrum* and *Tradescantia*.

Iris for Rock Gardens and Alpine Settings
If there weren't such a thing as rock gardens, they would have to be invented for the host of dwarf Iris. For where else do these iris show to better advantage than here? Of course, level plantings, or even border plantings, can also be very attractive, but in such places Iris can only be viewed from above. On the other hand, in a diverse rock garden with small eleva-

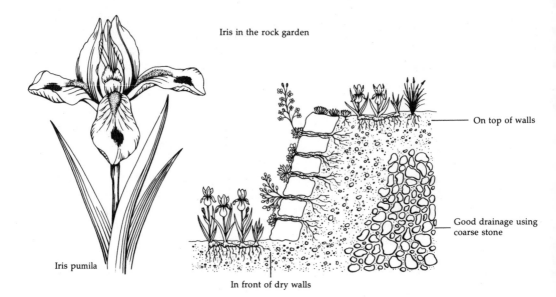

Iris in the rock garden

On top of walls

Good drainage using coarse stone

Iris pumila

In front of dry walls

tions, the charming dwarf Iris can be seen at eye level, if correctly planted.

Actually any iris can be used in such a setting, if they don't exceed a certain height, for even the most recently introduced dwarf Iris cannot hold their own against the high-bred impression made by Tall Bearded Iris. They are really appropriate in both types of gardens, the modern, natural-looking rock garden and the formal, stylized garden with its low walls, steps and geometric beds. I must, however, offer one warning: specially bred iris from the Iris Barbata Nana group should not be planted together with dwarf Pogon species. The latter, and their natural hybrids, usually cannot compete in form with the selectively bred iris. If they absolutely have to be together in the same rock garden, they should at least be planted far enough from each other to avoid any unfair competition.

The numbers of groups of iris suitable for rock gardens have now become so extensive that it is worthwhile concentrating on one group. One person may collect

Bulbous Iris, which are in full bloom in early spring; another specializes in small Pogon Iris with peak bloom from mid-April to mid-May. Another type of collection might be the beautiful hybrids of Iris Barbata Nana. Then there are the Juno Iris; however, seeds from the lesser known species are very difficult to come by and the bulbs almost impossible. There are the Beardless Iris, the Apogons, of which there are a whole series of dwarf species worth collecting. Not infrequently, gardeners will have a marshy area or a small pond in their rock gardens, in which case, of course, many of the species and varieties mentioned in the section "Iris and the Water Garden" can be used. This is just the right place for the slightly taller iris.

Another word about alpine gardens in the strict sense. This is the place for purely natural species and forms, not hybrids. Any of the dwarf plants that have pretty blossoms or attractive shapes and colors from the temperate zones of the Northern and Southern hemisphere, not just plants from the Alps, can be used here. Large alpine gardens, especially those in botanical gardens, are laid out according to geographic region. Thus, the small Iris would be together with plants from their native habitats. There are also a few alpine gardens which specialize only in plants from a specific region, e.g. the "Alpinium Julianum" in the Julian Alps in Slovinia (Yugoslavia). This collection includes *Iris illyrica*, *I. cengialti* and *I. pallida*, 3 closely related species with dry, membranous spathes, about which there is otherwise some confusion. In an alpine garden arranged according to geographic regions, local soil requirements for each group of plants have to be met if complete development is to be expected.

The following is a list of Iris for rock and alpine gardens.

Bulbous Iris
Iris from the Reticulata group (*Iridodictyum* according to Rodionenko) are, with few exceptions, all suitable. It would be superfluous to name them all (refer to "Iris Species" and "Small Bulbous Iris"). An exception is *Iridodictyum vartanii* 'Alba', which is frequently for sale, but is not hardy enough to plant outdoors in cool climates; it comes from Israel. The first five groups, below, include only *Iridodictyum* cultivars; because they are marketed as *Iris*, the Latin endings appropriate to that species are used. For example, Netted Iris is listed as *Iridodictyum reticulatum* or *Iris reticulata*.

The three most beautiful:
I. histrioides 'Major'
I. winogradowii
I. reticulatum 'Harmony'

Three reasonably priced iris:
I. reticulata
I. danfordiae
I. reticulatum 'Cantab'

Three early-bloomers:
I. histrio var. *aintabensis*
I. bakeriana
I. histrioides 'Major'

Three new hybrids and new introductions:
I. pamphylica
I. reticulatum 'Jeannine'
I. histrioides 'Katherine Hodgkin'

Three proven cultivars:
I. reticulatum 'Spring Time'
I. reticulatum 'Clairette'
I. reticulatum 'J. S. Dijt'

Dwarf Iris Species
All the lower-growing species are suitable. It's important that there be good drainage in the rock garden where the plants are to be placed and that the location receives full sun. I refer the reader again to the species list, as to enumerate them all again would be superfluous. There are so many, that specializing can be done here, too. The most important dwarf, *Iris pumila*, has so many local forms that making a small collection is worthwhile. There are species from many countries, in many colors, heights, forms and with various color patterns. The most beautiful and most vigorous ones are found among the Serbian *I. pumila*. A personal collection can also be made of *I. chamaeiris* and its natural forms, especially if one travels frequently and can collect seed and plants himself.

Three beautiful species:
Iris pumila (Serbian)
I. reichenbachii
I. variegata

Three recommended species:
Iris mellita
I. attica
I. arenaria (syn. *I. humilis* Georgi)

Three rare species:
Iris barthii (*I. pumila* form)
I. kamaonensis (*Pseudoregelia*)
I. bloudowii (*Regelia*)

Dwarf Bearded Iris Hybrids (Iris Barbata Nana)
After so many years when the only hybrids available were old ones such as 'Schnee-kuppe', 'Schwefelgeisir', 'Cyanea', 'Florida' and a few others, we now have many new hybrids to add to the list, though they still appear under the incorrect name of "*Iris pumila*". Some originate in the U.S., others in England, and more from Germany. Anyone wanting to collect them all would be hard pressed to acquire the land to accommodate them all. Besides, a rock garden should not be planted only in Iris Barbata Nana, so extra beds would be required. The variations in color are so unlimited that all kinds of combinations can be made. A list of cultivars will be found in the Appendices.

Juno Iris
These bulbs with fleshy roots are very attractive, with their blossoms emerging from the leaf axil. In a favorable location some of them will grow relatively tall. The following grow well and are the easiest to buy:
Juno bucharica
J. graeberiana
J. magnifica

Needing some protection:
Juno orchioides
J. willmottiana 'Alba'
J. aucheri (syn. *Iris sindjarensis*)

A few expensive hybrids, which are very tender but also very beautiful, are unfortunately almost impossible to obtain any more:

Iris cristata, Iris lacustris, Iris gracilipes, Iris verna, and Iris prismatica in partially shady, somewhat damp, neutral to slightly acid sites, with primroses, moss-type saxifragas, dwarf hostas and similar plants with the same cultural requirements.

Iris lacustris

Juno × *sindjareichii*
J. × *sindpers*
J. × *warlsind*

Dwarf Beardless Iris
A great many Dwarf Beardless Iris cultivars are suitable for the rock garden and for various other locations, not just for dry or sunny spots, but for damp or shaded to half-shaded ares of the rock garden, as well. *Iris ruthenica*, the Grass Iris from Siebenbürgen, is not particularly demanding, nor are the many dwarf Spurias, such as *I. pontica*, *I. graminea*, *I. sintenisii*, *I. urumovii*, and *I. pseudocyperus*. *I. minuto-aurea* from China is beautiful but rare, as are the various dwarfs of the Evansia group, such as *I. gracilipes* and *I. cristata* (slightly damp, half shade). *I. setosa* var. *arctica* grows best in moist, acidic soil. There are also *I. sibirica* species that stay fairly low and look well in a rock garden. The slender Grass Iris of the Chrysographes group fit into this part of the garden, especially *I. chrysographes* with its color variations, *I. forrestii* and its hybrids,

46

and *I. wilsonii*. Almost all the iris of the Californicae group can be used, as long as they are hardy enough, and, of course, the many named varieties and unnamed hybrids from them. For the avid collector we could mention many more, but let this suffice for now.

Iris may bloom in the rock garden from the end of February to the end of June. The individual species have an average blooming period of 10–14 days. But their needle-like, sword- or crescent-shaped leaves of delicate greenish yellow to dark blue-green, make them attractive even when they are not in flower. Nonetheless, the use of dwarf Iris should be kept proportionate to the other plants. The specially bred ones go particularly well with other colorful spring flowers, like *Aethionema*, Cushion Phlox, *Arabis*, sedums, and *Iberis*. Good companion plants with Bulbous Iris and Pogon species are the low-growing grasses, such as Sheep's Fescue, *Festuca ovina* cultivars F. 'Fruhlingsblau', F. 'Silberreiher' and F. 'Bergsilber'. The various species of *Sempervivum*, with their multicolored rosettes of leaves, or the encrusted *Saxifragas* make ideal partners. Finally, we have to remember that in a rock garden the placement of the rocks themselves is important. Attractive natural appearing stones can double the effect. Moreover, special Small Bearded Iris grow especially well on the south side of rocks.

Anyone who has assembled a collection of dwarf iris in a rock garden will rave about their beauty. Many people do what I do: first thing in the morning, before breakfast, I take a stroll through the rock garden to see what has opened since yesterday.

Iris in Stone Sinks and Tubs

Whereas relatively tall iris can be used in a rock garden—especially the Standard Dwarfs from the Bearded Iris hybrids and the taller, more slender Grass Iris next to rock garden bogs—stone sinks, tubs and other "portable gardens" are reserved only for the smallest dwarfs; some of the dwarfish Iris species and, the hybrids, the so-called Miniature Dwarfs, whose flower stalks do not exceed 8" (20 cm). These are the right plants for such situations, since their vigor is severely curtailed in containers and they won't outgrow their small plot overnight. The blossoms are small and dainty and begin opening very early, usually from the end of April to the beginning of May.

I. 'April Accent', *I.* 'Blue Beret', *I.* 'Bright White', *I.* 'Christine', *I.* 'Crispy', *I.* 'French Wine', *I.* 'Knick Knack', *I.* 'Lemon Puff', *I.* 'Little Sunbeam' and *I.* 'Three Cherries' are just a few of those available. And we mustn't forget the old *I.* 'Cyanea', which Goos & Koenemann introduced in 1899. Naturally there are an enormous number of new Miniature Iris hybrids. Their names can be found in the lists of the Dwarf Iris Competition in Vienna, which are printed in the back of this book.

But there is also a whole series of dwarf iris species which are suitable in such small areas; first and foremost, the genuine *Iris pumila* with its many forms, *I. attica*, *I. mellita* and similar species. The small-growing Low Iris (*I. humilis*) can be planted here too. In addition to Bearded Iris, other sections have something to offer, for instance *I. setosa* 'Dwarf Form', the tiny *I. lacustris* from the Evansia group and the not much larger *I. cristata*. The latter two, however, must have only half-sun and somewhat damper soil conditions. Attractive stone sink plantings can also be made in lightly shaded areas. Here small dwarf ferns can be used among *I. cristata* and *I. lacustris* (in larger containers *I. gracilipes* can also be used). There are many good ones, but *Athyrium filix-femina* 'Born-holmiense', a dwarf lady fern, is particularly noteworthy. Almost all the small Bulbous Iris (*Iridodictyum*) go well in such plantings.

There are, of course, many companion plants to go with iris in stone sinks and other containers. The best are those with flowers not their only attraction, but which also look well all year round. *Sempervivum* (Hen-and-Chicks or Common Houseleek), with its many species and varieties, makes an ideal partner since cultural requirements are almost the same. The small, slow-growing *Sedum* species belong here, too. Of the grasses, Dwarf Blue Sheep's Fescue (*Festuca valesiaca* 'Glaucantha') or Glacier Fescue (*Festuca glacialis*) are suitable, *Raoulia hookeri* (syn. *R. australis*) and *Raoulia lutescens*, the Raoulia species from New Zealand, form low-growing mats. All the encrusted species and varieties of *Saxifraga*, which remain dwarf, are also good accompaniments for container iris. Sinks and containers should usually be placed near the house, on or near the terrace. This way the early-blooming dwarf iris can always be easily covered by a layer of newspaper in the event of late frosts.

Having water in the garden in any form is becoming more and more popular. Barrel halves or large tubs made of concrete can be used to make a small natural-looking swamp. Many of the iris mentioned in the section "Iris in the Water Garden" are suitable for this purpose. Since these iris prefer a slightly acid soil, the walls of concrete containers should be coated with an indissoluble material (chlorinated rubber lacquer, plastic lacquer, epoxy-resin lacquer or polyurethane lacquer).

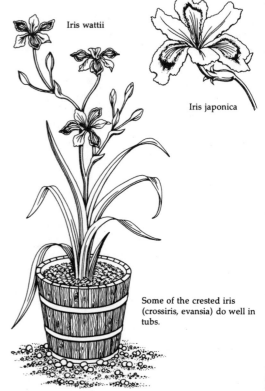

Iris wattii

Iris japonica

Some of the crested iris (crossiris, evansia) do well in tubs.

Dwarf iris in troughs and containers go well with Sempervivum and Sedum varieties.

48

Using Bearded Iris in the Garden Design

It is unfortunate that one sees Tall Bearded Iris in the garden all too seldom. One good reason for this is that they are somewhat difficult to work into the total garden design.

Severe, rectangular border hedges, which in earlier times were so popular, belong, at least in the private sector, to the past. Today's gardens are more informally laid out. And they are also less likely to be centered around specimen bushes, but rather combinations of shrubbery, perennials, and decorative non-plant elements.

However, if iris are wanted only for cutting, they should be planted, as in the past, in rectangular beds. Even strips along a walkway have their purpose, especially if beautiful, large-blossomed varieties are used. Hybrids should be looked at with this question in mind: are they going to be used more for background color or for close viewing? The former should be pure and luminous colors, so that even in the background, they add a brilliant splash of color. Such a dictum is also very important for parks and public gardens.

Whenever possible, iris varieties should be planted in masses rather than alone. The quantity depends, of course, on the size of the garden. In parks, 12 or more of each variety can be planted, whereas in small gardens 3 each can often be too many. In informal landscapes, 3 well coordinated colors are particularly effective. To look their best, these groupings should either stand out above low-growing plants or be placed at the upper edge of a gradually sloping embankment of small plants. In any case, Tall Bearded Iris should not be used between small plants. They can be combined with taller plants, in which case, one must provide sufficient spacing and a foreground that slopes forward. The focal point of many home gardens is a large lawn. Along its edge, usually between grass and pathway, iris can be very effectively used, even larger groupings of them. Bearded Iris of considerably differing heights (the Tall Bearded, Medians, and Dwarf Bearded) should not be mixed together in a planting, but grouped according to short, medium and tall, so each area blooms as a unit.

The blooming period for Tall Bearded Iris is limited. When they have finished blossoming, their beautifully-shaped, sword-like leaf structure still gives a decorative effect. They should be sprayed with a fungicide before and after blooming (don't forget the wetting agent), so that they do not develop leaf spot. They will retain their ornamental value into fall.

To avoid being without color in the garden for any length of time, groups of 3 varieties can be planted, leaving large spaces between these for low-growing summer annuals, again in groupings. The larger space for each of the annual groups, the more ornamental the planting. These "fillers" should have at least twice the area of their size available to them. In public gardens, where the arrangement is more strictly controlled, combinations of iris and summer annuals are also used, especially since much more space is usually available. Groups of iris by themselves can also be planted here. Light-colored iris blossoms show up particularly well against the dark background of a wooded copse. Combinations with fall-blooming ornamentals should also be considered.

It is also quite possible to have plantings in which Iris play only a minor role. There are any number of good companion plants and suitable combinations of them with Iris (see the following section).

Plantings With Iris

Granted, it is not that easy to place iris—especially Tall Bearded Iris and their tall hybrids—in just the right surroundings. It is preferable to lay out part of the garden with iris as the focal point, rather than to sprinkle a few here and there among a mixture of various plants and colors and hope that they fit in.

In newly planted gardens, 3–5 rhizomes per variety should be planted together. If the planting is not too narrowly laid out, 3 varieties of different colors should be combined: which makes a total of 9–15 rhizomes per garden feature. Obviously, this area should not be surrounded by tall plants. Even after blooming, the word is light, air and sun.

In a planting of this sort, for the foreground of the border lower-growing plants should be selected, although it must be remembered that iris leaves in mid-summer are not at their best. (Spray regularly with fungicide to prevent infections.) From time to time, brown leaves should be trimmed, but the garden owner should never feel like a slave. Dwarf Michaelmas Daisies, no more than 15–20″ (40–50 cm) tall, or similar plants, are ideal in front of groups of iris. They allow the Iris to get as much sun as they need and yet remain partially covered, so that the border gives an overall look of tidiness. Other low-growing plants include cushion-type chrysanthemums, Clove Pinks, Candytuft, the Santolinas, and *Stachys lanata.*

There are two choices available when looking for plants to accompany iris: those that bloom at the same time and those that bloom later.

There are very few spectacular, and at the same time colorful, plants that bloom simultaneously with iris: *Papaver orientale, Chrysanthemum coccineum* and peonies.

Some fabulous Turkish Poppy hybrids, which liven up any border planting at this time, are available. I would caution against planting them right next to iris, however. *Papaver orientale* fade quickly and as this happens, their untidy appearance detracts from the whole effect. *Chrysanthemum coccineum,* Painted Daisy, goes well with *Iris sibirica;* these, too, I would keep at a distance from Tall Bearded Iris, as they no longer look attractive after they blossom. Double peonies don't fit in as well stylistically, but the beautiful single forms make wonderful companions for iris. Some attractive and satisfying combinations can be made: white and blue iris with single pink peonies, yellow and blue iris with white peonies. Single yellow peonies are, unfortunately, still quite expensive. In selecting iris, clear, bright colors are preferable to *Plicatas* and other color mixes, which don't give the same dramatic effect. *Delphinium elatior,* tall delphinium, *Dicentra spectabilis,* Bleeding Heart, and *Aquilegia* hybrids, garden columbines also bloom with the Tall Bearded Iris.

The most important plant, of those not in bloom at the same time as iris, is the dwarf Michaelmas Daisy. Lower-growing chrysanthemum species are also recommended, e.g. C. 'Clara Curtis' (24″ or 60 cm), a single pink, or the low-growing pompon varieties, such as C. 'Roxy' or C. 'Altgold'. *Helenium* hybrids that are not too tall can be put in towards the back, e.g. *H.* 'Moerheim Beauty'. Only upright-growing plants should be placed right next to iris. *Hemerocallis* would be suitable if it didn't have such a mass of overhanging leaves. These can create too much shade in the summer for the iris rhizomes, preventing their proper development. All the Red-Hot-Poker plants (*Kniphofia*), with a range of colors constantly being broadened—there are even apple-green flowered varieties now—are suitable.

now—are suitable.

The whole question becomes much simpler if iris are to stand in the foreground of a planting. Areas planted with iris should be broken up by irregular drifts of low-growing plants. It is expedient to choose those plants that will thrive only on the natural rainfall, that is, those which do not have to be watered during the summer. Between groups of Iris, a mullein could poke up here and there, e.g. the stately white, felt-like *Verbascum bombyciferum* 'Polar Summer'; then there could be an island of bright yellow *Achillea* 'Coronation Gold', relieved by *Salvia nemorosa* 'Ostfriesland'. Canary-yellow *Potentilla recta* 'Warrenii', which can easily be grown in masses from seed, flowers tirelessly. There can never be enough grey and silver-grey among iris, such as low-growing *Artemisia* and all the varieties of *Festuca*. Species and cultivars of sedum, thyme and *Paronychia* are attractive; but the growth of creeping plants should be checked so they don't overrun the iris rhizomes. *Santolina chamaecyparissus,* the encrusted saxifrages, *Dianthus gratianopolitanus, Helianthemum* species, *Lavandula* and many more also fit in well.

All the lilies that tolerate sun are suitable, such as *L. lancifolium* (syn. *L. tigrinum*), *L. bulbiferum, L. davidii* var. *willmottiae* and the wealth of hybrids, e.g. *L.* 'Enchantment', *L.* 'Tabasco', *L.* 'Harmony' and many of the Aurelian hybrids, in any numbers will fill the space between iris that have long since faded. Today lilies have generally become common garden fare, and anyone who loves iris is very likely a fan of the noble lily.

Of ornamentals grown from bulbs, the many ornamental *Allium* species are noteworthy. They all go well with iris plantings and some of them even add a decorative note with their highly ornamental fruits.

Clumps of *Crocosmia* (Montbretia), especially *Crocosmia masonorum,* and, especially, the new Bressingham hybrids, are always effective. *Curtonus paniculatus* is an advance in both height and flower spectacle. The same applies to *Crocus,* either spring or fall blooming; the foliage yellows just at the right time, so that the rhizomes are not set back by being shaded. *Anemone nemorosa* cultivars are beautiful—though also frequently troublesome. Their foliage yellows as quickly as *Crocus.* But if you ever want to get rid of them completely, you have your work cut out for you. In my own garden I've twice dug it up and weeded it out, only to have a carpet of anemones appear again in the spring.

A word about the background for these plantings. The darker the effect, the better. Medium-tall groups of conifers, red Japanese maple, or perhaps just a garden wall are all good backgrounds.

The experts still cannot agree as to whether interspersing annuals is appropriate. I take the middle road. Use only plants that really go well with Iris and do not plant them too thickly. Any species selected should not require summer watering. *Lobularia maritima* var. *benthamii,* better known as Sweet Alyssum, just fills the bill. Seeds can be sown sparingly in place, lest the whole area be thickly covered with these cushions. The lowest-growing varieties are the best, e.g. *L.* 'Königsteppich', (2½" or 6 cm, deep violet), *L.* 'Rosie O'Day' (2½" or 6 cm, pink) and *L.* 'Carpet of Snow' (3" or 8 cm, white). Other annuals that can be sown between iris are California-poppies, not the tall variety, but one like *Eschscholzia caespitosa* 'Sundew', or the colorful *Portulaca, Nigella damascena* (Love-in-a-Mist), with their blue, white and old-rose colored cultivars can also be used, as well as *Nemophila. Dorotheanthus bellidiformis* (often still listed in catalogues as *Mesembryanthemum criniflorum*), or Fig-marigolds, are better planted as seedlings. An ideal flower for planting among iris is *Verbena peruviana*, which should be purchased as seedlings. They will form a large, long-lasting scarlet-red carpet, which will not become so thick as to damage the iris rhizomes. Both the large-blossomed *Dianthus c. heddewigii* (Pink) and the annual Baby's Breath (*Gypsophila elegans*) are suitable. If a larger space is available, a taller plant or two can be safely used, for instance the bizarre Spider Flower (*Cleome spinosa*), with new cultivars in improved violet and rose tones, as well as pure white. If iris are planted along a narrow strip against the house, annuals can also be interspersed. Annuals are a good complement to groups of iris at the corner of the patio, too.

Everything I have said so far applies not only to Tall Bearded Iris, but also, for the most part, to the somewhat earlier-blooming Median Iris. Of the plants blooming simultaneously with the latter, I should mention *Doronicum orientale*, Leopard's Bane, particularly the new compact cultivars. Late tulips also bloom at the same time, although I personally don't care for the combination of tulips and iris.

What does go well with Bearded Iris are—iris! It sounds a little strange, but Dutch Iris (Hollandica hybrids) are ideal for this. They can be planted among Bearded Iris in the fall, or even in the spring if temperature-treated bulbs are available. They cast almost no shadow on the Bearded Iris rhizomes, and when *Iris × hollandica* are finished blooming (2–3 weeks later for those planted out in the fall) they can be dug up and thrown on the compost heap, because in many regions they will not flower the following year

anyway and they are dirt cheap. Here too they should be planted in groups of solid colors rather than mixtures of colors. *Xiphium latifolium* (syn. *Iris xiphioides*), the English Iris, is often suggested for this kind of planting. But this is absolutely wrong! Granted, it is more of a perennial than the Hollandica hybrid Iris, but it is also the only Bulbous Iris that requires damp soil.

In conclusion, let us list a few more plants that go well with iris. One should use one's imagination and not be afraid to be a little daring: *Crocosmia masonorum*, *Scabiosa caucasica* (Scabiosa), *Artemisia* 'Silver Queen', *Aquilegia* (Columbine) in bright colors, *Asphodeline lutea* (Common Jacob'srod), *Linum narbonese* 'Heavenly Blue' (Flax), *Veronica spicata* ssp. *incana* (Speedwell), *Eremurus* (Desert Candle), *Heuchera* (Coral Bells), *Allium giganteum* (Giant Leek), *Armeria maritima* 'Alba' and *A.* 'Düsseldorfer Stolz' (Common Thrift). Ornamental grasses, include *Hystrix patula* (Bottle-brush Grass), *Stipa gigantea* (Giant Needlegrass), *Stipa barbata* (Bearded Needlegrass), *Molinia arundinacea* 'Fontane' and *Molinia arundinacea* 'Windspiel' (Moorgrass), and *Helictotrichon sempervirens* syn. *Avena sempervirens*.

Iris in and around water.

Above: Iris in boggy pond, which was originally a wading pool for the children when they were young. At left a white-blossomed Iris kaempferi and right Iris laevigata 'Albopurpurea' with white, blue-violet spotted blossoms. Lower left at the edge of the pond, Iris laevigata 'Variegata' in the budding stage.
Below: Iris at the edge of a lily pond. The violet iris at the lower left is Iris setosa ssp. canadensis (Iris hookeri). Behind it cultivars of Iris sibirica. The cream white Iris pseudacorus 'E. Turnipseed' stands in the water. In the background, Hemerocallis minor. The daylilies begin to blossom at the peak of the iris bloom.

Iris for the Meadow Garden

Today's iris are far too cultivated looking to try to recreate a completely natural meadow landscape in the garden, but one can imitate certain natural patterns found there. A large area should be available if such a planting is to achieve its full effect. In any case, isolated taller clumps of plants should rise above low, carpet-like plantings, and iris may predominate.

There are two groups of iris that go well in this type of planting: the various sizes of Bearded Iris and hybrids of the true meadow iris, Spuria Iris. The Bearded Iris species are common in Pontic meadow regions, as are Spuria species, which come from the inner Anatolian steppes. So it is not out of character to use modern garden hybrids in such plantings. Both like full sun and a warm, summery dry period. In the U.S., *Iris missouriensis* clumps stand in sunny, damp meadows, especially where winters are harsh; farther south *I. fulva*, the Louisiana Iris, takes its place.

Intersectional crosses.

Above: 'Fair Colleen' is a Calsibe (Californicae × Sibiricae). The delicate appearing blossom belies the plant's vigor and resistance. It thrives in eastern Bavaria.
Bottom left: The brownish 'Holden Clough' comes from a cross between Iris chrysographes and Iris pseudacorus and is a rewarding complement to any bank planting. Shown here with the more recent, white bordered Iris sibirica cultivar 'Silver Edge' in the foreground.
Bottom right: Iris 'Gerald Darby'. Its origin is not fully known, apparently it has Iris virginica as one parent or is a special form of it. In all respects an elegant, perennial garden iris, stem and segments with a violet cast also make it decorative.

Either one of the groups of iris may be used, or both together. It must, however, be kept in mind that in a meadow planting, openness must prevail and not the tall plant groupings that break it up. Further, these tall groupings should not be planted evenly throughout, but rather as irregularly as possible. There should be a mass of plants, then a large open space, then a single clump of iris, and so on. No matter what, it is important to work from a basic plan and let further variation arise from the plantings themselves.

Aside from the various height differences of the groups of iris mentioned, there are also other basic differences. The rhizomes of the Bearded Iris lie on the surface, while those of the Spuria Iris have to be covered by at least 1 in., (5 cm.) of soil. Thus, the latter are really less sensitive to the surrounding lower-growing plants which spread over and shade the iris roots. On the other hand, rhizomes of Bearded Iris should never be covered, otherwise the rhizomes will not mature properly. There are two alternatives: either use low-growing, clumping plants, which do not spread much laterally, as ground-cover plantings, or keep the area around the iris free by trimming back any vigorous low-growing creepers or sprawlers. This is not that much work and can be done fairly easily with an edger.

The types of plants that can be combined with iris in a natural meadow setting are numerous. Ornamental fescues which also thrive on sun and dryness are very good as the low-growing plants. There are lots of choices, all varying somewhat in leaf color and height. Different varieties can be used together, not jumbled up, but planted as groupings next to each other. Shades from dark green to pale silver-grey are available. To name only a few: *Festuca cinerea*, *F. ovina* 'Blaufuchs' and the lowest-growing fescue, *F. valesiaca* 'Glaucantha'. These grassy areas remain compact and are therefore ideal around Bearded Iris. Some other low-growing plants that can be recommended because of their colors have to be kept away from the iris rhizomes once they are established. For example, Speedwell (*Veronica spicata* ssp. *incana*): spikes of willowy, violet flowers adorn the attractive silvery-white cushions. Pussy-toes (*Antennaria dioica*) are more delicate and less silvery and grow well in a very light soil. *Sedum album*, particularly the red-leafed variety 'Coral Carpet', forms a beautiful ground cover. Annuals such as Moss Rose (*Portulaca grandiflora*), lower-growing gazanias like *Gazania* 'Minister', or low-growing *Felicia* also are suitable.

If Bearded Iris are being used for tall groups, Dwarf Iris can be massed with carpets of *Festuca*. Standard Dwarfs rather than Miniature Dwarfs should be used. They are more robust and spreading and, as they produce more blossoms per stem, are on average more free-flowering.

As already suggested, taller, upright plantings should be used sparingly. Nor is it necessary that they all bloom at the same time. On the contrary, the meadow is more interesting when blooming periods vary, so that the display of flowers does not go off in a single salvo at the same time the iris are in flower. It is far more important that soil and light requirements of all companion plants be similar to those of the iris.

A few wild tulips are a nice prelude to the iris. I prefer the genuine species of the so-called botanical tulip, but the species hybrids make a better show (*Tulipa* Fosteriana hybrids, *Tulipa* Greigii hybrids, *Tulipa* Kaufmanniana hybrids).

There are other bulbs which bloom at the same time or later than iris and that fit into a meadow garden, such as various *Allium* species (Ornamental Leek), preferably the tallest possible forms, such as *Allium christophii, A. gigantum, A. jesdianum, A. stipitatum* and so on. If a few early blooming *Hemerocallis* species (Daylily) are put in, such as *Hemerocallis minor* and *H. dumortieri,* they make lovely companions for blue or violet Tall Bearded Iris. *Hemerocallis thunbergii* and *H. middendorffii* follow somewhat later.

Poker plants (*Kniphofia*), which are similar in habit and soil requirements, are a good combination with later blooming iris. The spectacularly-colored varieties, such as *Kniphofia* 'Royal Standard', 'Mars', 'Alcazar', 'Fyrverkeri', 'Red Brilliance', 'Scarlet Cap', and others, should be used. Less striking, but equally suited to the location is common Jacob'srod (*Asphodeline lutea*), with its tufts of narrow leaves and slender rocket-like stems which are covered over a long period with yellow, star-shaped blossoms. A more gracious counterpart would be superior cultivars of the perennial *Scabiosa*, Pincushion Flower.

Eremurus, the Desert Candle, is another plant that should not be overlooked as an early summer bloomer. All the wild species, such as *Eremurus robustus, E. himalaicus, E. elwesii,* and *E. stenophyllus* ssp. *stenophyllus* (syn. *E. bungei*), can be used, as well as all their beautiful hybrids. Individual groups of lilies (Asiatic hybrids), especially those with up-turned or lateral blossoms, also combine well. Tall "thistles" standing alone emphasize the nature of the meadow, thus we have the various *Eryngium* species, the Globe Thistle (e.g. *Echinops ritro* 'Veitch's Blue'), which does not get too massive, or the occasional Cotton-Thistle (*Onopordum*), standing alone.

I have already mentioned grasses, but only as plants for drifts. There are many which recommend themselves as single specimens, such as *Sorghastrum arenaceum* (syn. *Chrysopogon nutans*), Yellow Indian Grass; *Molinia arundinacea* 'Karl Foerster'; *M. arundinacea* 'Windspiel'; *M. caerulea* 'Heidebraut' and 'Moorhexe', the Moor Grasses. The feather-grasses also belong here, mainly *Stipa barbata*, Heron's Feather Grass. *Panicum virgatum* 'Rehbraun' (Switch Grass) forms compact clumps, and lastly I can not leave out Oat Grass (*Helictotrichon sempervirens,* syn. *Avena sempervirens*).

There are so many good companions for iris that one is tempted to plant as many species as possible in a small area. But the right effect is achieved only when the low-growing plants predominate, and among the taller plants, iris play the main role.

As far as the iris themselves are concerned, there are so many beautiful species to pick from that the choice is difficult. At least in the case of Bearded Iris, bicolors or multicolors should be avoided in any meadow planting; selfs of very vibrant colors give a much better impression. A selection can be made from the lists at the back of the book.

Iris in Pots

It could easily be said that iris are not plants for pot culture. But here, as elsewhere, there are exceptions. Iris are planted in pots when the risks of setting them out directly is too great, that is, when dealing with small quantities of rare iris species or new hybrids. Such plants are kept in their pots in a small greenhouse or cold frame until roots are well established and they can be planted out in their permanent location with a strong rootball.

Pot culture with small Bulbous Iris is very popular. It is an inexpensive pleasure because the little bulbs do not cost very much. A few of these small beauties are always included on the lists of fall bulb offerings. As soon as they have been received, they should be put into pots or small containers, 5 to a medium-sized pot (4 in.), more for larger containers, depending on bulb size. Sink the pots in the group and protect from heavy autumn rains. They should be mulched with peat, so that even if it gets extremely cold and soil is frozen, the pots can still be brought inside for forcing. The inside temperature should not exceed 45–50°F (8–10°C) otherwise the exercise will be a fiasco! Once the flowers open, a moderately warm room will prolong their bloom. A good place is between double casement windows, which many older houses still have. Unfortunately this can not be done with modern windows.

Forcing can begin around Christmas time; the later one begins, the better will be the results. If one wants to combine containers of various blooming plants, the potted bulbs can be plunged in container trays. Just before buds open, assemble the container plants combining iris with forced crocuses, *Primula vulgaris*, or other blooming plants that were forced in the greenhouse. Coarse peat, bulb fiber, or even pebbles serve to fill round the pots plunged in the window box or jardinier.

Almost all the species and varieties of the Reticulata group are suitable for pot culture. *Iridodictyum vartanii* 'Alba', which is more frequently sold as a forcing bulb, has to be potted because it comes from Israel and is not winter hardy. Among

Iris in pots

Pots with
Iridodictyum
histrioides 'Major'
and Primula vulgaris

others, I wish to mention in particular are *Iridodictyum histrio* var. *aintabensis*, *Iridodictyum histrioides* 'Major', and the cultivars 'Harmony', 'Springtime', 'Violet Beauty', 'Joyce' and 'Clairette' (always sold as *Iris*).

Vacationers to Italy occasionally bring back *Juno (Iris) planifolia* from Sicily. Since it is not very vigorous, pot culture is the only solution for those who wish to experience its beautiful blossom at least once more; it is simply not hardy enough for our cold climates. *Iris unguicularis*, a winter-blooming species common to the Mediterranean region, and its cultivars, also lack cold hardiness. With this iris, too, pot culture is recommended for those without a cold house or cold frame. A species from this subsection, *Iris lazica*, a native of the Caucasus and also not too hardy, bloomed quite unexpectedly in my sunny basement window one February. The same is true of *Iris japonica*. This enchanting iris always has to be planted either in a box with peat to avoid being damaged by frosts, or else grown in a large pot or container. Dr. Hirao reports from Japan that many of the magnificent *Iris kaempferi* are

Grow rare Juno iris in pots in the coldhouse

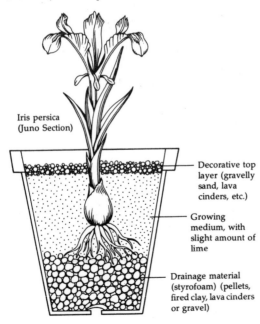

Iris persica
(Juno Section)

Decorative top layer (gravelly sand, lava cinders, etc.)

Growing medium, with slight amount of lime

Drainage material (styrofoam) (pellets, fired clay, lava cinders or gravel)

58

raised in pots there. It's surprising that such a robust plant grows and blossoms in a relatively small pot.

Finally, I must mention the small or Short Bearded Iris, many of which are not very vigorous and have to be cultivated in pots which is commonly done in England.

Despite these exceptions and special cases, iris are generally not plants for potting.

Iris as Cut Flowers

It is really inconceivable that iris are not used more as cut flowers. In looking at the many floral still lifes of the old masters, we are forced to conclude that iris were more popular as cut flowers then than they are now. Vases and jars of *Iris germanica, I. variegata, Xiphium vulgare* (syn. *I. xiphium*), *I. sibirica* and often even the Lady in Mourning, *I. susiana,* are frequently portrayed in old paintings.

What is the outlook today? Dutch Iris, mainly the standard blue variety 'Wedgewood', are for sale by the thousands in flower shops all year long. But what about Tall Bearded Iris?

The large-flowered stalks are obviously very difficult to transport in full bloom. In spite of the excellent substance of the new tetraploid hybrids, petals do get broken off or they arrive at their destination crushed or damaged. There is a very simple solution to this problem: the stems must be shipped while in bud. The ideal time is when the uppermost bud shows full color. The stalks should be packed in soft, absorbent paper (ten layers is usually enough) immediately after being cut; plastic wrap should never be used as it leads to decay. The iris can then be in transit without any further attention for 1–1½ days. When they arrive, the stems are trimmed and put in tepid water. At a temperature of 60–70°F (15–20°C), the uppermost bud should open fully within 24 hours.

Another objection one hears concerning iris as cut flowers is the short life of the blossoms. In defense, it must be said that individual Gladiolus blossoms do not last any longer, and modern, well-branched iris varieties have a large number of individual flowers per stem. A single stem will blossom for more than a week. If the beauty of the flower itself is taken into consideration, especially that of the latest hybrids, then no further argument can be raised against Tall Bearded Iris as cut flowers.

Wilted blossoms should be removed at once, of course, as blue and violet varieties will permanently stain a table cloth. The stems should also be trimmed frequently. I do not think much of the various chemical products on the market that are supposed to prolong blossoming. The best thing is a small piece of copper wire placed in the vase to retard the buildup of decay causing organisms (most penny coins can no longer be used as the core is made of iron so rusts when the edges are worn.)

What we have said about cutting Tall Bearded Iris applies to all the other iris species and varieties, which can, with few exceptions, also be used as cut flowers. If they are going to be transported, they also should be cut as buds. Dutch Iris, with their beautiful blossoms in all colors, have been, as we said, the most commercially successful. By using certain treatments, Dutch growers have been able to introduce the so-called "year-round iris" into the marketplace. It has been a boon to florists to be able to hold different varieties, notably the top sellers 'Wedgewood' and 'Prof. Blaauw', for 4–5 days in a cooler at 36°F. (2°C.), without detriment to the flowers. This process keeps the stalks fresh, whether they are put in water or not.

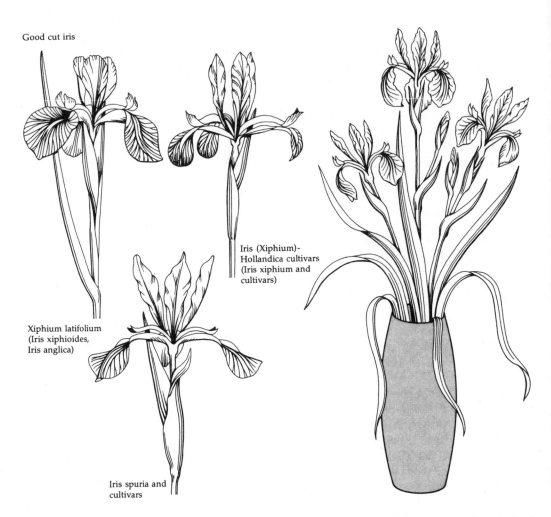

Good cut iris

Iris (Xiphium)-
Hollandica cultivars
(Iris xiphium and
cultivars)

Xiphium latifolium
(Iris xiphioides,
Iris anglica)

Iris spuria and
cultivars

If flowers in dry storage begin to droop, they can be quickly revived by placing them in water. The advantage of this process is that wholesale quantities of Hollandica hybrid Iris can be sold on the retail market over a longer period of time. After being treated, the flower will keep for about 5 days without any further attention.

Another important factor leading to the triumph of the Dutch Iris as a standard cut flower is its price. They can be inexpensively raised by the millions. We can purchase #2 bulbs in the fall, which bloom profusely, for a few cents a bulb. And wholesalers get them even more cheaply. Despite the cost of heating vast greenhouses, Dutch Iris remain an inexpensive cut flower.

There is a good future for Spuria Iris as cut flowers, now that more and more free-blooming varieties are becoming available. Its flowers are very similar to those of the Hollandica Iris, but its substance is even better, and the range of colors has been greatly expanded. However, their culture is completely different from that of Dutch Iris. Spurias grow naturally in open

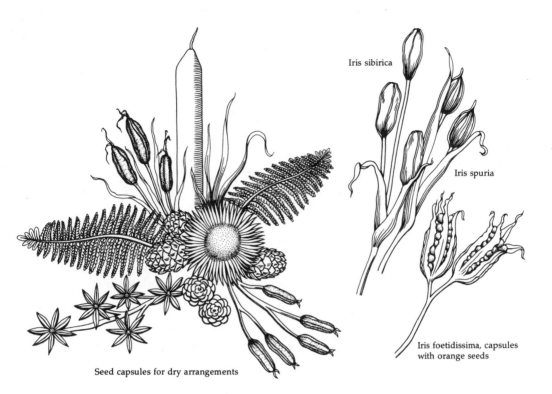

Iris sibirica

Iris spuria

Iris foetidissima, capsules with orange seeds

Seed capsules for dry arrangements

country and take a long time to develop. Old, established clumps, however, yield numerous stems for cutting. They bloom in July, just when cut flowers are plentiful. Whether they can be forced, possibly by using a portable greenhouse, is uncertain, so probably there will never be "year-round" Spurias. These beautiful and long-lasting cut flowers undoubtedly have a future, perhaps not so much in the commercial field, but all the more so in the hobbyist's garden, where everyone is his own cut-flower producer.

Iris sibirica is an important cut flower and will undoubtedly become even more so. Its new hybrids are more beautiful in form, are larger-blossomed, more vibrantly colored, and of better substance. When they are in bloom, they can be seen more frequently in florist shops than Tall Bearded Iris. The Japanese, American, and German hybrids of *Iris kaempferi,* with their sumptuous giant blossoms, last several days after being cut; moreover, they play an important role in the art of Ikebana.

We should call attention here to a new direction in Bearded Iris cultivation popular in the United States. These are the Table Iris—now called Miniature Tall Bearded Iris—which, as the name indicates, are meant for small vases and table decorations. They bloom abundantly and are free branching, derived from one of their antecedents, *Iris aphylla.*

I have not had much luck with the pretty *Iris japonica* 'Ledger's Variety', which is so often recommended as a cut flower, but which, for me, drops all its buds within 24 hours after being cut. *Iris graminea,* the small, so-called "plum-scented" iris, is enchanting in a small vase. One can smell it again and again and never tire of its

61

fragrance. Even in early spring, small Bulbous Iris are good cut flowers for small vases. The English Iris, *Xiphium latifolium*, also makes a good cut flower, even for commercial purposes, yet its importance is waning in the face of Dutch Iris. *Iris susiana*, an Oncocyclus iris, which is obtainable earlier than most others, makes an exotic and striking cut flower. As for the rest, we can only speak of "priceless" cut flowers, in that they are almost unobtainable and their culture is relatively complicated. I am reminded of a stalk of *Iris gatesii*, with its giant blossom, with enchanting stippling and streaking that is simply lost outside in the garden.

A few more tips about using cut iris indoors. Tall Bearded Iris blossoms look best in large vases or even floor vases and can be used alone or in combination with other flowers. Single peonies, for instance, are wonderful. If only the new yellow varieties weren't so terribly expensive! Lilacs also combine well with iris. Copper Beech leaves, which are still very red at the time iris are blooming, can be used to good effect. The many new hybrids of the Painted Daisy (*Chrysanthemum coccineum*) or Columbine *Aquilegia* make ideal partners for *Iris sibirica*, especially the white and yellow varieties. The various colors and shapes of *Hosta* foliage make a pretty addition.

Here, as elsewhere, there is no end to debate over taste and form. Some like masses of iris in huge vases and revel in a sea of colors, shapes, and fragrances. But more and more people prefer the spare style of Japanese flower arranging, which makes do with as little as possible—a shallow container, one or two stalks of iris, and a few other plant elements. It goes without saying that every horticulturalist, gardener, and iris fancier will have his own ideas of color, form, and style.

Iris are always the part of a bouquet that stretches out or reaches up. For this reason, great care should be taken in choosing and arranging the opposing horizontal elements. *Hosta* leaves (Plantain-lilies) are absolutely ideal and are available at this time of year in all sorts of colors and shapes: soft yellow, fresh green, bluish, variegated, with white or yellow edges, from almost lanceolate to ovate, or large heart-shaped leaves. New foliage sprays from woody plants can also be used, as can blooming ones such as the fragrant Dutchman's Pipe or False Jasmine (*Philadelphus*). Branches of the red-leafed Hazelnut offer a good contrast to yellow bearded iris. Combinations of iris and blooming azaleas can be captivating. Innumerable combinations are possible with filigreed ferns. *Allium* species also make a good play of opposites. The first lilies are often in flower when iris are blooming, and species lilies such as *Lilium monadelphum, L. szovitsianum, L. bulbiferum*, and a few others are almost always blooming at this time. Common Bleeding Heart (*Dicentra spectabilis*), either in its original pink form or with white hearts, is a good accompaniment for *Iris sibirica*. Great Solomon's Seal (*Polygonatum commutatum*) goes well with iris, as do a few bamboo shoots. Corkscrew Hazel is interesting, provided all the new leaves have been stripped off to allow the artistic form of the branches, with all their twists and turns, to appear.

Finally, one should not forget inanimate elements in creating iris bouquets. Artistically-shaped roots and pretty pieces of stone are favorites. But pieces of drift wood, old objects made of copper or other metals, such as an attractive lantern, can form the basis of an interesting iris arrangement. Even shells or broad, delicately shaped pieces of coral can be effective "extras", not to mention minerals or bird's feathers. Almost nothing should be rejected out of hand; almost any beautiful or interesting object can find a place in the right arrangement.

Iris Fragrance

It is a shame that fragrance in garden plants no longer plays the role it used to. The main thrust of hybridization was formerly for fragrant flowers. How did we almost lose sight of this goal? The main characteristics sought after in a new rose is an extravagant and flashy color—fragrance doesn't matter! Yet in times past, how flower fragrance was extolled!

In the case of iris, there are fragrant ones and those that have no odor. When and where the opportunity arises, fragrant irises should be used. There is an almost unbelievable range of aromatic nuances to choose from.

It begins in early spring with *Iridodictyum reticulatum* (syn. *Iris reticulata*); its fragrance is reminiscent of Sweet Violets under native hedges. Its yellow counterpart, *Iridodictyum danfordiae,* has a wonderful scent, something akin to the sweetness and richness of a honeycomb. The Junos are not to be left out either. *Juno bucharica* has an even more intense fragrance than *Iridodictyum reticulatum,* while *Juno aucheri* (syn. *Juno sindjarensis*) is reminiscent of almond trees in bloom. The genus *Xiphium,* Dutch Iris, while so colorful, is unfortunately almost all odorless, but the blue wild species has a pleasantly sweet fragrance. Many of the old Tall Bearded Iris species from peasant gardens are particularly notable for their pleasing fragrances. Some of their names make reference to this quality, such as the dull-colored "Elder Iris". *Iris pallida,* a Tall Bearded Iris of the southern Alps, has the synonymous designation *Iris odoratissima* and has, as its

name suggests, a pleasant fragrance. It is well known that *Iris florentina,* which is cultivated in fields, has not only a fragrant blossom, but the rhizome, too, marketed as orris root, smells like violets.

Bearded iris hybrids differ widely in their odors. Many of the newer varieties have a fine fragrance, but opinions vary about others. Strangely enough, even some iris fanciers refer to plants as "stinkers" if they have a somewhat stronger fragrance. I'd like to mention at least one dwarf species, *Iris humilis* (syn. *I. arenaria*), whose yellow flowers have a very sweet scent.

The blossoms of dwarf Spurias are often partially hidden by the foliage, but for their fragrance alone they should have a place in the rock garden. *Iris graminea* is rightly called the Plum-scented Iris. There could be no better description. When they bloom, a few blossoms should without fail be brought inside and put in a small vase. They really do smell like ripe plums on a sunny September day. The almost stemless *Iris pontica* (syn. *I. marschalliana, I. humilis* M. B.) has a similar odor. But there are also odorless clones. Among the Evansias, the Crested Iris, there are also those with nicely scented blossoms, e.g. the small *Iris cristata*.

There are many other fragrant species and cultivars. Anyone who wants can make his own expedition and discover differences. Sometimes the fragrance is similar to hyacinth, another time more like lilies or lily-of-the-valley. It's often necessary to get very close to the flower in order to discern the subtle differences.

Variegated Iris

Variegated shrubs and plants are not without controversy. There are a few specialists and gardeners, for instance, who reject them because they feel that the cause of this mottling is frequently a plant virus. But the majority of gardeners appreciate these natural deviations which enliven and break up the otherwise monotonous greenness that often prevails outside the blooming season.

Within the genus *Iris* there are a whole series of variegated species. This means that the sword-shaped leaves are more or less striped with white or a pale yellow, wherever chlorophyll is lacking. It's possible that such an iris will produce a completely pale fan of leaves. (But to try to vegetatively propagate this anomaly does not make any sense because an iris without any chlorophyll would not be viable.) The skillful use of variegated iris can make a big addition to any planting.

In Tall Bearded Iris plantings we are limited to *Iris pallida* 'Variegata'. Its yellowish-white variegation contrasts nicely with the grey-green background of its wide leaves. This iris from the southern Alps and the Adriatic has beautifully formed, pale lavender-blue blossoms which hug the bloom-stalk. It is not free branching. In larger iris plantings or when using newer varieties, this iris should be planted sparingly in clusters. Unfortunately, it is in short supply.

Besides the well-known, light-yellow variegated *I. pallida*, there is a pure white variegated form. It is prettier, but grows more slowly, is more prone to rhizome decay, and is almost impossible to obtain. It is so rare that the last specimens in Vienna were stolen from the iris beds of the Donaupark.

Iris foetidissima, the Gladwyn or Coral Iris, which has eye-catching red-orange seeds, also has a variegated form: *I. foetidissima* 'Variegata'. In this iris, part of the leaf surface cannot photosynthesize, so growth is minimal. The leaves are somewhat narrower than the species. The white variegation stands out handsomely against its dark green leaves. Unfortunately, this evergreen iris is delicate, does not tolerate frost very well, nor a soil with lime in it. It appreciates an application of slightly acid fertilizer. However, it will probably never become very widely used and is destined to remain a plant for iris specialists only.

The same holds true for a member of the Evansia group, *Iris japonica* 'Variegata'. It can however only make it through the winter in mild climates. Basically *I. japonica* and its variegated form are cold house plants. If the home gardener is fortunate enough to have a small greenhouse, this handsome colorful iris will make a good addition, for even the green plants in the greenhouse should be broken up a little. It is also possible to cultivate it in pots, but it then has to be divided and transplanted every 2–3 years. These plants should be more frequently used in local conservatories and in botanical gardens because they look attractive all year long. On top of that, their exotic flowers appear early in spring. Where more space is available, *I. japonica* and its variegated form should be planted outdoors. In a favorable location its roots roam a bit, but do no harm. Where winters are cold but sunny, this is a fine plant for the deep cold frame.

In comparison to the relatively limited uses of variegated iris already outlined, their value in the water garden is great. Even Yellow Flag (*Iris pseudacorus*) has produced a variegated form which is as vigorous as the species. *Iris pseudacorus* 'Variegata' has yellowish-white striped leaves which are especially attractive when they first come out and which later turn mostly green. But there are variations. One June, in a marshy area in the rock garden of the Edinburgh Botanical Gardens, I saw a highly variegated clump at a time when this iris had already turned green in Germany. It also seems that they do better in an acid substrate than in one which contains lime. They should be planted in groups, together with other standard aquatic iris and water and marsh plants with a horizontal orientation (e.g. water lilies). Their lengthwise striping goes well with the green and white variegation of the Zebra Bulrush, *Scirpus tabernaemontani* 'Zebrinus.'

The Japanese Iris (*I. kaempferi*) has also produced a form with green and white leaves, though these are rather narrow and the leaf veining is more pronounced than on the species. The variegation on *I. kaempferi* 'Variegata' is not very striking. It comes out more clearly in acid soils than in soils that are neutral or—undesirably— slightly alkaline.

The star among aquatic iris is *Iris laevigata* 'Variegata'. Its relatively broad leaves show a striking contrast between green and white. Anyone who has seen this iris is impressed. The variety blossoms as profusely as the species, is relatively vigorous, not as sensitive to lime as *Iris kaempferi,* and completely winter hardy. It is bound to become better known.

Anyone who writes about variegated iris cannot leave out a plant that indeed has nothing to do with iris but has beautiful, sword-shaped leaves variegated with white: the Sweet Flag, (*Acorus*). It can be used in all the same situations as water iris. There are two white variegated types, *Acorus calamus* 'Variegatus', which is approximately 24" (60 cm) tall, and the short *Acorus gramineus* 'Variegatus', which is often referred to as *A. gramineus* 'Aureo-

variegatus' and stands only about 6" (15 cm) high. Whereas tall Sweet Flag is completely hardy, *Acorus gramineus* 'Variegatus' needs good winter protection. (See also section on "Iris and the Water Garden".)

Iris Propagation

Harvesting and Collecting Seeds

If seeds are not going to be harvested, the iris stem should be cut off just above the base after the last flower has finished blooming. Not having to expend resources to develop seed will benefit the total plant and therefore next year's bloom. On the other hand, there are 3 reasons for letting seeds mature and harvesting them: first, to be able to sow them, and secondly, to have seeds for trading. Iris societies regularly hold seed exchanges, and botanical and public gardens maintain an international seed exchange mart. The third reason for harvesting seed is to start or complete a seed collection.

It is important to collect only true to parentage seed. This is not as easy as it sounds. In gardens and botanical parks, various species of iris, frequently from related groups, are often planted closely together. It has to be assumed, in such plantings, that uncontrolled pollination, especially by bumble bees, has occurred which of course leads to the creation of hybrids. Iris specialists usually have the advantage here of knowing that a cross between this species and that is not possible, or at least not likely, and so are able to harvest seeds which will be true without any hesitation. For example, if *Iris laevigata, I. fulva, I. graminea, Juno bucharica, Iris pallida, I. cristata, I. dichotoma* and *Xiphium latifolium* were to grow in the same garden, spontaneously produced seed from each species could be designated as species true. In contrast, species from individual sections and subsections often readily produce hybrids when grown in the proximity. We should bear in mind how easily the 40-chromosome Sibiricas cross with the Californicas. Even iris that are planted some distance from each other can produce hybrids, for instance *Iris pallida* (Pogon Iris) with *Iris tectorum* (Evansia); these are known a *Iris × paltec*. Uncontrolled crosses within sections and subsections are highly probable.

In order to avoid any mislabeling, seeds should be properly identified. If only the species name appears in the seed catalogue or on the packet, the person who contributed it must be certain that it is actually true seed. If the flower was pollinated by hand and protected against any incursion by insects (by removing the falls or, better yet, the falls and standards), the seeds should also be labeled "hand pollinated". If the seeds have been spontaneously produced, and it is not certain whether uncontrolled hybrid forms are present, the words "open pollinated" should be added to the species name.

From 25 years of experience I know what a sad story this can be. So many species have been raised from seed that turned out to be something completely different than was supposed. Seed from botanical gardens is no exception. We all know what problems they have with personnel, so this is just a statement and not a reproach. Only iris seeds which are guaranteed to be true or which were collected from wild species in their native habitats and which have been well documented should be procured from botanical gardens. Allowances have to be made for amateurs, but they too should be completely certain that the seeds in the packet are identical to what they have stated on the outside.

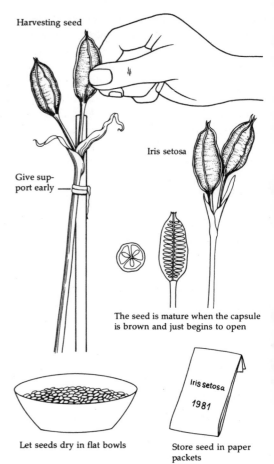

Harvesting seed

Iris setosa

Give support early

The seed is mature when the capsule is brown and just begins to open

Let seeds dry in flat bowls

Iris setosa 1981

Store seed in paper packets

Seeds should be harvested just before the seed capsule reaches complete maturity. If they are taken too soon, the kernel shrivels and germinates poorly or not at all. If harvesting is done too late, some of the seeds are usually lost or are completely scattered. These requirements are easier to write about than actually carry out, because at the time seeds are ripening there are so many other things to do in the garden.

Loss of seed can be prevented in part by staking any seed pod bearing stems which are not strong and erect. Use sturdy bamboo poles and a few twist-ems to keep stalks still and the seeds from falling out of the opened capsules in a strong wind. Tying a paper bag around the unripe seed pod will help retain seed.

Usually not a single seed will be collected if they are not harvested on time. The capsule may open up very wide or else the outer wall becomes paper thin, gets brittle and the seeds soon completely disperse. This is especially the case with many of the Pogon dwarfs, particularly *Iris pumila*, *I. missouriensis* and the Californicas. The opposite is true of the Spurias. After the seeds ripen, the beak on the top of the pod does open somewhat, but usually only very little.

Iris seed capsules themselves are a good way of identifying species, as these vary greatly from group to group. For example, the tip of the winged capsule of the Spuria Iris opens like a beak when ripe. The Evansias have smoother, more oval-shaped capsules and those of *Iris ensata* (Himalayan Iris) remind one of the first dirigibles. The seed pods of *Iridodictyum* are more membranous and lie just below the surface of the soil between the leaves. Those of *Iris kaempferi* are rounder, and the 40-chromosome Sibiricas are oblong-ovate with a worm-like appendage at the tip.

When the pod is completely ripe, it should be harvested, However, if the seed is not fully developed, the entire upper part of the stalk should be removed. Further handling depends on the degree of maturity. If the seeds are still rather green, the stalk should be put in a container of water. But if there are already signs of maturity, simply lay it on a piece of paper in a dry, shady place. It cannot be stressed enough that at no time should seeds or flower parts be without their complete labelling. You may have a good memory, but it's better to write it down!

Seeds offer good distinguishing characteristics

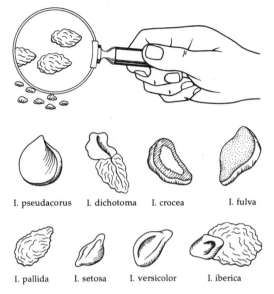

I. pseudacorus   I. dichotoma   I. crocea   I. fulva

I. pallida   I. setosa   I. versicolor   I. iberica

The best method is to tie a small tag bearing all pertinent data to each capsule while it still is in the garden.

When the seeds are mature, remove them from their capsules. Frequently the capsules are open so far that the seeds can simply be dumped into a seed packet. But sometimes as with Spuria Iris the opposite is true. In this case, the hard capsule can be broken with a rubber mallet without harming the seeds inside. Seeds should be as free as possible from stem and capsule particles. This can be quite easily done, even without a seed cleaning device, by putting the seeds and bits of capsule into a bowl and stirring them with the hand. The lighter contaminants rise to the top while the heavier seeds fall to the bottom. They can then be separated manually.

Storing the seeds in paper packets is a tried and true method. They may mold in glasses, jars, plastic bags, etc., even if left open at the top. Only when the seeds are absolutely dry should they be stored in air-tight containers. The paper packets shouldn't be so thin that they tend to break or tear; this is especially important when storing larger quantities of seed. Sometimes, however, despite being well dried, a seed will begin to mold. Its container should then be cleaned and the seeds wiped with a soft cloth slightly dampened with a light solution of Chlorox. Once in a while a stray insect or two has to be removed.

A seed collection is an interesting and useful thing. Iris seeds vary greatly from section to section, and even from species to species. One can learn to recognize the differences between seeds of various species. A good seed collection provides a handy way of comparing new, unknown seeds with known seeds. It is not unusual to obtain great rarities offered through seed exchanges, only to have them turn out, after 3 or 4 years of cultivation, to be some ordinary strain of *Iris sibirica*. Anyone who has an organized collection of seed can usually tell a false seed before it is sown, thus saving the waste of time and energy.

What should a seed collection look like? At first a few matchboxes, stacked up and glued together, will do for storage. The species name and maybe even the year of harvest should be written on the front of each "drawer". If the collection gets bigger, larger containers are necessary. Shallow, transparent boxes with lids, which hobbyists use for small parts, are useful. These clear little boxes usually have various-sized compartments so that the right size can be chosen, depending on the amount and size of the seeds. But we re-emphasize the seed must be totally dry before being put into its individual compartment. The morphological differences are especially apparent when seen side by side in these transparent boxes. Size, form, and color of

the seed grains all vary. Take care to label each compartment.

Then there are iris seeds with a so-called aril (Aril iris), a white, fleshy appendage or collar-like formation—a tasty morsel for ants and other insects, which collect the seed for a food supply and inadvertently propagate the plant. *Iris nepalensis* (syn. *Iris decora*), and species of Regelia Iris, Oncocyclus Iris, and Pseudo-regelia Iris all have an aril. Spuria Iris have a very characteristic parchment-like husk, while *Iris setosa* and its relatives have medium-brown, pear-shaped seeds with a shiny surface. Seeds of the subsection Laevigata, to which Yellow Flag (*Iris pseudacorus*) belongs, are remarkably large. Louisiana Iris (subsection Hexagonae) have even larger seeds which, in many of the species, are covered with an outer layer of cork so that they float. This adaption to their native habitat of the lower Mississippi River Basin has been a decisive factor in their region-wide propagation.

The bright, red-orange seeds of *Iris foetidissima* are unmistakable: when they are fresh they resemble pearls and as they get older they shrivel and turn brownish. This species' open capsule with red-orange seeds showing is used in dried bouquets.

These features are obvious, but many slight differences can be seen by direct comparison in a seed collection. Like a stamp collection, a collection of iris seeds can be fascinating. And it is often as difficult to acquire seeds for some rare species as it is to obtain a rare stamp.

Propagation by Sowing

Propagating iris by seed is usually the easiest thing in the world; there is only one catch, it requires patience. When is sowing called for and who should do it? Primarily it is a job for gardeners who are interested in hybridizing and who, therefore, have to sow the results of what has been crossed, namely the seeds produced. There are many people who just want to try it once and then can not give it up.

In this book the reader will be introduced to all the iris species. It is unfortunate that many of these treasures are not available in nurseries, just when the choices are steadily growing. In this respect nurseries abroad do have an advantage, but it's often so difficult to import them. Hence seed propagation is the only solution.

A good source of supply are the seed exchange programs run throughout the year by horticultural societies. The value of the seeds alone far outweighs the annual membership dues. Iris fanciers can easily exchange seeds all over the world using ordinary envelopes. Most botanical gardens, which also exchange seeds among themselves, will not turn a deaf ear to a serious amateur. But caution is in order. You wouldn't believe how many incorrectly labelled iris species are growing in botanical gardens. One piece of advice: only request seeds from plants native to the country of the botanical garden. They are almost always true.

Nature itself is a great source of seeds. In this age of the year-round migration known as the short vacation, there are opportunities to visit the natural habitat of most iris species and collect seeds. One's own garden should also not be overlooked. If an imported or exchanged rhizome has finally been brought to flower and seeds have started to form, iris fan-

Raising iris in pots (seed growing)

Square and round peat pots such as Jiffy-Strip for all iris species

Plastic pots and Jiffy 7 are especially suitable for moisture-loving iris

Peat pot inside a meshwork pot and clay pots particularly good for bearded iris

A Jiffy 7, dry and soaked

ciers are more than glad to start sowing it to ensure its continuation and increase.

As we have already seen in the section on seed harvesting and collecting, not only the blossom, but also the seed capsules and seed grains are very important identifying features for the vast range of plants belonging to the iris kingdom. The individual sections and series are clearly different from one another.

When should sowing be done? For iris, any season of the year is satisfactory, depending on facilities. Iris seeds are ripe at widely divergent times of the year, and when possible, immediate sowing is desirable.

Some hybridizers have had particularly good luck with Bearded Iris by sowing half-mature seed right after harvesting; but this should not be the rule. Generally speaking, sowing seed right after harvesting results in moldy seed. I

69

usually start sowing in the first 2 weeks of December, when all the outside work is finished. At this time, of course, only self-harvested seeds are available.

Iris are so-called "cold germinators". There are some exceptions, but we don't have to concern ourselves with them. Tall Spuria Iris, for example, germinate without the help of frosts, as do some Pacific Coast Iris, though these take a little longer. But then why change procedures, if no disadvantages arise from doing things the same way? Unfortunately seeds often arrive in spring or even summer, in which case they should be stratified in the refrigerator. Holding them like this for 4–5 weeks at about 40°F. simulates winter.

Different iris groups have special germinating behaviors. Rather than germinating in spring, the sown seed may only germinate in September, despite refrigeration or effects of frost. Pacific Coast Iris, for example, usually germinate only at the beginning or end of the following winter. And Dwarf Iris species usually only germinate in large numbers in their second spring. Sowing Oncocyclus Iris is a real test of patience, for even after 5 years a few seeds may still be germinating.

Now to the methods and techniques of sowing. Since the seeds are relatively large, sowing is easy if only a few seeds are involved, flower pots, small flats, or earthen pans can be used as containers. They should be kept as sterile as possible (with a 1:50 Chlorox solution, followed by thorough rinsing). Good drainage is a must. The seeds themselves should be treated with fungicide, which has been extended by the addition of talc. Such treatment is usually sufficient to protect against disease, and anyone who has lost valuable seedlings to disease won't skip this small chore of disinfecting seed.

If the seeds are being sown in a seedbed, sowing in furrows is the preferred method. But no matter where it is sown, the seed should not be covered by more than ⅜" (1 cm) of soil. To be absolutely precise, use the old rule: 3 times as deep as the seed is thick. Cover the seeds with sieved soil, then press it down lightly. The seeds should be kept evenly moist and never allowed to dry out. They should never be allowed to get bone dry—nor is a mini-swamp desirable. If seeds are sown in rows, a space of about 5½" (12 cm) should be left between rows.

Any weed-free, medium to heavy garden soil is suitable for seeds, but additions of peat and sand are advisable. If pasteurized or steam sterilized soil is available, use it by all means. A covering of snow in winter is advantageous, even if it melts again soon.

Iris sibirica cultivars. This plate includes both old and new to show their variations.

Top left: 'Ewen', a modern, large-blossomed cultivar. Like all reddish varieties, it is more sensitive to lime than blue or violet specimens.
Top right: 'Beth Ellen', an older cultivar, widespread in the U.S., similar in its blossom form to 'Eric the Red', which is one of its parent plants.
Center left: 'Amelia Earhart', an old brilliant blue variety with deep green foliage.
Center right: A group of newer cultivars. Back row left 'Sparkling Rose' hemstitched with a beautiful pinkish-red color; right 'Atoll', a large-blossomed cultivar by Bee Warburton; front row left 'Fortell' (McGarvey), the first successful cross between 28- and 40-chromosome sibiricas; right 'Lilienthal', a white, large-blossomed cultivar by Dr. Tamberg, Berlin; front right 'Nostalgie', a pure velvet, 40-chromosome cultivar by the author, without any trace of white or yellow.
Bottom left: Volunteer seedling from some Iris sibirica cultivar; these frequently self-sow in the garden.
Bottom right: 'Towanda Red Flair', an older, reddish type, used frequently in breeding. Prefers acid soil.

Cutting iris seeds

Cutting method

Cotton

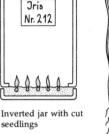

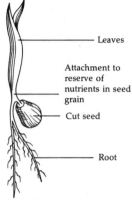
Leaves

Attachment to
reserve of
nutrients in seed
grain

Cut seed

Root

Seed in pre-soaked   Cut seed with   Inverted jar with cut
in water   embryo visible   seedlings

While good labelling is taken for granted, this is unfortunately not always the case. Neither cardboard tags nor the seed packet should ever be used, not even as a temporary measure for a few days. One usually forgets to replace them with waterproof tags and they soon cannot be deciphered. Plastic tags are a matter of course these days. A marking pen with waterproof black ink should be used to write on them. The most permanent tags can be made with a labelling gun. Labels stuck in the soil can be used for pots and small boxes, but in the seedbed labels wired to a sturdy rod are recommended, as markers stuck in the ground can be dislodged and jumbled. In my own garden, the birds have made a game of pulling out any loose labels. Just to be safe, a chart should be made showing the location of seeds.

The following procedure is recommended for speeding up protracted germination periods. Immediately after harvesting, put the seeds in a large plastic bag with a mixture of barely damp peat and river sand. The layer covering the seeds should not be more than 1⅛–1½″ (3–4 cm) thick. The bag is then tied shut and precisely labelled. Several bags can be put in a box and placed in a shady spot in the garden where they should be checked from time to time to see if seedlings are present. The new seedlings should be transplanted into beds or peat pots as soon as they have sprouted. Jiffy pressed peat pellets, which swell when placed in water and contain all the required nutrients, are good for this purpose. This method has the following advantages:

1. Large quantities of seed can be germinated in a small space.

Iris sibirica hybrids.

Top left: 'Weisschen' is a new, medium-tall, white cultivar by Dr. Tamberg. Such compact types are developed for foreground plantings.
Top right: In contrast, the white 'Iceberg' is an old, small-blossomed heavy bloomer, which is indispensible. Especially recommended for

natural plantings on a bank.
Below: This photograph reveals particularly well the change that Iris sibirica has undergone in the hands of breeders. Cultivars have become more "colorful" by increasing their visible petal surface. Here a new hybrid from the U.S., 'Deep Shade' (Bee Warburton).

2. Minimum care.
3. Invasion by insects and snails, attack by fungi, and drying out or becoming too moist are all eliminated.
4. The effects of frost or an unusual warming trend in winter can be easily controlled.
5. It is easier to combat the growth of moss on seeds that have to stratify for a long time.

Cutting the iris seed can significantly reduce the time required for germination, sometimes by more than a year, so that healthy seedlings are available in mid-winter. This method should be given a try by those too impatient to wait out the normal cycle. The seed is encouraged to germinate by a small operation. The method, in order of sequence, follows.

The seed is allowed to swell in a container of pure water, preferably in a test tube (well labelled!). The tube is sealed at the top with a clean cotton plug to prevent any air-born bacteria or fungi from entering. The water in the tube should be changed every day. After 3 days at room temperature, the seeds should be sufficiently swollen. At first the seeds may float on the surface of the water, but in time they will sink to the bottom.

The cutting operation itself has to be done with extreme care and under very sterile conditions. Chlorox is a good disinfectant. All the tools, as well as one's hands, should be treated with it. Every iris seed possesses a germinating cone which appears on the surface as a small protrusion. A few seeds will have to be sacrificed initially until one gets the hang of it and is able to find the cone immediately. The outer husk of some of the seeds will have loosened in soaking and should be removed if it can be done easily. This germinating cone is cut off with a razor blade under a strong light because cutting the seeds one by one is fine detail work. The off-white slice of endosperm is now visible, inside of which can be seen the pure white, rounded tip of the embryo.

Old canning jars can be used as culturing containers. The lid is filled with dampened vermiculite. The seed is laid in this substrate with the cut end up. The jar is turned upside down over the lid. Don't forget to constantly disinfect! Labelling shouldn't be forgotten here either.

The whole unit (lid and inverted jar) is then put on a kitchen shelf or on a windowsill close to a source of heat. Soon the embryo will start to push up and form a little seedling. There will still be some seeds that get moldy, despite all your best efforts. These should be removed immediately with tweezers. Initially, the tiny plants nourish themselves from the endosperm. When they are about 1⅛" (3 cm) high, they should be transplanted into small peat pots. Depending on what is available, their cultivation continues at a bright window, in a hotbed, or in a small greenhouse.

This method cannot unfortunately be used with Oncocyclus, Regelias, or their hybrids. But it is worth a try with the other iris groups. To be perfectly safe it is best to divide the risk. Sow half of each seed lot in the regular way and cut the other half.

All seedlings, no matter how they were produced, should be transplanted. Here one has several choices: transplanting flats, clay pots, plastic pots, seedling trays, or peat trays. I transplant all Apogon Iris into small plastic pots. There is usually not enough time for the care they need and their rootballs have to be kept relatively damp; in plastic pots they don't have to be watered as often and they can be planted out at any time. However, they will not grow quite as fast as iris transplanted into a seedbed, though they catch up quickly

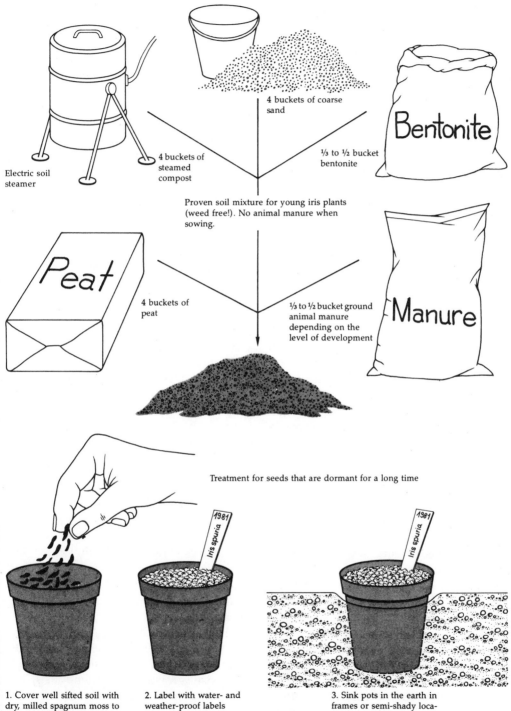

Electric soil
steamer

4 buckets of
steamed
compost

4 buckets of coarse
sand

⅓ to ½ bucket
bentonite

Bentonite

Proven soil mixture for young iris plants
(weed free!). No animal manure when
sowing.

Peat

4 buckets of
peat

⅓ to ½ bucket ground
animal manure
depending on the
level of development

Manure

Treatment for seeds that are dormant for a long time

1. Cover well sifted soil with
dry, milled spagnum moss to
prevent moss live build-up.

2. Label with water- and
weather-proof labels

3. Sink pots in the earth in
frames or semi-shady location

75

once planted in their permanent location. Clay pots are ideal for Bearded Iris. Rarities in limited numbers can go outdoors right from the pot. If hybrids have to be set out, the seedlings should go into a test bed. There is hardly ever enough room, but a distance of 8″ (20 cm) on all sides between Dwarf Iris and 10″ (30 cm) between Tall Bearded Iris should be maintained. Following the first blooming period, many of the seedlings that aren't completely satisfactory will end up on the compost heap anyway. Amateur breeders tend to save too many seedlings. Be ruthless; keep only truly outstanding hybrids.

A moderate fertilization program is in order for the young plants during this period, but here again, avoid using fertilizers with a high nitrogen content. A NPK ratio of 1:2:1 usually is suitable. Slugs are a major pest, so the young plants should be protected against them with slug bait.

You can never learn everything about seed propagation. Anyone who starts usually gets hooked, especially if he is holding a seductive packet of iris seeds in his hand.

Propagation by Division
The traditional method of vegetative propagation is division i.e., dividing the rhizome. True, it is not as productive as propagation by seed, but for private iris gardeners this is not an important consideration. The big advantage is that you always come up with an identical plant, whereas with seed an insect can upset your plans, by making an undesired cross.

Division, although a very old method, requires some understanding and care to be successful. In digging up the old stock, do not insert spade or fork too close to the plant. This is especially important with Bearded Iris because their roots grow almost horizontally from the rhizome. A garden fork is really safer for taking up the old clumps. The more functional roots that can be retained, the faster the division will be ready to bloom again. Also, in the case of Bearded Iris, there's no point in replanting the largest rhizome segment possible with lots of old pieces of rhizome. It has in fact been shown that single new rhizomes or 2 new rhizomes connected to one old one recover much faster than do those with a "line of ancestors" hanging on. To get the biggest return from new iris, the 2–3 year-old leafless rhizomes should not be thrown on the compost heap. There are so-called dormant growth buds on both sides of these. Because the front part, which is vegetatively more active, has been cut away, dormant buds will put out new shoots and roots will develop as well. That is why these older rhizomes should be planted in pots until their growth is fully established and then set out with rootball intact.

Dividing most Regelia Iris (Hexapogon) is a simple matter. They send out stolens on all sides just beneath the soil, on the ends of which new leaf buds form. These only need to be cut off and replanted. Just the opposite is true of many of the Oncocyclus Iris. Their rhizomes are knobby and grow together tightly. One has to be very careful when dividing them and then the results are unfortunately not very rewarding.

The mistake in dividing Apogon Iris lies in not taking enough of the rhizome. The segments chosen should *not* be too small, otherwise growth is tremendously retarded and the plants sometimes even die. Obviously, any dead parts of rhizomes

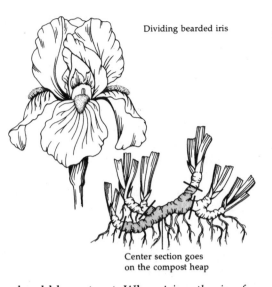

Dividing bearded iris

Center section goes
on the compost heap

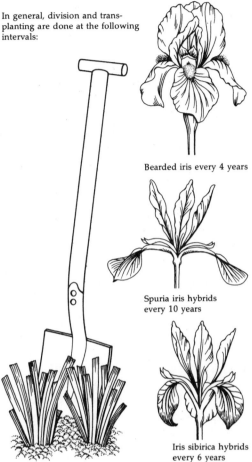

In general, division and transplanting are done at the following intervals:

Bearded iris every 4 years

Spuria iris hybrids
every 10 years

Iris sibirica hybrids
every 6 years

should be cut out. When *Iris ruthenica*, for example, has been growing in the same spot for several years it forms a sort of fairy ring: the middle of the clump dies out over time and only the outer edge survives to grow another green ring of leaves. This also is true of old *I. sibirica* clumps.

Bulbous Iris, that is members of the genera *Iridodictyum*, *Xiphium* and *Juno*, form side bulbs which have to be very carefully separated. With some of them (*Juno*), the yield is middling, whereas with others (*Iridodictyum danfordiae*, *Xiphium* ✕ *hollandicum*) quantities of little bulblets develop from the old one.

The iris grower should be aware that every division is a sort of operation which exposes more or less large areas of inner plant tissue. To prevent infection from entering these tissues, sterile conditions must be observed. All cuts should be made with a sharp knife, which has been dipped in sterilent, so that they are as clean as possible. As a precaution, the exposed tissue should either be dusted with a fungicide or the segment dipped in a mild solution of chlorox or potassium permanganate. I know this takes time and trouble, but any

bulb worth propagating deserves no less.

A great deal of success depends on the location of the garden. In milder regions one doesn't have to be as exacting as in cool, damp climates with heavy garden soils.

Replanting the rhizome segments is done in the same way as described in the sections on planting Bearded and Beardless Iris.

Shipping Bearded Iris rhizomes between distant countries is quite easy. They can travel for weeks or months without being the worse for wear. But it's very important that they be shipped dry and simply wrapped in newspaper; not in plastic bags in which they easily rot. Even shriveled up, almost bone-dry rhizomes will reawaken to new life. Apogon Iris segments are not as easily shipped over long distances, so it is preferable to ship them by air. The rhizomes should be left exposed and only their roots packed in slightly damp peat and then (roots only!) wrapped in plastic wrap.

It is precisely through this world-wide exchange of small gifts—for that is what iris rhizomes are—that international friendships can be sealed and made deeper.

Protecting Iris in Your Garden

Compared with other blooming plants, iris are really very disease free. The diseases and pests that do attack iris don't affect all groups of iris, and resistance from species to species and cultivar to cultivar differ widely. By keeping an eye on them and using a few preventative measures, which should be done routinely anyway, any serious damage can usually be avoided.

Animal Pests
Almost every plant genus has its "own" special pests that seem to increase proportionately to the number of plants put in.

We have already talked about rodents and Bulbous Iris. In gardens infested with mice and voles, traps can be laid or poison bait set out. A sure way of preventing rhizomes from being eaten is to treat them with red lead, then set them in the ground inside little baskets made of chicken wire.

One of the worst pests is slugs. Seedlings and rarities are especially at risk. One would almost think that the rarer a plant, the sooner it will be attacked and the more delicious it tastes. The usual methods are well known: scattering snail bait, putting out potato halves or flat stones, then picking the slugs from the underside the following morning. A really clever slug trap has been introduced recently that one fills with beer. The slugs (but not snails) in the near vicinity are magically drawn to it, crawl in, and are drowned.

The Iris Borer (*Macronoctua onusta*) is a dangerous insect. It is very rarely found in Europe, but is a nightmare for Americans. The real culprits are the larvae of the inconspicuous-looking moth, which lays its 150–200 eggs in the fall on the shrivelling iris leaves next to the rhizome. In the spring the caterpillars hatch and eat their way into the base of the leaves and on into the rhizome itself. They grow rapidly to over 1½" (4 cm) long. Often their unhappy presence goes unnoticed until the bloomstalk topples over. Then one can see that the bottom end has been completely riddled by their slimy feeding routes. One can attempt to remove all the larvae, but that's a lot of trouble and not always effective. An ounce of prevention is worth a pound of cure, so any newly received rhizomes should always be carefully checked over. If infestation is serious, the rhizomes should be sprayed once a month, beginning in spring, with Metasystox with a wetting agent added.

It would be quite wrong to shrug off aphids as annoying, but otherwise harmless insects. Both the black and the green aphids attack the base of the leaves and stem. In my own garden, they are primarily drawn to *Iris sibirica*, especially those in drier locations or when the early summer is very dry. *Iris setosa* seems to be a tasty morsel too, and here again the aphids prefer those which were bred from seeds

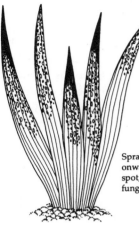

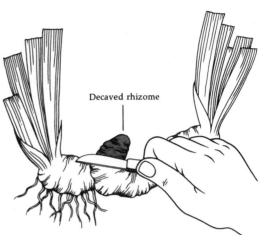

Decaved rhizome

Spray from early spring onward for leaf spot (leaf spot, leaf blight) with a fungicide as a precaution

For rhizome rot, cut back infected areas to healthy tissue and disinfect cuts with a bactericide-fungicide mixture, charcoal powder or some such agent.

The iris borer (here as adult moth) is a dreaded pest in the U.S.

from North Hokkaido, Japan. One hears a lot of complaints about infestations of Dwarf Iris and *Iris kaempferi*. When an infestation begins, and as long as the numbers remain small, the aphids can be stripped off with the fingers and squashed, if this is not too repulsive. Only spraying will work on heavy infestations, preferably with pyrethrum, which is relatively harmless to human beings.

It bears repeating that in treating iris with a spray, a wetting agent has to be used. All iris have a thin, waxy coating on their leaves and stems. If a wetting agent is not used, the spray will simply bead up and not cover the plant. Any kitchen detergent will also do.

Occasionally Weevils (*Mononychus punctum-album*) or Iris Leaf Miners (*Liriomyza urophorina*) will appear on Beardless Iris, attacking the buds and flowers.

In spite of the fact that I have an extensive collection of iris in my garden, I have yet to make the acquaintance of any of these insects.

From time to time white dots, which later run together as stripes, may appear on the leaves and flowers. The cause of this is thrips, which we already know due to their attraction to Gladiolus. But in this case it's usually the Iris Thrip (*Iridothrips iridis*). Depending on the extent of the infestation and the risk of damage being done, plants should be sprayed at intervals against this insect. One of the phosphoric acid ester compounds will do the job for sure, but their safety has lately been questioned.

Bacteria and Funguses
In my experience, bacterial wet rot in rhizomes is perhaps the nastiest of all iris diseases. U.S. hybrids are especially susceptible since they grow in a warm climate. In some of the cold, damp regions of the world where the soil is poorly drained, the danger is greatest.

Wet rot is caused by various bacterial organisms, the main one being *Erwinia carotovora* (recently: *Pectobacterium carotovorum*). In England they call it "soft rot". This rot is often a sign of improper care. The organism doesn't necessarily have to be introduced; it's already widely distributed attacking potatoes and carrots, regularly. The use of high-nitrogen fertilizer, against which we have warned, encourages the onset of this obnoxious disease. Anyone who has ever put his fingers into one of these mushy, foul-smelling rhizomes, knows what I'm talking about. One's hands smell terrible, even after repeated washings.

Frequently the tips of iris leaves turn yellow or the young shoots stop growing—the first signs of disease. But this is not absolute. Sometimes a fan of leaves is bright green and the stem laden with beautiful blossoms, only to topple over for no apparent reason. On inspection, it turns out to be rhizome rot. If not immediately attended to, the entire rootstock can rot.

All the affected rhizomes have to be ruthlessly cut out and the exposed tissue disinfected. This can be done by dusting them with charcoal, Sterosan, or best of all by dipping them in a 5% solution of Orthocide-50. An application of basic slag and fertilizing lime during the winter is a preventative measure. If the disease occurs after blooming, it is better to lift the whole plant and treat it as described above; usually it needs to be divided anyway. To be safe, iris should not be replanted in an area that has already been contaminated; at the very least, the soil in the old site should be replaced by new. The rhizomes will have lots of exposed cuts after being planted again, so do not water them! Both tools and hands, especially the knife used in making the cuts, should be disinfected afterwards.

Dry rot or scorch has not been common for some years. With this disease, the rhizomes die without softening. Treatment is the same as for wet rot.

Another disease which particularly affects Bearded Iris is Leaf Blight or Leaf Spot (*Heterosporium gracile*). It usually occurs on the leaves shortly after flowering, in the form of small, round, brownish-grey spots with translucent coronas, which quickly increase and spread. Susceptibility to blight varies greatly from cultivar to cultivar. First the tips of the leaves wither and then usually the entire leaf. This fungal disease does no long term damage and in my own experience has never had any effect on the following year's blossoms. However, it can, if nothing at all is done, soon ruin the beauty of an entire summer garden. Everything is in good order except the irises, which look pitiful with their withered leaves. If spraying is undesirable and one doesn't mind the work, all the affected brown parts of the leaves can be cut off 2–3 times from the time the plants flower until fall. But it's easier just to spray with Dithane (2%), Antracol (2%), or copper sulphate (3%) before and after flowering. Orthocide has proven successful, as have multiple sprayings with a diluted algaecide.

One always reads that diseased parts should be cut off and either burned or buried, never composted. This is good advice (since the fungus winters over in the old leaves), but who really has the time for this? Perhaps some retired person with 10 iris? I hold with Professor Alwin Seifert's thesis that a good compost heap will destroy disease germs. But just to be safe, I only use steamed compost on tender plants.

Apogon Iris are unfortunately prey to a still unidentified disease, which particularly attacks divided and transplanted plants. The leaves suddenly all turn brown. The damage actually begins in one spot and rapidly spreads. If noticed in time, cutting out the affected parts with a spade sometimes helps. The usual anti-bacterial and anti-fungal products are ineffective. Spraying with fenaminosulfate Dexon sometimes works.

In private gardens, small Bulbous Iris are more likely to get black spot. The leaves turn prematurely yellow or the plants simply stop sending out shoots. If they are dug up, the bulblets are partly or entirely blue-black. Nothing can be done at this point except to throw them in the trash can so that no other bulbs will be infected.

Viruses

Stunted, tightly-curled blossoms with off-colored specks on them are part of this sad picture, as are leaves covered with pale greyish or whitish spots.

Many viruses are transmitted by aphids and other piercing, sucking insects. It is impossible to combat viral diseases themselves, so the only defense is to take swift action against the transmitter.

I have tried repeatedly to obtain virus-free *Iris reichenbachii* and *Iris illyrica*, to no

avail. The important thing is good preventive measures. Especially in late fall, iris beds should be thoroughly cleaned up so that they go into the winter "clean". One of the oldest Sword Flags under cultivation, the Oncocyclus Iris (*Iris susiana*), is almost unobtainable virus-free. Its disease symptoms are not conspicuous, but there's always the danger that it will infect other iris. Many garden plants are virus carriers without showing any visible signs of disease themselves. Even in an apparently virus-free garden, one of these "symptom-less carriers" can be lurking and infect other plants. Any plants identified as having a virus should be immediately removed and destroyed. These definitely do not go on the compost heap. Viruses often go from genus to genus; some of the common "carrier" plants are lilies, daffodils, and, in America, the Pokeweed, *Phytolacca*.

Seasonal Care

Both general and specific care instructions are found throughout this book, but we will summarize the main points here. Basically, iris are "easy" plants.

A major cleanup should be done in March, if the ground has dried out, or in April if the winter has been long and wet. All the brown foliage should be removed, no matter what species of iris are involved. This is relatively easy with Bearded Iris. Leaves that have died back to the base can be removed with a slight tug and damage to the leaf tips can be cut off with a scissors. Cleanup is more difficult with some of the Apogons, and the water iris (*Iris laevigata, Iris pseudacorus*), with their tough, fibrous leaves. Nothing can be done without tools. An ordinary serrated knife or heavy scissors can be used to cut off dead foliage.

With various Apogon Iris the new shoots develop rather early so cutting should be done with care.

Plenty of fertilizer should be used until the flowers open. One need not be particular about the kind of fertilizer used. Naturally there are a few basic rules to go by. Bearded Iris should not receive much nitrogen. One can hardly go wrong with bone meal, horn meal, or guano. *Iris sibirica* respond to a top dressing of humus or an organic fertilizer, but avoid lime. This also applies to a whole series of species. If mineral fertilizer is used, one that creates an acid reaction should be chosen for alkaline soils, such as those used for marsh bedding plants. Ordinary garden complete fertilizer can be used, but here too moderation is advised. Spurias respond to cattle manure.

Until the possibility of really severe frosts has passed, protect the new spring shoots. These new tender shoots are injured by any kind of thick covering. A few pieces of newspaper arched over them turns the frost on windless nights. Be very careful about using plastic. It can do more harm where it comes in contact with the plant than if the plant were left unprotected.

During the growing season, water should be monitored carefully. This does not, of course, apply to Bearded Iris, which can easily survive long dry spells because of the reserves of moisture in their rhizomes. But 28- or 40-chromosome Sibirica iris have to be well watered during any extended dry period. Apogon Iris always need additional water in spring and midsummer during extended dry periods. Mulching with a coarse material, such as bark dust, also helps retain moisture. In areas where the soil has a high lime content iron sulfate, sulfur, or other acid producing agent should be applied to adjust soil pH.

The small Bulbous Iris (*Iridodictyum*) have one particular drawback. After they bloom, many of their leaves become disproportionately long and frequently already yellow by the end of May. Such leaves should be removed. During the blooming period, wilted flowers should be regularly removed and when the last blossom on a stalk wilts, the latter should be cut off just above the bulb unless you plan to collect seed.

Just before blooming, the plants should be sprayed with a fungicide to which has been added a wetting agent to prevent Leaf Spot (Iris Leaf Blight), which can be very unsightly. Spraying should be repeated right after the plant has finished blooming.

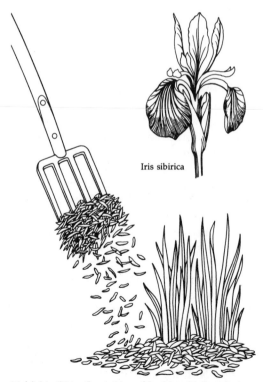

Iris sibirica

Mulch Iris sibirica, Spuria iris, and Louisiana iris in spring with half-rotted compost, well-rotted manure or a mixture of peat and manure.

Recommended preventive measures

In areas with lots of precipitation and mild winters, always remove dead leaves in late fall as a precaution against rhizome rot.

In cold winter areas (hard frost), cover rhizomes planted on the surface with sand, especially in exposed sites which get winter sun. Otherwise cracks form where diseases can start.

In exposed, windy sites, tall bearded iris have to be staked. Thin bamboo poles and plastic ties can be used.

In the case of Apogon Iris, most of which bloom after the Tall Bearded Iris, the stalk should also be cut off after all the flowers have finished blooming unless seeds are to be harvested for personal use or for exchange.

Keep on top of weeds, even after the blooming period. Shallow hoeing can be done between Apogon Iris with deeper-growing, but weeds are better pulled by hand around Bearded Iris because of their shallow roots.

Old, inactive rhizomes may be cut out of established clumps of Bearded Iris. Divide and transplant from July on. The earlier, the better, so that the plants go into the winter with well-established roots. Summer rains increase the danger of rhizome rot in Bearded Iris. Remove any affected parts promptly and watch for any other signs of disease and pests.

In the fall, prepare plants for the winter. Cut back leaves of Bearded Iris to where they no longer look unattractive. Apogon Iris can be cut back completely, but in cold climates 6–8" (15–20 cm) should be left on as winter protection. The use of chippers for making compost material has become popular lately. However, iris leaves can cause problems in these machines. Tough, half-dry leaves of *Iris sibirica* and others wind around the shaft and stop the motor. If the leaves have been freshly cut or are completely dry, there shouldn't be a problem. Only tender iris need to be covered with mulch.

Iris in the Wild

What a happy and satisfying thing it is to come across iris growing wild. These days, when frequent travel is taken for granted, such meetings are not rare—they have only to be sought out. A few recollections of the opportunities I have enjoyed are recounted here to perhaps serve as a stimulus to the reader.

The toughness of *Iris pseudacorus* was not to strike me though I had grown up with them as a boy until 50 years later in another setting. Right through the middle of property attached to a paint factory where I worked ran the White Main River restricted on both sides by high concrete walls. It was usually a gently flowing river, barely 13 ft. (4 m) wide, except during spring run-off from the Fichtel Mountains or extended rainy periods, when it became a torrent. An *Iris pseudacorus* had settled in close to one of the walls and bloomed there year round, without human involvement and in spite of being swept over by cascades of water, ice, and scree.

It was September on Crete. Hardly anything was left of the otherwise lush vegetation, even the Lassithi Plateau had been harvested and was dry. We were looking for *Iris cretensis* 'Janka', often called *Iris cretica* or *Iris unguicularis* var *cretensis*. According to our sources, this iris was supposed to be growing abundantly in the Dikti Mountains. We scoured the cliffs around the Diktean caves at a height of about 3,280 ft (1000 m)., where Zeus was supposed to have been born. Thyme and all kinds of low shrubs were growing among the scrubby, stunted oaks. After some searching, we came across the first sign, a dried rhizome in the typical shape of *I. unguicularis*. For some time we'd been seeing sporadic, half-dried bunches of grass growing between the stoney rubble. Indeed, I had known that the iris we were looking for had grass-like leaves, but somehow I had pictured them to be wider. After some hard digging, the thin fishbone-shaped rhizome, which is the earmark of *Iris cretensis*, was ours. It was a great moment and well worth the trouble.

Yet another story. It was summer in the interior of Bulgaria and we were looking for two irises: *Iris sintenisii* and *Iris reichenbachii*. We found ourselves in the Valley of Roses, where rose oil is extracted from *Rosa damascena*, which blossoms only once. The rose fields at this time had been harvested and were deserted. It was unmercifully hot. An extremely resistant strain of *Iris reichenbachii* was supposed to be found somewhere near the town of Kalofer, but to scour the slopes of the northern Balkan Mountains would have been impossible in the heat. It occurred to us that the natives of that tiny village had surely at one time or another gathered *Iris reichenbachii* for their own gardens. After looking around awhile, we found an old woman who, for very little money, was happy to part with half a square yard of them. Once back home in my own garden, the species was confirmed.

In another valley of the Bulgarian mountains, we made an excursion near the monastery of Drianovo. We crossed a little ravine and climbed up a small slope covered with all sorts of aromatic plants. There were tufts of *Helleborus,* deep yellow *Centaurea* in bloom, and *Clematis tangutica.* Species of *Daphne, Dianthus,* and *Gentiana* were growing there too, not in bloom, of course, but easily recognizable. In a low-growing stand of grass we came upon our goal: *Iris sintenisii.* It was a large clump, topped with typical seed capsules. Our previous exertions were as naught, compared to our attempts to dig part of it out of the red, almost brick-hard, scorched clay: a good piece of work. Sweaty, dirty and covered with dust, but overjoyed, we returned to the monastery with a small rhizome of *Iris sentenisii* in hand.

It was the beginning of March. The beaches of Grand Canary were full of frolicking vacationers, very few of whom thought about visiting the interesting volcanic landscape in the interior of the island, even though there were bus connections between all the little villages. We went up into the mountains, where wisps of clouds and clear skies were changing places with each other in rapid succession. Sometimes we were completely swathed in clouds, then they would pass and the sun would shine through on the gentle slopes, covered in part with *Vinca major.* Then suddenly we saw it: a whole slope covered with iris, bright-green Bearded Iris, not blooming, but clearly identifiable as *Iris albicans,* the white Bearded Iris species from Arabia that followed the spread of Islam to Spain and then to the Grand Canaries, where it had naturalized.

On a February morning in Lebanon, a taxi had taken us up to Sofar, a small village in the Lebanese Mountains. We felt refreshed in the clear morning sun, while down in Beirut, which we could see off in the distance on an indentation in the coastline, it had been 70°F (20°C). Yet up here we could still see snow several hundred meters away. Not a hundred meters from where we left the taxi, a small miracle awaited us. Among all sorts of vegetative remains from last year stood *Iridodictyum histrio* (syn. *Iris histrio*) in full bloom. It was an enchanting sight, the wonderful contrast of these flowers daubed blue with a yellow streak on the falls. Not far away a species of *Ornithogalum* and *Anemone coronaria* were blooming. It was a picture of spring one seldom has a chance to see.

The Biokovo Mountains jut sharply up from the sea on the Dalmatian coast. The mostly deserted towns, where a few old people still live, hang like swallows' nests on the steep slopes. The summer sun was burning down and the stones were red hot. Clumps of *Moltkia, Campanula, Dianthus,* and *Allium* were growing everywhere. There were also stands of iris on the embankments, undoubtedly *Iris pallida* var. *dalmatica,* which is now being increasingly cultivated in fields around Florence instead of *Iris florentina.*

Iris fanciers from all over the world were assembled near Prague for a symposium, and, of course, there were field trips to look for native iris. A bus took us as far as Litomerice (previously Leitmeritz). We walked a few kilometers down the Elbe to a bend in the river, where a steep slope rose up on the right side. We clambered up this with some difficulty, but not without reward. There in front of us, growing among rounded *Jovibarba* and silvery-grey *Festuca,* was *Iris aphylla,* one of the most northerly Bearded Iris species. The Czech botanists then drove us to a swampy wasteland. Tank tracks indicated that the area was used for military exercises, but, nonetheless, just beginning to bloom between the tracks was *Iris sibirica.*

Naturally the Sibirica specialists among us were enthralled.

We were on Cyprus. A taxi had taken us from Famagusta to the northern limestone mountains of Cyprus, and into the Kantara Mountains. I had never seen so many anemones, *Ornithogalum* species, *Cyclamen,* and orchids growing together in one place. Wherever we walked, one of these plants was in front of us, but of iris were there none. Yet in the garden of the village inn was one of the Near Eastern tetraploid, tall Pogon Iris, sometimes known as *Iris cypriana.* It was not in bloom, but we recognized it by its extremely large, wide leaves. We came to a quick arrangement with the tavern keeper, and it was ours.

We were a few kilometers from the International Airport in Beirut. The sun was still strong in the coastal lowlands despite the fact that it was the end of February. Brilliant red *Anemone coronaria* was growing between the rocks and the fresh, green grass, as were a few *Cyclamen persicum,* with their delicate pink blossoms and subtle odor. Then came another surprise: growing here and there in this poor soil was *Juno palaestina,* with its white flowers. Each plant had only one or two blossoms, but what a charming dwarf! Spring had come to the Eastern Mediterranean!

We had just landed in Srinagar, the capital of Kashmir, and were glad to have escaped the oppressive monsoon heat of India. Even on our way from the airport to the houseboat, we could see we had arrived in the land of iris. The embankments along the streets were covered with *Iris kashmiriana* and a type of *I. germanica* that did not have a very good substance. These iris were to be seen all over the plains of Kashmir, especially on the graves of Moslems. The sheep and goats that graze there don't seem to be interested in the leaves of these plants.

Taxis had taken us up to the subalpine zone of the Himalayas, to Pahalgam. At the 13,120 ft (4000 m) level, thousands of pilgrims passed by on a pilgrimage. Not far from a bridge, clumps of narrow-leafed iris, typical of *Iris ensata* (the correct botanical name of this species has not yet been clearly established), were growing in a sort of depression. These iris could frequently be seen in low-lying areas, but they simply could not be separated from the rock-hard soil. But here in this damper spot we could at least dig with a trowel. We wrapped the rootballs in damp paper towels and put them into a plastic bag, ready for the flight back to Europe.

Another time we rode ponies up to the 12,500 ft (3800 m) level. The alpine flora of the Himalayas was in full bloom. Even at about 9,800 ft (3000 m) we crossed an alpine meadow, a short grass carpet with a few huts. The grass had been grazed to nothing, but there were two tall clumps of plants that the grazers had avoided: *Iris hookeriana* and *Euphorbia wallichiana,* the former already with mature seed capsules and the latter with tall sulfur-yellow leaves. The seed capsules were quickly collected before our climb up to Apharwat continued.

I was sitting with an injured ankle in the Mogul Gardens of Verinac on the southeast side of the Kashmir plateau. I had been forced to give up a hike to a place where *Iris notha* was supposed to be found. Since the other members of this botanical expedition knew about my interest in iris, they brought me back a stalk with seed capsules on it. There was no doubt. The thin stem zig-zagging from node to node was indeed *Iris notha,* whose occurrence so far east had not been suspected.

It happened on a trip along the

Ammersee. What was growing on the banks were not reeds, but *Iris sibirica*, still shrouded in the morning fog.

Iris experienced in the wild are always delightful, whether far away or close to home.

These little field notes should encourage any interested reader to look for irises where they naturally grow, whenever the opportunity arises. There are iris all over the temperate zone of the Northern Hemisphere. Just the experience of tracking down these natural habitats is worth the trouble. But a lot of useful information can be gathered about habitat, soil composition, neighboring plants, and more. Photographers are enticed to the plants in bloom. When the seeds become ripe, it's worth collecting a few. Where plants are plentiful and if seed is only for private purposes and done in moderation, nobody objects. More plants, however, are added to the endangered species lists each year, and such plants should be left quite undisturbed, including seeds.

The question of removing entire plants is a more difficult one. It is a matter of principle for plant lovers and specialists to obey the environmental protection laws of whatever country they are visiting. (There is not enough space here to enumerate them all.) In Germany all wild iris species are protected by law. On the other hand, there are countries where iris grow in such abundance that they don't need to be protected and a rhizome may be taken without feeling guilty. Familiar species that are obtainable on the market should be left alone. But variant specimens, which might be of interest to collectors and hybridizers, are a great temptation, and the removal of a small division by an iris specialist might be justified.

Transportation and care of rhizomes on the way home from vacation is very easy.

Many Pogon Iris can simply be put in a paper bag. If new, active roots are present, they should be wrapped in a damp piece of Kleenex. Bearded Iris species should never be put in air-tight containers or closed plastic bags (danger of rot!). This is different for moisture-loving iris: wrap the cut-back plant in moss and put it in a plastic bag, but leave the bag open at the top! In my long years of collecting I have never lost a single iris in transport; adapt your method to your means. The iris should be planted immediately when one gets home again, smaller pieces first, in clay pots.

Purchase, Customs, Exchange, Shipment

The acquisition of iris, no matter by what method, can sometimes be irritating. Iris fanciers should limit themselves as much as possible to species plants and this is very much in vogue. A modern assortment of iris is available from local gardening specialists, from iris importers, and from breeders. The beginner can quickly find these sources through advertisements in horticultural journals and periodicals. But he must understand that not every nurseryman has his burning interest in iris. There are many whose offerings consist of varieties long since surpassed. The ordinary consumer does not realize this, nor does he care or need to know about the latest iris.

If named cultivars are indicated, older ones are still acceptable, if only as reliable mass bloomers in the background. But nobody, not even beginners, should buy iris through the mail, if they are designated as *Iris germanica*, blue, yellow, violet, and so on. This is very common in the case of The Netherlands iris. Other flowering bulbs, tulips, etc., are as clearly and precisely described as iris are unclearly described. Usually such selections consist of ancient but vigorous not very attractive cultivars that grow somewhere on the edge of other cultivated fields.

Even when dealing with reputable firms, it is best to order Bearded Iris as early as possible so that they can be planted between the end of July and the end of August. This also applies to importers who offer rhizomes at different times of the year. One should always make sure that iris are received by the earliest date possible. This applies particularly to those who live in regions where cold sets in early, so that the iris go into winter with established root systems. The supply is usually more than sufficient to take care of public gardens and ornamental plantings in botanical gardens as well.

There are always people who, for whatever reason, make purchases abroad. These can be groups of iris fanciers for whom the selection of imported iris is too narrowly limited to the plants of specific breeders or they can be passionate collectors who always want the latest thing in their gardens; but they can also be systematic breeders who wish to learn if this or that hybrid will have a positive effect on his breeding line. Many iris

species are difficult to obtain and generally not available commercially. For such name species, botanical gardens, specialist plant societies, and collectors turn to the import market.

Plants are not as easy to import as, say, books. There are basic laws set up to protect the importing country's agriculture against the introduction of plant diseases and pests. In principle, nobody really objects to this, even if in practice it does not quite work out that way. For example, one single head of cabbage in an entire trainload is inspected, from which is it assumed that the other 4,000 heads are okay. On the other hand, out of 3 iris rhizomes, each will be inspected with a magnifying glass, even though health certificates from the country of origin are attached. It would be welcome if smaller orders of imported plants (as long as they are free of any soil) were somewhat more magnanimously treated, as they are in Switzerland. Shipments accompanied by health certificates should be expedited as soon as possible, as should small shipments between plant collectors. It is often impossible for the mailer, especially if a private party, to obtain phytosanitary certificates, as the nearest government plant office may be miles away.

Very small shipments do not present a

Tall bulbous iris (Xiphium).

Top left: Xiphium latifolium, sometives listed in the catalogues as English Iris or Iris anglica, is the only species of this genus that needs a damp situation. Here the variety 'The Giant'.
Top right: Dutch iris (Hollandica Cultivars) are the most important bulbous horticultural group. 'Synphonia' is the cultivar shown here.
Center left: Xiphium latifolium (Iris anglica) is native to the Pyrenees, where it thrives in moist soils. Lack of success is almost always due to a site that is too dry. Shown is a delicate violet cultivar.
Center right: Xiphium latifolium 'Montblanc', a white cultivar of this moisture-loving species.

Unlike the Hollandica cultivars, there are no yellow varieties.
Bottom left: Hollandica Cultivar 'Imperator'. This iris has taken over as a cut flower to such an extent that people who don't know much about gardening, always associate this cultivar with the term "iris".
Bottom right: Xiphium vulgare var. lusitanicum (Iris lusitanica) is unfortunately not hardy in Germany. But over-wintered in a coldhouse or frost-protected container, it has no problems and blossoms intense golden yellow.

problem. Rhizomes sent in envelopes or in small packages reach their destinations without any trouble. Except for gift packages, plants sent this way cost only the amount of duty, which is very reasonable and everyone is willing to pay—if no other stumbling blocks are put in the way.

Problems can arise with rhizomes that have been privately collected. If shipped by air, the inspection is more random and the chance that they might be held up very slight. However, if one runs into an over-zealous official, who first wants to send the rhizomes to the airport plant inspector's office, all one's patience has to be mustered.

Iris are gladly exchanged across borders. These shipments are usually so small that, with the soil removed, their weight doesn't exceed that of a foreign packet (2.2 lb. or 1 kg.). The label should be filled out correctly. It should read something like *Oncocyclus* rhizomes, *Pogon* rhizomes, *Juno* bulbs, and so on.

If this is done properly, usually neither the sender nor receiver will have much trouble. All iris are not alike, which is true even in shipping them. An iris I was importing from Israel sat in some government office of a neighboring county for 7 weeks before anyone notified me! Fortunately they were Oncocyclus Iris, which

usually come from hot, dry, desert-like countries, which is the only reason the knobby rhizomes, dried up in their little packages, survived their long ordeal in a hot office. This kind of situation should be avoided at all cost with moisture-loving iris! Pogon Iris tolerate dryness well. Between July and September they can be shipped completely dry, without any soil, simply wrapped in newspaper, even if a 3–4 week journey is involved. This is also true for *Juno, Xiphium* and *Iridodictyum* bulbs. However, with the little Junos, care must be taken that the fragile, fleshy roots don't get broken off during shipment. Bearded Iris can also be shipped like this, outside the usual dates, if only short distances are involved.

A few precautions should be taken when shipping Bearded Iris outside the prescribed dates—i.e. when the roots are fresh, long, white, and active—especially over long distances. The rhizome itself and the fan of leaves are left bare; the long roots are bound with a rubber band or twist-em, then wrapped in slightly damp sphagnum moss and aluminum foil. Stick tags should not be used for labelling as they interfere with the stump of leaves; it is better to put the wire of a wooden tag through the stump of leaves and twist it closed.

Apogon species for diverse uses in the garden.

Top left: Iris ruthenica, the Siebenburgen grass iris, is a long-lived perennial and can be used in the border because of its small size. Perfect for the rock garden.
Top right: Iris nepalensis is interesting for its strange rootstock otherwise it is only for collectors. Blooming period is very short.
Center left: Iris kamaonensis. This iris from the Himalayas belongs in the rock garden. It does not do well in all locations and does not bloom reliably in all areas but it is valued by iris lovers for its patterned blossom.

Center right: Iris uniflora is closely related to Iris ruthenica—not the European species, but the Central Asian one. It is somewhat more attractive than its European relative.
Lower left: Iris foetidissima is important as a late bloomer. The blossom of the typical species is not particularly attractive, but now there are white, blue and yellow selections without the muddy tones of the original. Tolerates semi-shade.
Lower right: Iris foetidissima. This species is interesting for its striking cluster of seeds, if not for its blossom. The reddish-orange seeds cling tightly to the burst capsule, making them very useful in the art of dry flower arranging.

Tall Spuria Iris can also be shipped without any special protection, but all the other groups are more problematic. Certainly *Iris sibirica* have been shipped as described above and has made it safely, but there is always a risk. The tender roots should really be wrapped in damp sphagnum or peat, dampened cheese cloth or similar material, covered with plastic and held tightly with florist's wire, rubber bands, or a twist-em. The plants will not have used up all their strength just to survive and should grow again with little set-back at their destination.

Public Gardens, Iris Competitions and Awards

When a gardener becomes an iris fancier, his interest will turn to new hybrids and rarities and how they can be used and displayed. This is really no different than any interested specialist gardener who wants to keep up with the latest. Sources of information about iris are not all that plentiful. A good overview of what is available can be obtained from specialist nurseries which carry a broad and plentiful stock of iris and whose addresses can be found in the list of suppliers.

Iris are obviously the focal point of the iris societies which have been formed in various countries. The German Iris Society was founded in Berlin after World War II as the Deutsche Iris-Gesellschaft. A later expansion, to include all perennials, led to today's name, Gesellschaft der Staudenfreunde. The extremely active iris group within the Society fully represents the special interests of iris enthusiasts.

It is the dream of iris fanciers and breeders to create comparative gardens, where all the species and new cultivars may be seen. The center for iris display in

Germany is at the Palm Garden of the City of Frankfurt. In addition to Dr. Gustav Schoser, the Director of the Palm Garden, and Hermann Hald, President of the Gesellschaft der Staudenfreunde, and his very active wife, many iris enthusiasts from the Frankfurt area helped make this iris garden a success. The first plantings were made in the fall of 1971 and in 1973 the first judging took place. Today this iris planting has become one of the most eminent, primarily for its collection of the latest German and foreign hybrids as well as some of the valuable older varieties.

Iris plantings can also be found in the various gardens that were created by the Federal Garden Show Program. A prime example is Hamburg's "Planten un Blomen", where international garden shows take place every ten years. An extensive display of all the latest iris was planted in Munich at the I.G.A. (International Garden Exposition) 83. Proven older varieties, Dwarf Iris and wild iris are planted in the viewing gardens in Weihenstephan/Friesing, a regular Eldorado for plant lovers. Iris plantings in botanical gardens should also not be overlooked. The most memorable botanical garden planting for me is the hillside of iris in the Botanical Garden in Tübingen.

In the Donaupark in Vienna, vast iris plantings have been in place since the International Garden Exposition there (1964). Collectors of rare Dwarf Iris will find a fine display in the Alpengarten in the Belvedère.

The Swiss Iris Society, Schweizer Iris- und Lilienfreunde, is very active, opening their private gardens to visiting specialists, and assisting Swiss botanic gardens with their iris collections. The largest collection of wild species and hybrids can be found in the Iris Garden in Brüglingen near Basel. Countess H. von Stein-Zeppelin's Bearded

Iris collection, which contains about 1400 different varieties, is located here too. Her iris garden comprises an area of some 27,000 sq. ft. (2500 sq. m). In Bern there is a nice planting of recent Bearded Iris in the "Rosengarten" and a lovely show planting has been laid out in Wallisellen near Zurich. There is an iris collection in the Jardin Botanique in Porrentruy in the Jura Alps as well as in the old castle gardens of the Chateau de Vuillerens in the vicinity of Lake Geneva.

The extensive iris plantings in the Botanical Gardens of Pruhonice near Prague, Czechoslovakia, exist thanks to the efforts of M. Blazek. These plantings are unique in that the iris are arranged historically. One can observe iris strains from the Middle Ages to the newest hybrids, all laid out according to time periods.

England abounds in iris gardens. The iris plantings of the Royal Horticultural Society in Wisley and those in the Botanical Garden in Kew are surely the most famous. But there are lovely plantings in Barrington Court near Ilminster, Somerset and another in Poleseden Lacey near Dorking, Surrey. The iris plantings in Sezincote, Moreton in the Marsh, Gloucestershire are interesting, as are those in Waterhouse Plantations, Bushey Park, Hampton, Greater London. Admirable collections, especially of Apogon Iris, are found in a number of Scottish gardens. The Botanical Garden of Edinburgh should not be missed.

Wherever intensive breeding or growing is going on, competitions where growers, amateur and commercial vie with each other in a friendly spirit have sprung up. The competition in Germany for Tall Bearded Iris, is held at the Palmgarten in Frankfurt. If a strictly objective judgment is to be rendered by the show judges, there must be guidelines for judging. These vary somewhat from country to country, but we can take the Frankfurt guidelines as typical.

Only new cultivars introduced and registered within the previous 3 years may be entered for judging. This is a way of encouraging the introduction of new cultivars. Breeders from Germany and abroad may enter up to 6 hybrids per year each. Two healthy rhizomes per cultivar must be submitted. The entries aren't judged for 2 years, in order to give the plants time to become established and grow to their full potential. If, after two years, an entry has not yet bloomed, it is removed but may be replaced by 2 new rhizomes, which are then treated as if they are a new submission. There is no entry fee, but the plants entered become the property of the Palmgarten. Judging is usually done when the iris are in bloom and is done by differing numbers of iris judges. A point system is used. There are seven separate categories to be evaluated each of which can be assigned 10, 15, or 30 points, depending on the category:

1. Formation of the clump and overall healthiness
2. Inflorescence (blossoms per stem, stems per clump)
3. Stem (strength, branching characteristics)
4. Color of blossom
5. Form and substance of blossom
6. Special features and balance
7. Advancement in breeding

As the breeder wishes recognition, various levels of awards have been instituted. The first level is a commendation (*Highly Commended*), which any cultivar receiving a minimum number of points automatically gets. The best cultivar from the German-speaking countries receives the *Countess Zeppelin Cup* (donated by Frau von Stein-Zeppelin) as a challenge trophy. The best cultivar from abroad receives a Gold Medal from the Palmgarten; while a Silver Medal goes to both the best early bloomer and the best late bloomer. Every cultivar receiving a commendation is judged again the following year according to stricter criteria. The top 6 cultivars, assuming they have accumulated a specified minimum number of points, receive an *Award of Merit*. The next 6 cultivars are also singled out to receive *runner-up* commendations. Finally, the cultivar judged best overall receives the *Karl Foerster Medal*. This is the highest distinction the Gesellschaft der Staudenfreunde has to award. Chief judge is Herr von Heydwolff.

What this competition in the Frankfurt Palmgarten is to those interested in Bearded Iris, the Vienna Dwarf Iris Show is to those who grow Dwarf Iris. Breeders from all over the world take part in this competition. The Viennese climate is ideal for Dwarf Iris, indeed *Iris pumila* still grows wild on the outskirts of the city. The Vienna Dwarf Iris Show is closely connected with the name of one man: Professor Franz Kurzmann. He deserves much of the credit for his years of tireless work in establishing the primary of the Viennan Show. The iris submitted for judging are planted in long beds under identical conditions at Kagran, the college for landscape architecture in Vienna. Four different groups are judged:

1. Dwarf Iris (up to 9" or 25 cm tall) = Miniature Dwarfs
2. Small iris (up to 15" or 40 cm tall) = Standard Dwarfs
3. Median iris (up to 28" or 70 cm tall) = Intermediate Bearded
4. Oncobreds

The highest award is the Staatspreis (National Award). For advances in breeding (color, form, etc.), there is the special award of the Gesellschaft der Staudenfreunde. In addition, gold, silver, and bronze medals are awarded in each category.

The most sought after trophy for iris breeding in Europe may be the "Premio Firenze", the golden florin awarded in Florence. The competition for the best new Tall Bearded Iris hybrids is an annual event. Those who attend will see new cultivars in their full array.

The greatest number and the most diverse iris competitions take place in England and the United States. To make your way through them, you almost have to be a specialist. In England every year the B.I.S. (British Iris Society) conducts a Dwarf, Median and Species show, the Chelsea Show and the Main Iris Show. Trophies presented include the Dykes Medal, the Foster Memorial Plaque, the Pilkington Award, The Hugh Miller Trophy, the Souvenir de M. Lemoine, and The Fothergill Memorial Trophy.

In the U.S. there is also a Dykes Medal, as well as the Knowlton Medal for Border Iris, the San Medal for Intermedias, the Cook-Douglas Medal for Standard Dwarfs, the Caparne Award for Miniature Dwarfs, the White Award for Aril Iris, and the William Mohr Award for Arilbreds.

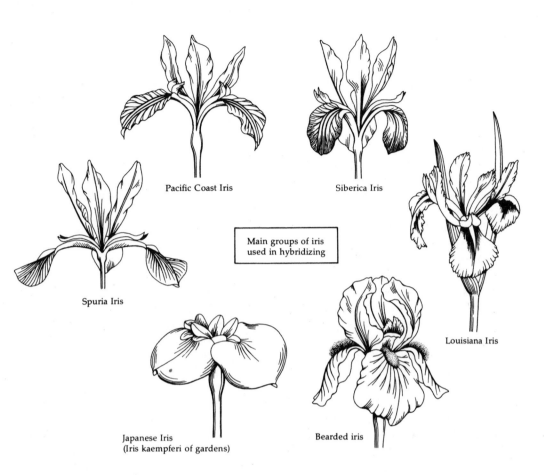

Pacific Coast Iris

Siberica Iris

Main groups of iris
used in hybridizing

Spuria Iris

Louisiana Iris

Japanese Iris
(Iris kaempferi of gardens)

Bearded iris

Cut Iris Flower Shows

Cut Iris Flower Shows have long been a tradition in England and the U.S.A., but for the past several years have also been held in West Germany by the Iris Specialty Group of the G.S. In England these are run by the British Iris Society (B.I.S.) and in the U.S. by the American Iris Society.

Obviously there is no hope of winning a prize or medal with ordinary plants. There are, however, two possible ways of coming up with award winning blooms. The first is really a matter of luck. Shortly before the iris come into bloom, one looks over one's garden and selects the stem which appears to be above average.

The second, more methodical approach begins with special preparations a year in advance. Quality cannot be achieved from old established plants that have become overgrown and form tangled clusters of rhizomes. The best stalks are obtained from plants planted as healthy rhizomes 2 years previously, although it's very possible to get show-quality flower stalks from 1-year plants but only if they have been transplanted in July. During this 1–2 year period, the plants selected should be protected and receive the best nutrients.

It is just as difficult to bring iris blossoms to a show in perfect display as it is to set the date of the show or a conference when iris will be blooming. It all has to be decided months or even a year in advance, before the weather conditions are known.

Unless it is a Dwarf Iris or species show, as they have in England and the U.S., Tall Bearded Iris are always the focal point of any cut-iris show. The blooming period of iris fluctuates tremendously, depending on the weather. Flowering time commonly varies by 2–3 weeks from year to year, so cut-iris shows offer at best an opportunity for only some of the exhibitors to cut show-quality stalks the day of the show. The weather even in the last few weeks before a show can have a major effect on iris development.

However, there are a few tricks for manipulating the blooming time of show iris. If one intends to participate in a cut-iris exhibition, the iris stalks should be inspected 1–2 weeks before the show to see how they are developing. Usually one can tell just by the thickness of the stalk which plants have any chance at all. This becomes routine for those who have exhibited often and indeed they can predict just how long it will take a particular flower to develop fully, which is unfortunately different for each variety. There is no certainty that the blossoms will be wide open tomorrow, if the buds show color today. There are so many different categories in a cut-iris show, some advance consideration should also be given into which category this or that iris will be entered. A great deal depends on how many show quality iris one has of any one variety.

It is legitimate to manipulate blossoming. Often individual buds must be prevented from opening, because the stalk chosen for showing should have three branches and at least 2, but preferably 3, fully opened blossoms at judging time. To prevent rapidly developing buds from opening, wrap them in a piece of Kleenex tied in the middle with a soft, thick piece of yarn (thread is too thin and cuts; rubber bands leave visible deformities in the blossom). The point is not to bring development to an abrupt standstill, but to allow the buds to go on swelling, though somewhat more slowly, beneath this mantle. A light touch is needed for this operation because buds break off very easily.

Other means of retarding or speeding up development of iris blossoms are available from professional gardeners and plant importers. Most commercial nurseries have a greenhouse which any iris hobbyist, who himself does not have a small greenhouse, can use to speed up the development of flowers. The stalk is cut a few days beforehand, put in water, and then exposed to the humid warmth. But this obviously should not be done too far in advance. To reverse the process, iris can be put in a florist's cold storage facilities.

Blossoms opening 2 days before a show will probably not arrive in prime condition. This fact must be considered when choosing the flower stalk, so do not rely on the last blossom on a branch. Stalks should be cut just above the rhizome. The same applies to cut iris for personal use. The cuts can then dry out quickly and so are less prone to infection. Exhibitors have wide latitude in selecting stem length for a show exhibition, so any buds which show color should be carefully wrapped in soft paper.

Transporting cut iris can be difficult, especially if the show is at some distance. Obviously it's simpler when the show is taking place in one's own city and more difficult if a trip of hundreds of miles is involved. Iris can easily be transported by automobile.

The iris are placed on a layer of smooth or corrugated cardboard. The first layer of iris should have all the stems going in one direction, then comes a layer of newspaper or tissue paper, and then another layer of iris with buds at the opposite end. This layering is repeated, if space permits, but two layers are optimal. More imagination is required to transport open blossoms. I made a frame out of a grate with legs welded to it. The stalks are stuck through the holes in the grate and held upright. On hot days, a plastic tub filled with damp moss or peat, rather than water which would slosh out is put under the rack to keep the ends of the stems moist. Racks can also be made from bamboo sticks or large stalks of pampas grass or giant reed (*Arundo donax*). Individual stalks are secured with rubber bands. Orchid tubes can be used to provide water or several stalks may be put in a water-filled plastic bag fastened at the top with a rubber band.

Once at their destination, take the iris out of the car immediately, especially if it is hot. The evening before the show opens, all the iris should be completely set up in their vases. This extra time should be allowed for in the planning for the show. One can never count on everything that one needs being available at the exhibition site. Vases and materials for flower arranging, such as florist's wax, gravel, florist's foam, etc. must be provided. But knives, scissors, florist's wire, extra iris leaves, white pieces of cardboard, and felt pens should all be brought by the exhibitor in case there are not enough utensils for everyone.

The vases needed should be cleaned and filled with water. Stationary, round inserts slightly smaller than the bottom of the vase should be cut out of florist's foam with holes, corresponding to the number of stalks to be displayed, punched in. The stalks are then stuck in these holes. Florist's wax or pebbles can also be used

for holding the iris upright. In an emergency, crumpled newspaper will also do. Any buds which have been "bound up" should be unwrapped, i.e. the pieces of yarn should be cut and the paper removed. Unattractive blossoms, unwanted parts of blossoms, and forming ovules should be removed. The spathe valves should be brushed forward so that the amputation is not so noticeable. In most American iris shows the primary (first bud on the stalk) flower must be in bloom, or the stalk is disqualified. The leaves should be examined carefully for damaged brown tips which must be trimmed off.

The ornamentation should harmonize with the vases and display. Viewers see either florist's wax and foam inserts or a vase appropriately decorated and hiding the mechanism. Good decorative materials include peat, sphagnum, bark dust, or expanded clay. The flower stalks should be arranged in the vase and the distance between vases planned so that all the blossoms have enough room to open.

Each individual vase must get to its respective judging area without being mixed up with others. If a single vase can qualify for more than one class, it is wise to concentrate on the classification where it has the best chance of winning and the least competition.

Standard cards are usually supplied at such competitions. But to avoid any confusion either with your own entries or those of others showing the same iris—the stalks should be labelled with paper tags, wooden twist tags or simply a small cardboard sign stuck in the vase. This is the reason for bringing white cardboard and a felt tip pen. The tag should carry the name of the iris, the class, and the exhibitor's name.

Organizational details vary from competition to competition. So I won't deal here with preregistration, participant's tickets, exhibition lists, etc. Just one more tip: Shortly before judging begins, half-open blossoms can be quickly opened so that they look their best when the judge comes around. Add warm water to the container and blow gently but steadily on the center of the flower.

We have talked about displaying iris in competitions, but many local garden clubs hold spring or early summer shows exhibiting all the products of the garden. If iris are in bloom, they should be included. They can be beautifully shown, when not in competition, with other late spring or early summer flowers. There should be no limit to one's imagination here.

Even cut-iris competitions usually offer a so-called creative category, in which iris from any of the sections can be used with flowers of other genera, as long as iris predominate in the arrangement. Sometimes these arrangements have to be made around an announced theme. One can use Japanese principles (e.g., Ikebana), traditional arrangements, or flights of fancy. The main point is that iris of the most disparate groups can be combined with each other or with other genera blooming at the same time (see section on "Iris as Cut Flowers").

Dwarf Iris and, to a degree, iris species are often exhibited as potted plants. Here too, retarding the flowers in cold storage 36°–37.5°F. (at 2–3°C) or forcing them is necessary. Because the number of buds is so limited, having an open blossom on the day of the show can't always be guaranteed. Thus, as many of the same species or cultivar, as is practical, should be potted up and forced so that at least one good blossom can be exhibited.

The precise system of categories used in competition varies greatly from one show to the next so no purpose is served in reporting a specific system here. But the usual divisions are Tall Bearded Iris, often subdivided into domestic and foreign hybrids; other taller Bearded Iris, such as Dwarf Iris, Intermedias and Border Iris; Arils and Arilbreds; Sibiricas; iris species and interspecific hybrids; other Iridacae; and finally the so-called creative category already mentioned. These main groups (usually called divisions) can be further subdivided into iris hybridized by the participant, iris registered by the participant, foreign hybrids, and finally into the number of flower stalks and the number of varieties. The rules for exhibiting in a specific show should be learned beforehand as there is usually not enough time on the day of the show to do so.

Iris Species

Classification of Iris (Systematics)

Some plant genera contain only a few, sometimes even one, species, while in others hundreds of species are included. For example, more than 1600 species are contained in the genus *Euphorbia*. To get a better overall view, botanists try to subdivide these huge genera into groups (series) containing plants with specific morphological features in common.

Iris is one of the very comprehensive genera. Not just the amateur but even experts have difficulties distinguishing the various species. There is an enormous number of species, subspecies, varieties, forms, and natural hybrids. If one adds cultivars, the number of distinct taxa goes into the thousands. There are well over 200 different *Iris* to which botanists have given the status of species. The larger its range, the more diverse the individual species. Where these ranges overlap, numerous natural hybrids occur. And every year new ones are being bred by growers and breeders. Gardeners and plant-lovers all over the world participate in the breeding of Iris cultivar's. To be sure, nature does not allow all Iris to be crossed. It depends on the number of chromosomes, how closely related they are and many other factors. But potentials for crossing are vast, and successful combinations are being achieved more and more frequently— often by using highly technical methods— which have been impossible until recently. From these efforts crosses between members of different sections have even been achieved.

Beginners should not be put off by the number of names and classifications. One soon realizes that unless one proceeds systematically, it is impossible to try to comprehend the entire realm of iris. First of all, it is necessary to bear in mind the hierarchical division used with plants in general:

Genus (gen.)
  Subgenus (subgen.)
    Section (sec.)
      Subsection (subsec.)
       Series (ser.)
        Species (sp. on spp. plural)
         Subspecies (ssp.)
          Variety (var.)
           Subvariety (subvar.)
            Form (f.)
             [Cultivar (cr.)
             = man-made
             variety]

The classification, subvariety, is rarely used within the genus *Iris*. The scope of each systematic unit can vary considerably. The hierarchy also proceeds further back from genus (family, order, etc.), to include longer and larger categories of plants, but that does not really concern us here. Various systems for categorizing plants have existed in some form for centuries. Perhaps the most familiar plant system is the one developed by Carolus Linnaeus (Carl von Linne) (1707–1778). To avoid confusion, only the more recent systems to categorize *Iris* taxa will be mentioned here. The Dykes-Diels classification of the genera was made in

1930, and another classification was made in 1953 by George H. M. Lawrence. There was a subsequent classification made by Lawrence and Randolph (1959). The Iris latest classification is the work of Rodionenko (Leningrad, 1961). All three systems are presented at the end of this section; the comparison is interesting. This book is based on the classification made by Rodionenko because, in my opinion, it is the most successful.

Lay gardeners may wonder how the work of individual botanists has so greatly changed the system of the genus *Iris*. As time passes and more research is done, our knowledge, even about phylogenesis, keeps growing, and from decade to decade chromosomal relationships, which furnish key data, are being more and more clearly understood.

It should be pointed out here that G. H. M. Lawrence and the American Iris Society have classified Pogon Iris according to size. We accept this division only for the bearded hybrids, not for the species. However, for the sake of completeness we shall repeat this classification of the species.

1. Miniature Dwarf Bearded
   I. alexeenkoi Gross
   I. astrachanica Rodionenko
   I. attica Boiss. et Heldr.
   I. balkana Janka
   I. barthii Prod. et Buia
   I. binata Schur
   I. bosniaca Beck
   I. chamaeiris Bert.
   I. furcata M. Bieb.
   I. griffithii Baker
   I. mellita Janka
   I. pseudopumila Tineo
   I. pumila L.
   I. reichenbachii Heuff.
   I. scariosa Wild. ex Link
   I. taurica Lodd.

I. timofejewii Woronow
2. Standard Dwarf Bearded
   I. aphylla L.
   I. benacensis Kern.
   I. italica Parl.
   I. lutescens Lam.
   I. olbiensis Henon
   I. subbiflora
   I. virescens
Intermediate Bearded:
   I. albicans Lange
   I. aphylla L.
   I. florentina L.
   I. germanica L.
   I. kashmiriana Baker
   I. kochii Kern.
Miniature Tall Bearded
   I. cengialti Ambrosi
   I. illyrica Tomm.
   I. perrieri Sim.
   I. reginae Horvath
   I. rudskyi Horvath
   I. variegata L.
Border Bearded
   I. alberti Regel
   I. bartonii M. Foster
   I. belouinii Boiss. et Corn.
   I. imbricata Lindl.
   I. junonia Schott et Kotschy
Standard Tall Bearded
   I. croatica Horvath
   I. cypriana Baker et Foster
   I. mesopotamica Dykes
   I. pallida Lam. with the hybrid forms amoena, *I. plicata*, *I. squalens*, *I. sambucina*
   I. trojana Kern. ex Stapf
   I. varbossiana Maly

This classification contains a large number of species whose species status is doubtful, as at least some given species rank are of hybrid origin. However this division is useful for breeding Bearded Iris. In this classification the old *I. ger-*

manica became the Iris Barbata Elatior group; the old dwarf varieties, which were formerly called *I. pumila* in the catalogues, became the Iris Barbata Nana group, and the hybrids between the two became the middle-sized Barbata Median group. The American classification differentiates still further by designating precise sizes in centimeters. Whether this classification is ideal is a moot point, since iris that fall near the dividing lines can belong to one group or the other, depending on soil conditions.

Classification according to size

up to 8" (20 cm)	Miniature Dwarf	Dwarf Iris group
8–15" (21–40 cm)	Standard Dwarf	Barbata Nana group
15–28" (41–70 cm)	Intermedias Stiff, upright branching stems standing well above upright leaves. Blossoms 4–5" (10–12.5 cm). Blooming period between Standard Dwarfs and Tall Bearded Iris.	Median Iris (Iris-Barbata Median group)
15–28" (41–70 cm)	Table Iris (Miniature Tall Bearded—MTB) Flowers no larger than 6" (15 cm) when height and width are combined. Flowers on slender, flexible, branching stems. Leaves upright or overhanging.	
15–28" (41–70 cm)	Border Iris Diameter of blossom 4–5" (10–13 cm). Upright stems, leaves shorter than stems. Similar to Tall Bearded Iris, only smaller overall, in proportion to size of flower.	
above 28" (70 cm)	Standard Talls	Tall Bearded Iris (Iris Barbata Elatior group)

Classification of the Genus According to Dykes-Diels
(Engler-Prantl, *Naturl. Pflanzenfam.* ed. 2, 15a, 500–505, 1930)
Section I.   Apogon Baker, Gard. Chron. 1876, 2, 143.
          Subsection 1. Sibiricae (also: Prismatica)
          Subsection 2. Tenuifoliae
          Subsection 3. Californicae
          Subsection 4. Syriacae

Section II.   Pardanthopsis Hance in *Journ. Bot.* 13, 105 (1875)
Section III.   Evansia Salisbury, *Trans. Hort Soc.* 1, 303 (1812), s. t. gen.
Section IV.   Oncocyclus Siemssen, *Bot. Ztg.* 4, 705 (1846), s. t. gen.
Section V.   Regelia Dykes, *Genus Iris* 124 (1913)
Section VI.   Pseudoregelia Dykes, *Genus Iris* 129 (1913)
Section VII.   Pogon Iris Baker, *Gard. Chron.* 1876, 2, 647 (A. Unbranching stem [also: *flavissima*!]; B. Branching stem)
Section VIII.   Nepalensis Dykes, *Genus Iris* 184 (1913)
Section IX.   Juno Trattinnick (s. t. gen. ex Roemer & Schultes, *Syst.* 1, 471 [1817])
Section X.   Xiphium Miller, *Garden Dictionary* ed. 7 (1759), s. t. gen.
Section XI.   Reticulata Dykes, *Genus Iris* 220 (1913)
Section XII.   Gynandriris Parlatore, Nov. gen. & spec. *Monocot.* 49 (1854)

Classification of the genus according to Lawrence (Lawrence, *A Reclassification of the Genus Iris, Gentes Herbarum* 8, fasc. 4, 195)

I. Subgenus Iris (the rhizomatous species)
    1. Sect. *Pogiris.* Tausch (the bearded species)
        a) Subsect. Pogoniris, (Spach) Bentham
            1. Series Pumilae, Lawrence
            2. Series Elatae, Lawrence
        b) Subsect. Hexapogon, Bentham ("Regelia-Iris")
        c) Subsect. Oncocyclus, (Siemssen) Bentham
        d) Subsect. Pseudoregelia, (Dykes) Lawrence
    2. Sect. Spathula, Tausch emend. Lawrence (the non-bearded species)
        a) Subsect. Pardanthopsis, (Hance) Lawrence
        b) Subsect. Foetidissima, Diels
        c) Subsect. Apogon, Bentham
            1. Series Sibiricae, (Diels) Lawr. stat. nov.
            2. Series Tenuifoliae, (Diels) Lawrence stat. nov.
            3. Series Californicae, (Diels) Lawrence stat. nov.
            4. Series Syriacae, (Diels) Lawr. stat. nov.
            5. Series Chinensis, (Diels) Lawrence stat. nov.
            6. Series Ruthenicae, (Diels) Lawrence stat. nov.

7. Series Unguicularis, (Diels) Lawrence stat. nov.
8. Series Spuriae, (Diels) Lawr. stat. nov.
9. Series Laevigatae, (Diels) Lawrence stat. nov.
10. Series Prismaticae, Lawrence stat. nov.
11. Series Hexagonae, (Diels) Lawrence stat. nov.
12. Series Ensatae, (Diels) Lawr. stat. nov.
13. Series Longipetalae, (Diels) Lawrence stat. nov.
14. Series Tripetalae, (Diels) Lawrence stat. nov.
15. Series Vernae, (Diels) Lawrence stat. nov.

    d) Subsect. Evansia, Bentham

II. Subgenus Nepalensis, (Dykes) Lawrence
III. Subgenus Xiphium, (Miller) Spach
       1. Sect. Xiphion, Tausch
       2. Sect. Reticulata, Dykes
IV. Subgenus Scorpiris, Spach (Juno)
V. Subgenus Gynandriris, (Parlatore) Lawrence

Classification of the genus Iris and related genera according to Rodionenko
(*Rod. Iris*, Akad. Nauk, SSR, Moscow 1961)

Genus	Subgenus	Section	Subsection	Series
Iris L.	I. Limniris (Tausch) Spach	I. Limniris Tausch	a) Apogon Bentham em. Rod.	Sibiricae (Dykes) Lawrence Prismaticae Laevigatae Chinensis Californicae Hexagonae Longipetalae Tripetalae Vernae
			b) Ensatae Diels c) Tenuifoliae	Ensatae Diels Tenuifoliae (Diels) Lawr. Ventricosae Rodionenko
			d) Syriacae	Syriacae Diels
		2. Unguiculares (Diels) Rod.	e) Unguicularis Diels (Genus Siphonostylis W. Schulze)	Unguicularis (Diels) Lawr.
		3. Ioniris Spach em. Rod.		Ruthenicae (Diels) Lawr.

Genus	Subgenus	Section	Subsection	Series
	II. Xyridion Tausch Spach em. Rod.	1. Xyridion Tausch		Spuriae (Diels) Lawr. Gramineae Rod.
		2. Spathula Tausch	(I. foetidissima L.)	
	III. Nepalensis (Dykes) Lawr.		(I. nepalensis D. Don)	
	IV. Pardanthopsis (Hance) Baker		(I. dichotoma Pallas)	
	V. Crossiris Spach	1. Crossiris Spach		Japonicae Rod. Tectores Rod. Cristatae Rod.
		2. Lophiris Tausch		
		3. Monospatha Rodionenko	(I. gracilipes A. Gray)	
	VI. Iris (Pogoniris Spach)	1. Iris (Pogoniris)		Pumilae Lawr. Elatae Lawr. Dykes Rod.
		2. Hexapogon (Bunge)	a) Regelia b) Pseudoregelia (Dykes) Lawrence c) Oncocyclus (Siemssen) Bentham	
Xiphium Miller Iridodictyum Rodionenko		1. Iridodictyum Rod.	(I. retic. M. B.) (I. kolp. Regel)	
		2. Monolepis Rod.		
Gynandriris Parlatore Juno Trattinnick			(Genus Sisyrin-chium [L.] Parl.)	
		1. Juno s. nov. Rod.	(I. persica, bucharica, stocksii)	
		2. Physocaulon s. nov. Rod.		Drephanophyllae Rodionenko Rosenbachianae Rodionenko
		3. Acanthospora s. nov. Rod.	(I. alata I. palaestina)	

Key to the Identification of the Genus *Iris* and Closely Related Genera, according to the B. I. S. Species Group:

Plants with bulbs   A + B
Plants without bulbs   C—Z

A | Bulbs with robust, fleshy roots........................... Juno
    | Bulbs lacking robust, fleshy roots........................ B

B | Bulbs with smooth outer skin .... Xiphium
    | Bulbs with rough, netted outer skin .... Iridodictyum

C | Rootstock tuberous with rough, netted outer skin.......... Gynandriris
    | Rootstock tuberous lacking rough, netted outer skin .... D

D | Rootstock tuberous, strangely finger-like, lacking dry outer skin, leaves square in cross-section...................... Hermodactylus
    | Rootstock rhizomatous .... E

E | Rhizomes joining at points of growth (like a dahlia) .... Nepalensis
    | Rhizome clearly horizontal............................. F

F | Falls with crest-like structure .... Evansia
    | Falls lacking crest.................................... G

G | Falls with beard .... H
    | Falls lacking beard .... K

H | Seed lacking aril (fleshy, white appendage on seed)........ Pogon Iris
    | Seed with aril I

I | Aril small, blossoms open when leaves are still short........ Pseudoregelia
   | Aril large, blossoms open when leaves are well-developed... J

J | Unifloral... Oncocyclus
    | Unifloral or several flowers on one stem.................. Regelia

K | Seed noticeably winged .... Pardanthopsis
    | Seed not winged..................................... L

L | Seed coral-red, attached to capsule..................... Foetidissima
    | Seed not firmly attached to capsule .... M

M | Capsule hexagonal in cross-section..................... N
    | Capsule triangular in cross section .... R

N | Capsule with doubled rib at angles .... Spuriae
    | Capsule with single rib at angles....................... O

O | Rhizome slender, with long, stolon-like shoots on the ground .... Prismaticae
    | Rhizome without stolons .... P

P	Blossoms sessile in leaf axil	Hexagonae
	Blossoms not sessile in leaf axil.	Q

Q	Capsule short, tube-shaped, spherical in cross section	Ensatae
	Capsule broad in cross-section, pointed towards the ends. . . .	Longipetalae

R	Seeds with aril	S
	Seeds lacking aril	T

S	Seed with white aril in fresh condition, dwarfish, grass-like growth	Ruthenicae
	Seed lacking white aril, rhizome slender, form like Pogon Iris. . .	Vernae

T	Perianth tube long, falls narrowing abruptly into the haft	Unguicularis
	Perianth tube short, falls with gradual transition to haft.	U

U	Stigma in form of a triangular tongue	V
	Stigma not in form of triangular tongue	W

V	Rhizome slender, reddish.	Californicae
	Rhizome strong, brown.	Sibiricae (incl. Chrysographes)

W	Ring-shaped rhizome, with stiff bristles.	Syriacae
	Rhizome not ring-shaped	X

X	Rhizome slender, growing wide-spread.	Chinensis
	Rhizome not slender	Y

Y	Standards reduced almost to bristle	Tripetalae
	Standards not reduced to bristle	Z

Z	Seed more or less D-shaped with smooth, shiny surface	Laevigatae
	Seed cube-shaped with coarse, wrinkled skin	Tenuifoliae

A Word About Nomenclature

A gardening book, which in many respects relies heavily on botany, should attempt to use the latest nomenclature. I say attempt, because even nomenclature is not absolutely immutable or eternally valid. Botanists themselves do not agree on many names, and all of them pull on the same rope of priority, with sometimes one name being valid, sometimes another.

I have tried to adapt myself as much as possible to current usage, but there are

Bearded iris old and new. Between fanatics who have to have the latest cultivars and collectors of historical varieties, there are all shades of iris fanciers. Not everything new is better, and not everything that has been around a long time is necessarily good.

Upper left: This border iris with the name 'Brown Lasso' is new. The color combination is interesting.
Upper right: The tall bearded iris 'Margarita' seems to have the resistance to put up with poor European climatic conditions. A modern iris that is universally praised.
Below: 'Gudrun', an old, classical variety, developed by E. Dykes in 1931, now almost numbers among the historical varieties, although its garden value is still indisputable.

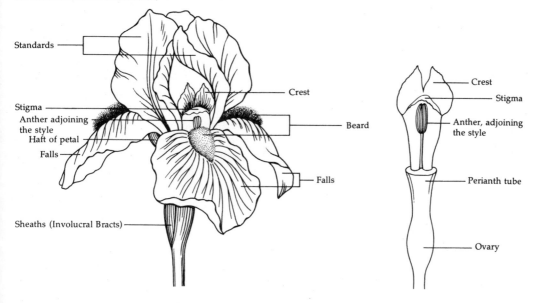

Iris blossom structure (bearded iris)

Standards

Crest

Stigma
Anther adjoining
the style
Haft of petal

Beard

Falls

Crest

Stigma

Anther, adjoining
the style

Falls

Perianth tube

Sheaths (Involucral Bracts)

Ovary

some very difficult complexes in which I do not follow normal botanical usage, but consciously use conventional names.

The whole complex of Japanese Iris, *I. kaempferi* Sieb. ex Lem. is very difficult. I shall stay with this common name, as this is first and foremost a gardening book. A name like Japanese Iris, so common among gardeners, cannot be eliminated just like that. *I. kaempferi* Sieb. ex Lem. is

New colors of tall bearded iris.

Upper left: 'Leo Haven', already a somewhat older hybrid, which nonetheless has an enchanting display of colors. It should be said that not all possible color combinations are beautiful, but this combination is.
Upper right: 'One Desire', shown together with Jacob'srod, Asphodelene lutea. Today we rarely take notice of the fact that not very long ago this color of tall bearded iris did not exist.
Below: This pretty pink hybrid was developed by the author from a cross between 'Rosenquarz' (Dr. Werckmeister) and 'Geliputz' (Victor von Martin). It shows stress in the damp, cold weather of upper Franconia, but it serves as an example of the many pink varieties.

called *I. ensata* Thunberg today, because it was given the name *I. ensata* Thunberg in 1794 and the name *I. kaempferi* Sieb in 1858.

Until now the tall, slender, small-blossomed iris of subsection *Ensatae* has been incorrectly known as *I. ensata* Thunberg. In the publications of the B. I S., it is now called *I. lactea* Pallas. I do not follow this precedent, but stay with *I. ensata*, though not *I. ensata* Thunberg, but *I. ensata* auct. non Thunb. In *Flora of the Iranian Highlands and Surrounding Regions* Professor D. Reichenberg named this Iris *I. oxypetala* Bunge (syn. *I. moorcroftiana* Wall, ex D. Don and *I. ensata* auct. non Thunb.) In Volume V of *Flora Europaea*, it is called *I. triflorum* (Balbis) Cesati because this plant grows wild in northwestern Italy, although its homeland is Central Asia. In the future, when a priority has definitely been established, I shall gladly use the official name, but this is not the case at present.

Rodionenko, whose classification system I am following, shows *Xiphium* as an

109

independent genus. In Miller's original description (1753), the name was spelled *Xiphion*, presumably the standard Greek form. I prefer the Latin version *Xiphium*—used by other writers and hence established—as an orthographic variant without any particular significance in nomenclature, and so in this book we will stay with the term *Xiphium*.

Any other special problems with nomenclature will be considered along with the individual species they affect.

Genus Iris
   Subgenus Limniris
      Sect Limniris
         Subsect Apogon
            Series Sibiricae

Gardeners call these iris the Sibirica group or simply Grass Iris. They all make attractive garden plants and have been very intensively cultivated, especially the true *I. sibirica*. All told, there are 10 different species known, of which the origin of 2 is obscure; the native habitats of both *I. bulleyana* and *I. dykesii* are unknown. Another species, *I. phragmitetorum*, is little known and rarely cultivated. Difficulties concerning species purity among garden specimens occur with *I. sibirica* and *I. sanguinea* because they look so similar and cross freely with each other. The series itself is divided into 2 groups, according to the number of chromosomes. *I. sibirica* and *I. sanguinea*, each with 28 chromosomes, belong to the first group. The second group is made up of species with 40 chromosomes, such as *I. bulleyana*, *I. chrysographes*, *I. clarkei*, *I. delavayi*, *I. forrestii*

and *I. wilsonii*. There is no data on chromosome count for *I. dykesii* or *I. phragmitetorum*.

The native range of *I. sibirica* (the name is misleading) extends from Europe to Japan and southwest China, while *I. sanguinea* is its counterpart in central-northern Asia (Siberia), China, and Japan. The other species are native to the region in and around Yunnan Province in China, including the Himalyas east of Nepal, upper Burma and southeast Tibet. At various times *I. prismatica*, from North America, has been assigned to this series too, but it now comprises its own series. All members of this group have strong, gnarled, cespitose, brown rhizomes with many roots and tough remains of fibrous roots. The leaves are narrow and linear and not reddish at the base, as with the series Californicae (Pacific Coast Iris). They turn yellow-brown in the fall and die back. Stems are hollow, with the exception of *I. clarkei*. The color of the blossoms is yellow or blue to reddish violet, with a short perianth tube. The crest has a triangular, tongue-shaped stigma. The seeds are D- to cube-shaped.

None of the species of this series thrive in hot, dry climates, but require a minimum of moisture in the soil to flourish. They grow particularly well where the air is somewhat more humid. The lighter the soil, the damper it should be. Soil pH should be neutral to slightly acid; sensitivity to lime varies. *I. sibirica* is largely insensitive, whereas *I. clarkei* becomes chlorotic when there is even a small amount of lime in the soil. Some species can tolerate a great deal of moisture in the soil. *I. sibirica*, for instance, can tolerate standing in a few centimeters of water year round. The plant native to Germany also prefers damp meadows.

None of the species transplants well; divisions are slow to reestablish, taking several years to become really splendid bloomers again. Opinions differ about the best time to plant and divide these iris. In my experience, early spring is better than fall. In any case, they must be well watered for a long time. Small amounts of compost, humus, and mineral fertilizer are well tolerated.

Subseries Sibiricae

Iris sanguinea Don. (Hornem. is also given as the author)
Synonyms: *I. orientalis* Thunb. (Caution, not to be confused with the present *I. orientalis* Mill., the current valid name for *I. ochroleuca*!), *I. extremorientalis*, *I. sibirica* var. *sanguinea*.

Native to Siberia, especially southern Ussuria, Dauria, also China, Manchuria, Korea, and Japan.

Botanists find it difficult to distinguish between *I. sanguinea* and *I. sibirica*. The distinction is rendered difficult because both hybridize freely. However, a number of features simplify identification. The height of the flower stalk is one of them. In the case of *I. sanguinea* it is shorter than the leaves, the upper ⅓ of which arch over. *I. sibirica* is generally taller, with the blossoms held above the leaves. The flower stalk of *I. sanguinea* is non-branching and produces only 2 terminal blossoms. The spathes are green when the flowers are in bloom, rather than papery, and often tinged with pink or a reddish color at the base. Its blossoms are larger than those of *I. sibirica* and have erect standards and conspicuously wide, round falls. Typical blossom color is deep blue-violet with the ground color of the falls white, covered with a network of blue-violet veins that blend at the margins to form a pure blue-violet band. The width of the falls is 1½–2" (4–5 cm). Seed capsules

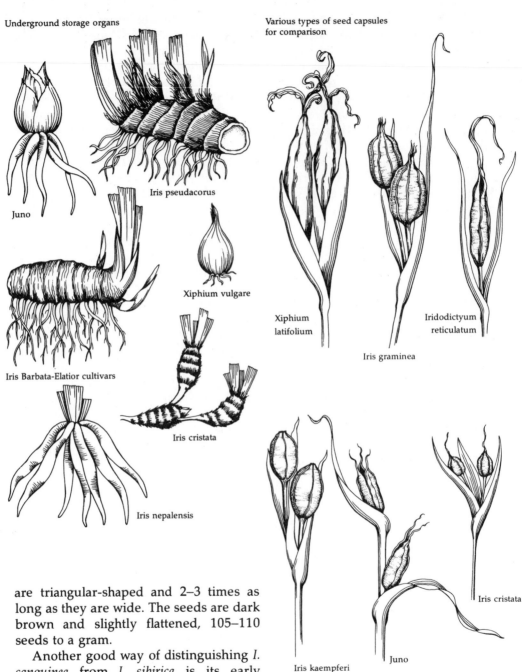

Underground storage organs

Various types of seed capsules for comparison

Juno

Iris pseudacorus

Iris Barbata-Elatior cultivars

Xiphium vulgare

Xiphium latifolium

Iridodictyum reticulatum

Iris graminea

Iris cristata

Iris nepalensis

Iris kaempferi (of gardens)

Juno

Iris cristata

are triangular-shaped and 2–3 times as long as they are wide. The seeds are dark brown and slightly flattened, 105–110 seeds to a gram.

Another good way of distinguishing *I. sanguinea* from *I. sibirica* is its early blooming period, which is about 7–10 days earlier than the latter. Blossoms from end of May to beginning of June (in Bavaria).

112

In addition to the species there are several other significant forms. *I. sanguinea* var. *alba* is a beautiful white type. A particularly attractive selection is known by the name of *I. sanguinea* 'Snow Queen'. *I. sanguinea* var. *violacea* comes from Japan and is characterized by deep purple-violet blossoms. There are numerous hybrids in gardens from crosses between *I. sanguinea* and *I. sibirica*. The surest way of obtaining genuine plants is to grow them from native seed. Germination presents no problem if seed is stratified at 40°F. or planted in a cold frame in the fall.

In general *I. sanguinea* is a good garden plant, even in the pure, wild species. Because it is not very tall, it can be used in a variety of settings. It is ideal combined with the white *I.* 'Snow Queen'. In every respect it is the equal of *I. sibirica*.

I have already pointed out its breeding value. Number of chromosomes 2n=28.

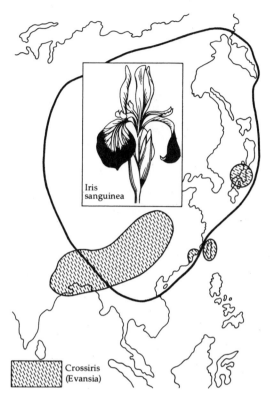

Iris sanguinea

Crossiris (Evansia)

Iris sibirica Linne

Synonyms: *I. pratensis* Lamarck, *I. angustifolia* Gilberti, *I. stricta* Moench, *I. maritima* Miller, *I. atracoerulea* Lynch, *I. erirrhiza* Pospichal, *I. acuta* Willdenow, *I. trigonocarpa* A. Br., *I. triflora* Redoute.

This extensive list of synonyms leads us to 2 conclusions. First, it is a plant with a long history and secondly, *I. sibirica* is very widespread. It is native to Germany (Lake Constance, Rheingau, northwestern Harz, Hannover, Osnabrück, Ammersee, Saxony, and the Havel region), Czechoslovakia, Carinthia, in European Russia (outskirts of Leningrad, east into western Siberia), the Balkans, and Asia Minor.

Compared to *I. sanguinea*, *I. sibirica*'s blossoms are bluer, with more slender falls (width ½–1" or 2–2.5 cm) and the spathes do not have a reddish tinge. The flower stalk is longer than the leaves and often more heavily branched, with 3–5 blossoms. Spathes are papery when the plant is in bloom. The seed capsules are rounder and are usually not more than twice as long as wide. If these features are noted, it can be readily differentiated from *I. sanguinea*.

The height of the flower stalk varies from 24–48" (60–120 cm), depending on the local form and habitat. The thin, grasslike foliage (3/16–7/16" or 0.6–1.2 cm wide) is slightly bluish green and forms dense clumps. Leaves have raised ribs. The rhizomes form creeping, gnarled rootstocks, which are covered with fibrous roots. Each fall has a small, white haft and the outer part is bluish with lighter veins

Iris sibirica and related species thrive in damp soil

Plant below soil line in a slight depression

Lots of peat and loam

running through it. Crests are pale lilac and are often spotted. This species blooms in June.

In spite of all the magnificent new hybrids, the wild species is still a worthwhile garden plant, thriving in slightly moist, rich soil. A bit more moisture and fertilizer are advised for light soils. Also needs a slightly acid soil reaction, but grows moderately well in soils with a slight lime content. *I. sibirica* grows particularly well with a top dressing of compost or old manure in the spring. Full sun will increase the number of blossoms, though it will also grow in semi-shade. Do not transplant until old clump begins to die out in the center. Planting time spring or fall; in colder regions early spring is preferable, but otherwise plant in fall. When dividing, about 6 shoots should be cut from the exterior of the clump; discard the woody center. *I. sibirica* need more room than Spuria Iris because the leaves spread outwards. They should be kept well watered after planting. It is not difficult to grow them from seed if they are treated like a "cold germinator". After being harvested, seeds should be sown in fall and covered with ⅜–¾' (1–2 cm) of earth. Fast growers, blossoms often appear by the second year.

I. sibirica var. *lactea* (milk-white, with a solitary black vein). Good companion plant to other larger pink, white, and red plants blooming at the same time, such as *Papaver orientalis, Paeonia* hybrids, *Chrysanthemum coccineum,* and Russell lupines. If combined with plants that bloom at different times, these should require the same kind of location or have contrasting leaf forms (*Hosta, Ligularia, Trollius, Caltha*).

I. sibirica is the most important species used in hybridizing modern Grass-Iris and this process is ongoing. Number of chromosomes 2n=28. Tetraploid types and forms with red and yellow blossoms are being sought.

Iris phragmitetorum Handel-Mazzetti

Native to northwest Yunnan Province in southwest China. Unfortunately very little is known of this iris; probably not in cultivation and only collected once. Named after Phragmites Swamp where it was found.

The leaves are narrow, about ⅜" (1 cm) wide and about 18" (45 cm) long. Spathes are papery. Blossoms somewhat larger than those of *I. chrysographes*, with upright standards. The color of the blossom is dark blue; the falls have a white spot in the center, from which veining radiates. In general, this iris is similar to *I. sanguinea*, the chief difference apparently being its remote geographical habitat.

Subseries Chrysographes

Iris bulleyana Dykes

The origin of this series is rather obscure. It was described in 1910. The original plant was collected by A. K. Bulley and sent to Dykes. In spite of intensive searching, Forrest did not find this plant on later expeditions and it was suspected that *I. bulleyana* was no more than an accidental seedling from Bulley's garden, a joint product of *I. forrestii, I. chrysographes,* and *I. wilsonii*. There had not been, however, enough time to produce such a hybrid, given the fact that it had only recently been introduced, and that this species blossomed almost immediately. Nonetheless, due to a number of features, it is probable that *I. bulleyana* was originally a hybrid, although it cannot be proved. (Even hand-pollinated seedlings do not come true, but vary and look similar to *I. forrestii*. The purplish-blue veins against a yellow background resemble the hybrids of *I. forrestii* and *I. chrysographes;* the seed pod and the form of the blossom resemble that of *I. chrysographes*.) Thus, if *I. bulleyana* is of hybrid origin, its parent plants are probably *I. chrysographes* and *I. forrestii*.

The flower stalk, with 2 more or less terminal blossoms, is about 20" (50 cm) tall; it is hollow and unbranched. The leaves are narrow and linear, glossy above, dull below. The spathes are bright green during the blooming period but papery at the tip.

The form of the blossom is the same as *I. chrysographes,* the standards slanting outwards at an angle of 45 degrees. The oval falls slant downwards. The light yellow area is larger than that of *I. clarkei,* but it is not separated from the deep purple-blue veined and spotted lower area by a darker zone, as is the case with *I. clarkei*. The standards are light blue-violet with dark veins. There are seedlings which vary not only in color but in other ways as well. Seeds are small, thick, D-shaped disks. The upper part of the stem is shorter than that of the second blossom.

Flowers during the first half of June. Should be planted in a sunny, open location in slightly damp soil. In general, *I. bulleyana* is somewhat less vigorous than other members of the same group nor is it as attractive, though it looks good in the foreground of borders and on some of the larger banks of a rock garden. Propagation by division; generative propagation is almost impossible because seeds are seldom fertile. Number of chromosomes $2n=40$.

Iris chrysographes Dykes

Its name comes from the golden yellow pattern on its falls. Native of southwest China, specifically Sichuan Province and upper Burma. The plant was discovered in 1910 by Stevens.

Leaves are narrow, up to ½" (12 mm) wide and about as long as the flower stalk, 15–24" (40–60 cm) and greyish-green on both sides. The stem is hollow and unbranched. Spathes are narrow and green. Blossoms are medium-sized and a dark velvety violet color. The standards are rigid and spreading. The pendulous falls have an elongated, sharply contrasting blade; the style is also elongated with golden yellow markings. The upper part of the stem is very short, a little over

2″ (5 cm). The stem that bears the first blossom is even shorter. Blossoms in June; in upper Franconia about mid-June.

Probably the prettiest species of the subseries, though sometimes less reliable than close relatives. Needs sufficient moisture in the soil during the growing period; dry soil during its first year can kill it. Full sun and plenty of room are essential for good development. Takes a rich, humusy soil. A slightly acid soil is ideal, but it will also grow in slightly alkaline soils. A light top dressing in spring is beneficial. Basically, *I. chrysographes* grows better in more humid regions than in those with a dry continental climate. Best planting time is September.

Many hybrids are being used in gardens, especially *I. × chrysofor*, the cross with *I. forrestii*. Seedlings from it are quite variable. *I. × chrysowegii*, a cross with *I. hartwegii*, is well known. Another well known hybrid is *Iris* 'Margot Holms', a cross between *I. chrysographes* and *I. tenax*. The very widespread *I.* 'Gold Mark' is a cross between *I. chrysographes* and *I. delavayi*. *I.* 'Mirza Citronella' is an attractive garden hybrid from *I. chrysographes* and a yellow-blossomed species (*I. forrestii* or *I. wilsonii*). There are also different forms from the true species which do not have a hybrid origin. *I. chrysographes* var. *rubellum* (also known as 'Rubellum') is a red-violet natural form which was collected in southwest China by Kingdon Ward. Aksel Olsen, the Danish plant importer, found *I. chrysographes* 'Stjerneskud' among seeds sown naturally in their native habitat. It is a lovely dark violet specimen with a golden yellow streak on the falls. *I. chrysographes* 'Black Form', also called *I. chrysographes* var. *nigra*, is dark reddish black. In some kinds of light the blossom could almost be described as true black. *I. chrysographes* 'Inshriach Form',

'Knew Black', and 'Mandarin Purple' are also well known. Sowing them presents no problems following a cold spell. Fast growing, often blooming in its second year. Number of chromosomes 2n=40.

Iris clarkei Baker
Synonym: *Iris himalaica* Dykes

Native to eastern Nepal, Sikkim, and Bhutan in extreme southern Tibet, northeast India (Tongo near Darjeeling) and in upper Burma. This species is somewhat isolated within the subseries (Chrysographes group). The flower stalks are not hollow like the other species, and the leaves are considerably broader; begins branching quite low on the flower stalk. Thus, botanically this species could form its own subsection.

Usually found at an elevation of about 9,800 ft (3000 m), where it grows in extensive clumps on rocky slopes in the company of scattered rhododendron species and conifers. Half the year it lives in high humidity, while during the other half it is covered by a protective layer of snow.

I. clarkei is about 20–24″ (50–60 cm) tall. The flower stalks have 1–2, or even 3 branches, in contrast to other species of this subseries. The leaves are glossy above, blue-green below and about ½–¾″ (1.5–2 cm) wide. 1–2 blossoms appear on the tip of each branch of the flower stalk, at about the same height as the leaves. The standards are wavy and held almost horizontally. The color of the blossoms varies considerably from medium blue to red-violet, but could generally be described as a smokey violet. There is a white spot on the upper part of the fall which varies in size, but is quite distinct. This area is surrounded by a smaller, darker zone. Sometimes white veins are present. Spathe is bright green during the blooming period. The seedpod is flat on the sides with a raised middle rib. The seeds are thin disks which lie in rows in the seed case.

I. clarkei has some lovely forms which are extremely attractive in the garden, though they do tend to be more ponderous and not as graceful as the other species in the series. In Europe, at least in Central Europe, the plant is not very long-lived, probably for want of high humidity. The soil should be kept evenly damp. After extensive observation, it has been determined that *I. clarkei* is more sensitive to lime than any other plant in the series. It becomes chlorotic very easily, so soil with lime must be treated with sulfur or iron sulfate or as organic iron compound. Prefers sun, but half-shade gives tolerable results.

Blooming period is the first half of June. Propagate by division (September) and by seed which presents no problems. Beautiful forms should be propagated by vegetative means. A highly praised form grows in the open forest of the Chumbi mountain range in Tibet together with *Meconopsis paniculata*, but so far it has been of little importance for breeding. Number of chromosomes 2n=40.

Iris delavayi Micheli

Native to southwest China, particularly southwest Sichuan and northern Yunnan Provinces. This plant was first introduced in Europe in 1892 by Abbé Delavay. Swamplands are its natural habitat. The flower stalks are 38–50" (100–130 cm) tall and hollow (it is the tallest species of the series) and extend far above the foliage. The leaves are fairly broad, compared with *I. forrestii* and *I. wilsonii*, and are ornamental. They are dull blue-green to dark green on both sides. The flower stalks have 1–2, sometimes 3 branches with 2 blossoms each. The spathes are wide and grass-green during the blooming period, though papery at the tips. Blossoms are dark red-violet to pure violet with a white spot and white markings. None are yellow. The form of the blossom resembles that of *I. wilsonii*. Standards are narrow-lanceolate, spreading outward at more than a 45° angle. The seedpods have a small depression along each side. Seeds are small disks similar to *I. clarkei*.

Grows in full sun and a relatively damp, humusy soil, neutral to slightly acid. Should be planted where the soil will not dry out, even in summer. On the other hand, it can tolerate more dryness in the fall than *I. forrestii* and *I. chrysographes*. Divide and replant in September, removing old portions of the thin rhizome that are no longer capable of growth. Once the plant is established, it has to be divided regularly. Raising plants from seed is not difficult and similar to *I. sibirica*. If other species of the Chrysographes series are in the garden, they should be pollinated by hand to obtain pure seed and to protect them from any outside pollination.

Blooming period with me is June to beginning of July. *I. delavayi* is recommended as a good garden plant for sunny but damper locations. Also grows well in bog settings. It is particularly beautiful at the edge of pools and ponds. Combines well with yellow-blooming species of this series. Produces good effect as companion to broad-leafed plants such as *Hosta, Ligularia,* and *Bergenia*.

An *I. delavayi* var. *pallida* is also mentioned in the literature. It differs from the original form only in its more blue-violet blossoms. It is often used for crossing with other 40-chromosome species of this series. *I. delavayi* × *wilsonii* produces violet-purple blossoms with a yellow background color on the falls. Number of chromosomes 2n=40.

Iris dykesii Stapf

As with *I. bulleyana*, there is considerable confusion about the origin of this plant. Dykes, after whom it was named, said shortly before his death that it was a species. But he had never seen the plant in bloom. Some say it is native to China, but this is highly speculative. In all probability, it originated as a hybrid. The plants we see in most gardens are not uniform.

The original plant is bushy and more robust than *I. chrysographes*, with leaves longer than its flower stalk. The latter are unbranched and bear 2 blossoms. The leaves are dull green above and below, about ½" (1.5 cm) wide and about 30" (80 cm) long. They even encircle the flower stalks, which is quite unusual for this group. The blossoms are larger than those of *I. chrysographes*, with standards that are somewhat incurved. The color of the blossoms is a vibrant, dark purple-violet. The falls have whitish-yellow veins in the center. Blooming period is June to beginning of July. Plant in September. Number of chromosomes indeterminate.

Iris forrestii Dykes

This iris, named after the horticulturist George Forrest, is a native of southwest China. It can usually be found on mountain meadows in Yunnan Province (9800–13,120 ft. or 3000–4000 m). The height of the plant greatly depends on its location and varies from 13–22" (35–55 cm). The leaves are shorter than the flower stalk, linear, grass-like, about 3/16" (0.5 cm) wide. They are glossy above and dull beneath. The flower stalk is unbranching and bears 2 blossoms, or occasionally only 1, at the tip. Flowers have a diameter of 2¼–2¾" (5.6–7 cm), butter-yellow in color making this and *I. wilsonii* the only yellow blossomed plants in the series. In contrast to *I. wilsonii*, the standards are upright and somewhat closed. The narrow, oval falls have a dark yellow spot marked with discontinuous brownish red veins. The spathes are grass-green. The flower stalk is hollow and has 2–3 small leaves. The seeds are small, thin, discs, D-shaped, with a dark center and pale edge.

Being a meadow plant, *I. forrestii* grows in full sun and very damp soil, even during the growing period. If these requirements are not met, the plant becomes stunted and fails to bloom. It can be divided and transplanted equally well in spring or fall, but spring is preferable in colder regions and fall in warmer climates. Soil reaction is not critical, but a slightly acid one is preferred.

I. forrestii is an attractive and recommended garden plant. It is particularly effective next to pools or in other garden settings with water. Two different types are common in gardens, a smaller one similar to the species description and a somewhat taller one. Crosses between them result in various intermediate forms. Blooming period in my garden is about mid-to end of June.

Since *I. forrestii* crosses so readily with other members of this subgroup, there are many hybrids, particularly with *I. chrysographes*. These hybrids are known as *I.* × *chrysofor*. In addition, *I. forrestii* can easily be hybridized with species of the Californicae series, the results are known in the U.S. as Calsibes. It is hoped that the wild form will be introduced again sometime, since the present stock is probably no longer pure. Number of chromosomes 2n=40.

Iris wilsonii C. H. Wright

Brought from western China in 1907 by Wilson, its range is fairly extensive: western Hupeh, Shen-Si, southwestern Sichuan and central Yunnan Provinces, at 6500–7550 ft or 2000–2300 m. The plant has yellow blossoms like *I. forrestii,* but can be easily distinguished from the latter by its standards, which spread outward at more than a 45° angle, and its flower stalks. These are as long as the leaves, but since the leaves arch over at the top, the flower stalks stand well above the foliage. Becomes 24–28″ (60–70 cm) tall. The leaves are dull green above and below, with a somewhat raised central rib, usually in the mid-section. The flower stalk is hollow and unbranched and bears two terminal blossoms, with one leaf in the middle of the stem. Spathes are grass-green. Blossoms are somewhat larger than those of *I. forrestii,* pale yellow, with falls held stiffly at an angle, as mentioned. The broad, oval fall has a semi-circular brown veined spot and a red and brown veined haft. Seeds are small, thick, and D-shaped. A sturdier form is known as *I. wilsonii* var. *major.*

It takes a sunny location and damp, rich, humusy soil. Moisture in the fall is required for normal development. But in general it, like *I. wilsonii,* will survive drought better than *Iris forrestii.* Blooming period is end of May to beginning of June.

A handsome plant, recommended for the garden, especially at the edge of water and interspersed with other lower-growing wild plants. Unfortunately, many plants known in the garden as *I. wilsonii* are hybrids. Should be divided in September. No problem with seeds after being cooled. Can be easily cross-bred, especially with *I. forrestii* and *I. delavayi.* Number of chromosomes 2n=40.

Development of Iris Sibirica Hybrids

The natural form of *Iris sibirica* is a very old garden plant. It was collected from its native habitat in the Middle Ages and planted in monastery and royal gardens. It is represented in the flower still-life paintings of the Dutch masters. Because of its extensive range there were habitational variations, so different types already existed in the garden without really being able to call them cultivars.

In 1876, a red-violet type, *I. sibirica* 'Atropurpurea' appeared in the lists. When *I. sanguinea* was imported from east Asia in the last century, the entire complex began to undergo changes. Because it had the same number of chromosomes it could be crossed with *I. sibirica.* The albino form of *I. sibirica* had long been known, but in 1900 Barr collected a white *I. sanguinea* in Japan. It was later commonly known under the name *I.* 'Snow Queen' and is still available in many nurseries today. The base having been enlarged, more and more hybridizers, especially in Great Britain and the U.S., jumped into the field to work with *I. sibirica,* such as van Houtte, Damman, Wallace, Dykes and Perry. A hybrid from this early period, which still holds its own, is the light blue *I.* 'Perry's Blue' (E. Perry, 1916) and also his *I.* 'Mrs. Rowe', a silvery-white lavender. In 1928, E. Barr introduced *I. sibirica* 'Superba', which is important for its early blossoms.

Of the many *I. sibirica* hybrids, *I.* 'Caesar' and *I.* 'Caesar's Brother', both bred by Morgan, deserve special mention. *I. sibirica* 'Caesar' was awarded 3 stars. It is indeed astonishing that a hybrid from 1930 could take top honors in the 1970's. It should also be noted that *I.* 'Margot Holmes', a hybrid of *I. sibirica* and an iris of the Californicae series, received the first

Dykes Medal of the British Iris Society in 1927.

Hybridizers in Germany were also working with *I. sibirica* in those early years. One of their landmarks was the cultivar *I.* 'Strandperle' by Goos and Koenemann (1927). The ivory-white *I.* 'Möve' also stems from this period. *I.* 'Phosphorflamme', bred by Steffen in 1935 and introduced by Karl Foerster, is also worth noting.

In the 40's and 50's hybridizing *I. sibirica* shifted increasingly to the U.S, building on the work already done by such hybridizers as Cleveland, Craigie, Farr, Gersdorf, Kellogg, Morgan, Preston, Spender, Sturevand, Wallace, Washington, Waymann, and others. A large number of new cultivars were registered. There was *I.* 'My Love' (Scheffy, 1944) and one of the most important cultivars for subsequent breeding, *I.* 'White Swirl' (Cassebeer, 1957), to mention only a couple of outstanding ones.

Max Steiger (Lauf an der Pegnitz), working in Germany, developed *I.* 'Apfelblüte' and *I.* 'Weisser Orient'. The latter is particularly valuable as a garden and breeding plant, as well as for its late blossoms (*I. s.* 'Tunkhannock' ✕? 1958).

I. 'White Swirl' was a most important breeding cultivar, one of its first great descendants being the enchanting *I.* 'Cambridge' by Mrs. Brummitt (Great Britain). Things were progressing in the U.S. too, where McEwen and McGarvey, two outstanding breeders, were working. Many new hybrids by these breeders also go back to *I.* 'White Swirl'. A great deal of work was also done with the old cultivar *I.* 'Gatineau', which came from *I. sibirica* 'Maxima' ✕ *I. sanguinea* 'Snow Queen'.

Since 1960 these breeders have also been working with tetraploid *I. sibiricas*. Their original breeding material was

Flower modification in Iris sibirica

'Sea Shadows'

Iris sibirica
(wild form)

created by colchicine treatment. The seeds were taken fresh from sterile capsules and put in petri dishes, on filter paper moistened with a 0.02 to 0.05% solution of colchicine, for 12 hours. The seeds were then washed 2–4 times and placed in a sterile growing medium. After 3–5 weeks, between 60–90% of them had germinated, of which some 10% were tetraploid or chimeras. Crosses among the tetraploid seedlings resulted in a stable tetraploid *I. sibirica*. The tetraploid forms of *I. sibirica* have larger blossoms, better substance, and a broader color spectrum.

The most significant difference between the modern *I. sibirica* and the old garden varieties, apart from the size of the flowers and the substance, is the horizontal position of the falls. These are very wide and present a large surface to view.

Hence *I. sibirica* is "much more colorful" when in bloom. Mr. McEwen has recently bred a yellowish *I. sibirica*. This is not a descendant of the 40-chromosome yellow *I. forrestii* and *I. wilsonii*, but a pure *I. sibirica*. The yellow color of the haft, which was present especially in white *I. sibirica*, was gradually increased until it spread over the entire blossom.

I. sibirica is also being hybridized in Germany, though to a far lesser extent. Dr. Karl Mildenberger has been working with this group since 1960. One of his early efforts was the cultivar *I.* 'Wellenspiel'. Crosses among members of the Chrysographes group (subseries) with 40 chromosomes resulted in the variety *I.* 'Goldauge'.

Dr. Tamberg (Berlin) and Eckard Berlin (Biberach) have recently been working intensively with the Sibiricas. Eckard Berlin has raised a robust cultivar named *I.* 'Laurenbühl', as well as a cultivar similar to the wild plant, *I.* 'Elmeney', formerly 'USO', which has abundant, long-lasting blossoms. Dr. Tamberg and others are working assiduously on *I. sibirica* 'Cambridge'. He has achieved considerable success with his hybrids. *I.* 'Wide White' (1978), tetraploid white; *I.* 'Kobaltblau' (1978), which won the Wisley prize, has a vibrant blue color with lighter crests; *I.* 'Lichterfelde' (1978), tetraploid, medium-blue, white-striped blossoms; *I.* 'Lilienthal' (1978), white, fertile diploid hybrid with good branching; *I.* 'Breiter Start' (1978), particularly good as breeding stock, induces fertile diploids, outstanding branching. We should also mention two dwarf cultivars, *I.* 'Cambrita' and *I.* 'Weisschen', which are only 13–15" (35–40 cm) tall. 'Cambrita' has a flower form like *I.* 'Cambridge' and *I.* 'Weisschen', but is a product of *I.* 'Ego'.

Even though hybridizing the 28-chromosome *I. sibirica* was always the top priority—and more recently its tetraploid forms—much work has also been done over the years with 40-chromosome species of this series, which hybridize easily among themselves. One of the oldest of these hybrids is *I.* × *chrysofor* (*I. chrysographes* × *I. forrestii*). Other cultivars like *I.* 'Diamond Jubilee', *I.* 'Yellow Apricot', and *I.* 'Yellow Court' also appeared on the market. Max Steiger bred a tetraploid *I. forrestii*. Dr. Tamberg was successful with his *I.* 'Berliner Riesen' (*I. delavayi* × *I. clarkei*) and more recently with *I.* 'Yellow Chrys' (1978), a fertile, large-blossomed, 40-chromosome diploid variety. In my own garden I bred *I.* 'Nostalgie', a plant with uniform velvety, violet blossoms but no trace of yellow or white. Many attempts have been made to cross 28-chromosome with 40-chromosome iris. Isolated successes like the cultivar *I.* 'Moonscape' were sterile. But a few years ago, Mr. McGarvey succeeded in breeding a fertile cultivar with the cultivar *I.* 'Fortell', which opens up other avenues for the future.

It will be many years before all possibilities are exhausted with the Sibiricaes. New colors will certainly be added to the palette. Reddish colors have existed for sometime, but *I.* 'Sparkling Rose', *I.* 'Ewen', and *I.* 'Ruby Wine' are new enchanting reddish cultivars. The series will undoubtedly be expanded with bicolors, with cultivars having different color patterns, and with earlier and later bloomers. Blossom form and carriage can hardly be improved upon.

One group that should not be forgotten in this discussion on cross-breeding is the hybrids from the 40-chromosome Sibiricae and the series Californicae, called Calsibes for short in the U.S. Despite the fact that their seedlings are sterile, there are many attractive garden plants among them, and the immediate interruption of the breeding line is at least partially compensated for by the tremendous number of breeding partners. It is hoped that a fertile seedling with double chromosomes will occur, either accidentally or with the aid of colchicine. But for now the F1-generation alone is worth growing.

All the hybrids are more or less blends of both parents, even though the appearance of the blossoms is more like that of the Californicaes, while the total form of the plant resembles the Sibiricas. Parents on the one side are the genuine species of 40-chromosome Sibiricas, such as *I. clarkei, I. delavayi, I. chrysographes, I. forrestii,* and *I. wilsonii.* The other parents are the hardier Californicaes which grow in northern climates, like *I. tenax, I. innominata, I. douglasiana,* and *I. chrysophylla; I. bracteata, I. purdyi,* and *I. munzii* are also used, but not as frequently. The number of new combinations is being increased by color variants, such as *I. chrysographes* by *I.* 'Rubellum' and *I.* 'Black Form', or by making use of the somewhat obscure species of *I. bulleyana* and *I. dykesii,* or hybrids with species or hybrids with hybrids. It is still too early to say how far the new fertile hybrids from the 28-chromosome and 40 chromosome Sibiricas will expand future possibilities.

The first known hybrid was *I.* 'Margot Holmes' from a cross of *I. chrysographes* with a Californicae. Crosses between *I. chrysographes* and *I. douglasiana, I. tenax* and *I. innominata* produced good seedlings. Combinations of *I. clarkei* and *I. tenax* are mostly successful; the well-known *I.* 'Space Child' by Leona Mahood came from such a cross. None of these hybrids have any problems with their stems, which have usually not been very strong. *I.* 'Fair Colleen' is a very common *I. douglasiana*

hybrid, which also grows well in my garden in cool upper Franconia. Crosses with *I. innominata* produce elegant blossom forms; these hybrids also have a very wide range of colors. *I.* 'El Tigra', for instance, is an interesting yellow-brown iris.

And there are still other possibilities. In the U.S. and England, a number of hybridizers are working with the Calsibes. Hopefully there will be further experimentation among these lines in Germany. This would be of considerable importance for us in Central Europe because the hardiness of the pure Californicas leaves much to be desired. In most cases the sensitivity to lime could also be improved. This was confirmed by *I.* 'Fair Colleen'. Moreover, the number of blossoms is being increased.

'Berliner Riesen' and *I.* 'Berliner Riesen' × *I. fernaldii*) were completely sterile, they were changed into tetraploids by colchicine and have extremely fertile pollen. This proved for the first time that changing Calsibe hybrids into tetraploids leads to recovery of fertility and that breeding at the tetraploid level opens interesting prospects for the future. *I. douglasiana* × *I. ensata* also resulted in sterile hybrids, but treatment with colchicine has been so successful that it is hoped there will soon be fertile tetraploid Calsata hybrids. Crossing tetraploid Calsibe hybrids with tetraploid Calsata hybrids promises even more. The influence of Ensatae Iris on this whole complex will show up mainly in resistance to drought, winter hardiness, and rhizomes that definitely grow underground.

Subsection *Apogon*
Series *Prismaticae*

Iris prismatica occur in the U.S. in swampy soil and sandy beaches along the Atlantic coast from North Carolina north to Rhode Island and Massachussetts into the state of Maine. Also in the interior mountains of North Carolina, Georgia and Tennessee. The Prismaticae are hardy, thriving in high humidity and ample rainfall. They grow best when planted in partially-shady locations. The soil must be acid or the plants become chlorotic. A sandy, clay soil that does not dry out in summer is preferred. These plants—if they are the pure species—are hard to grow in the garden (often quite different plants are being used in gardens under the name *I. prismatica*). *I. prismatica* is difficult to transplant, but if this must be done then only in the spring or fall. Better yet grow it from seed.

The Prismaticae series is represented by only one species, namely *I. prismatica* Pursh. In contrast to *I. sibirica,* the rhizomes do not form tight clumps, but are free-running, putting up grass-like clusters of leaves here and there. The flower stalks are some 11½–20" (30–50 cm) tall, slender, wiry and filled with pith. They are usually twisted rather than straight. Every stem produces 2–3 blossoms, often with a branch that bears one blossom. The basal foliage is dull green, slender, 11½–20" (30–50 cm) long, and ⅛–⅜" (3–9 mm) wide. Spathes are opposite, very slender and 1–2" (2.5–5 cm) long. The blossom is similar to that of *I. sibirica,* only much smaller. Falls 2" (5 cm) long, the blade oval, ½" (1.5 cm) wide, whitish or pale-violet with striking dark-violet veins. Standards up to 1½" (4 cm) long, wide-lanceolate, upright, pale violet. The capsule is triagonal, elliptical to elongated and about 1¼" (3.5 cm) long. Seed is dark reddish brown, smooth, varies in shape, either D-shaped or rhomboidal, thick at the center, 1½–2" (4–5 cm) long. There are also some shorter forms up to 11½" (30 cm) tall. Blooming period June. Number of chromosomes 2n=42.

Subsection *Apogon*
Series *Laevigatae*

The species of the series Laevigatae are very common in the Northern Hemisphere. One of them is the European Yellow Flag, *I. pseudacorus,* native to western Asia as well. The east Asian species *I. laevigata* and *I. kaempferi* also belong to this series. And finally, *I. versicolor* and *I. virginica,* which are natives of North America.

All the species of this series are hardy enough to be grown in cooler climates.

In spite of the different climatic conditions under which these iris grow, they all are found on wet soil. Some virtually are dependent on it; others will grow in dry soils, but not very well. An acid soil is ideal; some will thrive only in acid conditions, others (*I. pseudacorus*) will even tolerate lime. All need full sun to produce their most beautiful blossoms. Divided plants grow well if the soil is well prepared. They can be planted in either spring or fall.

Iris kaempferi Siebold (botanically correct: **Iris ensata** Thunb.)
Although *I. ensata* Thunb. is the correct name according to priority rules, I will use the name familiar to everyone, *I. kaempferi* Siebold, so as not to add any further confusion; the horticultural name takes precedence in this book. For more details, see the section on nomenclature.

Occurs in east Asia, into Siberia though not as far west as *I. laevigata*. Major range:

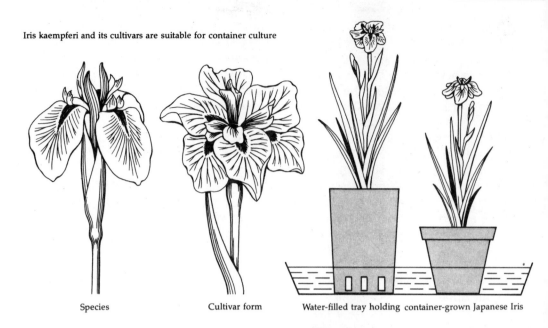

Iris kaempferi and its cultivars are suitable for container culture

Species   Cultivar form   Water-filled tray holding container-grown Japanese Iris

Japan, China (Ussuri), Manchuria, Korea.

Iris kaempferi is hardy enough for continental gardens, although it can't quite compare in this respect to *I. laevigata*.

Full sun and ample moisture during the growing period are important. However, *I. kaempferi* is by nature a meadow rather than a marsh plant. Pictures from Japan always seem to show small temples and streams with *I. kaempferi* in bloom.

The Japanese usually flood their gardens, but only shortly before the iris blossom and only for aesthetic reasons. Some varieties thrive in normal soil, but others develop optimally only if they are kept dry in winter and very moist in summer, which is, of course, difficult to accomplish. Best planting time is September to November, but in colder regions this should be done early to give new roots time to develop before winter. If possible, plant clumps with 5–6 shoots at a depth of about 2" (5 cm). Divide every 3–4 years. A heavy clay soil is preferred. *I. kaempferi* is extremely sensitive to lime, more so than *I.*

laevigata, so even tap water that contains lime should not be used for watering. If chlorosis occurs, cover the plant with peat, and water with a solution of aluminum sulfate or Fetrilon iron sulfate. Sow seed from September to October, larger quantities in rows 4–5" (10–13 cm) apart. Under favorable conditions, *I. kaempferi* will blossom in its second year.

A collection of bearded iris. This plate shows the spectrum of this group. New cultivars are added every year. Interested gardeners should check the catalogues of specialty nurseries and growers annually.

Upper left: Older yellow cultivars. These shades may be used between iris of other colors.
Upper right: 'Blue Lustre', a self; even the beard is the same color.
Middle left: 'Lucky Number', white and delicate pink tones predominate.
Middle right: 'Smart Barbara' has deeply frilled margins, which has its admirers, but also its detractors.
Lower left: There are many similar plicatas, of which the most familiar is 'Stepping Out'. Shown is a seedling from 'Stepping Out' × 'Newport'.
Lower right: A Media iris called 'Pink Reverie'.

I. kaempferi is 24–40″ (60 cm–1 m) tall, the leaves bright green, and the slender stems usually having one lateral branch and 3–4 blossoms. The leaves have a very prominent center rib (unlike *I. laevigata*) and are about ¾–1¼″ (2–3 cm) wide. The spathes are 2–2¾″ (5–7 cm) long, green, and have a narrow rim. Color of blossoms varies, even in the wild, ranging from pale blue to deep violet. Standards are considerably smaller than the falls. Individual blossoms last for several days and flowering peaks in July. The leaves wither in fall, but should only be cut off in spring. Number of chromosomes 2n=24.

In addition to *Iris kaempferi* 'Alba', the white wild form, there is the ornamental, variegated *Iris kaempferi* 'Variegata'.

Oncocyclus iris, the dream of all iris enthusiasts. They come from a unique environment—the Near East—which makes the culture of these exotic plants very difficult. It takes a lot of work and dedication to keep them alive and to get them to blossom, though they thrive in the Pacific Southwest, U.S.A.

Upper left: Iris samariae, from the Israel province of Samaria, as its name implies. It stems from the time of Christ and grows on scorching hot hillsides.
Upper right: Iris paradoxa var. coshab looks almost unreal with its standards reduced to a minimum.

Middle left: Iris gatesii has to be observed close up to see the delicate pattern of dots and lines. The blossoms are enormous.
Middle right: Iris iberica ssp. elegantissima does not carry its varietal name without reason. This is among the most beautiful blossoms in the iris kingdom. It grows well under favorable conditions.
Lower left: Iris atrofusca from Israel has a blackish-brown color. Its velvety sheen makes the blossom particularly elegant.
Lower right: Iris susiana was brought to Central Europe as early as the Middle Ages, where it got the popular name "lady in mourning". Numerous cultivars and hybrids grow in southern California.

Iris kaempferi hybrids
Iris kaempferi, with its many hybrids, is to the Japanese what Tall Bearded Iris are to us. It's hard to understand why we don't grow them more widely. With their considerably later blooming period, one would assume that no garden is complete without at least a few varieties. Their flowers are extremely attractive. Perhaps we don't grow them due to the myth that *I. kaempferi* is an aquatic plant.

I. kaempferi has been cultivated in Japan for more than 500 years. There are 4 breeding types called Tokyo, Ise, Higo and Edo. The smaller Higo type with large blossoms is often used in pot culture. We don't make these type distinctions, possibly because their varietal names sound so strange to us.

Japanese Iris have been cultivated in the U.S. for 4 years. Walter Marx (Boring, Oregon) is well-known for his large-blossomed 'Marhigos'. In the U.S., where some cities have large Japanese populations, *I. kaempferi* cultivars are more common and nurseries offer long lists of cultivars. *I.* 'Summer Storm', with its deep-violet saucer-like blossoms, has achieved great repute and I especially remember the heavily veined *I.* 'Sorcerer's Triumph' which took top honors. W. A. Payne (Terre Haute, Indiana) has also bred cultivars with large single and double blossoms in appealing colors and forms. Both these men started with the Japanese Higo type. In fact, most of the *I. kaempferi* hybrids found in our gardens are derived from this type, regardless of where they originated.

The late hybridizer Max Steiger bred Japanese Iris in Germany from 1953 until he moved to Teneriff. His goal was to produce lime-resistant varieties, and in 1959 he came out with the first one. It should really be called a "lime tolerant" *I. kaempferi* and not lime resistant because soils that

127

have a high lime content still produce symptoms of chlorosis. He grew more than 10,000 seedlings for several years to breed the familiar named varieties. Selections were made from a field containing 21% lime and a pH-value of 7.4. The original seed came from the Japanese Higo Hybrid. After being neglected for almost 10 years, many of these varieties are now widely grown.

I. 'Biedermeierzeit', I. 'Blaue Stunde', I. 'Sturmwind', I. 'Windjammer', and I. 'Tropennacht' are familiar names. My personal favorites are I. 'Operettenstar', I. 'Lustige Witwe', I. 'Grosse Parade', I. 'Festrobe', and I. 'Roter Burgunder'.

The original blossom form of the wild species is no longer recognizable in the hybrids. In most cases, the falls are enormous and flair horizontally. The standards on the so-called single blossom are tiny and point upward; on the doubles the standards are broad and also horizontal. The range of colors is tremendous: white, pink, blue, violet, and purple in all shades, most of which offer a strong contrast to the yellow signal spot at the base of the style. The blossoms often have prominent veins of contrasting colors.

Yellow is one color that has not been achieved. Many attempts have been made in the past to get yellow-brown into the Japanese Iris through I. pseudacorus, but this will probably only be realized through tetraploid forms produced by using colchicine.

Fertilization is an important part of raising Japanese Iris successfully. Only newly planted I. kaempferi varieties should not be fertilized, as fertilization in this case retards root formation. Old, established plants need an application of manure before the onset of winter. In my artificial bog, I make holes with a dibble in the spring and put dried, ground steer manure in them. Primroses are particularly effective planted among Japanese Iris and give that part of the garden a dressed up look even in spring.

Iris laevigata Fischer

Occurs in many parts of eastern Siberia, particularly in Daurien, in the Ussuri region, and on the banks of Lake Baikal. But it can also be found in China, Japan, and Korea.

I. laevigata is exceptionally hardy. Losses due to frost are unheard of. It is as frost-resistant as I. setosa, renowned for its hardiness.

Even more than I. kaempferi, it needs moist, fertile loam to thrive. It can tolerate standing water year-round if the level does not exceed 6" (15 cm). It can be grown in pots sunk in water. To blossom abundantly, I. laevigata requires an open, sunny location. It also needs an acid soil, but tolerates lime better than most I. kaempferi. I. laevigata is sensitive to any disturbance, even to work around its roots to amend soil. Transplant in spring or, if this is not possible, in the fall. Propagation by seed is easy; self-sown volunteer seedlings often occur in favorable locations.

Because its range is so vast, the species cannot possibly be uniform. Among plants growing in the wild are specimens with the bluest blossom color of any iris. On the Sakhalin Peninsula plants with small blossoms are found, while in central Siberia some have a diameter of 6" (15 cm). Generally the blossoms have no scent; however, some fragrant Iris laevigata are known. On the average the plants are about 30" (80 cm) tall. The scope is usually unbranched. Standards of the blossoms stand stiffly erect. Falls have a yellow stripe down the middle. Seed capsules are blunt, the seeds D-shaped with a thick, light brown, glossy seedcoat. Can easily be distinguished from *I. kaempferi* as the leaves of *I. laevigata* are smooth, while those of *I. kaempferi* have a raised central rib. The blossoms of the wild form of *I. laevigata* are blue, those of *I. kaempferi* violet-purple. The two irises can also be distinguished by the interior of the seed capsule and by the seeds themselves. It is more difficult to separate the hybrids of either species. Blooming period June to July, before *I. kaempferi*. In a favorable location it will blossom a second time. Number of chromosomes 2n=32.

Various forms and named cultivars are available:

I. l. 'Variegata', with white variegated leaves, is very effective in gardens and much more striking than the variegated forms of *I. pseudacorus*.

I. l. 'Alba', with white blossoms, is particularly ornamental in small garden ponds.

I. l. 'Monstrosa', dark blue, large with a white center.

I. l. 'Rose Queen' is an attractive pink.

I. l. 'Albopurpurea', white flecked with purple spots.

I. l. 'Colchesterensis', white double with blue dots.

I. l. 'Niagara', bluish white.

I. l. 'Snowdrift', white.

Iris pseudacorus Linné

This single European representative of the section Laevigatae can also be found in countries outside of Europe—Asiatic Russia, Asia Minor, Syria, and North Africa. It was introduced into the U.S. and now grows wild there. It can be seen everywhere, often together with reeds, along streams, on the banks of ponds, or other swampy places. Grows to a height of 28–38" (70–100 cm). The leaves are deep green, reed-like, up to 1⅛" (3 cm) wide. The flower stalk is branched and somewhat pinched. The yellow blossoms have a black-brown pattern in the center. Standards and crests are narrow, erect, and about the same size. Falls are much larger, have a long haft, and spread out horizontally.

Although it is a swamp plant, it thrives in gardens, even in dry locations, and often blooms more abundantly than in its native habitat. With time, *I. pseudacorus* develops into large stands. Although the fruits, with their hanging seed capsules, are very decorative, they should be cut off early to prevent unwanted seedlings from springing up as a result of broadcast seed. *I. pseudacorus* makes a good cut flower, especially in Ikebana-type arrangements. Blooming period generally coincides with Tall Bearded Iris, from end of May to June.

Because it is a heavy feeder and leaches the soil badly, an application of cattle manure, as well as a bone or blood meal fertilizer, is recommended in the fall.

There are a large number of garden and natural forms that can be used effectively: *I. p.* 'Variegata' has greenish yellow variegated leaves which are particularly striking in the spring. Seedlings have green leaves, therefore propagate only by vegetative means. Not nearly as effective as *I. laevigata* 'Variegata'.

I. p. var. *bastardii* is a natural form found in Great Britain near Llanfairfechan in North Wales. It has distinctive pale sulfur-yellow blossoms. The cultivar *I.* 'E. Turnipseed', which is similar, has cream-colored blossoms.

I. p. var. *superba* also known in the trade as *I.* 'Golden Queen', is a richer, fuller-blossomed self, without the usual brown markings. Especially recommended.

I. p. 'Flore Pleno', also known as 'Double', a plant with double blossoms, more curious than beautiful.

I. p. 'Typ Keukenhof', a dwarf form that only reaches 10" (30 cm).

In older publications synonyms such as *I. lutea, I. palustris,* and *I. longifolia* are often used for this species. Number of chromosomes 2n=34.

New tetraploid *I. pseudacorus*

These tetraploid *I. pseudacorus* from Eckard Berlin (Biberach an der Riss) have breeding value as well as being attractive plants for water and garden. The plants are the result of colchicine treatment of seeds: *I. p.* 'Beuron', pale medium-yellow, about 46" (120 cm) tall, large blossoms fertile.

Grows best in clay soil. Leaves slightly arching. Blossoms particularly beautiful in damp location.

I. p. 'Ilgengold', medium to golden yellow, 35–40" (90–100 cm) tall, leaves stiffly upright, in contrast to *I.* 'Beuron'. Not as fertile as the latter.

I. p. 'Fahle Ilge'. The blossom color corresponds to the hybrid Yellow Flag (*I. pseudacorus* var. *bastardii*). Light grey-greenish yellow with very pale markings. Petals almost floating, large. Partly fertile. Blossoms a little later than the 2 aforementioned cultivars. Foliage slightly arching.

Iris versicolor Linne

Native to the northeastern U.S., including northern Virginia and Ohio, Great Lakes region, southeastern Canada (from the coastal provinces and offshore islands to Winnipeg).

The height of the stem is about 24" (60 cm) and has 1–2 branches. The leaves are a little taller than the blossoms and about 1⅛" (3 cm) wide. The blossoms appear in clusters of 2–4. Spathes are bright green, often with brownish markings. The round to oval falls are medium-sized, mostly pale blue-violet with darker venation; at their base is a dull greenish gold signal spot covered with a faint down. But in the wild rich violet blossoms occur. Standards are very narrow and slanting. Capsule is 2" (5 cm) long, oblong-ovate, with a warty surface. Unlike *I. virginica,* it overwinters. Seeds are dark brown and D-shaped.

I. versicolor flourishes in moist soils, but—like *I. pseudacorus*—does not fail in dryer conditions. This iris responds to an application of cattle manure in the fall and returns the favor with luxuriant growth. Lime in the soil causes chlorsis. Blooming period is the first part of June. *I. versicolor* var. *kermesina* is particularly recommended for the garden for its almost red blossoms. It is probably the best known American iris in Europe. There are also forms with pure white blossoms and others that are white with rich blue veining. Other forms called *I. versicolor* var. *elatior* and *I. versicolor* var. *arkonensis* (medium blue with violet spots) are listed. Named cultivars such as *I.* 'China Blue' and *I.* 'Royal Purple' are widely planted.

They can all be easily propagated by division. Number of chromosomes 2n=106–108 (Luscombe) is not quite clear—data in the literature varies. *I. versicolor* is probably a natural hybrid, not a genuine species, possibly the result of a cross between *I. virginica* var. *shrevei* (2n=72) and *I. setosa* ssp. *interior* (92n=38).

Iris virginica Linne

Synonyms: *I. georgiana* Britton, *I. carolina* Radius, *I. caroliniana* S. Watson (all probably crosses with *I. versicolor*).

This iris is found on the eastern seaboard of the U.S. South from Virginia along the Atlantic coast, including Florida, Georgia and the Carolinas, and southeast Louisiana. It occurs abundantly on coastal plains. *I. virginica* and its forms are also hardy in cooler climates.

Since this Iris occurs in the wild only in sites with very acid soil—i.e. swamps and flood plains with fairly sandy soils where water often covers their roots for several months of the year—similar conditions should be provided in the garden. Recommended more for connoisseurs and enthusiasts than for the general gardeners. For the latter, *I. virginica* var. *shrevei*, now usually classified as a separate species, *I. shrevei,* is much better suited and easier to grow in the garden.

Scapes vary from 11½″ (30 cm) to 40″ (1 m). Unbranched or with a single, very small branch. There are 1–4 nearly ter-minal blossoms on each stalk. Basal foliage also varies considerably and can be anywhere from 8–35″ (20–90 cm) long, rich dark-green in color, and conspicuously ribbed. Spathes compact, inner valve usually longer than the outer; they have a fairly thick, leathery substance. The blossoms are relatively large, lavender or violet-blue, veining purple-blue. The falls are 1½–3″ (4–8 cm) long. On the upper base of the blade, which is up to 1½″ (4 cm) wide, is a striking yellow signal spot covered with a dense, fine bloom. Standards 1⅛–2¾″ (3–7 cm) long, almost spherical, with a warty surface. Seeds rounded or D-shaped, large; outer coat is very corky with a dull surface. Seed capsules and their stems are not very durable so they are often destroyed before the seed ripens. There is also an *I. virginica* with white blossoms. Blooming period June. Number of chromosomes 2n=70 to 72.

I. virginica var. *shrevei* Small, is, as I have said, a much easier garden plant. It is ubiquitous in the Mississippi Valley, on both sides of the river, even north to the Great Lakes region, including Minnesota, Wisconsin and Michigan and in the Canadian province of Ontario. It differs from the typical species by being somewhat weaker and having fragrant blossoms. The blossoms themselves have broader, more rounded parts. It usually grows in moist meadows and doesn't require such an extremely acid soil as the type *I. virginica*. Grows well in gardens if ample moisture is provided.

I. versicolor and *I. virginica,* though often confused, are distinguished chiefly by the size of their standards. The standards of *I. virginica* are almost exactly the same size as the falls, whereas with *I. versicolor,* the standards are considerably smaller and shorter than the falls, clearly veined, and broadened through the blade. The falls of *I. virginica* are more oblong-ovate, with indicator mark that fuses with the veining.

I. 'Gerald Darby', is probably a form of *I. virginica*. A good grower, the leaves are heavily spotted with purple-red at the base. The flower stalk is purplish-black as are the spathes which enclose the unopened bud. Blossoms are a blue similar to that of *I. virginica*.

Hybridizes easily within the series Laevigatae. The plants most frequently seen in the garden are crosses between *I. kaempferi* and *I. laevigata*, since several varieties of Japanese Iris have both in their ancestry. Crosses of *I. pseudacorus* with *I. virginica* and *I. versicolor* have been made, but are not of any great garden value.

Subsection Apogon
Series Chinensis

Species from China, Manchuria, Korea. Only those iris which are native to Manchuria and Korea are hardy in continental climates, not those from southern China.

Soil not too dry, sunny location. Difficult to transplant, but once established, quite tenacious. Propagation by seed is best, if obtainable. This is the least known series and only very few iris lovers have plants from this group in their gardens.

I. cathayensis Migo, native to Kiangsu province, China, not in cultivation.
I. grijsii Maximowicz, not in cultivation. White with purple-red veins. 4–6" (10–15 cm) tall. Produces 2 flower stalks side by side.
I. henryi Baker, Hupeh, Szechuan, Provinces, not in China cultivation, 2–8" (5–20 cm) tall. Similar to *I. minutoaurea*.
I. kobayashii Kitagawa, from Manchuria,

not in cultivation. Yellow, speckled with violet, 6–11½" (15–30 cm) tall.
I. koreana Nakai. Occurs in Korea and abundantly in moist locations on the northeastern Manchurian plateau. Rarer in the mountainous regions of North Korea and southern Manchuria. Closely related to *I. minutoaurea*, save that *I. koreana* has a taller flower stalk and more slender rhizomes. Attractive yellow blossoms. Is cultivated by a few enthusiasts. Often confused with *I. sibirica* var. *koreana*.
I. minutoaurea Makino, probably the best known iris of this series (syn. *I. minuta* Franchet et Savatier). Probably native to Japan, where it has long been in cultivation. *I. minutoaurea* has a certain similarity to *I. ruthenica*, but the former has yellowish-brown blossoms. The haft of the falls has a raised edge on both sides of the middle rib. The roundish blade of the falls has a brown pattern. Standards are pale yellow. When the plant is in flower, the leaves are 4" (10 cm) long and 3/16–7/16" (0.6–1.2 cm) wide. When mature, they are 11½–13" (30–35 cm) long. Flowers stalk 4" (10 cm) tall. Slow-growing but very persistent. Best time for planting September. Suited for rock garden groupings in full sun, good drainage. Number of chromosomes 2n=22.
I. polysticta Diehls, from Sichuan Province, China, not in cultivation. Pale lilac, heavily spotted, 6–20" (15–50 cm) tall.
I. proantha Diehls, also from Sichuan Province, China and not in cultivation. Ground color violet, 3–4½" (8–12 cm) tall.
I. rossii Baker, from Manchuria, cultivated occasionally in Japan. Lilac or pink-lilac, 1½–4" (4–10 cm) tall. Looks like an *I. ruthenica* with a long pollen tube.
No hybrids known.

Iris innominata   Iris tenax   Iris douglasiana

Subsection Apogon
Series Californicae

This series contains a wealth of very attractive iris. However, they are somewhat tender for continental climates and cannot be easily grown. They had been difficult to classify, until Dr. Lee W. Lenz, Director of the Rancho Santa Ana Botanic Gardens in southern California, worked out a new system in 1956. The series now contains eleven species and five subspecies. Their natural occurrence is confined exclusively to the west coast of North America, within the U.S. borders. Hence these iris are known popularly as Pacific Coast Iris or Pacific Coast Hybrids. They are found in the foothills of higher mountain ranges but are not high mountain plants. Nor does their range extend into the vast lowlands of central California. *I. tenax* goes north into the state of Washington, almost to the northern Olympic Mountains. The southern limit of its range is the southern foothills of the Sierra Nevada and the Coast Range of California. *I. hartwegii* ssp. *australis* reaches even further south into the San Gabriel and San Bernadino Mountains east of Los Angeles.

The series Californicae generally contains small, clumpy species with thin, hard roots and short, tangled, delicate rhizomes. The foliage is narrow, grass-like, and as sturdy as leather, with the exception of two species which have somewhat longer, wider, sword-shaped leaves. The scapes are unbranched, except for *I. douglasiana*. The height of the blossoms relative to the foliage differs greatly, even within a single genus. The majority of the species have 1–2 flowers per stalk. Exceptions are *I. munzii*, which can produce up to

133

4 blossoms from each spathe, and *I. hartwegii* ssp. *columbiana*, which usually has 3 blossoms per stem. The type species, *I. douglasiana*, often produces 3 blossoms from each spathe, and since the flower stalks of older plants are branched, 8–9 flowers can grow on each flower stalk. Blooming period is from about the beginning of May till June. The species native to California bloom earlier, those from Oregon somewhat later. This also applies to the formation of seeds in the capsule.

The blossoms, even of the species, are relatively large. Standards and falls are well-developed, often beautifully veined or patterned with strong colors. The colors may vary greatly, even within a species. It should be noted that some of these iris have a richer color in their natural habitat than they do after being transplanted into a garden. Most species have crests that are rounded or trapezoidal and generally toothed on the end. Two species have extremely long, narrow crests. The stigmas are triangular and tongue-shaped, with the exception of *I. purdyi*.

These Iris are tricky to grow in continental climates not only because of their southern origins, but because of climatic conditions. Continental climates do not have the long, dry periods in the summer that last 2–3 months in the north and up to 6 months in California, to which they are accustomed. And just as significant as the dry period is the extended rainy season from fall to spring. The total rainfall during this time is 1½–2 times that in continental climates. In areas where *I. douglasiana* and *I. innominata* grow, dormant season rainfall is even 3 times as great. Since precisely these species were used to produce hybrids, it is no wonder they do so well in England, with its persistent winter rains. Winter temperatures, even in the northern part of their ranges, are mild, despite the fact that

the temperature can occasionally get down to −15°F (−25°C) in the states of Washington and Oregon. Temperature in the summer ranges from 30–50°C or sometimes lower. The California species enjoy higher summer temperatures, of course.

The secret of cultivating these iris successfully seems to be excellent drainage. The soils in their natural habitats vary greatly, but all are exceptionally porous. Only *I. douglasiana* grows on more compact soils. The pH balance of these soils is neutral or slightly acid. In addition, the soil is normally well mulched with humus from natural leaf fall, and sometimes is sandy or gritty with small pebbles. As to the amount of sun, it depends on the geographical location of the garden. In cooler regions full sun is required for good growth; in warmer regions, light semi-shade is recommended. As mentioned, *I. douglasiana* is a special case. Just as it grows well in any soil and even tolerates a certain amount of lime, so it grows equally well in a sunny or shady spot. It does not even seem to mind the salty fogs of its natural habitat near the ocean.

The species from Oregon and Washington (*I. tenax*) will obviously do better in continental climates than those from California, but it is futile to try to grow *I. munzii* in northernly latitudes.

Planting these Iris prevents some problems. Older plants are often difficult to transplant, and sometimes it's not possible at all unless it is within one's own garden or not over any great distance. Young plants, on the other hand, packed in damp sphagnum moss, usually withstand air transport well. When they are shipped from nurseries in Oregon in the fall, the young plants or small offsets should be potted up in a suitable substrate and kept in a cool place over the winter. Thorough watering (lime-free) when planting is necessary for the plant's survival. They do not need much water in the summer, but plants should be sprayed periodically so that the soil stays relatively cool, particularly if they are planted in full sun. Soil composition should meet the plant's natural requirements (drainage, slightly acid). The use of shredded bark serves this purpose. The northern species can withstand continental winters, but the evergreen sorts need protection from winter sun. In colder regions keep collections in a cold frame or use them for cut flowers in the summer. In regions with alkaline soils, soil amendments have to be used. Flowers of sulfur should also be added to the planting bed, as is done with rhododendrons. Periodic watering with iron sulfate will help prevent lime chlorosis.

Propagation from seed is relatively easy. All species grow true from seed, as there are no hidden hybrids among them. However, since they cross readily with one another, they have to be protected from outside pollination. In spite of their warm climate origins, the seeds should be treated as cold germinators. Snow on seed pots and trays has a positive effect. Seeds of most species then germinate freely in spring, although some remain dormant until late fall. After being transplanted, they should be put in small pots, then later planted out with their rootballs intact, taking care not to injure the sensitive root systems. Too rich a soil spells trouble for these iris. So fertilize only lightly, and with slow-release, low nitrogen, acidic fertilizers.

There are many desirable ways to use Californicas in the garden. These iris make attractive companions for rhododendrons, especially the lower-growing species and cultivars. They have the same requirements: slightly acid soil and protection from winter sun. Larger rock gardens or a slightly raised bed are both good sites for Pacific Coast Iris.

In England, these are frequently planted in long strips along a pathway. Larger sinks and pots may also be used, but the outer walls have to be well insulated to prevent winter damage from frequent freezing and thawing.

Iris of the series Californicae definitely have a greater future in our gardens, maybe less so for the species than for selected hybrids. Number of chromosomes $2n=40$.

Iris bracteata Watson
Limited to a small region in the Siskiyou Mountains of southern Oregon, in dry pine woods. Occasional also in northern California.

Usual ground color is yellow, but there are individuals which vary from reddish cream to reddish yellow. The blade of the falls has a golden yellow center, and the falls have a beautiful reddish or purple venation covering their entire surface. The plant has relatively large blossoms with flaring falls and wavy standards held erect. The crests are lanceolate, recurved, and toothed. The ovary is triangular; the perianth tube short, stout, and funnel-shaped. Spathes are large and closed. The scapes are up to 13" (35 cm) tall, with short, overlapping bracts, hence the name I. bracteata. The latter are often spotted with red (rusty), the color intensifying at the base and on the spathes. I. purdyi has similar bracts, but a much longer perianth tube. The leaves are stiff, relatively wide, bright green and glossy. There is a still smaller form in the wild and a hybrid between it and the type form.

This species with its large blossoms is very attractive in the garden, but unfortunately it is more difficult to grow than I. douglasiana, though not with regard to temperature. *I. bracteata* is particularly sensitive to being transplanted; propagation by seed is recommended. It also hybridizes in the wild; hybrids with *I. chrysophylla* can be seen in its native habitat. On the north coast of California, there are natural hybrids between *I. innomata* and *I. douglasiana* (=*I. thompsonii*). These hybrids penetrate farther north into the range of *I. bracteata*, increasingly approaching the appearance of *I. bracteata*, both in form and color. It should therefore be assumed that all 3 species participated in the creation of these hybrids.

Iris chrysophylla Howell

Iris chrysophylla is an Oregon species, but extends farther inland than *I. tenax*. Sometimes both occur together. In the south, *I. chrysophylla* pushes into the territory of *I. bracteata*, where they form hybrids. *I. chrysophylla* is particularly common in or near pine or fir forests, especially on steep slopes or embankments.

The blossoms are mostly white or cream-colored, often with a pattern of dark-yellow veins, more rarely violet. This iris is closely related to *I. tenuissima*. The very long perianth tube is swollen at the top where it meets the blossom parts. In some plants the perianth tube is more than 4¼″ (11 cm) long. The long crests are narrow and only slightly curved. The blossom segments are narrow and the standards often flared. The scapes are up to 6–9″ (20–25 cm) long, but there are also forms that have only a very short bloomstalk. The evergreen leaves are narrow and light green, often with a glaucous bloom. Sometimes red or pink at the base.

I. chrysophylla grows in a somewhat sunnier location than the other Californica species. Not as good in the garden as the others. Blossoms are weak and fragile, so it is only recommended for collectors.

Iris douglasiana Herbert

Synonym: *I. beecheyana* Herbert, *I. watsoniana* Purdy

Its habitat is a very long, narrow strip of about 750 mi. (1200 km) in southern Oregon and northern California, from Gold Beach to Santa Barbara. It usually grows on grassy slopes and rocky outcroppings, often facing the ocean; in fact it frequently grows right up to the sandy beach.

Occasionally 2 but usually 3 blossoms grow from each spathe. But since *I. douglasiana* is the only one of this series that is free branching, it must be called multi-blossomed: 8–9 blossoms per stem. The individual blossom varies considerably in circumference and size. The color of the blossoms also varies greatly. Purple-red, light lavender, blue, cream, and all shades between are represented. In addition, they often have attractive patterns of golden yellow, blue, or purple veins. Light blue and delicate ivory colored specimens have also been found.

The tube is medium long (¾–1⅛″ or 2–2.7 cm). The spathes can be open or closed, offset or opposite, broad-lanceolate, green, sometimes tinged with purple, up to 3″ (8 cm) long. The crests are round or elongated, recurved and toothed at the edge. The flower stalk is shorter than the foliage (ca. 11½–20″ or 30–50 cm), with 1–4 branches. The width of the leaves varies from ¼–1⅛″ (0.7 to 2.7 cm). There are also taller-growing forms, whose leaves reach 1 m. One such form was once called *I. watsoniana*. The color of the leaves also varies from dark blue to yellow-green, glossy or dull on the surface. The base of the leaves displays a deep reddish color and is evergreen.

Natural habitats of *I. douglasiana* include heavy soil in some locations; this species is not demanding as to soil in the garden. It grows best in semi-shade in warm regions. As with all evergreen iris, the leaves should be protected from winter sun when there is frost. Old established plants will tolerate longer dry periods. Blooms end of May to middle of June. Being the most robust species of this series, it is a good garden plant. Its tolerance of a small amount of lime bears repeating.

Iris fernaldii R. C. Foster
Has a relatively limited range, about 62 mi. (100 km) north of San Francisco. True, *I. fernaldii* had been found in numerous counties, but the pure form occurs principally in Sonoma County near the Petrified Forest. There the plants grow in tangled underbrush together with grasses and other ground covers, mostly in the bright shade of trees.

A typical feature of this species is the dark grey-green basal leaves, intensely colored and spotted beet-red. Sometimes the color extends to the scapes and the broad spathes. The leaves themselves are narrow, usually only to 5/16" (7 mm) wide, and longer than the flower stalks. The blossoms are light cream-yellow, with some having pale lavender falls. There are even types where the blossom is entirely lavender. But compared to the type form, these are some divergent characteristics, and plants exhibiting them tend to be more vigorous. The perianth tube is funnel-shaped at the top, forming a wide throat up to the base of the blossom. Each crest is shaped like a long, recurved lance, deeply toothed. The entire blossom shows a delicate veining, partly yellow, partly light-lavender. Spathes are broad and closed. The flower stalk is 8½–13" (22–35 cm) long, with one or more leaves. Foliage is evergreen.

Plant *I. fernaldii* in slightly acid, humusy soil in the garden in light semi-shade.

Probably only a plant for collectors. *I. fernaldii* is rarely true because it hybridizes so easily. Even in its native habitat, a number of natural hybrids can be found. Particularly attractive hybrids grow along the road from Mark West Springs to Kellogg. Fairly compact, the leaves are no longer than 7–8" (18–20 cm) and the stout, short flower stalks reach about the same height. All the herbaceous parts are spotted purple-red. The spathes are very broad, and the shape of the perianth tube is somewhere between that of *I. fernaldii* and *I. macrosiphon*. It has a tremendous range of colors, from white and lavender to mauve, purple, purple-red, and dark violet. The lighter colored blossoms are striped and veined. The majority have a golden-yellow signal spot. Since this species hybridizes so readily, there is a chance that it will become extinct in its own habitat.

Iris hartwegii Baker
Synonym: *I. pinetorum* Eastwood
This California species grows mainly in the western foothills of the Sierra Nevada. In the northern part of its range it grows at about the 1,970 ft (600 m) level, whereas in the south it can be found at 3,280 ft (1000 m). This plant grows in sunnier sites than most of the other species of this series. In its native habitat it is commonly found along the sunny margins of pine forests; it does not grow in the shade. In the northern end of its range it appears together with *I. macrosiphon* (compare p. 139). The plants are scattered in the wild.

The foliage can be described as almost scanty. The ground color of the blossom is pale cream or straw-colored, sometimes with golden yellow venation. The perianth tube is short, stout, and broader than the cylindrical ovary. The frail scape usually has 2 blossoms which are relatively slender. The individual blossom is quite small, the standards upright. The flower stalk has one or more leaves, which are narrow (up to 5/16" or 7 mm wide), light green, without any red tones at the base. Plants die back every year.

This species is not important for the typical gardener and only of interest to collectors. This is not true of *I. hartwegii* ssp. *australis*. It needs a sunny location and porous, slightly acid soil.

Iris hartwegii ssp. *australis* (Parish) Lenz
This iris has produced a number of very distinct forms. *I. hartwegii* ssp. *australis* is geographically isolated from the type species and from the other subspecies. It is found in the San Bernadino and San Gabriel Mountains, not far from Los Angeles. It is the southernmost iris of this series. Its botanical status was unclear for a long time. Because its flower form resembles that of *I. tenax,* it was classified with it. But *I. hartwegii* ssp. *australis* forms a loose circle of leaves, as opposed to the compact, tufted foliage of *I. tenax,* and the color of its leaves is much greyer and harsher. In its natural habitat it grows at heights of 5,250–7,550 ft. (1600–2300 m), occurring in the semi-shade on the margins of pine groves. The color of its blossoms ranges from purple-blue to violet-blue. Unlike the type species, it can be called attractive. It also has broader spathes than the species and a slightly reddish color at the base.

Iris hartwegii ssp. *columbiana* Lenz
This subspecies occurs along a small strip in Toulumne County, California at the edge of Yellow Pine forests. Its locality is not far from the old gold-mining town of Columbia, hence the name. The leaves are remarkably long, often up to 30" (80 cm), and bluish green. Their base either has no color or is tinted very delicate pink. The

scape, however, is only 13–14" (33–37 cm) tall, usually with 3 blossoms, more rarely 2. The color of the blossoms is pale cream-yellow with golden yellow veins. Blossom substance is superior to that of the species. At the Rancho Santa Ana Botanical Gardens, it is grown in full, hot sun. This plant was once suspected of being a hybrid between *I. hartwegii* and *I. munzii* because replanted hybrids had a similar appearance. But this conclusion is questionable, for although *I. hartwegii* is found in the vicinity, the nearest *I. munzii* occurs 80 mi. (200 km) away.

Iris hartwegii ssp. *pinetorum* (Eastwood) Lenz
This unusually small iris occurs in Plumas County, California. It grows in the semi-shade of Yellow Pine forests at elevations of 4,300–5,250 ft. (1300–1600 m). It has similarities to the type species and also to *I. tenuissima*. This subspecies is unusual in that both blossoms at the top of the stem open simultaneously. The slender perianth parts, as well as the long, slender crests, resemble *I. tenuissima* (perhaps it is a hybrid of this species). The perianth tube is much longer than that of *I. hartwegii*. The blossoms are smaller than those of *I. hartwegii* ssp. *columbiana,* but similar in color.

Iris innominata Henderson
This is among the most attractive iris of this series. Even in the wild, its color range is considerable. One of the most beautiful forms, with a golden yellow blossom, grows along the Rogue River in south-western Oregon. Not far away are individuals with orchid colored blossoms. A purple blossom form can be found in northern Del Norte County, Calif. In the interior of southwestern Oregon, it often grows together with *Rhododendron macro-*

138

phyllum, R. occidentale, and *Xerophyllum tenax.* There are other types with light cream, apricot, orange, and light pink shades. Some are covered with Venetian-red veins. In coastal areas, *I. innominata* occurs with *I. douglasiana* on wooded slopes in porous soil.

Two blossoms may grow from the spathes, but 1 is far more common. The crests are rounded, curved, toothed, or slightly lobed on the edge. The perianth segments are relatively broad and usually rounded. The perianth tube is medium-long (about ¾" or 2 cm), slender, and slightly tube-shaped at the end. The spathes are identical in size and closed. The scape is slender and hidden among leaves, which are narrow, about 1½" (4 cm) wide, dark-green and glossy, with purple-red spots near the base. The whole plant is short and compact, forming attractive tufts. The plant is evergreen, sprouting additional new leaves every spring.

This, the prettiest iris of the series, has done well in gardens. Good drainage and neutral to slightly acid soil are important. It thrives in a sunny to partly shady locations. Many hybrid garden iris are incorrectly called *I. innominata.*

Iris macrosiphon Torrey
Synonym: *I. californica* Leichtlin, *I. amabile* Eastwood

Native to central and northern California, *I. macrosiphon* is widely distributed over 18 counties. Found particularly on both sides of the Great Valley. East in the foothills of the Sierra Nevada only lavender individuals occur. In its 280-mi. (450 km) long western range, it displays an astounding palette of colors. No other iris exhibits such diversity. This species alone contains almost all the colors that occur in the entire series.

The same diversity is obtained relative to the height of the scape. Some plants are almost stemless; others have flower stalks up to 11½" (30 cm) long. The perianth tube is very long, 3" (8 cm) or more; very slender, most of its total length swelling at the top as it merges with the blossom segments. The long, slender spathes are closed. Each flower stalk bears 1–2 blossoms, in most cases 2. Variations occur not only in the color of the blossoms and the height of the flower stalk, but also in the blooming period. In one region, dark violet-blue specimens blossom at the end of April, while a month later white ones and a cream-colored colony bloom. The crests are lanceolate, toothed, and curving. There are always several leaves on the stalk. The dull, evergreen leaves are always longer than the stalk and vary in color from grass-green to dark green. Foliage of the great majority of plants is white at the base; only the yellowish blooming plants show a delicate pink. *I. macrosiphon* usually grows in forested foothills on road embankments, in open grassy areas, and along forest margins, but rarely in shade.

I. macrosiphon is seldom found in gardens because it is not easy to grow. It requires slightly acid, humusy soil, good drainage, and winter protection.
I. macrosiphon var. *elata* (Eastwood) = *I. purdyi*
I. macrosiphon var. *purdyi* (Jepson) = *I. purdyi*

Iris munzii R. C. Foster
Grows in the southern Sierra Nevadas in California, particularly in Tulare County near Coffee Creek Camp in the vicinity of Springville near citrus groves. A very mild climate prevails and for that reason this is the Californica most sensitive to cold weather. It cannot be grown outdoors in harsher climates. In California it grows in

relatively shady spots, beneath trees on mountain slopes.

The size of the blossoms is impressive. They stand beautifully upright on strong, stiff stems. Two to four blossoms develop from the spathes. The perianth tube is short and compact, funnel-shaped and narrowing as it merges into the ovary. The blossoms themselves are well-proportioned and, despite their size, very elegant. The color varies from pale blue and lavender to purple, usually beautifully veined with shades of violet or turquoise-blue. In many cases, the blossoms are also beautifully ruffled. Crests are recurved, roundish and toothed on the tip. The large spathes are separated and distinct. The tall flower stalks have 1 or more leaves. The evergreen leaves are up to 22" (55 cm) long, noticeably shorter than the stems. Leaves are about ¾" (2 cm) wide, green or grey-green with no coloring on the base. It is an outstanding plant, if given protection from frost.

Iris purdyi Eastwood

Synonyms: *I. macrosiphon* var. *purdyi* (Eastwood) Jepson, *I. landsdaleana* (Eastwood)

I. purdyi is indigenous to redwood country in northern California, especially in Sonoma, Mendocino, Humboldt, and Trinity Counties. It is one of the rarest of the Californicae species, although it used to be quite common. There is even danger that it may become extinct because it hybridizes so easily. Natural crosses with *I. douglasiana* and *I. macrosiphon* are taking over. In its natural habitat, this beautiful iris grows almost exclusively in the high shade.

Usually 2 blossoms per scape. The blossom color of the true species is rich creamy yellow or white, washed pale lavender, with well-developed veins and stippling in purple and cherry-pink. Falls are very

large and the standards lie flat, so the flower resembles a clematis blossom. The stigma is twisted, which is unique to this series. The crests are elongated, narrow, triangular, curved, toothed, and turned up at the tip. Has a long perianth tube, occasionally funnel-shaped at the top. Large, very broad spathes, distended and closed. The flower stalks are from 9–13" (25–35 cm) long, slightly flattened and have a number of short, bulging, bract-like leaves. The leaves are grey-green with a partial bloom. Striking pink and mahogany-red spots on leaf bases, the scape, the stem leaves, and the spathes. The leaves are evergreen.

I. purdyi is an extremely attractive plant both for gardeners and collectors as well. It needs partial shade, good drainage, and slightly acid soil. Winter protection is necessary in harsh climates.

Some of the hybrids with *I. macrosiphon* have dark-red blossoms.

Iris tenax Douglas

Synonyms: *I. gormanii* (identified by Lenz as a yellow local form of *I. tenax*)

This iris was one of the first Californica iris discovered. David Douglas discovered it 150 years ago on his travels through Indian territory. Its native habitat is southwestern Washington and western Oregon. It is the northernmost iris of the series, but is not found beyond the Olympic Mountains or the crest of the Cascades; south to the range of *I. innominata.* Occurs more frequently in sunny than shady situations.

Normally every scape has only 1 blossom, but occasionally plants with 2 blossoms will occur. Blossom color varies greatly, though usually no more than 2 shades occur in any given locality. In the southwestern part of its range, deep purple-blue shades prevail, while northwest of Portland only pale lavender *I. tenax* are found. To the west of Portland, along Scoggin Creek and up to the crest of the Coast Range, yellow local forms, formerly described as *I. gormanii,* occur. It is considered by some to be the most beautiful of the wild Pacific Coast Iris. The light cream-colored blossoms have a golden-yellow throat, but there are also white forms of *I. tenax.*

The standards are large and erect, but the falls are recurved so that the whole flower is in proportion. The perianth tube is very short (about 5/16″ or 7 mm). The crests are rounded and recurved with toothed margins, and the stigma is triangular. The blossom rises elegantly above the 2 open spathes. The flower stalks are weak and have one or more stem leaves. The narrow, grass-green foliage is up to 5/16″ (7 mm) wide, and the plant grows in dense, grass-like tufts. The base of the foliage is spotted pink to purple-pink. The flower stalk is usually shorter than the leaves. Old established, fully developed plants blossom profusely. The leaves die back every year in the fall. Blooms in May. Plant height 9–11½″ (25–30 cm).

This iris has been cultivated in gardens for years, longer than the other members of this series, and yet it has remained a stranger even in North America. According to Dr. Lenz, it cannot be kept alive, even in the botanical gardens of southern California, probably because of the heat. They have had better results in England. I also found it difficult to grow in my garden in upper Franconia, but this may result from its extreme sensitivity to lime. It is more sensitive to lime than either *I. douglasiana* or *I. tenuissima.* The soil must be acidic. Some soil from the forest with bits of primary rock in it, mixed with regular non-alkaline garden soil, makes an ideal planting medium. Good drainage is also important. Because of its northern origin,

winter protection is not necessary. It should be fertilized with a weak solution of a slightly acid mineral fertilizer (rhododendron-type fertilizer). Working well-rotted oakleaf compost into the soil also has had positive results.

Iris tenax ssp. *klamathensis*
Restricted to a very small area around the town of Orleans in northern California, *I. tenax* ssp. *klamathensis* can be found in forest clearings and in the wooded hills on both sides of the Klamath River.

Blossom color ranges from light cream to light apricot with a yellow throat spot and beautiful brown-red veining on the falls. The standards are narrower and smaller than those of the species, and the perianth tube is longer. The leaves of the plant are very similar to those of *I. tenuissima.* They are evergreen. The flower stalk reaches a length of from 6–11½″ (15–30 cm). The leaves are somewhat longer than those of the type species. It grows close to the range of *I. tenuissima.*

I. thompsonii Foster = according to Lenz, *I. douglasiana* × *I. innominata* of Smith River Canyon.

Iris tenuissima Dykes
Synonym: *I. citrina* (Eastwood), *I. humboldtiana* Eastwood.

I. tenuissima grows in northern California from the end of the Great Valley to the southern part of the Siskiyous and east to the Cascades in fairly dry forest soil. The color of the blossoms is normally a light cream. The falls have brown or purple veins. In 1942 Miss Eastwood described a light yellow form without a stem. A typical distinguishing feature is the very long perianth tube, which spreads out at the top so much that it can be compared to an inverted red-wine bottle. There are types with long and with short stems. Ordinarily there are 2 blossoms per scape. The crests are very long, narrow, and strongly recurved. The stigma is triangular, the blossom segments rather narrow. This iris has broad, closed spathes and an oval ovary. The evergreen leaves are narrow, grey-green, and reddish at the base. Blooms first part of June.

An attractive iris for the garden, but only if cultural conditions are suitable, otherwise for collectors. It grows particularly well in partial shade and, like all the other species of this series, it grows in light, porous, slightly acid, humusy soil. Gravel is also a good addition. Takes very little fertilizer and then only one which produces an acid reaction. Needs protection from winter sun.

Iris tenuissima ssp. *purdyiformis* Lenz
This subspecies grows in a narrow region in the northern part of the Sierra Nevada, near Feather River Canyon (Plumas County). It has stem leaves like *I. purdyi,* but they do not overlap. Grey-green, evergreen leaves, the blossom is cream to light-yellow. It looks like a hybrid between *I. tenuissima* and *I. purdyi.* The upper part of the perianth tube also widens like *I. tenuissima.*

Iris watsoniana = not a separate species, but an *I. douglasiana* with particularly large blossoms.

Pacific Coast Hybrids

Most of the species in this series are very attractive, but their hybrids are even more so. All Californicae have 40 chromosomes and, therefore, crossbreed very easily. Since the ranges of individual species often overlap, many natural hybrids have

come about, to which 2 and often 3 species have contributed. Before Dr. Lee Lenz did his work on this group, it was quite difficult to identify the true species because many of these natural hybrids had been given species names. After working for more than 10 years, Lenz finally clarified this matter in 1958.

These iris hybridize just as easily in the garden if several species are present. The hybrids are usually more vigorous growers than their parents. One disadvantage is that they don't come "true" from seed, so they can only be propagated by vegetative means. This poses certain problems, because offsets from the hybrids don't take root as easily as other iris, often leading to a total loss. This is particularly true for plants imported from abroad, which have had to withstand the additional stress of being transported.

The best time to divide Pacific Coast Hybrids is when new roots are forming. In a mild climate this is in late autumn or early winter, but in continental climates only in spring. One can be sure that the plants will keep growing when the new roots have grown to about 2½" (6 cm) long. The mother plants are lifted, washed clean of any soil, and divided. Small offsets

Apogon iris from North America.

Upper left: Iris longipetala is unmistakable, with its extremely long sheath bracts. It combines well in the garden with many other wild plants, and is, in addition, very hardy.
Upper right: Iris missouriensis var. pelogonus is better known in gardening circles by its synonym Iris montana. It is only half as tall as the species.
Lower left: Iris missouriensis 'Dark Form' has a darker blossom. Within the relatively large area where this species occurs, there is an enormous variation in form.
Lower right: Iris missouriensis 'Alba' is a pretty near-albino form that is very effective in the garden, especially when well established.

142

must have some of the newly formed roots to be used. The offsets are planted in small pots and later, after they are well-rooted, planted in their permanent location.

Root formation can be encouraged by creating an artificial dry period, followed by heavy watering. This can be done by covering the plants at the beginning of June in a wooden frame under a sheet of glass to dry them out and then watering them heavily from the middle of August on. New roots start forming in early fall, and they can then be divided. But the offsets have to be kept in a coldhouse during the winter.

For many years I have been growing a selection of Pacific Coast Hybrids in upper Franconia in a cold frame using a porous substrate made of expanded clay pebbles and styrofoam pellets, made slightly acid with the addition of flowers of sulfur and iron sulfate. The walls of the cold frame are insulated with ¾" (2 cm) styrofoam insulation, and the frame is covered in winter. This minimal effort is richly rewarded by small, delicate cut flowers. Shredded bark should be used to mulch them.

Mrs. Brummit is one of the most outstanding European cultivators of these beautiful iris. Her newer varieties are I. 'Banbury Festival', I. 'Banbury Dream', I. 'Banbury Candy', I. 'Banbury Pageant', I.

Dwarf iris, wild species and cultivars.

Upper left: Iris reichenbachii is one of the dwarf iris species of the Balkans. Many forms are listed. The vigorous ones are very good in the garden, especially the rock garden.
Upper right: Iris glockiana (Schwartz) is closely related. Photographed here in its natural habitat in Turkey. It is still uncertain whether it deserves its species status.
Bottom: 'Tonya' is a somewhat older dwarf iris cultivar with tremendous growing power. Shown here growing from a carpet of sedum.

'Banbury Gem', and I. 'Banbury Princess'. A few other English varieties also deserve mention: I. 'Arnold Sunrise' (Humphrey), I. 'Alex Back' (Alex Back), and I. 'Founding Father' (Service).

The varieties of the 40-chromosome Sibirica group are closely related to the Californicas and cross readily. Unfortunately, these hybrids have always proved sterile. But they are very pretty plants, known as Calsibes (for details see the Sibiricae series). Since there are already tetraploid I. sibirica, it is only a question of time until fertile hybrids result from tetraploid Californicas.

Subsection Apogon
Series Hexagonae

The iris of the Hexagonae series produce both terminal flowers and lateral flowers from the leaf axils. They have leaf-like exterior spathes, a double-lobed stigma, a six-ribbed seed capsule, and large seeds with a corky teste.

These iris are relatively new as garden plants. Fifty years ago only 3 species were known: *I. hexagona, I. fulva,* and *I. brevicaulis.* Their native habitat is the central and southern part of the U.S., particularly the large Mississippi drainage area from the mouth of the Ohio River southward. A number of plants were gathered in the wild between 1920 and 1940 by various collectors, particularly by Small. He classified them and gave many the status of species. Only later was it discovered, after the individual types had been selfed, that save for one plant, they were all natural hybrids. The one confirmed species was *I. giganticaerulea* Small. Beautiful iris with reddish blossoms were also found and became known as "Abbeville Reds". These plants proved to

Iris brevicaulis

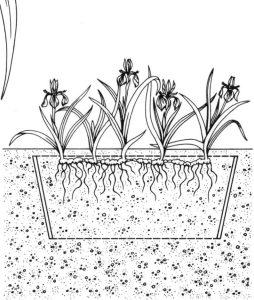

Iris with runner-like rhizomes such as Iris brevicaulis,
Iris prismatica and others, can be controlled by planting
them in halved barrels, buckets or similar containers
with their bottoms cut out.

represent a stable species and received the
name *I. nelsonii* (Randolph). The requirements of each species are different; information about their cultivation is
provided under the individual species.

Iris brevicaulis Rafinesque
Synonyms: *I. foliosa* Mackenzie et Bush, *I.
hexagona* var. *lamancei*

Grows mainly in the Mississippi River
basin and along its tributaries, from
Louisiana north to central U.S., especially
in damp grasslands.

The scapes are usually 9–11½" (25–30
cm) long and zig-zag back and forth at 45°
angles. The rhizomes are oval rather than
round in cross-section and grow rather
rampantly. The flower stalk produces 2 terminal blossoms and additional free-
standing blossoms from the axils of the
relatively large scape leaves. The leaves
are 10–20" (30–50 cm) long and ¾–2" (2–
5 cm) wide. The spathes are grass-green,
opposite, and unequal in size, about 2" (5
cm) long. The outer spathe sometimes
looks like a foliage leaf. The perianth tube

146

is ⅜–¾" (1–2 cm) long and sturdy. The blossom is medium-sized and varies in color from purple-blue to light violet-blue. Falls are 3–3¾" (7.5–9.5 cm) long and have a width of up to 1⅛" (3 cm). The blade is oval with a whitish yellow to whitish green triangular basal spot. The end of the center ridge is yellow and covered with downy hairs. The widely flared standards are shorter and lanceolate. The 6-ribbed seed capsule is 1½–2" (3–5 cm) long and oval-eliptical. The large seed is spherical or D-shaped, brownish and covered with a corky testa. Similar in many respects to *I. hexagona*, the main difference is the shorter bloomstalk of *I. brevicaulis*.

A pretty iris, easy to grow and completely winter hardy, it is actually a marsh plant, but also grows in normal, slightly moist garden soil. Ample moisture is especially required through the blooming period. Grows best in sun, but also partial shade, though producing fewer blossoms. Needs neutral or slightly acid soils, but also is tolerant of some lime.

Easily increased by division, sowing seed is rarely done. Plants can be divided spring or fall. If greater quantities are desired, offshoots can be cut immediately after blooming in June. Splitting the stem lengthwise is also possible.

This interesting, resistant iris should be planted in the cutting bed or out of sight. Its beautiful blossoms do not show to advantage in a usual garden situation because they are hidden by taller foliage. But it makes a good cut flower, as the blossoms last a relatively long time. Number of chromosomes 2n=44.

A pure white natural form is known by the name *I. brevicaulis* var. *boonensis*. A natural hybrid with *I. fulva* is widely grown in English and American gardens under the name *I.* × *fulvala*. Its blossoms differ from cultivars like *I.* 'Dorothea K. Williamson', despite identical parentage. The flower stalks of *I.* × *fulvala* are taller than those of *I. brevicaulis*, but not taller than their own foliage.

A number of cultivars have been developed. *I. brevicaulis* 'Brevipes' (syn. *I. brevipes* Alexand.), has pinkish-lavender, oval falls and smokey lilac veining. The standards vary from light violet to light blue-violet. Then there is *I. brevicaulis*

'Flexicaulis' (syn. *I. flexicaulis* Small), with an extremely zig-zagging scape. The falls are obovate, narrower than the type, dark violet. Standards narrow, spatulate, violet. Thirdly, *I. brevicaulis* 'Mississippiensis' (syn. *I. mississippiensis* Alexand.), falls semicircular, lavender to lavender-violet with olive-brown veins, standards lavender to lavender-violet with whitish base.

Since *I. brevicaulis* is completely hardy, the cultivars mentioned should be more widely used in harsher climates.

Iris fulva ker Gawler

Synonyms: *I. cuprea* Pursh, *I. rubescens* Rafinesque

Very common in the Mississippi Valley, from Louisiana north to Missouri and southern Illinois. Grows especially well in moist, clayey, alluvial soil, usually at the edges of delta bottomlands and cypress swamps. Much of this habitat is completely dessicated in summer, but when these iris are in bloom (in April), the soil is very damp, often completely covered by water.

Their slender flower stalks are 28–30" (70–80 cm) tall, often a little taller, have short branches, leaves, and often zig-zag. The scapes bear 2 subterminal blossoms, and 2 solitary blossoms emerge from the axils of the upper stem leaves. The spathes are grass-green and noticeably uneven. The exterior ones are 4–4¼" (10–11 cm) long, the others about 3" (8 cm). The linear, equally sturdy perianth tube is about 1" (2.5 cm) long. The delicate blossoms are mainly a copper-pink-terra cotta, a rather unusual color for an iris species. But there are also atypical shades, usually from pale to clear yellow, and sometimes covered with light brown veins. The yellow type is known by the name "Arkansas Form". The falls are 2–2½" (5–6 cm) long and 1¼–1½" (3.5–4 cm) wide.

The blade is elliptical-lanceolate. The standards are also pendulous and only slightly smaller than the falls. The 3 flesh-colored crests are sometimes almost succulent. The capsule is 6-ribbed, about 2" (5 cm) long, large, and oval-elliptical. The seeds are relatively large, D-shaped or irregular, pale brown with a corky aril. Blooming period is June, a week to 10 days earlier than *Iris brevicaulis*.

This attractive iris, with its unusual blossom color is unfortunately not very hardy, hence could only be recommended for collectors in harsher climates.

In the wild it is found in partial shade, but in continental climates must have full sun. When sending out new growth in the spring, it requires a great deal of water. Grows best in a moderately heavy, slightly moist, humusy, neutral to slightly acid soil. Responds to fertilizer, and a top dressing of compost, especially leaf mold. Since this iris is a heavy feeder, it should be transplanted every 3 years.

The vegetative method of propagation is recommended. Dividing is not difficult, and especially successful after blooming. The rhizomes can also be split lengthwise. Since vegetative propagation is done in the summer, offsets should be planted in a partially shaded, open bed, kept very damp to encourage growth. These slender rhizomes should be planted just barely below the soil line. If planted in the fall, give good winter protection. Chromosome count 2n=42. Important component of the modern Louisiana Iris; important for backcrossing.

Iris giganticaerulea Small

Synonym: *I. hexagona* Walter var. *giganticaerulea* (Small) R. C. Foster

Grows in the Mississippi lowlands, mainly the Gulf Coast regions of Louisiana and from there west to the Lake Charles area, where it is most common at the edges of fresh water marshes and in slightly brackish swamps in full sun.

The scape varies in height from 28–40" (70 cm–1 m). Vigorous, upright growth habit, always straight, never zig-zagging as with other species of this series, and produces 2 terminal blossoms, held well above the foliage. In addition, 2–3 blossoms, single or paired, emerge from the leaf-axils of the upper stem leaves. The spathes have large ridges, are grass-green, with a membraneous papery edge. The outer valve is elongated. The very large blossom has an excellent substance and a musk-like scent. Falls are 3½–4½" (8.6–11.5 cm) long and 1½" (4 cm) wide. The blade is semicircular to oval. The raised, slender, elliptical haft has a downy middle rib and is yellow, yellow-orange, or a very pale shade of green. The zone leading to the blade is yellowish or cream colored and combed with white veins, which extend into the blade. Standards are semi-erect, 3½" (8.5 cm) long and about ¾" (2 cm) wide. The blossom color varies from alkaline-blue, lavender, lilac, and violet to white or yellowish-white. But usually it is some indefinable shade between violet, lavender, and brown.

The capsule is ovate-elliptical to cylindrical, with a blunt end; its size is between that of *I. brevicaulis* and *I. fulva*. The capsules are a striking dull green, with a broad, rounded ridge. The seeds are large, D-shaped, usually very thick, with a cork-like seedcoat. This iris is similar to *I. hexagona*, but its blossoms are larger and very differently shaped; the capsules and seeds are also different, as well as its habitat. *I. giganticaerulea* blooms at the same time as *I. fulva*.

An atypical form is known as *I. giganticaerulea* 'Miraculosa' (syn. *I. miraculosa* Small) and differs only in color.

It is not completely hardy, but not as sensitive to frost as *I. hexagona*. Can be grown outdoors in milder climates, if it gets winter protection. It is basically quite a robust plant and not very demanding. Grows in a slightly acid soil. Division and propagation by seed are equally successful. Number of chromosomes 2n=44.

A few other natural forms occur, such as *I. giganticaerulea* var. *citricristata* Small, in which the central ridge of the haft and the adjoining area are lemon-yellow. As with *I. giganticaerulea* var. *elephantina* Small, the blossom is yellowish white, the haft lemon-yellow flanked by yellowish green veins, which also extend into the blade of the falls.

Iris hexagona Walter

I. hexagona grows in the southeastern States of the U.S. bordering the Atlantic Ocean and Gulf of Mexico, South Carolina, Georgia, Florida and Alabama. As an aquatic iris, it grows in wet ditches, marshes and bogs, in both sunny and shady sites.

The length of the scape is 11½–35" (30–90 cm), strong, rigid and erect, or sometimes slightly zig-zagging. It is either single-blossomed or may have short branches. Two blossoms grow from the terminal buds, but only 1 from the axils of the upper stem leaves. The yellow-green leaves are 24–35" (60–90 cm) long and 1" (2.5 cm) wide. The spathes are grass-green and often of different sizes, in which case the outer valve is the longer (6–8" or 15–20 cm long). The perianth tube is about 1⅛" (3 cm) long and barrel-shaped. The blossom color is a rich, dark purple. The falls are 3¼–4" (9–10 cm) long and about 1½" (4 cm) wide. The blade is obovate and has a striking yellow stripe or spot on its central ridge. The outer end of this ridge has a whitish-yellow spot combed with deep purple veins. The erect, spatulate standards are 2¾–3″ (7–8.3 cm) long and smaller and narrower than the falls. The blossom is fragrant. The oval capsule is perfectly hexagonal and 1½–2½″ (4–6 cm) long. The D-shaped or irregular, light brown seeds have a thick, corky seedcoat. There is also a white form. Blooms relatively late in June/July. Its rhizomes are sturdy, very branching, and spreading.

This iris is not hardy in continental climates so must be grown in a coldhouse or container. Needs moist, humusy soil. Grows in the sun and semi-shade. Increase by division or seed.

I. hexagona is quite variable in the wild. *I. hexagona* var. *savannarum* Small can be found in the interior of Florida, where it blossoms relatively early. It differs from the type mainly in the shape of its large blossoms. The blossom segments are not as wide and about 4¼″ (11 cm) long. The American common name is Prairie Blue Flag.

Iris nelsonii Randolph
Formerly known as "Abbeville Reds" or as "Giant Fulvas", these plants grow in the Abbeville Swamps and their drainage basin in the Gulf Coast region of south central Louisiana. *Iris nelsonii* is not a true species, but probably a hybrid from *I. giganticaerulea, I. fulva* and *I. brevicaulis*. It is, however, different from these species. It grows true from seed, so the hybrid has stabilized itself. Prof. L. F. Randolph justifies his classification by drawing parallels to other plant genera.

The upright scapes are 28–42″ (70–110 cm) tall and have short branches at the upper end, with 2 terminal blossoms on each. The basal leaves are 30–35″ (80–90 cm) long and ⅜–1⅛″ (1–3 cm) wide; they are yellowish green and often dull. All 6 segments of the very large blossoms hang down and are blunt at the ends. The falls are 2½–2¾″ (6–7 cm) long and 1⅛–1½″ (3–4 cm) wide. The standards (hanging!) are 1¾–2¼″ (4.8–5.5 cm) long and ¾″ (2 cm) wide. The unique, magnificent purple-red color of the blossoms is eye-catching. There are also yellow specimens, though they are rare. The capsule is oval or lanceolate (2–2¼″ or 5–5.6 cm long), usually coming to a point on both sides. The seeds are irregular or D-shaped, light brown, ⅝″ (1.5 cm) in diameter, smooth, and irregularly pitted.

Despite its striking color, it is not recommended for continental climates. It is extensively planted in England, and the southern parts of the U.S. It grows in a moist location and somewhat more shade than other iris of this series. Can be propagated by division or seed. Blooming period is a little later than *I. fulva*. Number of chromosomes 2n=42.

Louisiana Hybrids

I have already mentioned the natural hybrids *I.* × *fulvala* Dykes, a hybrid from *I. brevicaulis* and *I. fulva*. Another is *I.* × *vinicolor* Small, resulting from a cross between *I. fulva* and *I. giganticaerulea*. This hybrid has a scape about 40″ (1 m) tall, usually branching. The basal leaves are from 15–40″ (35 cm–1 m) long and are a striking green. The blossom color is purple-wine-red. It has two cultivars: *I.* 'Chrysophoenica' (syn. *I. crysophoenicia* Small) and *I.* 'Lilacinaurea' (syn. *I. lilacinaurea* Alexand.), with dark lilac blossoms. I already mentioned many of the other natural hybrids.

One of the first cultivars, *Iris* 'Dorothea K. Williamson', was introduced in 1920 and also a cross between *I. fulva* and *I. brevicaulis*. It differs from *I.* × *fulvala*, although it has the same parents. It is the only hybrid widely used in continental climates. A pretty plant with velvety purple blossoms and a yellow stripe on the falls. The low, horizontal scapes are well branched, with the blossoms opening up one after the other on the end of each branch. So it can also be recommended for cutting. It is not demanding as to soil, except that it should not be entirely dry. Grows in partial shade, but tends to be rampant in a location that is too favorable.

In catalogues from the 20's many natural hybrids were listed, as were the results of the first successful crosses. Between the wars, many plantsmen in North America, gardeners and botanists alike, worked with the Louisiana Hybrids, e.g. Foster, Reed, Riley, Randolph, and Viosca. Today a tremendous number of hybrids in magnificent colors and forms exist. The Louisiana Iris Society founded in 1948 is associated with the American Iris Society. Breeding is going on in England, too. *I.* 'Wheelhorse', *I.* 'Dixie Deb', *I.* 'Elizabeth the Queen', *I.* 'Contestant', *I.* 'Pristine Beauty', *I.* 'Cajun Joyeuse', *I.* 'Bienville', *I.* 'Cherry Bounce', *I.* 'Gay Deceiver', and *I.* 'Marjorie Brummit' are praiseworthy cultivars.

Many of these cultivars are not hardy in cooler climates, since completely hardy species are not involved in the breeding. Fortunately, hybridizers are now working on this magnificent iris group (Dr. Tamberg), so that we can look forward to having a completely hardy Louisiana Iris in the foreseeable future.

Completely hardy hybrids do not need any unusual attention, though adequate fertilization with an organic fertilizer is important. Louisiana Iris are voracious feeders, so sufficient fertilization is necessary to bring out their full blooming potential. Before planting, the soil should be

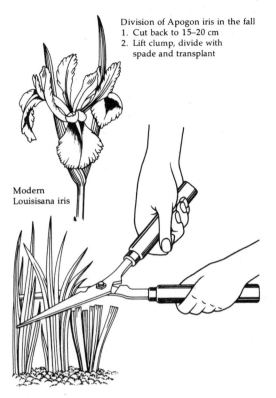

Division of Apogon iris in the fall
1. Cut back to 15–20 cm
2. Lift clump, divide with spade and transplant

Modern Louisisana iris

enriched with organic matter to be sure it is on the acid side. If mineral fertilizer is used, it should be one with an acid reaction (rhododendron fertilizer). Planting time in southern regions is from August to October, in the north, April is recommended.

Sufficient moisture is important during the growing and blooming periods. Louisiana Iris bloom best in a sunny location, but some flowers appear on partial shaded plants, if shade is filtered and not too dense. Louisiana Iris fail if subjected to competition from tree roots. Competition can be prevented by sinking plastic containers with their bottoms cut out in the ground.

These iris should be lifted and replanted after 3–4 years, regardless of their location. If they are going to be planted in the same place again, the soil should be enriched. Old, weak rhizomes lacking active roots go to the compost heap. Mulching has proved very beneficial, especially for plantings in sunny spots, where the sun burns down on the partly exposed rhizomes. All commonly used materials, such as shredded bark, conifer needles, leaf mold, grass cuttings, and wood shavings are suitable.

An ideal location is at the edge of water. It should not be forgotten that these iris are extremely satisfying cut flowers, the blossoms lasting from 7–10 days. Louisiana Iris are rarely affected by disease, though now and again they may have rust, in which case the leaves then look as if they have been covered by red dust. Where this disease exists, preventive spraying with a fungicide is advisable. In soils containing lime, chlorosis sets in. As soon as this is noticed, the plants should be watered with an acid fertilizer (such as Miracid) and fertilized with an organic iron compound (such as Sequestrene). In gardens that are visited by rabbits, protective measures have to be taken, as rabbits adore the leaves and rhizomes of this iris.

Subsection Apogon
 Series Longipetalae

All the species of this series are native to North America. *I. longipetala* grows in the coastal hills of California. *I. missouriensis* has its origins along the upper Missouri River and is very common in higher country. Its range crosses the Rocky Mountains in British Columbia south to New Mexico, Arizona, and California and east to the Dakotas. *I. missouriensis* var. *pelegonus* grows in Montana and the region east of the Rockies. *I. missouriensis* var. *arizonica* occurs only in the Arizona hills.

The Montana State University College of Agriculture recommends the species and types from northern Arizona, northern New Mexico, and southern Colorado as particularly suitable in the garden due to the intense color of their foliage and superior branching.

All the iris of this series are hardy and have few requirements. Being meadow and hill dwellers, they thrive in open spaces and full sun. Adequate moisture is desirable, particularly during the growing season. This is even more important for *I. missouriensis* var. *pelogonus* (the name "pelogonus" means clay-loving). But all the species of this series require dry soil after the blooming period. The soil in their natural habitat always contains some lime and moist clay.

I. longipetala is a precarious, hardy garden plant with an attractive appearance. *I. missouriensis* is equally attractive; its dark blue and white forms are highly recommended. Propagation by seed and division are not difficult.

Americans recommend stratifying the seed at 40°F (+5°C) for 90 days, but seeds from southerly regions for a shorter time.

These iris are easily transplanted, even while in bloom. After they bloom, it is more difficult, and losses occur when planting in the fall.

Iris longipetala Herbert
A robust species with scapes 18–24" (45–60 cm). Some forms reach 35" (90 cm). The flower stalks are large, strong, either single or branching, and produce 3–6 blossoms. The basal leaves are somewhat longer, slender, about ⅜" (1 cm) wide and evergreen. The spathes are grass-green, very narrow and up to 6" (15 cm) long. The blossoms have a slender form with falls up to 4" (10 cm) long. The center

152

ridge is yellow with purple-violet dots. The base of the blade is white, flecked with violet, and the outer part whitish with striking violet veins. The violet standards are semi-erect, elongate, and bluntly rounded and notched at the tips. The capsule is lanceolate-oval, fairly rounded in cross-section, 6-ribbed, and 3½" (9 cm) long. The seed is smooth, dark brown, spherical, or pear-shaped. Blooming period is May–June.

I. longipetala is a tetraploid. Number of chromosomes differs (2n=80, 86 or 88, including incomplete chromosomes and fragments). The origin of this polyploid plant is obscure, probably the result of a cross between species. One parent seems to be *I. missouriensis* and the second a species of the Californicae series (perhaps *I. douglasiana*).

Iris missouriensis Nutall
Synonym: *I. tolmeiana* Herbert

Strongly resembles *I. longipetala,* but the parts are all more slender. The scape is 18–20" tall (45–50 cm) rising 2–4" (5–10 cm) above the foliage, simple or branched, with clusters of 2–4 blossoms. The basal leaves are slender and ⅜" (1 cm) wide. Spathes opposite, grass-green at the base, pointed, 1½–2¾" (4–7 cm) long. Falls of the blossoms are 2½" (6 cm) long and ¾" (2 cm) wide. A striking, deep lilac-purple veining covers the lighter ground of the blade, at the base of which is a white spot. Standards are shorter, ⅜" (1 cm) wide, notched, solid lilac-purple. Capsule up to 2" (5 cm) long, oval, with 6 ribs. There are forms with white blossoms. Unlike *I. longipetala,* this plant dies back in the fall. Blooms May–June. Number of chromosomes 2n=38.

Iris missouriensis var. *pelogonus* (Goodding) R. C. Foster
Synonyms: *I. montana* Nutt. ex Dykes, *I. pelogonus*

A small plant, scape less than 11½" (30 cm) tall and unbranched, 1–3 terminal blossoms. Basal leaves thick, upright and ribbed, 4½–9" (12–25 cm) long and up to ¼" (6 mm) wide. The falls of the blossoms are about 2¾" (7 cm) long and ¾" (2 cm) wide. The blade is pale lavender-blue, more darkly veined, with a yellowish basal spot. Standards upright, with a pointed tip, blunt or notched, pale violet, 2" (5 cm) long, ⅜" (1 cm) wide. Plants die back in winter. Number of chromosomes 2n=86 to 88 (Simonet 1934).

Iris missouriensis var. *arizonica* (Dykes) R. C. Foster
Synonym: *I. arizonica* Dykes

Scape to 29" (75 cm) tall, produces 3–5 blossoms. Stem with short branches and clusters of 2–3 blossoms. Basal foliage as tall as the flower stalks, yellowish-green, 7/16" (1.2 cm) wide, ribbed. Blossoms small and fairly weak. Falls are 2" (5 cm) long and ¾" (2 cm) wide, broad-lanceolate. Blade heavily veined in violet-purple on a white or pale lavender base. The basal spot is yellowish. The standards are shorter, narrow-lanceolate, and markedly pointed. The foliage dies back in winter. In contrast to the others, this species is particularly drought tolerant. Not very good for gardens.

Iris missouriensis f. *angustispatha* R. C. Foster
A form with slender, usually open and dissimilar spathes.

Crosses with other series:
I. 'Longwat' = *I. longipetala* × *douglasiana* (description from *I. watsoniana,* an old description for *I. douglasiana*).

I. 'Monwat' = *I. montana* (correctly: *I. missouriensis* var. *pelogonus*) × *I. douglasiana*.

Other cultivars are *I.* 'Longsib' (*I. longipetala* × *I. sibirica*) and the crosses by Ingwersen between *I. forrestii* and *I. longipetala*.

Subsection Apogon
Series Tripetalae

The two species of this series have vastly different ranges. *I. setosa,* which is important in cooler climates, occurs in many northern countries. It grows in northern parts of Siberia and China, on the northern islands of Japan, crosses to Alaska via the Aleutian Islands, where it is found chiefly in coastal regions. Toward the southeast its range covers large parts of Canada. The other species, *I. tridentata,* grows in the warm, southeastern states of the U.S. (North and South Carolina, Georgia, Florida and particularly Tennessee).

I. setosa is the cold hardiest of all the iris species. It can be found even in regions where the soil never completely thaws out, so this plant is very hardy in the garden where summer heat is no problem. *I. tridentata,* on the other hand, is fairly tender. What we see in botanical gardens under this name is not the true species.

I. setosa needs full sun and soil that is not too dry. If it grows in the shade, the blossoms lack contrast. Acid soil is the most important requirement for good growth. Lime in the soil or water soon leads to yellow, chlorotic plants. *I. setosa* var. *canadensis,* the Canadian form, is particularly sensitive to lime. It grows in leaf mold and responds to ample water in spring. In its native habitat, *I. tridentata* grows in rich, moist, slightly shaded sites.

I. setosa is a very responsive garden plant. Large-blossomed cultivars are particularly recommended, as are dwarf forms for the rock garden. Propagation by seed after frost is not difficult. Healthy plants can be divided in spring or autumn, September being ideal.

Iris setosa Pallas ex Link
Synonyms: *I. brachycuspis* Fischer ex Sims, *I. brevicuspis* Fischer ex Sims, *I. yedoensis* Franch. et Savat

The height of the stem of *I. setosa* is variable. It is about 18″ (45 cm) on the common form, but can reach 30″ (80 cm). The stem is usually branched. The foliage forms thick clusters, is arched, and about 1″ (2.5 cm) wide. Leaves are prominently ribbed and reddish at the base. *I. setosa* has short, thick rhizomes. Flower falls are 2–2¾″ (5–7 cm) long, and the blade is always rounded, with a spreading network of dark-violet or red-violet veins on a pale ground. There is a white spot at its base. The standards are reduced, erect, pale greenish, stippled with violet, and have bristly ends. There are forms with white blossoms. Seeds can easily be distinguished from those of other species. They are medium brown, narrow, glossy, with a noticeably raised middle rib along the smooth underside. The seeds could be described as pear-shaped. They are fairly loosely arranged in the capsules. Blooming period, end of May to middle of June. Number of chromosomes 2n=36.

Iris setosa ssp. *canadensis* (M. Foster) Hulten
Synonym: *I. hookeri* Penny

Compared with the type species, this subspecies is a good deal smaller. The blade has a larger white spot. In relation to the falls, the standards are smaller yet. The leaves are not as luxuriant and somewhat narrower, usually wavy at the margin. Occurs in northeastern North America

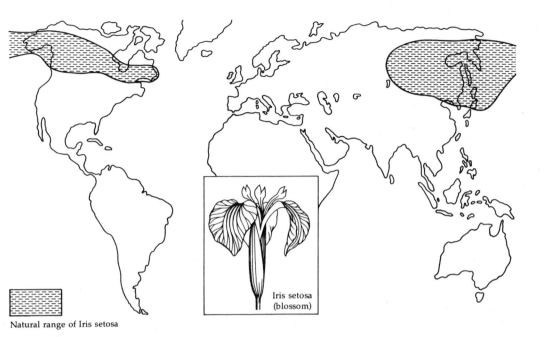

Iris setosa
(blossom)

Natural range of Iris setosa

from Labrador to Maine. There are two other forms of this subspecies: *I. pallidiflora* Fernald, larger overall and with bluish white blossoms, native to Newfoundland and *I. zonalis* Eames, leaves with yellowish white and whitish transverse bands, sometimes with a reddish margin, native to Newfoundland and Quebec.

Iris setosa ssp. *hondoensis* Honda
or Kurosawa
Velvety purple blossoms. Standards to 1⅛" (3 cm) long. Tall growing plants to about 28–30" (70–80 cm) less branching. Kirigamuel District of Japan. It is thought to be a hybrid with *I. laevigata* Fischer et Meyer. Number of chromosomes 2n=52, 54, 56 or 67.

Iris setosa ssp. *interior* (Anderson) Hulten
Free blooming, well branched form. The papery, violet-tinted spathes are shorter than the flower axil. Occurs in Alaska and isolated in northeastern Siberia.

Iris setosa var. *arctica* Eastwood
Synonym: *I. arctica* Eastwood
Very small variety, probably identical to "Dwarf Form" common to the garden. Blossom color violet with a white spot on the blade. Found in Alaska.

Iris setosa var. *nasuensis* Hara or Kurosawa
Broader leaves than species, flower stalk up to 40" (1 m). Large blossoms with standards ¾" (2 cm) long. Found in Middle Honshu. Probably a hybrid. Number of chromosomes 2n=54.

Iris setosa var. *tricuspis*
A taller-growing variety from the east coast of Canada. Blossoms are more reddish violet.

Iris setosa f. *alpina* Komarov
The scape of this plant is quite short. Found in Siberia.

Iris setosa f. *platyrhyncha* Hulten
A single-blossomed form. In contrast to the species, the standards are larger and wider with a pointed or rounded tip. Found in the coastal regions of Alaska and the Aleutian Islands.

Iris setosa f. *serotina* Komarov
Scape almost unelongated. Native to Siberia.

Iris tridentata Pursh
Synonym: *I. tripetala* Walter
   The scape of *I. tridentata* is about 13½" (35 cm), usually with one fairly large blossom. The leaves grow above the flowers. They are linear with a brownish reddish margin, ⅜" (1 cm) wide, stiff, dull dark green, growth irregular. Blossoms are purple-blue, the blade is round, (1½") (4 cm) in diameter. The veins are a pretty, dark-purple color, and the basal spot is yellowish-white. The standards are very narrow and erect. The capsules are about 1⅛" (3 cm) long, rounded or lanceolate, and have a beak. Seeds round or D-shaped, thick, flat, russet colored.
   Crosses with other series:
Simonet crossed *I. sibirica* and *I. sanguinea* with *I. setosa*, and *I. tenax* with *I. setosa*. Foster obtained seedlings from a cross between *I. setosa* and *I. kaempferi*. Eckhard Berlin obtained an accidental seedling by crossing *I. sibirica* with *I. setosa*. It is similar to *I. setosa* but has larger blossoms, scape about 42" (110 cm); a descendant of *I.* 'Elmeney'. The plant is almost sterile. Commonly known as *I.* 'Stilles Wasser'.

Subsection Apogon
   Series Vernae

This monotypic genus occurs in the mountain ranges of the eastern and southeastern states of the U.S., common in the areas of Washington, D.C., Maryland, Virginia, Georgia, and Alabama. *Iris verna* is also very abundant in the foothills of the southern Appalachians.
   I. verna is hardy enough to grow in continental climates. Grows in acid soil in its native habitat, in partial shade or open woodlands, and in underbrush.
   This charming iris should be used much more frequently, especially in rock gardens and natural gardens. Unfortunately, its requirements make it one of the fussiest iris. The soil must be completely lime-free and sandy-humus, similar to some forest soils, and it should remain wet even in summer. In England this iris survives at least briefly provided the above requirements are met. But even there it is difficult to maintain for any length of time. Best planted in spring when shoots are beginning to form.

Iris verna Linne
This is the only species of the series. It looks somewhat like an *I. pumila* without a beard. It is a dwarf plant with an usually short and crooked scape. The perianth tube is about 2–2⅝" (5–6.5 cm) long, rather slender and elongated towards the throat. The spathes are overlapping bracts, up to 2" (5 cm) long, usually herbaceous, green but sometimes purple-red with pale lines. The tip of the blossom extends up to 5½" 14 cm. The blossom itself is violet, the falls are 2" (5 cm) long, broad-lanceolate, deep lilac with dark violet spots at the base of the blade. There is a wide, orange-red sap mark along the mid-line of the blossom segments that extends onto the blade. The standards are about 2" (5 cm) long, semi-erect, spatulate, pale bluish lilac with translucent, darker colored veins. The foliage reaches about 8¼" (21 cm) in length. The inside of the fan is light green, the

outside reddish purple with white lines. The oval, dark brown capsule is 7/16" (1.3 cm) long and each seed has a white aril similar to a crest. Blooming period is April to May. Number of chromosomes 2n=42.

A mountain form occurring in South Carolina and West Virginia has a distinctly different rootstock, larger blossoms, larger leaves, and usually lacks fragrance. These atypical features suggest a separate species, nonetheless it is usually classified with *I. verna*.

Subsection Ensatae
Series Ensatae

Afghanistan, Siberia, the Himalayas: Tibet, Mongolia, China, Japan; in the West, its range extends to the Caucasus.

The only species of this series, *Iris ensata* is very hardy and robust. As a plant of the steppe, it is very easy to grow under varying conditions even in moist, clay soils. Because of its deep root system, it does not seem to be affected by extreme dryness.

Propagation from seed is easy; division in autumn or preferably in spring. This iris quickly forms dense clusters of leaves. The forms common in cultivation are not very impressive, so are more highly valued for their ornamental leaves. According to Rodionenko, specimens from the arid southern regions of its range carefully cultivated and well watered can change beyond recognition and are very ornamental.

Iris ensata auct. non Thunberg
For more than a century, this small-blossomed iris of the Himalayas was known as *I. ensata* Thunberg, until more recent study, based on comparisons with other plant materials, showed that this name is proper to the Japanese Iris generally known as *I. kaempferi* Sieb. But since the valid name cannot be established with absolute certainty for this small-blossomed iris, I shall stick to the old description—however, not *I. ensata* Thunb. but *I. ensata* auct. non Thunb. In English language publications, it is now often referred to as *I. lactea* Pallas. In *Flora of the Iranian Highlands and Neighboring Regions*, edited by Dr. Karl Heinz Rechinger, in the series *Iridaceae* by P. Wendelbo and B. Mathew, it is called *I. oxypetala* Bunge (syn. *I. moorcroftiana, I. ensata* auct. non Thunb.). In Volume V of *Flora Europaea* on the other hand, it is described as *I. triflora* (syn. *I. ensata* auct. non Thunb., *Xiphion triflorum* [Balbis] Cesati). In the midst of all this confusion I prefer to stay with the old name.

The leaves are fairly stiff, about 20–24" (50–60 cm) long (some forms grow taller). The branching scapes nestle in the leaves and are 11½–15" (30–40 cm) high. The small flowers have a very short perianth tube. The shades of the petals vary; there are whitish ones with darker veins, pale blue ones, cream colored, and also rich violet ones. The standards are usually somewhat darker than the falls, lanceolate, erect, and about ¼" (6 mm) wide. *I. ensata* has strong, healthy rhizomes that rapidly form good clumps. The capsules are 6-ribbed, narrow and long, and are easily distinguished from other species. Seeds rounded, smooth, and glossy. Dormant plants begin to grow very early. The shoots are yellow at first, later turning green. In Asia *I. ensata* is sometimes used as a fiber plant. Blooms in early summer. Number of chromosomes 2n=40.

I. pallasii Fisch., a synonym for *I. ensata* according to Dykes, grows wild in Mongolia, but must be considered a distinct species due to the completely different shape of the seed.

157

A number of varieties are grown—*I. ensata* var. *chinensis* Maxim., *I. ensata* var. *pabularia* Naudin and others. But there seems to be as much confusion in the varieties as in the type species so clear distinguishing features cannot be described.

Subsection *Tenuifoliae*
Series *Tenuifoliae*

Native to Asia *I. iliensis* grows in Kazakstan on the Ili River, from which the name derives. *I. loczyi* comes from the Pamir mountains in China, at elevations up to 13,120 ft. (4000 m). *I. tenuifolia* grows in western and eastern Siberia, as far west as the lower Volga, as well as in Central Asia, in Mongolia, China, and Turkestan.

The species of this series are steppe plants and by nature accustomed to great fluctuations in temperature. Nevertheless, some are difficult to grow in northern regions, due to winter wetness.

These iris grow well in normal garden soil or a sandy soil to which leaf mold has been added (some grow on sand dunes). They will grow in semi-shade, but do better in full sun.

Propagation from seed is recommended; the seedlings, however, grow very slowly. Best time for planting is September. The species of this series have no great value as ornamental plants. The stems bear inconspicuous blossoms which poke out between the leaves after they have withered. *I. iliensis* is slightly more ornamental. According to Dykes, it is difficult to bloom any of the plants of this series in continental climates.

Iris iliensis P. Poljakow
This plant has only recently reached us in the form of seeds and still needs to be tested as a garden plant. Some writers think it is identical to *I. lactea* (= garden *I. ensata*).

Iris loczyi Kanitz
This iris is closely related to *I. tenuifolia*. *I. tianschanica* was recently found in the Tien Shan region and described as another xerophilic iris. But it is probably the same iris that Kanitz described in 1891, under the name *I. loczyi*. *I. loczyi* has the same ornamental value as *Iris tenuifolia*, but is much more resistant to fluctuations in temperature and soil moisture. The blossoms are pale purple-blue; the plant only reaches a height of 2¾–6″ (7–15 cm).

Iris tenuifolia Pallas
In its natural habitat the plant always bears a layer of dead, fibrous leaves on top of the rhizomes. The leaf is grass-like, ⅜–¾″ (1–2 cm) wide. The scape is 2″ (5 cm) long with two pale blue or lilac blossoms, reported to be fragrant. Blooming period April to May. Total height 2¾–6″ (7–15 cm).

Subsection *Tenuifoliae*
Series *Ventricosae*

These are Asiatic species. *I. bungei* is a Mongolian plant, typical of the Gobi Desert flora. *I. songarica* is found on the loamy desert steppes of Turkmenia and Afghanistan, as well as along the edge of the desert between Teheran and Meshed. Migrates up to elevations of 3,900–4,900 ft. (1200–1500 m). *I. ventricosa* occurs generally in Dahurien and the trans-Baikal region.

In their native habitat these iris are exposed to extreme temperature changes, yet they cannot be grown in continental climates for any length of time, again due to winter moisture. They need full sun, but grow in any good garden soil which is not too damp.

Propagation from seed is best, although only a few seeds will germinate and those very slowly. Germination after 5 years has been recorded. Gardeners with cold frames may try their luck with these iris. They have to be protected from moisture in fall and winter.

Iris bungei Maximowicz
This species, with its short stem, falls between *I. tenuifolia* and *I. ventricosa*. A Mongolian postage stamp depicts the blue blossom color. One scape bears several blossoms.

Iris songarica Schrenk
Wherever this species grows, it dominates the entire landscape. When it blossoms in the spring, it really looks from an airplane as though one is flying over a blue sea. In dry regions, *I. songarica* can be used as an ornamental plant. 6–8 silvery blue blossoms stand on a rather tall scape (15–20" or 40–50 cm). The falls and standards are narrow, with a brownish green central stripe on a silver grey-lilac ground. Leaves are narrow and grass-like. In the wild, dead leaves lie all around the plant, similar to *I. grant-duffii*. When the plant is mature, it should be protected from winter moisture and summer rains.

Whether *I. songarica* var. *multiflora* O. Kuntze is really a separate form has not been clearly established.

Iris ventricosa Pallas
Unlike any other iris, *I. ventricosa* has extremely large, reticulated bracts. The blossoms are light blue. The standards have a long stem and a short, wide section. The short flower stalks, 4–8" (10–20 cm) long, bear 1–2 blossoms. The spathes are distended. Needs full sun and sandy soil. This plant is probably more valuable for its use in textiles than as a garden ornamental.

Subsection Syriacae
Series Syriacae

Iris grant-duffii Baker
This series is represented by only one species, but there are a number of varieties, such as *Iris caeruleoviolaea* Foster, *I. masia* Dykes, and *I. melanosticta* Bornmüller, species status for which cannot be justified.

I. grant-duffii is a rare and unusual iris which occurs in northern Israel, Syria and Lebanon (on the road to Baalbeck), and Turkey. It grows in marshy soil that dries out in summer almost to the consistency of stone. It may be the botanical link between rhizomous and bulbous iris. In the wild the plants are surrounded by dry, dead leaf parts. This yellow-blossomed iris is very rarely cultivated. There are also violet specimens, especially in eastern Turkey. Height of the flowerstalk 6–9" (15–25 cm).

Section Unguiculares
Subsection Unguiculares
Series Unguiculares

The natural range of this species is the eastern Mediterranean to the Caucasus. *I. cretensis* grows only on Crete and Rhodes; *I. lazica* in the Caucasus and around the Black Sea. *I. unguicularis* has the widest range, from Algeria to Israel, Turkey, and Greece. In Italy, *I. unguicularis* does not grow wild, but is widely planted in public parks. Some writers have recently discounted *I. cretensis* and *I. lazica* as independent species, but have classified them as

159

varieties of *I. unguicularis*, which I find unacceptable. One almost gets the impression that these writers have not ever seen these morphologically different plants before.

Not generally winter hardy outdoors in continental climates, *I. cretensis*, which I have been able to grow outdoors with winter protection for over 3 years, is hardier than others in this group.

Unlike many Bearded Iris, which grow in neutral or acid soil, these iris thrive in lime soils. They should be planted in a sunny location; the drier the plants in summer, the more abundantly they will flower the following winter. *I. lazica* grows where there is some shade.

In colder latitudes these iris can only be grown in a container or coldhouse. They will bloom in the coldhouse in January–February, often earlier, at a temperature of 40–45°F (5–8°C). Larger containers put in a well lighted spot in the basement will also start to bloom around this time; they should then be moved to a cool room. I have learned that in a moderately heated bedroom, they will blossom for about 2 weeks. The best time for transplanting is April. At that time they have a number of active, white roots. If transplanted in the fall, on the other hand, only wiry, dead-looking roots are present and the development of new rhizomes is quite slow. All three species have firm, linear, evergreen leaves. The blue blossoms have a very long pericanth tube.

Iris cretensis Janka
Synonyms: *I. cretica* Herbert ex Baker, *I. humilis* ssp. *cretensis* (Janka) Nyman

In its native habitat, *I. cretensis* grows on open grassy, alpine meadows. In contrast to the other two species, the leaves are small, narrow and stand upright. The blossoms are violet with a yellow veina-tion. Not to be confused with a small Pogon Iris called *I.* 'Cretica' that was bred early in the development of Dwarf Iris cultivation in North America and was never native to Crete.

Iris lazica Albow
On coastal hills of the Black Sea, *I. lazica* forms extensive carpets with its evergreen leaves. In late autumn and winter it has pale, sky blue, odorless blossoms. It is planted along the Black Sea to prevent shoreline erosion, as well as for beautification. The blossoms of *I. lazica* cannot be distinguished from those of *I. unguicularis*, but their foliage is another matter. That of *I. lazica* is shorter and not quite as stiffly erect as *I. unguicularis*. *I. lazica* has overhanging fans. Number of chromosomes 2n=32.

Iris unguicularis Poiret
Synonym: *I. stylosa* Desf.

I. unguilicaris often is called the Winter Iris or Algerian Iris. It has very sturdy rhizomes. The scape is very short or quite unelongated. The blossoms have a perianth tube 4–8½" (10–22 cm) long and only show between the long leaves, which may grow to 24" (60 cm) long, but are usually shorter in the garden; their width is about 7/16" (1.2 cm). The obovate petals, 1" (2.5 cm) wide, are spotted yellow on a violet ground at the throat. The standards are 5/8" (1.8 cm) wide, and the crests appear to be dusted with gold on the back, the result of a fine glandular secretion. The falls are usually held out horizontally.

The blossoms have a pleasant fragrance, in contrast to those of *I. lazica*. The triangular capsules lie close to the leaf bases. Grown outdoors in temperate areas of England, in the U.S. it is found mostly from California to British Columbia. Experiments have shown that it can grow even in regions with lows of 15°F (−10°C), if covered by snow. A number of cultivars are grown, especially in England. The popularity of this iris will certainly increase as more gardeners acquire small greenhouses than can be used as cold-houses, and hence maintain a temperature of 40–45°F (5–8°C) in winter. The following cultivars have been developed:

I. 'Alba', white blossoms
I. 'Miss Ellis Variety', dark violet
I. 'Winter's Treasure', white
I. 'Winter's Snowflake', white
I. 'Mary Bernard' natural forms collected in Algeria
I. 'Walter Butt'
Also *I.* 'Speciosa', *I.* 'Lilacina', *I.* 'Imperatrice Elizabetta', I. 'Marginata', *I.* 'Peacock', *I.* 'Bridal Pink' and *I.* 'Marbled'.

Section Ioniris
Series Ruthenicae

The species of this series grow from the Carpathians east across Asia to the Pacific Coast. *I. ruthenica* grows in Transylvania and neighboring regions. A few years ago, the botanist Vvedensky split off a new species from *I. ruthenica,* and named it *I. brevituba.* The latter occurs in the mountains of Kirghiz and has a short perianth tube. More precise study will confirm whether this plant deserves the species status. *I. uniflora,* a recognized species, grows in eastern Siberia and Mongolia.

The representatives of this series are completely hardy; frost damage is unknown. They show tolerance to dryness as well as long rainy periods.

These iris are not particularly demanding plants. They grow best in a heavy, sandy-clay soil, but will also get along in rocky soils, and should be planted in full sun. Use in clusters in the rock garden, as border plants, or with other groupings of wild plants.

They are hard to transplant because their rhizomes have so few roots, but they can easily be grown from seed. The best time for transplanting is shortly after they bloom, from the end of April to the middle of May, depending on climatic conditions. Their roots are actively growing only shortly before or after the blooming period.

Iris ruthenica Ker Gawler
Synonyms: *I. caespitosa* Pallas, *I. nana* Maxim

Known to many iris lovers as Transylvanian Grass Iris, the leaves can easily be mistaken for a tuft of grass when the plant is not in bloom. The leaves are about 8" (20 cm) long and ⅛–¼" (0.3–0.6 cm) wide. The color is bright green, with a glossy upper surface. The rhizomes are thin and multi-branched. The scapes vary from 1⅛–8" (3–20 cm) in length, depending on location and the amount of available moisture. The blossoms usually emerge between the leaves, except in dry springs when they may stand above them. Each pedicel has only one white blossom with heavy dark blue to blue-violet veining. The petals are uniform in length, the falls are held out horizontally, and the standards are upright and pale violet. The falls are about 2" (5 cm) long, ovate-cuneate and, of course, beardless. The seed capsules, which contain only 6–14 seeds, burst open when ripe and disperse the seeds in the grass. Each spherical seed has a white aril, which later shrinks and disappears, but when fresh it becomes sticky in the rain and clings to the feet of animals, thus scattering the seed over long distances.

Both poorly- and profusely-blooming clones of this cushion-forming iris exist in the wild and in gardens. It is not morphologically uniform throughout its vast range.

Iris uniflora Pallas

The blossoms are not noticeably different from *I. ruthenica;* but the ends of the petals are slightly blunter, the leaves are usually more compact and wider (5/16–7/16" or 0.8–1 cm), and the fans a bit more arched. Another distinguishing feature are the bracts which, on *I. ruthenica,* wither immediately after the plant blooms and decay very quickly, whereas they remain green on *I. uniflora* until the seeds are completely mature. *I. uniflora* is the more attractive species, always holding its attractive blossoms visibly above the foliage. Height about 4" (10 cm).

Subgenus Xyridion
Section Xyridion

The species of this section are generally called Spuria Iris, or Steppe Iris. Both series are also known as Tall Spuria Iris and as Dwarf Spurias. The species of this section inhabit a relatively wide range. On closer inspection, however, even those species having a larger range grow in relatively isolated patches within that range. The Tall Spuria Iris grow in a few areas of Spain; in France; the east coast of England; vary locally in southern Germany; lower Austria; Moravia; the Danish islands; Corsica; North Africa; the Balkans; southeast Soviet Union particularly around the Caucasus; Turkey; Iran; Afghanistan; and China. I have even seen *I. crocea* and *I. notha* in Kashmir. The Dwarf Spurias do not occur as widely. They grow naturally in France, in Tessin; Bavaria; Czechoslovakia and the Balkans; southwest Soviet Union up to the Altai Mountains and in the south, particularly in the Caucasus.

Climatically speaking, the entire range lies on the southern edge of the temperate zone. Experience shows that all members of this section are completely winter hardy, even though a certain paucity of flowering in colder regions is noticeable in some of the species from the extreme south.

In North America the Tall Spuria Iris are divided into two groups, based on their chromosome counts. One includes *I. crocea* and *I. orientalis* (syn. *I. ochroleuca*), the other the balance. Modern Spuria hybrids are derived from both species of the first group. All Spuria species are relatively easy to grow and are valuable garden plants.

Briefly, full sun and a warm location are requisites for growing Spuria Iris successfully. The idea soil is neutral to slightly alkaline. The tall species blossoms particularly well in clay soils. But summers must be hot and dry so the soil can really "bake". In regions with heavy summer precipitation, good drainage must be provided and the soil should generally be more porous, since the plants will suffer in standing water. Dwarf Spurias are not as sensitive in this respect. The tall species, especially, thrive with ample fertilization. Excellent results are obtained with well-composted steer manure, but a slow-release complete mineral fertilizer is also recommended.

The Tall Spurias have relatively thick rhizomes similar to those of Bearded Iris. This leads people to plant them at the surface. However, the rhizomes of Tall Spuria Iris should properly be covered with about 2" (5 cm) of soil. Planting in fall is preferable to spring planting, although both can be done. If possible, Dwarf Spuria Iris should be planted with their rootballs intact, unless compact offsets are available. All the iris in this section should remain undisturbed for a long period of time. The negative effects of transplanting and dividing can be noticed for years. Special requirements of individual species are mentioned in the species descriptions.

Series Spuriae

Iris carthaliniae Fomin

I. carthaliniae grows in Georgia, particularly west of Tiflis, in the Kuban region east of the Caucasus and in Transcaucasia. The soil in its natural habitat is often moist. This

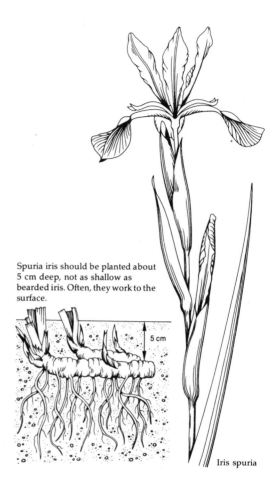

Spuria iris should be planted about 5 cm deep, not as shallow as bearded iris. Often, they work to the surface.

5 cm

Iris spuria

species has the broadest leaves of all Spuria Iris, 1–1⅛" (2.5–3 cm) wide, and they are light gray-green. The length of the leaves is 50–55 in. (1.3–1.4 m.) The height of the scapes is about 43" (110 cm), and they are slightly kinked, in contrast to those of *I. notha* which are noticeably bent. The whole plant stands straight up and presents a somewhat stiff appearance. Each stem has an average of 5 flowers which bloom in sequence, one below the other. They have a diameter of about 4¼" (11 cm) and are a beautiful shade of blue. The blade has a golden yellow central stripe with radial white stripes. There is also a rare pure white form which is a rewarding plant, excellent for the garden. The tips of the leaves rise slightly above the blossoms, but the latter makes a very good effect nonetheless. Its robust growth (somewhat slower when the plant is young), firmness, and beautiful blue of the blossoms are pluses. The soil should be heavy sandy loam and not too dry (in contrast to *I. orientalis* Carr. = *I. ochroleuca* of gardens and *I. crocea*). It blossoms mid-May to mid-June. It can be propagated by division or from seed which usually germinates readily. Plant in September. Number of chromosomes 2n=44.

Iris crocea Jacquemont
Synonym: *I. aurea* Lindley

I. crocea may occur in Kashmir and Turkey, although this is not completely certain. It was introduced into Kashmir, but no natural localities are known, only stands in or near villages. Those native to Turkey are probably an independent species, not yet described: seeds were collected at Haydar Bagda near Ankara, and the plants differ from the true species. *I. crocea* reaches about 33–46″ (85–120 cm). The leaves are sword-shaped and stand stiffly upright; they are about 1″ (2.5 cm) wide. The firm stem bears a cluster of terminal blossoms that are about 4¾″ (12 cm) in diameter. The are attractive, golden yellow, and the margin of the blade on the falls is delicately ruffled. The perianth tube is slender and about ⅜″ (1 cm) long. The blade is 1″ (2.5 cm) wide and about as long as the haft. The standards are shorter and much narrower. The blossoms stand a little higher than the foliage. The rhizomes are thin, hard, and compact.

In the garden plant in a soil that tends toward clay-loam, slightly acidic, and moist. A light top dressing in spring, especially with well-rotted cattle manure, is very effective. An open location in full sun is preferred. This is a gorgeous species that deserves to be more widely grown. It is not as robust as *I. orientalis* (syn. *I. ochroleuca*) and takes a longer time to blossom after being planted. September is the best time for dividing and transplanting, but this should not be done too often, as there is a wait of 1 or 2 years afterwards for blossoms. Blooms in second half of June to beginning of July. Number of chromosomes 2n=40.

Iris demetrii Achverdov et Mirzoieva
Synonym: *Iris prilipkoana* Kenularia-Natadze

From the mountains of Azerbaidzhan in Nakhichevan ASSR, *I. demetrii* grows at an altitude of 5,250 ft. (1600 m). It is similar to *I. klattii* Kemularia-Natadze (syn. *I. violacea* Klatt); differing from it morphologically only slightly, but ecologically very much. *I. demitrii* grows in high mountain meadows, while *I. klattii* is found in lower-lying marsh meadows. The flower is a very beautiful, pure violet-blue, considerably more beautiful than the various local forms of *I. spuria*, with which *I. demetrii*

Small bulbous iris (Iridodictyum) are the earliest blooming of all iris. Their blossoms are often surprised by a snowfall.

Upper left: Iridodictyum danfordiae (Iris danfordiae) is reasonably priced and can be found in all the lists of fall bulb offers. Unfortunately they may rapidly divide into many small bulblets that take a long time to blossom again. However, they can be replaced often because of their low cost. Upper right: 'Blue Veil' is the name of this cultivar of Iridodictyum reticulatum. Its beautiful blue blossom goes well with early wild tulips and species of narcissus, with heather and primroses. Bottom: 'Clairette', a descendent of Iridodictyum bakerianum (Iris reticulate var. bakerianum), has a gaily patterned blossom. Reputed to be from the cross I. reticulatum × I. bakerianum.

shares both the form and arrangement of its blossoms. Unlike other Spuria Iris, the blossoms are held well above the foliage. The leaves are medium-wide (wider than those of *I. notha* and narrower than *I. carthaliniae*) and stand upright without the tips hanging over too much. Height of the plant 28–35″ (70–90 cm).

In this case too, a fertile clay soil is ideal, but with good drainage. Desirable planting time is September. The rhizomes should be covered with 2″ (5 cm) soil. Means of propagation is the same as with other Spurias. A beautiful natural plant. Good companion plant is Golden Yellow Achillea. Unfortunately, very prone to a fungus disease common to Spuria Iris, which often causes them to die.

Iris halophila Pallas
Synonyms: *I. spuria* ssp. *halophila, I. gueldenstaedtiana* Lepechin.

Completely different iris are often sold on the market as *I. halophila*.

I. halophila is native to Rumania and the Soviet Union to Central Asia. Particularly large-blossomed individuals are found in the Moldau region, according to Rodio-

Small bulbous iris (Iridodictyum).

Upper left: Iridodictyum histroides 'Major' is without a doubt the most rewarding species of this now independent genus. It has large, early blossoms, a vibrant color and relatively low price. No one should be without it.
Upper right: Iridodictyum histrio var. aintabensis. Whereas the true I. histrio from the Lebanon mountains is not completely hardy, this variety survives even Germany's severe winters. It is the earliest-blooming small dwarf iris.
Below: 'Katharine Hodgkin' was the first successful cross between I. histrioides and I. danfordiae, made by S. B. Anderson in 1958. Rix and Phillips suggest that the yellow parent may have been I. winogradowskil. It has a somewhat strange beauty. It is a much sought after rarity for pot culture.

nenko. They inhabit low-lying meadows, where their roots can reach ground water. In the Moldau region, this iris is found along the Kaghilnik River for miles at a stretch. In Asia some stands reach the Himalayas and the western slopes of the Altai Mountains. On the Asiatic steppe, this iris occurs commonly where there is salt in the soil, hence its specific name, "salt-loving". It is not completely clear whether these types belong to *I. musulmanica*.

The true *I. halophila* is a strong, free-blooming plant, which usually differs from *I. spuria* and other related forms and species distinctly, but not essentially. It has smaller, narrower blossoms, many yellow and yellow-blue, in contrast to *I. spuria*. In addition, *I. halophila* has a larger ovary and a longer perianth tube. The fruit is more winged and with a longer beak. The falls are shortened, and the circular to oval blade extends horizontally. The blossom color varies, usually yellow or yellow with shades of blue, gray, or white. There are also blue speciments with yellow veining. The height of the plant is 15–30″ (40–80 cm). The blossoms stand at the same height as the leaves or a bit higher. They are arranged on the stem in tiers, with usually several open at the same time. The width of the leaves is about ⅜″ (1 cm).

I. halophila usually blooms at the same time as the Tall Bearded Iris, making it one of the earliest-blooming Tall Spuria Iris. It grows in full sun and a fertile, clay-loam soil; slight moisture in the soil during the growing period is **advantageous**, but basically it has no special requirements. It does not have especially large, attractive blossoms, but since it grows well and blooms freely, it is a satisfying garden plant. As with other Spurias, it should be planted in the fall rather than in spring. Don't plant too shallow! Not difficult to divide. Develops strong, volunteer seed-lings and germinates readily after effects of frost; often self-sows. A white natural form also exists. Since it is the northernmost spuria, hybridizers are greatly interested in it, particularly the large-blossomed Moldau form. Number of chromosomes 2n=44.

Iris klattii Kemularia-Natadze
Synonym: *I. violacea* Klatt

Native to the Caucasus, along the Samur River, *I. klattii* grows also in eastern Transcaucasia, in Azerbaidzan, and even into the region of Persian Azerbaidzan. There it is found in tremendous stands, particularly in low, marshy meadows.

Different specimens have differing heights, varying between 15 and 35" (40 and 90 cm). But this may only be the result of location. The Botanical Garden of Moscow produced a dwarf form. The blossoms of *I. klattii* have the same striking blue-violet color as *I. notha,* but not their elegance and the leaves are also con-siderably wider. There is a reddish stripe on the haft. In the wild there are types with various shades of the blossom color. Pure white ones were found west of Baku.

Like most of the Spuria Iris found in the Soviet Union, *I. klattii* is extremely good in the garden, although it is not very common. Blooms in June. Number of chromosomes 2n=44.

Iris monnieri D. C.
Synonym: *I. spuria* var. *monnieri*

Information about natural habitats on Crete and Rhodes for *I. monnieri* was mostly inaccurate. Its whole origin is shrouded in mystery; despite its species status, it is probably a hybrid. It was first discovered in a French garden, but occurs nowhere in nature. According to Lenz's researches, it is a hybrid between an iris similar to *I. crocea* found near Ankara ("Turkey Yellow") and *I. orientalis* Mill (=garden *I. ochroleuca*). Others maintain that it is a mutation of *I. spuria.*

The color of the well-formed blossoms is a light, clear yellow (daffodil yellow), without any veining or patterns. Multiple buds bloom either serially or simul-taneously at the end of the stem. The form of the blossom is similar to *I. spuria,* the blossom color somewhat lighter than *I. crocea,* without a wavy or ruffled margin. The dark green foliage keeps its color for a long time and withers only towards the end of the year. It is somewhat shorter than *I. orientalis* (=garden *I. ochroleuca* var. *gigantea*) and somewhat taller than *I. spuria.* When it is not in bloom, the plant resembles *I. ochroleuca* because of the dark-green color of its leaves (the leaves of *I. spuria* are narrower and a more off-gray shade). Height of the leaves is 24–38" (60–100 cm); height of the scape 40–60" (100–150 cm).

Plant in full sun and fertile, loamy soil. Can easily be propagated by dividing the clumps. Sowing seed after effects of frost yields good seedling crops. Cutting method is successful. A stately garden plant, the light yellow is very effective in the background. It is also valuable because of its relatively late bloom, end of June to beginning of July, later than most other Spurias. Number of chromosomes 2n=40. Other hybrids are *I.* × *monspur* (=*I. monneiri* × *I. spuria*) and *I.* × *monaurea* (=*I. monnieri* × *crocea* syn. *I. aurea*). Many plants being sold as *I. monnieri* are not genuine.

Iris musulmanica Fomin
Synonym: *I. spuria* ssp. *musulmanica*

Native to southwest Asia, particularly Armenia, in the vicinity of Eriwan, often at the edge of salt marshes. Closely related to *I. halophila* but shorter than the *I. halophila* from Bessarabia and Bukovina. Perianth tubes of the two iris also differ in length. Number of chromosomes 2n=44.

Iris notha M. B.
Synonym: *I. spuria* ssp. *notha*.

I cannot agree with the proposal that this is a subspecies of *I. spuria* because the morphological differences are too great. If the proposition were true, all the other blue-blossomed, tall Spuria Iris from the Soviet Union would also have to be considered subspecies of *I. spuria*.

I. notha occurs in the Caucasus and in Transcaucasia (Kabarda-Balkar ASSR) around Neussk, Urodschai, Nalchik in the northern Caucasus. Grows in steppe-like valleys at higher elevations. Possibly also occurs farther to the east. I was able to positively identify *I. notha* in Kashmir (Verinac near the Banhial Pass).

Elegant, narrow, often arching leaves, 26–30" (65–80 cm) long, 7/16–1/2" (1.3–1.5 cm) wide. The height of the scape is 40–43" (100–110 cm). Blossoms are large and have a diameter of up to 6" (15 cm). Almost vertical standards, falls held horizontally, color medium blue to light blue-violet. The medium blue type has the most beautiful blue color of all the Spuria Iris. There is a yellow stripe down the middle of the falls. The flower stalks usually bear 3 blossoms, are relatively thin, and change direction somewhat from node to node, so that they zigzag slightly, which is particularly noticeable on stems which are bowed over. The plant is more elegant in every respect than *I. carthaliniae* or *I. spuria*, even though it is not as hardy.

Being a plant of the high steppe, it grows in full sun and a heavy clay loam; surviving extreme drought. Best planted in autumn. Offsets are often hard to grow and losses must be expected; it is better to propagate them by seed, even though it takes longer. This elegant plant must not be cramped. Blooming period: mid June to early July.

Iris orientalis Mill
Synonyms: *I. ochroleuca* L., *I. gigantea* Carr.; not to be mistaken for *I. sanguinea* Hornem (syn. *I. orientalis* Thunb.). Here again there has been a botanical change of names because of priority rules. But to avoid confusion, this is the garden *I. ochroleuca* var. *gigantea*.

Its habitat is scattered through Asia Minor and Syria. It grows in places that are fairly wet during the rainy season, but completely desiccated in summer. The species is 24–30" (60–80 cm) tall, the scapes reach about 40" (1 m). The sword-shaped leaves stand stiffly erect, are dark green and ornamental. The blossoms are white with a large yellow spot in the middle of the recurved falls. Standards have a median yellow stripe. A blue wild form is reported but is uncommon. A somewhat taller sort known as *I. ochroleuca* 'Gigantea' or as *I. ochroleuca* var. *gigantea* is found in gardens. The bloomstalk of this iris can reach a height of 5 ft. (1.5 m). Whether this is a taller-growing natural form is not known.

This iris is not a heavy feeder; like other Spurias it thrives in a fertile, humus-rich clay loam, but grows quite well in light soils. During the growing period in spring it should have sufficient moisture. Like all Spurias, it takes a long time to become established. Best time for planting is in September. When replanting, leave 9" (25 cm) between rhizomes.

This is a very rewarding plant, suitable for cutting. It is particularly attractive as a specimen among low-growing perennials or at the edge of a pond (it shouldn't come into direct contact with the wet banks). Combines well with larkspur. It begins to bloom between June 25 and July 1. There is also a lighter-colored form known as *I. ochroleuca* var. *sulphurea*. Number of chromosomes 2n=40.

In accord with botanists, we have classified this as *I. orientalis*, although it will be called *I. ochroleuca* in nurseries and gardening circles for years to come.

Iris sogdiana Bunge
Synonym: *I. spuria* var. *sogdiana*

I. sogdiana is native to central Asia and the southern part of Kazakstan. Whereas *I. halophila* has relatively large, though narrow blossoms, 3–4" (8–10 cm) in diameter carried at the height of the leaves or above, the flowers of *I. sogdiana* are only half as large, have a pale blue or dingy violet color, and are borne on short stems among the foliage. There are, however, specimens in its large range with better coloring. The short stems are a typical feature of the wild species.

I. sogdiana does not seem to be particularly sensitive to salty soils. It is found in gardens in North Turkmenia, but has no great value as a garden plant in the west. The dark green leaves are indestructible, even surviving very high temperatures. Grows in full sun, but otherwise has no requirements.

Iris spuria Linne
Synonyms: *Iris spathulata* Lamarck, *I. dierinckii* Baker

Iris spuria is a very complex group because of its tremendous range, in which many local forms are present, all varying in height, ease of culture, blossom, and color. Among the many varieties, the following have "justified" their existence: *I. spuria* ssp. *maritima*, *I.s.* var. *danica*, *I.s.* var. *hispanica*, *I.s.* var. *reichenbachiana*, and *I.s.* var. *subbarbata*. Some publications list *I. notha*, *I. halophila*, and *I. musulmanica* as

varieties of *I. spuria*. But if this were true, all the other spuria species from the southern USSR would have to be added to *I. spuria*. Morphological differences give these iris their species status.

It should be noted that *Flora Europea*, Vol. V, has a completely different classification.:

I. spuria ssp. *spuria*: The upper stem leaves are shorter than the stem internodes; falls are more than 1¾" (45 mm) long. The blossom is violet-blue.

I. spuria ssp. *maritima*: The upper stem leaves are longer than one internode. The falls are less than 1¾" (45 mm) long. The blossom is violet-blue.

I. spuria ssp. *halophila*: Basal leaves 5/16–½" (7–12 mm) wide, falls usually less than 2½" (60 mm) long. Color of blossoms whitish, yellowish, often tinted with violet.

I. spuria ssp. *ochroleuca* (*I. orientalis*): Basal leaves 7/16–7/8" (10–20 mm) wide, falls more than 2½" (60 mm) long. Blossom whitish with yellow center.

I do not agree with this classification because it ignores all the species of southwestern Soviet Union. On the other hand, information on the distinguishing features is very useful.

We have already mentioned its vast distribution: North Africa, Spain, southern France, West Germany (the Rhineland near Mainz), Denmark (Salthomen Island), lower Austria, and Hungary are only the most important areas. There *I. spuria* grows in river meadows, in marshy areas, and on the banks of lakes (not in the water).

Average height is 24" (60 cm), and if all varieties are included, it is 13–28" (35–70 cm). The lower figure applies more to *I. spuria* ssp. *maritima*, a native of Western Europe, the higher to *I. spuria* ssp. *subbarbata* found in the region of Neuseidl Lake in eastern Austria. The leaves are shorter than the stem, which has few branches and are narrow (about ⅜" or 1 cm wide), and stand rather stiffly erect. They have an unpleasant odor when crushed. Every scape bears several buds (2–4) that open sequentially. The spathes have double or triple folds. The perianth tube is about ⅜" (1 cm) long. Falls with a pendulous blade, ⅜" (1 cm) wide and half as long as the haft. The standards are somewhat shorter, ⅜" (1 cm) wide and flaring. The anthers are purple with a yellow border. The crests lie close above them. Coloration varies according to origin. Some are pure violet with a yellow mid-stripe on the falls; others have violet standards and yellowish, blue-veined falls. The white form, *I. spuria* 'Alba', is very beautiful. The capsule is 1–2" (2.5–5 cm) long, elongated, with a beak. The seed is smooth, brown and covered by a cellophane-like skin. This species has thin, hard rhizomes.

Does well in the garden, except *I. spuria* var. *danica* from Saltholmen Island. Plant in medium-heavy loam and grow somewhat wetter than the *I. crocea-orientalis (ochroleuca)-monnieri* group. It will grow well even in sandy soils, if given sufficient water in the summer. *I. spuria* is a heavy feeder and responds to well-rotted steer manure. Blooming period in June follows that of the Tall Bearded Iris and lasts into July. Number of chromosomes 2n=38.

Iris spuria var. *subbarbata* Joo
Among the large number of *I. spuria* types, this one deserves special mention as one of the prettiest. It grows in lower Austria in damp, but not marshy places. Up to 4 blossoms are borne on an almost unbranched stalk, about 24" (60 cm) tall. In some plants these are a pure azure blue. The blossoms are 3–4" (8–10 cm) in diameter. The somewhat nodding falls are scalloped in the shape of a heart, and the

standards spread out in the familiar V-shape. This variety is wholeheartedly recommended for the garden, despite its slow growth. It rewards patience with its beauty. The brown, hard, old roots do not die off that quickly, but hang like wires to the old rhizomes. The leaves become somewhat wider (½–⅝" or 12–15 mm).

Series Gramineae

Iris brandzae Prodan
Synonym: *I. sintenisii* ssp. *brandzae* (*Flora Europea*)

I. brandzae is a dwarf Spuria from Rumania (Bessarabia near Noua Sulita in the vicinity of Marsnita). While Prodan describes this as a separate new species and compares its relationship to *I. sintenisii* with that of *I. pseudocyperus* to *I. graminea*, other botanists subordinate *I. brandzae* as a subspecies of *I. sintenisii*.

The leaves of *I. brandzae* are narrower and with different substance than those of *I. sintenissi*; its veins protrude more and are attenuate and spiked at the upper end. The leaves of the typical *I. brandzae* are almost twice as long as the scape, whereas the leaves of the typical *I. sintensisii* are at the most 4" (10 cm) longer than its scape. Three natural forms of *I. brandzae* are known. Apart from the typical *I. brandzae*, there is a form with the scape ¾ the length of the leaves. The blossoms of the third form stand as high as the leaves (*I. brandzae* f. *topae*). The spathes of *I. brandzae* are wider and more distended than those of *I. sintenisii*. It blooms in May, violet-blue. Height 9–13" (25–35 cm).

Much less important for the garden than *I. sintenisii*, the latter being much more ornamental. Number of chromosomes 2n=20.

Iris colchica Kemularia-Natadze
Grows at an elevation of about 5,900 ft. (1800 m) at the summit of the Atshishka Mountain Range, Adzhar, USSR, and is probably a form of *I. graminea.*

Iris farreri Dykes
Native to southwestern China. This iris too might be considered a form of *I. graminea.* The blossoms, certainly, strongly resemble that species. The rounded scape of *I. farreri* differentiates it from *I. graminea,* with its flatter scape. It differs from *I. sintenisii* by its narrower, thinner leaves and its outer spathe valve, which is always weaker and ridged.

Iris graminea L.
Synonyms: *I. sylvatica* Balbi, *I. lamprophylla* Lange

With very extensive range, *I. graminea* has many different forms. From the Bay of Biscay to the mouth of the Volga, on both sides of the Caucasus. Also native to Central Europe, particularly in forest meadows (in southern Tyrol, Carinthia, Wurttemberg, southern Bavaria, in Franconia near Nurnberg, in Silesia, Bohemia, Moravia, in the Crimea, in Switzerland, etc.).

The Central European species has narrow, grass-like foliage and the typically flattened stem with two blossoms. It also has the erect scape bract with a sharp end. In the Caucasus there are forms with very narrow leaves and others with wider ones. Height varies from form to form, between about 8–18" (20–45 cm). The width of the leaf also varies correspondingly from 1/8–5/16" (3 to 7 mm). The blossoms are hidden deep in the foliage. The short scape, which is usually 4–8" (10–20 cm) tall and solid through, bears two terminal buds. Blade of the violet falls oval to circular, contrasting distinctly from the yel-lowish-white, blue-veined, oval haft. The standards are shorter, broadly-lanceolate, and purple-blue. There are specimens with shades varying from blue-violet to purple-violet.

Although the blossoms of this iris are usually buried in the foliage, *I. graminea* is an old favorite in the garden. It is widely used under the name Plum-scented Iris. The blossoms have a pleasantly sweet, fruity fragrance, reminiscent of ripe plums. The dense, grassy clumps are an embellishment to the garden, even when they are not in bloom.

Transplanting every 3 or 4 years helps prevent the blossoms from sitting too deeply in the foliage. Young plants have more blossoms than older ones; leaves become too crowded on older plants. The blossoms are attractive in small vases. Useful in rock gardens or in borders. Sunny location, tolerates lime but grows better in neutral to slightly acid soil. Needs an open spot in full sun. The planting site should not be too dry. Blooms in June, but a few second blooms appear even in September. Can be easily divided, in September. Also easy to propagate by seed.

Iris kerneriana Ascherson et Sintenis ex Baker
Occurs in European Turkey, particularly around Amasya, and in Armenia. Has slender, short, branching rhizomes. The upright leaf clusters are quite crowded. The leaves are linear, 5/16–7/16" (8–10 mm) wide at the base, 15/16" (7 mm) in the middle, growing straight up and ending in a sharp point. Leaf color is dull medium-green, turning light gray-green towards the base. The longest leaves are about the same height as the blossoming scape. The stem is elliptical in cross-section and unbranched; varying from

11½–17" (30–45 cm); and usually with two flowers. The outer spathe is slightly ridged and 2–2¾" (5–7 cm) long. The blossoms open sequentially. The ovary has six wings, as with all Spuria Iris. The blossom color is primrose yellow, partly washed with a bright daffodil yellow, especially on the falls, except for a narrow margin and along the middle rib and the standards. The falls are 2" (5 cm) long and about ⅝" (1.8 cm) wide at the widest point. The whole fall is violin-shaped. The blade is elliptical-ovate, slightly ruffled on the margin; the haft is slender and channeled. The standards are about 1½" (4 cm) long. The slightly twisted crests are 1½" (4 cm) long and slender.

Blooming period is May–June; beautiful, freely-blooming iris; the only Dwarf Spuria with yellow blossoms. Unfortunately, only too rarely for sale in nurseries. Planting time is spring or autumn, but September is preferable. Transplanting is possible even after blooming. The plant dies back completely in fall. The soil should never completely dry out. Requires neutral soil and no mineral fertilizer; compost is suitable. In some locations the plant can be very erratic. Propagation by seed is not difficult, but requires patience as germination often occurs only after 18 months! Rarely used for hybridizing. Number of chromosomes 2n=18.

Iris ludwigii Maxim

Native to the Altai and surrounding steppes, where this iris is often associated with *Stipa splendens*. Counterpart in this region *I. pontica* Zap., with which it has much in common; however, morphological differences justify a separate species status. The blossoms of *I. ludwigii* are more or less without stems, as are those of *I. pontica* Zap. Two blossoms, enclosed between two shortened leaves, emerge from the papery spathes. Differentiated from *I. pontica* mainly by the shape and type of rhizome, which is very narrow and free-running, in contrast to the compact, crowded rhizomes of *I. ludwigii*. Difficult to obtain and not as beautiful as *I. pontica* Zap. Height 8–10" (20–30 cm). Best time for transplanting is September. Sunny rock garden with good drainage.

Iris pontica Zapalowicz

Synonyms: *I. humilis* M. B., *I. marschalliana* Bobrov, *I. humilis* var. *pontica*.

I. pontica, in the garden, often is identified as *I. humilis* (this description is also found in Zander). However, since the small, yellow Pseudoregelia, which is also known as *I. flavissima, I. arenaria*, is now officially called *I. humilis* Georgi, I am compelled to follow the botanists. *I. pontica* Zapalowicz should also not be confused with *I. variegata* var. *pontica*.

I. pontica is native to European Soviet Union, especially in Besarabia and in the region of the Caucasus, also in Bakarda-Balkar USSR, in Rumania, and particularly Transylvania.

The narrow, dark-green leaves are strikingly ornamental. The flowers are borne on short stalks, but appear to grow directly out of the ground. Usually one blossom per scape. The blossoms stand somewhat taller in fertile, moist places. Blossom color is violet-blue with reddish tones. The diameter of the relatively large blossoms is about 4–5½" (10–14 cm). The outer perianth segments are constructed. The blade of the falls is circular with a white, veined spot; and yellow tones appear at the outer edge. Blooms at the end of May. Some of the various local forms have a slight fragrance.

Because of its short rhizomes, the plant forms mats. The height of the plant is 11½–

15″ (30–40 cm). The leaves themselves are handsome and larger than those of the closely-related Plum-scented Iris, *I. graminea*. They are 3/16″ (5 mm) wide with protruding veins. In the case of *I. humilis* var. *pontica*, the leaves reach 6–8″ (15–20 cm) tall and are narrow, about 1/16–3/16″ (2–4 mm). On the other hand, the blossoms reach a diameter of about 6½″ (16 cm)! There are other varying local forms.

Plant in a fertile, clay loam in the garden; a moderate amount of clay mixed with crushed limestone is good. Protect from a too soggy root run with good drainage. A sunny site is important. Soil that is too fertile distorts the typical form.

Plant in spring with rootball intact. Vegetative propagation is not very easy because, unlike other dwarf spurias, offsets do not grow very well. Propagation from seed is more dependable, but also more protracted.

The genuine plant can rarely be obtained in nurseries because it is often confused with *I. graminea*. Although its blossoms sit even deeper than those of *I. graminea*, the plant should be used in the a rock garden, especially next to low cushion plants.

Number of chromosomes 2n=72.

Iris psuedocyprus Schur
Synonym: *I. graminea* var. *pseudocyperus* Beck

This iris occurs particularly in Rumania and Transylvania and in eastern Czechoslovakia near the border of the Soviet Union. Since this iris was described, there has been a tug-of-war among botanists about whether its species status is deserved, or if it should only be considered a variety of *I. graminea*.

Clear, light blue, very striking blossoms appear deep in the foliage like those of *I. pontica* Zap. and *I. graminea*. Standards grow stiffly upright and are oblanceolate. The blade and haft of the falls are about the same size and the narrowing between the two barely indicated. The blade is blue on the surface, with a yellow line in the middle from which white veins radiate; The underside is yellowish, with a blue edge. Its shape is obovate. The haft is reddish violet. The crests are light violet with a dark center. The intensity of this color fluctuates between individual local forms more than the color of the rest of the blossom. The diameter of the blossom varies from 2½–3″ (6–8 cm). The length of the scape likewise differs between 4 and 12″ (10–32 cm) including the blossom. Hexagonal capsules usually contain only a few seeds or are empty. *I. pseudocyperus* can easily be distinguished from *I. pontica* Zap. and *I. graminea*, to which it is related, by its decidedly winged ovary and its short perianth tube. The leaves, which are gray-green in the wild, turn greener under cultivation. The width of the leaves, from 2¾–8″ (7–15 cm), is also a definite distinguishing feature. The leaves of *I. pontica* Zap. and *I. graminea* are much narrower.

Blooming period is June. A genuine plant is rarely obtainable. Best planted in a rock garden. A rewarding ornamental.

Iris sintenisii Janka
Native to the Dobrutscha, in Bulgaria, in the vicinity of Istanbul. There are also differing southern Italian forms, which vary in height from 4–6″ (10–15 cm), the lower forms being more spreading, the taller ones more erect. Rhizomes are thin and hard; leaves evergreen, linear and pointed, about 3/16–¼″ (4–6 mm) wide. Stems are round and bear two blossoms; the spathes are ridged. The blossoms are slender; the ground color of the falls is white, covered

with deep violet-blue veins, and the standards are dark violet-blue. The blossoms and tips of the leaves are about the same height. *I. sintenisii* differs from *I. graminea* and *I. pseudocyperus* by its small blossoms with narrower haft and longer perianth tube, as well as by narrower, stiffer leaves with prominent leaf veins. Easy to differentiate from other Dwarf Spurias by its blooming period (about middle of June), which is about 2–3 weeks later than the others.

Thrives in a sunny to partly shady location in the garden, in heavy soil with lime. Fertilize with compost. Transplant with care to avoid damaging the roots. Divide in fall or spring; this too is somewhat tricky. The rhizomes have to be kept constantly moist when they are being transplanted. It is preferable to grow *I. sintenissi* from seed and to plant out seedlings with rootballs intact. Seeds lie dormant for about a year, germinate often only in the fall.

I. sintennisii is without a doubt the most valuable Dwarf Spuria for the garden. Of particular note is its evergreen foliage, its free-flowering habit, and its display of blossoms above the foliage. It also provides good cut flowers for small vases. Number of chromosomes 2n=16.

Iris urumovii Velenovsky

I. urumovii is native to Bulgaria. About 6–11½" (15–30 cm) tall. Altogether a more delicate plant than *I. graminea* or *I. sintenisii*, to which it is closely related. Differs from *I. sintenisii* by its spathes, which are not ridged, by its more slender, upright form, and leaves which die back in the fall, while *I. sintenisii* is more or less evergreen. In all its parts it is more delicate than *I. brandzae* (blossoms, leaves, sheaths). The rhizomes are almost tuberous and very dark, while those of *I. brandzae* are longer and lighter. The leaves, particularly brownish-green

towards the base, are almost blue-green. *I. pontica* Zap. and *I. graminea*, on the other hand, have more yellowish-green leaves. The width of the leaves is about ¾" (2 cm). The stems usually bear 2 blossoms, more rarely 1 or 3. The violet blossoms are 2¾–3¾" (7–9 cm) in diameter and are very similar to those of *I. graminea*. The crests and standards are a more reddish violet. No noticeable scent.

Blooming period is second part of May and first part of June. Good in the rock garden. Number of chromosomes 2n=20.

Development of Iris Spuria hybrids

Iris spuria species have long been cultivated. In the Middle Ages they were used in the gardens of princes and monasteries. Without doubt a Dwarf Spuria Iris is illustrated in the *Hortus Eystettensis* under the fantastic name—according to today's notions—of *Chamaeiris angustis folys minor*. Whereas *I. spuria* was used in gardens fairly early on, the work of actually cultivating it did not begin until comparatively late. *I. monnierii*, which is classified as a species, is probably a hybrid, though it cannot be established positively whether it is a natural or a cultivated one. It was found, in any case, in France in the garden of a M. Monnier. In 1890, Sir Michael Foster crossed it with *I. spuria* to produce the hybrid *I.* 'Monspur', a basic variety of great importance to the work of breeding which began intensively much later. An early hybrid from this time and still very valuable as a garden plant is the pure blue *I.* 'Cambridge Blue', as well as *I.* 'Premier', grown by Barr in 1899 and widely known as *I.* 'Violacea'. Other varieties from this period are *I.* 'Lord Wolsely' and *I.* 'Monaurea', a cross between *I. monneiri* and *I. crocea* (=*I. aurea*). After that no hybridizing was done for a long time. Only in the past 30–40 years have Spuria Iris been intensively hybridized in the U.S.

Aside from the basic crosses mentioned, two groups of Spuria Iris were available as original breeding stock, the Spuria Iris of Asia Minor, to which *I. orientalis* (=garden *I. ochroleuca*) belongs, and the so-called European Spuria Iris. The Spuria Iris of Asia Minor are fairly resistant to virus. Depending on local climatic conditions, they die back in early summer and no longer look attractive. But in the fall they again grow fresh green leaves. In wet summers, which do not occur in their native habitat, they may rot, especially at growing points, thus destroying next year's blossoms. This can lead to a total loss of newly planted species. The European Spuria Iris are completely hardy and die back late, but are unfortunately prone to viruses. On account of inexplicable poor-seed germination, this iris can usually only be used as a pollen parent.

T. A. Washington of Nashville was probably one of the first American breeders who used *I.* × *monspur* and *I. monnieri*, as well as *I. halophila* and *I. orientalis* (=garden *I. ochroleuca*). He produced *I.* 'Blue Acres', *I.* 'Monteagle' and *I.* 'Blue Zephir'. T. A. Washington's hybrids have the typical decidous foliage, which comes from *I. halophila* and *I.* × *monspur*. Somewhat later Eric Nies tried various crosses. He crossed *I.* × *monspur* with *I. orientalis* (=garden *I. ochroleuca*). The seedlings were backcrossed with each other again, since the first generation only resulted in individuals from only *I. orientalis* (=garden *I. ochroleuca*). Then later a very colorful seedling mix arose, dominated by the *I.* × *monspur* types. White, brown, and blue colors were present, among them the familiar brown *I.*

'Bronce Spur', *I.* 'Azure Dawn', *I.* 'Saugatuch', *I.* 'Dutch Defiance' and *I.* 'Cherokee Chief' (ca. 1949). All had 40 chromosomes. Another *Iris spuria* pioneer was Carl S. Milliken of Pasadena, California. He cultivated the well-known varieties *I.* 'White Heron' and *I.* 'Wadi Zem Zem'. As they were particularly vigorous, they were later frequently used in other hybridizing efforts. The cultivar *I.* 'Wadi Zem Zem' was also unusually virus-resistant. It has given rise to the beautiful varieties *I.* 'Golden Lady' (Combs 1957) and *I.* 'Oroville' (Walker 1955).

Up to this point, all hybrids stemmed from the varieties mentioned above. Various *I. spuria* varieties were almost certainly used also. It's too bad that *I. crocea*, with its large pure-yellow blossoms, a native of Kashmir, was not used at all in hybridizing. But with *I. carthaliniae*, a new impetus was given to breeding. It was crossed with *I.* 'Morningtide' and *I.* 'Golden Lady'. Hager's *I.* 'Neophyte', which gets to be more than 5 ft (1.6 m) tall, and *I.* 'Protege', which only attains a height of 35" (90 cm) are two seedlings from it. *I. demetrii*, from southern Soviet Union, has recently been used in the U.S. It is hoped that its dark blue-violet will result in particularly rich colors. In the meantime, other breeders are busy with further crosses, and slowly but surely a higher standard is being achieved.

However, these activities cannot in any way compare to those surrounding the Bearded Iris. A checklist of Spuria Iris was published in 1973, which lists 317 cultivars and 48 hybridizers. But there are at the most only 10 or 12 really active Spuria Iris breeders, and they all live in the most climatically favorable regions of the U.S., namely Texas and California. Hence, it is obvious that in the colder climates, some of the new breeds will always die, simply because of the weather, while others may grow, but not blossom. It is, therefore, important that good bloomers be bred for colder regions too. At the same time, susceptibility to viruses, as well as tenderness in wet summers, must be bred out. Crosses with species from the Soviet Union appear promising.

There are still many avenues to pursue with Spuria Iris. Several species have not been crossed at all. But we must be patient. We cannot hope to attain results as quickly as with the Tall Bearded Iris because the Spurias grow so much more slowly. For years I have occupied myself with Spuria crosses, but it's hard going in the harsh climate of eastern Bavaria. Only a relatively short type, with blue, brown, and yellow shades in the blossom, was selected from many seedlings and named 'Steppenkerze'. I hope that younger people who are prepared to think in terms of long periods of time will undertake the breeding of Iris Spuria hybrids.

Subgenus Xyridion
  Section Spathula

Iris foetidissima Linne
Native to the Mediterranean countries, especially northern Italy, Yugoslavia, as well as Western Europe and north Africa.

The Latin name *I. foetidissima* means "stinking iris". But that is an exaggeratiion, because there is only an odor if the leaves and stems are crushed between the fingers, and it is not a stench by any means. This iris is England's "Gladwyn" and is often called "Coral Iris" for the clusters of red seeds.

Completely hardy in harsh continental climates. The plants do not die, but they are weakened when frost kills their ever-green leaves. (Indeed, most iris do not die directly from the cold, but because of fluctuations in soil moisture.) Winter protection is therefore necessary where weather is inclement.

A location in partial shade is ideal in cooler climates, as this is one of the few iris that can thrive in shade. A somewhat moist, humusy soil contributes to better growth, although *I. foetidissima* also grows fairly well in sunny dry spots.

Division in spring or fall presents no problems (in climatically unfavorable regions, only in spring). It is also easy to grow from seed. However, the seeds germinate somewhat erratically. The blossom is usually not very attractive, but planting this iris is worthwhile, if only for its very decorative capsules.

The tender rhizomes of *I. foetidissima* grow slowly. The dark green leaves are 13–22" (35–55 cm) long and about 1" (2.5 cm) wide. They have pronounced linear veins. Scapes reach a height of 10–24" (30–60 cm), depending on growing conditions, and have a number of shortened stem leaves (2–3). The unbranching stem bears a number of blossoms. After the flowers fade, the lateral branches bearing capsules elongate. The beardless blossoms are not very decorative nor of great garden value, being a sort of washed lilac. The background color of the blossoms is white, yellowish, bluish, or pink-lilac, overlaid with a thick network of violet veins. The lanceolate spathes are about 2¾" (7 cm) long, green, and rigid. Their 3-part capsules, which are filled with orange-red seeds, are very ornamental in the garden when they burst open. They look like a string of coral beads. Unlike many other iris species, they do not drop out. Cut and dried in the fall, seed stalks make beautiful additions to dried floral arrangements. Blooming period for *I. foetidissima* is June–

July, depending on location.

There is one form with green and white variegated leaves, 'Variegata', a pretty ornamental plant for shady and semi-shady places, but it grows even more slowly than the original species.

'Lutea' has very pretty light-yellow blossoms. It probably comes from the yellow-blossomed form found in the Madoni. Recently, blue-violet and white types have also appeared in the lists.

Subgenus Nepalensis

Native to the Himalayas, especially in the mountains of Nepal, these species grow at elevations of 4900–6500 ft. (1500 to 2000 m), but have been found up to 12,000–13,800 ft (3600–4200 m).

These iris are not always completely hardy in cooler climates, though they grow natively at high elevations. It is, therefore, recommended that the rootstock be stored in the cellar during the winter.

Plant in full sun. The soil should be deeply cultivated, despite the fact that it is rocky in their native habitat. Division is difficult and unsuccessful because of the dahlia-like rootstock. Propagation from seed, on the other hand, is very easy. These are plants for collectors, not for the general gardener, because the blossoms, though attractive, are very short-lived (not even half a day, hence "Vesper Iris").

Synonym: The most important feature of this subgenus is its rootstock; it is not a rhizome or a bulb, but a fleshy dahlia- or hemerocallis-like rootstock.

Iris collettii Hooker
Synonyms: *I. nepalensis* var. *letha* Foster, *I. nepalensis* f. *depauperata* Coll. et Hemsley. *I. duclouxii* Leveille.

The native habitat of *Iris collettii* is Burma, Thailand, and Yunnan Province of China. It is probably only a smaller form of *I. nepalensis*. There are several transitional forms. Number of chromosomes 2n=28.

Iris nepalensis Don
Synonyms: *I. decora* Wallich, *I. fasciculata* Jacquemont, *I. sulcata* Wall, *I. yunnanensis* Leveille.

Even though vigorous plants do exist that produce several pedicels, the plants of *Iris nepalensis* generally remain quite weak and never form large clumps. They reach a height of 8–15" (20–40 cm) and bear a number of rather small, pretty blossoms on multiple branches. The pale lavender-violet ground color is fairly consistent. The falls are attractively veined, and the standards, which are a somewhat darker shade, spread horizontally, making a plate-like blossom.

Iris staintonii Hara
Grows in Nepal in the Siwalik Range at elevations of 11,500 ft (3500 m). A species with tuberous roots, it has a low growth habit and pale yellow blossoms. It is only 1⅛–3" (3–8 cm) tall when blooming, with a short rhizome and 1 or 2 oval or elliptical tubers with the fibrous residue of old leaves around the base of the stem. It has four leaves; the outer ones are short and involucral, the inner ones 6–10" (15–30 cm) long and 3/16–¼" (4–6 mm) wide. The flowers bloom one at a time and have a spread of 1⅛" (3 cm). The perianth tube is ¾–1" (2–2.5 cm) long. The blossoms have no beard.

Differs from *I. nepalensis* by its very small form, small beardless blossoms and short stamens. It differs from *I. collettii* by its shorter perianth tubes. Only rediscovered in 1974.

Subgenus Pardanthopsis

Iris dichotoma Pallas
Synonym: *Pardanthopsis dichotoma* Lenz.

This lone species occurs in eastern Siberia, in the Transbaikal, and in other southern regions of the Far East; mainly on slopes and crevices where the soil is warm and dry.

The plant is hardy, but usually grows for only one year; it exhausts itself and dies.

I. dichotoma grows in full sun, in any good garden soil, except that it should have ample moisture before it blossoms.

This is purely a collector's plant with no ornamental value, since each blossom only lasts a short time and the plant itself is short-lived. Division not possible, but it produces abundant seeds which germinate easily. It will bloom the same year, if planted in spring. Planting time September.

The stem is 24–30" (60–80 cm) tall, much forked, and rises above a fan of broad leaves. The small, pink-violet blossoms, 2½–3" (6–8 cm) in diameter, open in the afternoon and last only till evening. However, one plant has many buds and will bloom for a total of 3–4 weeks. Two hours after opening, the blossoms emit a slight, but pleasant fragrance. The haft of the falls stands upright, and the blade is held out horizontally. They are reddish purple with white spots at the base, or white with a brown pattern. The standards are small, erect; the perianth tube is short. Blooming period July–August.

In 1972, the American botanist Lenz split this iris off to form a new genus, *Pardanthopsis*. Samuel Norris crossed *I. dichomota* with *Belamcanda chinensis* (syn. *Pardanthus chinensis*) in 1967 and got fertile hybrids. This underscores the unique position of this plant. Because of the work done by Lenz, *I. dichotoma* ought to be called *Pardanthopsis dichotoma*. Hybrids with *Belamcanda chinensis* are attractive garden plants, but they are not long-lived, at least in colder climates. These hybrids are sometimes listed in publications as *Pardancanda* × *norrisii*.

Subgenus Crossiris

The iris which are not classed under the subgenus *Crossiris* were formerly called Evansia Iris. Their common distinguishing feature is a comb-like formation on the falls.

Section Crossiris
Series Japonicae

East Asia is the native habitat of iris of this series: *I. japonica* in Japan and central China, *I. wattii* in Assam and southwestern China, *I. speculatrix* around Hong Kong, *I. confusa* in Sichuan and Yunnan Provinces, and *I. formosana*, as its name indicates, on Formosa.

These enchanting plants are unfortunately not hardy in harsher climates, although there are differences in hardiness among individual species. They are plants of moist, warm mountain regions.

The iris of this series should not be planted in full sun; in summer they grow in a cool, semi-shady spot; bright tree-shaded sites are ideal. The soil should not be too heavy and with a high humus content; the reaction should be slightly acid. Good results are obtained by adding oak leaf compost.

As mentioned, these plants are demanding because they lack winter hardiness; but their beauty justifies additional work. This is especially true of *I. japonica*. It grows outdoors without protection in southwestern England. But it is important that the evergreen leaves get through the winter without damage, otherwise it will not bloom. I am able to grow them in a deep cold frame covered with boards and filled with peat in the winter; they blossom faithfully every year. Those who own a coldhouse have it easier. These species are sometimes treated as potted plants, or are dug in the fall and overwintered in a basement window in a box filled with barely damp peat.

I. wattii is grown in North European gardens only in containers because it is exceptionally tender. *I. confusa,* a closely related species, can also be overwintered in a box filled with peat. *I. formosana* and *I. speculatrix* behave similarly. They can be propagated easily by vegetative means, since they all have rooted offshoots which need only to be cut off. Propagation by seed is not difficult, but several species set inviable seed.

Iris confusa Sealy
Similar in character to *I. wattii* and included by some breeders in that species. The differences, however, are so great that independent species status seems justified. The rhizomes spread widely, forming scattered clumps; these grow only at the tips of new shoots. First a strong shoot emerges from the ground, and the foliage cluster, with its alternate, densely crowded leaves encircling the stem, usually starts at 11½–15″ (30–40 cm) above the ground. In a cold frame, it will get 30″ (80 cm) tall. The leaves themselves attain a length of 15″ (40 cm) and a width of 2″ (5 cm). The leaf color is medium green, lighter than *I. japonica,* the top being glossier than the bottom. As they are evergreen, maintaining this foliage is a precondition for flowering. The small, branching blossoms are similar to those of *I. japonica.* They are white with a touch of lilac, show no blue markings, and have a yellow crest. The standards are much smaller than the falls, which are attractively waved. The crests are heavily fringed. The habit of this plant is "bamboo-like". Blooming period is mid-June. Number of chromosomes 2n=30.

Iris formosana Ohwi
This plant, which received a separate species status fairly late, is rarely cultivated. *I. japonica* and *I. formosana* look very much alike. *I. formosana* is a little more robust. It has small basal stalks (4–8″ or 10–20 cm), somewhat reminiscent of *I. confusa,* which *I. japonica* lacks. The blossoms of *I. formosana* are larger than those of *I. japonica* (2¾–3½″ or 7–9 cm diameter) and more like those of *I. wattii.* Flowers are white, suffused with a very delicate blue. Yellow-orange flecks dot the falls, which are dabbed with violet towards the outside. There are also specimens without the yellow-orange spots. These bloom very early in the coldhouse (in February); in very mild climates and protected places in April–May. Seed germination is much better than *I. japonica.* Various chromosome counts are reported (2n=28 Yasui, 2n=35 BIS Species Group Bulletin Mar. 1969).

Iris japonica Thunberg
Synonym: *I. fimbriata* Vent.
The rhizomes of this iris spread widely. The leaves are up to 24″ (60 cm) long, evergreen; they have a fan-like arrangement, with tips arching over. The dark green leaves are fairly wide. The scape is 20–24″ (50–60 cm) tall and branches widely. Blossoms average 2″ (5 cm) wide; falls are white, becoming azure blue at the edge, with a serrated, wavy rim. The comb

has three ribs, the middle one yellow, the crests are delicately frayed. The whole flower is orchidlike. One pedicel will often bear up to 30 blossoms, which means that it blooms for up to four weeks. Blooming period May to beginning of June; if other methods of cultivation are used, it can be much later.

I. j. 'Variegata', with its cream-striped foliage, is an attractive ornamental plant. The blossoms are somewhat smaller and whiter than the original form.

I. j. 'Ledgers Variety' is a popular commercial iris, somewhat hardier than the species. In England it is quite hardy. Another type is known in the U.S. as *I.* 'Uwodu'.

Anyone who has seen *I. japonica* in bloom in parks and gardens in southern England or on the Canary Islands will work hard to grow this pretty iris, no matter how great the effort. Chromosome count: a number of figures are given: 2n=34, 2n=36, and for 'Ledgers Variety', 2n=54.

Iris speculatrix Hance

Rarely cultivated. This iris, which grows in the vicinity of Hong Kong, differs markedly from the previous species, especially because of its much narrower, tall, and hornlike leaves (max. ⅜" (1 cm) instead of ¾–1½" (2–4 cm) as with *I. japonica* and *I. formosana*). *I. speculatrix* does not form offsets. Its growth is somewhat like that of the North American Evansia *Iris tenuis*. The blossom is a uniform mauve-lilac with a yellow comb, that ends in a white Y and is bordered by a lively shade of violet. The scape is about 13" (35 cm) tall and bears two blossoms. The blossom is reminiscent of *I. cristata*.

Apart from *I. verna*, it is one of the most difficult species to grow, according to Dr. Boussard, the foremost French iris species specialist. It occurs natively in stands of conifers in moist, acid soil with good drainage, in semi-shade. The evergreen foliage is really the only characteristic the three species—*I. japonica*, *I. formosana*, and *I. speculatrix*—have in common.

Iris wattii Baker

As I have said, this iris has many things in common with *I. confusa*. It grows taller than 35" (90 cm) and is well branched. Blossom color is bright lavender-lilac, with violet-blue spots on the falls and an orange comb. The individual blossom is considerably larger than that of *I. japonica*. Can be cultivated only in a large container. Number of chromosomes 2n=30.

The variety *I.* 'Nada', a cross between *I. japonica* and *I. confusa*, or *I. japo-watt = I. japonica* × *I. wattii*, has become well known. *I. japonica* × *I. milesii* should also be mentioned.

Other forms, such as *I.* 'Queens Grace', from seed self-sown by *I. wattii* (Jean Stevens, New Zealand), are common in the U.S. The other parent is probably *I. tectorum*. Another hybrid is *I.* 'Bourne Graceful'. It is a creation of Dr. Ellis, Great Britain (*I. japonica* 'Ledgers Variety' × *I. japonica* 'Capri Form'). The latter parent cultivar seems to be a hybrid of unknown parentage.

Section Crossiris
Series Tectores

The two species of this series are natives of East Asia. *I. milesii* is found in the eastern Himalayas, near Burma and southwestern China. *I. tectorum* is widespread in Japan and China, and also in Burma, where the plant Dykes described originated.

Both are much hardier than the iris of Series Japonicae, even though they cannot be considered completely hardy. The abundance of blossoms will suffer if plants are not protected in the winter, at least in the case of *I. milesii*.

These can tolerate more sun than the Japonicae Series, especially if the soil is somewhat moist and humusy. The soil reaction should be slightly acid, otherwise the leaves become chlorotic. *I. tectorum* is a heavy feeder and should be given an application of compost in the fall or a top dressing throughout the year. Both division and propagation from seed are easy. Young plants raised from seed usually bloom in their second year. Divide in spring or fall, or—as I have done—after flowering in July. These are very versatile and *I. tectorum*, in particular, can be used effectively in the rock garden, at the edge of ponds, and in natural plantings. In very damp places, good drainage is essential.

Iris milessii Foster
This tall iris, which grows on slopes in open woodlands at an elevation of about 5,900 ft (1800 m), forms strong rhizomes. The fans are about 24" (60 cm) long and light green, dull on both sides. The leaf is 1–1⅛" (2.5–3 cm) wide. The scapes are 28–35" (70–90 cm) tall, branching, with each branch cupped by a leaf surrounding the stem. Flower standards are erect and held at a slightly incurved angle. They are washed delicately with violet, a bit darker in places. The falls have good form and are almost horizontally held. Their violet is paler yet, with dark veins that become darker towards the white comb. 3–3½" (8–9 cm) wide blossoms are borne, several at the tips of the branches, opening sequentially. The crests are very heavily fringed. A description from India mentions rather small, purple-reddish blossoms; apparently a few such forms exist. This iris blooms long and profusely beginning in mid-June in my garden. It is incomprehensible to me that this beautiful iris is not more commonly used. Number of chromosomes 2n=26.

Iris tectorum Maximowicz
Called the "Roof Iris" because in earlier times it was often found growing on the thatched roofs in China and Japan. It is about 15–20" (40–50 cm) tall. The upright leaves, about 1⅛–1½" (3–4 cm) wide, light green and prominently ribbed, come from thin, brown, fleshy, spreading rhizomes. The somewhat wobbly, lilac blossoms are about 4" (10 cm) wide. The falls are more

Tall bearded iris species and historical forms. They cannot be compared in beauty to the modern hybrids, but the collector of iris species would not be without them.

Upper left: Iris pallida has beautifully shaped blossoms but unfortunately its branching is not good. Vacationers love to bring them home from a holiday on the Istrian Peninsula or the Dalmatian Coast. The species is easily identified when in bloom by the papery sheaths.
Upper right: Iris alberti, a species from the Soviet Union that appears to be valuable for breeders of Pogocyclus and Pogoregelia iris. An unusual feature of this species is its brown throat veining, which extends into the violet area.
Below: From a botanical point of view, Iris florentina and Iris flavescens are not strictly speaking pure species, but rather, ancient, stabilized hybrids. Iris florentina is grown in fields in Tuscany, and Iris flavescens is a pale yellow form that can be seen in many old country gardens. The modern term "iris" is really not appropriate in these cases, as they are more reminiscent of the old German name Schwertlilie (Sword Lily), or, in America, Flags.

darkly veined, have a white comb, and are held almost horizontally. But atypical forms exist that have different colored combs. When in full bloom, standards and falls spread out like the spokes of a wheel. The stem is poorly branched; several blossoms bloom one after the other at their tips. The crests are delicately frilled. Blooming period is shortly before or during that of Tall Bearded Iris. Number of chromosomes 2n=28.

'Alba' is an attractive form with white blossoms.

Species hybrids:

I. gracilipes × *I. tectorum*
I. cristata × *I. tectorum*

I. tectorum has been used in a number of crosses with bearded iris. *I.* × *pal-tec* is a well known cross between *I. pallida* (*I.* 'Edina' is often indicated too) and *I. tectorum*. When these come into flower, they really look like *I. pallida,* only shorter. In full bloom the standards separate, and then this floral chameleon looks like *I. tectorum.* It is sterile. Crosses between *I. chamaeiris* and *I. cengialti* are also known. The variety *I.* 'Lucilla' comes from a cross between *I. tectorum* and a Dwarf Bearded Iris. Darby crossed a tetraploid form, treated with colchicine so that it had 56 chromosomes, with Tall Bearded Iris. Such crosses produce fertile amphidiploid hybrids.

Section *Lophiris*
Series *Cristatae*

The iris of this series are found in North America. *I. cristata* grows particularly in the southeastern and central States of the U.S., increasing around Washington, D.C. and Ohio, south and westward to eastern Oklahoma. Also in the Allegheny and Appalachian Mountains, often stretching to the coast. They grow on rocky mountain slopes, in canyons and ravines, in forests. *I. lacustris,* on the other hand, grows only in the Great Lakes area: Wisconsin, Michigan, Ohio, and in the province of Ontario. It grows in sandy and gravelly soils where there is no grass, but also in forests and thickets. *I. tenuis* is found only in a small area of northeastern Oregon and in Clackamas County. It grows in cool, shady, damp spots rich in peat or leaf mold, mostly on valley floors or slopes covered with conifers.

Except for *I. tenuis,* the iris of this series are winter hardy. High humidity works in their favor; some species are difficult to

Tall bearded iris species and historical forms.

Upper left: Iris albicans is a true species, thought to originate on the Arabian Peninsula in Yemen and spread first by the Moors, then later by the Spaniards. Distinguished from I. florentina by its more compact blossoms.
Upper right: Iris schachtii was discovered relatively late near Ankara. It is difficult to grow and even harder to get to blossom in a North temperate garden. This is a challenge for experienced growers, shown here in a clay pot.
Lower left: Iris sambucina, known as the "Elder iris", also a medieval form, with a later blooming period and somewhat dingy blossoms. For collectors. While others have blossoms with more violet tones.
Lower right: Iris varbossiana probably is not a true species, but a stabilized form that was often seen growing wild near castles and fortresses. This example is from the Botanical Gardens in Zagreb.

grow in a dry climate.

I. lacustris, a small ornamental plant, rapidly forms a broad mat in a favorable location. It is found in cool, acidic, moderately moist, slightly gravelly sites. Watch out for slugs! They consider *I. cristata* a delicacy. *I. lacustris* is less demanding, tolerates more dryness and even full sun. It also grows on slightly alkaline soil. *I. tenuis,* on the other hand, is difficult to keep in a garden due to cultural requirements.

Easy to raise from seed, although not many germinate. Best method of propagation is to remove offshoots early in summer after the plant blooms.

Iris cristata Solander

Karl Foerster called this dwarf the "Painted Indian Dwarf Iris". This species has a rootstock of spindle-shaped, woody rhizomes, with nodes producing leafy fans. The scape is very short (1–1¾" 2.5–4.5 cm) or lacking altogether, foliate, bearing one or two blossoms. The basal leaves are wide, light green, conspicuously ribbed, up to 9" (25 cm) long and 1" (2.5 cm) wide, sometimes longer after blooming. The perianth tube is very slender and linear, enlarged towards the top, and about 2–2¾" (5–7 cm) long. Blossoms are pale blue-violet, often with ruffled edges. Falls are up to 1¾" (4.5 cm) long and about ½" (1.5 cm) wide. The blade is oval-lanceolate, often blunt and with a white central spot bordered by dark-violet spots. Comb is white-orange. Standards are shorter and widely flared. The small seeds have a small, sticky appendage, and the capsules are oval, triangular in cross sections. Blooming period is April-May. It should be noted that this iris is slightly variable in form, especially the size of the leaves. Number of chromosomes 2n=24 × (also indicated 2n=36).

'Alba', with white blossoms, is a very rare and difficult form to grow.

Iris lacustris Nuttall

This smallest of all Evansias forms beautiful mats. In spite of its similarity to *I. cristata,* it can be distinguished easily by its significantly smaller size, which remains constant, in contrast to the other variable species. The wedge-shaped, dark violet standards and falls, very similar, are also features of *I. lacustris.* The scapes are very short and slender, 1⅛–1½" (3–4 cm) long, and leafless. The basal leaves may grow to 6¼" (16 cm) long, but are usually shorter during the blooming period. Perianth tube 7/16–¾" (1.3–2 cm) long, gradually broadening from the base. The light blue-violet falls have a white central spot and an orange and white frayed comb. Standards shorter, blue-violet, semi-erect or slanting. The capsule is about 7/16" (1.2 cm) long, rounded-oval. Seeds small, brown, oval with appendage. Blooming period is May. This Dwarf Iris often flowers again in the fall. Number of chromosomes 2n=42 (also 2n=36). A white form also exists.

I. lacustris has been crossed with *I. speculatrix.*

Iris tenuis S. Watson

This iris was classified for some time with the Californica Iris. It was correctly classified with the Evansias in 1959 by Lee W. Lenz. It does not form thick clumps. The very slender rhizomes spread widely, producing fans of leaves at their tips. The slender scapes are up to 11½" (30 cm) tall, deeply forked, with 1 or 2 branches. Each produces 1 blossom. The blossoms on the lateral branches stand as high as those on the central stalk. The basal leaves are pale-green with papery edges, up to 13" (35 cm) long, ½" (1.5 cm) wide and ribbed. Blossoms small, whitish, tinted faintly blue, and covered with strange violet veins and spots. The comb is whitish yellow. Standards bluish white, spreading widely. Not completely hardy. Blooming period May. Number of chromosomes 2n=28.

Section Monospatha

Iris gracilipes A. Gray

The Monospatha section is represented only by this one species. It grows in China and Japan in moderately moist soils in open forests. It is reasonably hardy, but suffers from extreme temperature fluctuations in spring. Needs high humidity.

I. gracilipes is suitable for rock gardens and for border plantings. It grows in a moderately moist, but not wet soil. Semi-shade is preferable to full sun. Propagate by removing offshoots shortly after blooming.

The grassy leaves, about 3⁄8" (1 cm) wide, rise from spreading rhizomes. Total height of plant is about 6–8" (15–20 cm), with leaves about 11½" (30 cm) long, but overarching. They are light green, turning a beautiful yellow in the fall. Branches low on the scape. The pink-lilac blossoms are about 1½" (4 cm) wide, the falls obovate, with a dark-veined white spot. The comb is orange. The standards are 3⁄4" (2 cm) long and only half as wide as the falls. Number of chromosomes 2n=36.

'Alba' is a beautiful white form.

Species hybrids: *I. gracilipes* × *I. cristata* and *I. gracilipes* × *I. tectorum*.

The classification of the following species is unclear:

Iris pseudorossii Chien

This iris grows largely in the Chinese coastal regions of Jiangsu, Anhui province, in the environs of Shanghai and in the hills around Nanking.

The rootstock is formed by spreading, knobby, branching rhizomes covered with many stiff, stringy root fibers. The leaves form discreet clusters with a fibrous sheath at the base. The leaves are linear and pointed, rigid, with a green-blue to gray-green color; they are whitish and papery on the edge near the base; 2–6" (5–15 cm) long. The scape is short, about 6" (15 cm), and bears a single flower. Spathes are lanceolate, pointed, green with papery edges and papery toward the tip, about 2" (5 cm) long. The perianth tube is slender-linear, 1⅛–2" (3–5 cm) long and abruptly funnel-shaped near the tip. The blossoms are medium-large and quite variable in color: blue, purple-blue, white, covered with blue or pink. The whitish shades have a ring of darker color around the yellow comb on the lower part of the blade and on the haft of the falls. The latter are either widely flaring or completely horizontal, up to 1" (2.5 cm) long and 3⁄8" (1 cm) wide. The blade is obovate, the longish haft being shorter than the blade. The standards are 3⁄8–3⁄4" (1.5–2 cm) long and 1/4–5/16" (6–7 mm) wide. The crests are pale blue. The outer edge of the longish, narrow comb is more or less toothed or notched. Produces abundant seed.

The variety *I. pseudorossii* var. *valide* Chien. comes from this species, also growing in eastern China west of Zhejiang. Blooming period there is April. This plant is larger and the leaves, in contrast to those of the species, not as rigidly erect, but more arching, longer and wider (up to 5/16" or 7 mm), with a purple, papery margin. The blossoms are also larger. The plant in general is more robust and taller (up to 11" or 28 cm). Very difficult to maintain in a garden.

Observe the nomenclature closely. Not to be confused with *I. rossii* of the series Chinenses of subsection Apogon.

Subgenus Iris (Pogoniris)
Section Iris (Pogoniris)
Series Pumilae

Iris alexeenkoi Grossheim
A Dwarf Iris from the southeastern
Transcaucasus, especially found on the
Shiraki steppe.

Closely related to *I. pumila*. Main differences are its larger rhizomes and larger
blossoms. Blossom color dark violet.
Needs an extremely warm location. Grows
poorly in cooler climates. Better for coldhouse cultivation. Rarely obtainable.

Iris attica Boissier et Heldreich
Occurs only in a relatively small range in
southern Greece, in Attica, and on Mt.
Parnassus. This species falls into one of
those gray areas where it is difficult to tell
whether it is a species in its own right or
simply a dwarf *I. pumila*.

The beard of *I. attica* is always one color,
in contrast to *I. pumila*, whose beard is
always bi-colored. The small, very
crescent-shaped leaves are striking. The
entire form of the blossom is similar to that
of *I. pumila*, but the plant is only 4–4¾"
(10–12 cm) tall. The perianth tube is long.
The color of the blossoms varies; there are
purple-violet, as well as straw-colored
types.

Charming dwarfs for sundry planting
places such as rock gardens, sinks, and
bowls. More difficult to grow than *I. pumila*.
The location must get full sun. *I. attica*
thrives in rocky, porous soil, possibly
enriched with volcanic slag or pulverized
processed clay. A light mulch in spring or
fall is recommended. Wet sites are fatal to
this iris. Blooming period is end of April.
Propagation by seed (if hand-pollinated
material or seeds from wild plants are
available) is much better than using offsets
that are slow to resume growth. Important

in the field of Dwarf Iris for its early blossom time. Number of chromosomes
2n=16.

Iris balkana Janka
A dwarf iris of the Balkans; precise
classification is difficult, probably because
it does not have its own species status,
although specimens in the U.S. were used
for hybridizing. There are both diploid
and tetraploid forms. Should probably be
considered a variety of *I. reichenbachii*.
Number of chromosomes 2n=48, 2n=24;
there are still other numbers, probably
because various iris called *I. balkana* are
found in gardens.

Iris bosniaca B. Beck
Grows in the Balkans, specifically on
Mount Trebevic near Sarajevo. Very difficult to obtain. Also probably not a pure
species, but a variety of *I. reichenbachii*.

Scape up to the blooming period is 5"
(13 cm) long and rather thin, elongating
later. The blossoms are yellow. The leaves
are slightly crescent-shaped. Only for
experts and collectors because it cannot be
grown easily in cool climates. Needs a very
sunny location with good drainage.
Number of chromosomes 2n=24.

Iris chamaeiris Bertoloni
Now described as *I. lutescens* Lam. in
Volume V of *Flora Europaea*. Until recently
this name had been reserved for a type
from southern France found specifically at
Le Luc near Draguignan in Provence. It is a
yellow-blooming Pogon species which,
depending on its location, grows anywhere from 3–8¾" (8–23 cm) tall. In continental climates, very sensitive to rot. In
Flora Europaea this species is subdivided
into ssp. *lutescens* (*I. pumila* auct. non L. incl.
I. chamaraeiris Bertol) and ssp. *subbiflora*
(Brot.) D. W. Webb. et Charter. But I will

stay with the familiar name among gardeners and follow the example of Zander.

Native to Spain, southern France, northwestern Italy, and Switzerland (as *I. virescens*). *I. chamaeiris* includes a great number of subspecies with differing forms and sizes. The actual Bertolinii type is the smallest form with an approximate height of 6½" (16 cm). *I. chamaeiris* is the latest-blooming genuine Dwarf Iris. Most types grow taller, about 8–8½" (20–22 cm), making *I. chamaeiris* the tallest species of genuine Dwarf Iris.

The color of the flowers varies greatly. There are purple-blue, red-purple, medium and pale yellow, and even white types. Spots produce beautiful one- and two-colored forms. The falls on the bicolors are always darker than the standards. The beard is usually yellow, but plants with blue, violet, or white beards can be found, and often their color contrasts sharply with the color of the falls. Blossoms are held above the foliage. *I. chamaeiris* differs from the other important Dwarf Iris, *I. pumila,* by its short perianth tube, which is not even twice as long as the ovary. *I. chamaeiris* has a scape, whereas *I. pumila* has one, though it barely shows (about 3/16" or 0.5 cm long). *I. chamaeiris* becomes twice as tall as *I. pumila* and blooms 1 or 2 weeks later. The leaves are often evergreen. *I. chamaeiris* has one or two blossoms, and the ovary is always at the top of the scape, whereas in *I. pumila,* the ovary is directly above the rhizome. In general, *I. chamaeiris* is easier to grow than *I. pumila.*

Because of its ease of cultivation, its winter hardiness, and its abundance of blossoms, *I. chamaeiris* is among the most rewarding Dwarf Iris. An additional attraction is the great variety of flower color. Its form is, unfortunately, not as elegant as that of most *I. pumila.* Its falls are often curled inward. Good, sunny locations can be found in rock gardens. It is important to provide good drainage, even though *I. chamaeiris* is less sensitive in this respect than *I. pumila.* Blooming period is beginning of May, 1 to 2 weeks later than *I. pumila.* Number of chromosomes 2n=40 (*I. chamaeiris* is amphidiploid, with two sets of 8 and two sets of 12 chromosomes = 40 chromosomes).

Division and propagation by seed present no problems.

There are different varieties or subspecies, which are often classified as species with doubtful justification. Among these is *I. italica* Parlatore, a dark violet, tall-growing type (about 12½" or 32 cm tall); various origins. *I. virescens* Delarbre (syn. *I. chamaeiris* var. *virescens*), typically found on the Tourbillon near Sitten (Sion) in the Vlaid, Switzerland, reaches a height of 8¾–13¾" (24–36 cm); falls and standards are lanceolate-elliptical, blossoms are yellowish white to yellowish green. *I. olbiensis* Henon (syn. *I. chamaeiris* var. *olbiensis*) occurs in Liguria and Tuscany, specifically in the province of Lucca and on Mount Calvi. It is a form of *I. chamaeiris,* with sulfur yellow blossoms. Number of chromosomes 2n=40.

Iris griffithii Baker

Often mentioned in older publications, *I. griffithii* is rarely found anywhere as a pure species. It grows in northwestern India, Afghanistan, Kafiristan.

Differs from *I. kashimiriana* by its short, unbranching bloomstalk. It can be compared with an *I. chamaeiris* with purple-violet blossoms. But it differs in that it has a long perianth tube about 2" (5 cm) long and long green spathes. Rarely obtainable.

Iris mellita Janka

Now described in *Flora Europaea* as *I. suaveolens* Boiss. et Reuter. But we will stick to the common name that is also used in Zander.

Widespread across the Balkans, from the Mediterranean (Albania), Yugoslavia, Bulgaria, and parts of Turkey, up to the Black Sea coast. The height of the scape is 4–5¾″ (10–14 cm). The leaves are extremely crescent-shaped, with a slight bloom sometimes with a reddish margin. Spathes are green, long, and strongly ridged. The blossom color is a smokey purple-red; smokey color mixtures of purple and shades of yellow also occur. The falls are shorter and narrower than the standards and rolled inward. The standards are tall and rigid. The beard is bluish, its base off-white. There are usually 2 blossoms on the stem, rarely 1 and even more rarely 3. Slender, wiry perianth tube standing well above the leaves, which curve toward it.

A curious, attractive little iris, which should be grown like *I. pumila*. Very prone to rhizome rot in rainy regions. It needs full sun, good drainage, and a lime supplement. A pebble mulch is recommended. Good in large containers. Blooms at the beginning of May, about 2 weeks after *I. pumila*.

I. mellita var. *rubromarginata* (also known as *I. rubromarginata*) is another form. Found specifically near Scutari on the Bosporus. The crescent-shaped leaves spread widely, are slightly wavy, and have a distinct reddish margin.

Iris pseudopumila Tineo

Native to Sicily and southern Italy. There are two distinctly different forms, Sicilian and Calabrian. They are so different in appearance that it is even questionable whether they belong to the same species.

The San Martino form (southern Italy) has greenish yellow standards, and the falls are dingy purple-violet with a fringe. Grows to about 8½″ (22 cm) tall. The ovary stands at about 4¼″ (11 cm); the perianth tube is about 4¼″ (11 cm) long. The standards are open, the falls curved inward. The stem is slender. The leaves are rather broad and pointed, not curved inward. The beard of the falls is greenish yellow.

The Sicilian form reaches about the same height, grows more slowly, and the leaves are extremely crescent-shaped, similar to those of *I. mellita*. The standards are light yellow and the falls are pale dark brown, but there have also been types with lilac-colored falls. The plant has 1 blossom per scape. The feature which most distinguishes it from *I. pumila* is the presence of a short, but distinct scape. So the height is not determined only by the perianth tube.

It is an iris for Dwarf Iris lovers and for collectors. Blooms in the first half of May. Should be planted in a rock garden with low-growing, spring-flowering cushion plants. The location must get full sun and be dry, with good drainage. More robust than most local forms of *I. pumila*. Ideal planting time is after blooming, otherwise fall planting is preferable to spring.

Not desirable for hybridizing as the poor blossom form with the falls rolled tightly inwards is passed on. Number of chromosomes 2n=16.

Iris pumila Linne

I. pumila has the largest range of any similar species. The Danube flows through or borders a great part of its range, such as Austria, Czechoslovakia (Moravia and Slovakia), Hungary, Yugoslavia (Serbia), Rumania, Bulgaria. From the Black Sea its range pushes into the Soviet Union, the Ukraine, into the Donets and Kuban Basins, the Crimea, and finally south of the Black Sea to Anatolia. *I. pumila* can generally be described as a typical plant of the Pannonian steppe.

Because of its vast range, there is no typical *I. pumila*. For example, in Austria forms are found with broader and longer leaves, contrasting to the *I. pumila* of the Soviet Union, with its short, narrow leaves and generally more slender shapes and smaller blossoms.

It is really incorrect to speak of *I. pumila* as a single species, but better to call it a species complex, within which many specific factors vary. Individual types can vary in size of the plant and blossoms, blossom color, length and form, and condition (herbaceous or papery) of the spathes, length of the stem leaves, size and substance of the basal leaves, length and form of the perianth tube, form of the ovary, form and substance of the seed capsule, as well as form, size, and color of the crests. The exact size of the seed is important, so is the form and size of rhizome segments, the form of the falls (e.g. held horizontally or rolled in at the end). And there are certainly other distinguishing features. The subspecies, varieties, and forms mentioned below attest to this.

In general, the main characteristic features of *I. pumila* are unbranching stem; dwarf form; distinct, large, separated rhizome segments; the extended perianth tube; and the strongly contrasting oval color spot on the falls. The falls narrow abruptly at the base to a very slim, long haft. A large, thick beard is present on the falls. The plant produces a single blossom. Height of the scape is 3/16–3/8" (5–15 mm), (sources that state *I. pumila* has no bloomstalk at all and that the ovary rises

directly from the rhizomes are incorrect; scape is at least 3/16" (0.5 cm) long). But there are varieties with longer bloom-stalks, 3–4" (8–10 cm) long. The spathes are greenish-membraneous, with the outer valve mostly herbaceous and ridged toward the outside half. The 2 spathe valves enclose the short stem, the ovary, and most of the perianth tube. There are 4 leaves on both sides of the spathes (5 on types with a taller bloomstalk). All this applies only to the typical *I. pumila*.

When considering the entire *I. pumila* complex, only 2 features distinguish it from all the other dwarf Pogon species: the striking, diverse blossom colors and color combinations, and the color contrast of the *Iris pumila* spot. Its vast range should also be mentioned as another feature in common.

No other bearded iris, whether dwarf or tall, shows such a great variety of colors. The oval spot of color on the blade of the falls is characteristic. It contrasts sharply with the ground color and is usually some shade of purple-violet or brown. The main colors of the blossoms are yellow, true blue, red-purple, dark ruby red to black. The ground color is often overlaid by traces of another color, producing further shades, such as bronze, brown, delicate pink, and grayish and greenish tones. There are amoenas and variegatas, but no genuine plicatas. Also lacking is, of course, pure pink. Some specimens show a good contrasting network of fine veins on the falls. The color of the beard also plays a part in the total color effect. It is usually a combination of 2 colors, mostly whitish yellow towards the throat and another color towards the blade. Some off whites show a slight greenish coloration on the falls. Plants with pure white blossoms are rare. Some specimens, particularly those from Bessarabia, emit a mild but pleasant scent of violets, heliotrope, vanilla, or honeysuckle.

The blossoms are in harmonious proportion to the rest of the plant, which is why *I. pumila* is often called the King of the Dwarfs. However, there are some among the many varieties for which this title would not be apt. I have already mentioned the diversity within its large range. This peaks in Rumania. The following are listed in Vol. XI of *Flora Republicii Socialiste Romania* (1966):

I. pumila L.

I. p. L. var. *scapifera* Borb.

I. p. L. ssp. *sintenisiiformis* Prod.

I. p. L. *albiflora* Schur.

I. p. L. *atroviolacea* Schur.

I. p. L. *dobrogensis* Prod.

I. p. L. *dobrogensis* f. *romania* Prod. et Borza

I. p. var. *rozaliae* Prod.

I. p. L. var. *latispatha* Prod. et Borza

I. p. L. var. *lutea* Ker-Gawl. (syn. *I. pumila* var. *ochroleuca* Prod. et Borza)

I. p. L. f. *acuta* Prod.

I. napocae Prod. (syn. *I. sarajovensis* Prod.)

I. n. Prod. var. *macrocarpa* (syn. *I. pumila* L. var. *macrocarpa* Prod.)

I. pluriscapis Prod.

I. suaveolens Boiss. et Reut. with the forms *aureo-flava* Prod. and *flavo-barbata* Prod.

I. barthii Prod. et Buia (syn. *I. pumila* L. var. *barthii* Prod. et Buia)

I. barthaeiformis Prod. (syn. *I. pumila* L. var. *barthaeiformis* Prod.)

I. b. Prod. var. *violacea* Prod. (syn. *I. pumila* L. var. *barthaeiformis* Prod. f. *violacea* Prod.)

I. pseudopumilaeoides Prod. (syn. *I. pumila* L. var. *pseudopumilaeoides* Prod.)

There are also others, probably hybrids, such as:

I. guertleri Prod. (syn. *I. pumila* L. var. *guertleri* P.)

I. g. Prod. var. *moldavica* Prod. (syn. *I. pumila* L. var. *guertleri* Prod. f. *moldavica* Prod.)

I. g. and f. *moldavica* are undoubtedly natural hybrids between *I. pumila* and *I. aphylla* var. *hungarica*.

I. binata Schur (syn. *I. pumila* L. var. *binata* Schur)

This has also produced the forms *I. sulphurea* Prod. and *I. purpurea* Prod., in all probability natural hybrids between *I. pumila* and *I. aphylla*. So the correct description should really be *I.* × *binata*.

All the above iris, even if they have their own species names, belong to the *I. pumila* complex. Apart from those noted in the Rumanian *Flora*, a few other *I. pumila* should be mentioned: *I. pumila* L. var. *heliotropii* Prod. et Borza (syn. *I. pumila* L. f. *heliotropii* Borza) and

I. aequiloba Ledeb. (syn. *I. longiflora* Ledeb.).

Various forms from the past have also become well known, such as the Kuban Pumila, which was sent to the U.S. by Hanselmeyer and used extensively in breeding dwarf iris, some of which were even registered. A very large-blossomed form called *I.* 'Piroschka' was developed by Eckard Berlin and is a rewarding garden plant. A type known as *Iris pumila* 'Cretica' was often used for hybridizing. In the U.S. many dwarf iris hybrids go back to the types "Nana" and "Sulina". Other natural hybrids also occur in regions where *Iris pumila* and other Pogon Iris grow.

Volume V of *Flora Europaea* makes a simple subdivision into *I. pumila* ssp. *pumila* and *I. pumila* ssp. *attica*. But the group is more complicated than that!

The various *I. pumila* are rewarding plants in the garden, though they cannot be grown equally well everywhere. I have learned in my own garden that *I. pumila* is easier to maintain than *I. chaemaeiris*, which is not what I have read in many publications. They thrive in an open, sunny location with good drainage. Some do well in light, sandy soils and some in clay soils. If soil is clay, small pieces of limestone should be mixed in with it. There are ideal spots in the rock garden (be careful that *I. pumila* is not overgrown by rank cushion plants). It is also good for cultivating in large containers. Too much winter moisture is debilitating. Plants may have to be divided every 3 years or they may remain undisturbed for a long time, depending on what type. This can be determined by the density of the rhizome mass. It has often been said that yellow-blooming types are easier to grow than blue-violet ones.

Over the years, I have been able to try out many in my own garden, and I have learned that the Serbian types, with their horizontal falls, are particularly attractive. But many died, and it was always necessary to raise replacement plants from seed. Division is recommended for fast-growing specimens. Violet specimens from Bulgaria and *I.* 'Piroschka' from Hungary have been particularly robust for me. Number of chromosomes 2n=32.

I have purposefully devoted a lot of space to *I. pumila*. Although the true species, with its many varieties, is a charming, small garden plant, its greatest contribution has been as a breeding plant. *I. pumila* is one of the most important parent partners in the hybridizing of Dwarf Iris (Miniature Dwarfs, Standard Dwarfs, Median Hybrids). Even though hybridizing will proceed at the current high level of these varieties, backcrossings with the *I. pumila* complex will always be necessary to introduce new elements into the breeding line. It should be pointed out that the old Dwarf Iris, referred to in iris catalogues as *I. pumila*, are not *I. pumila* at all, but probably hybrids of *I. pumila* and *I. chamaeiris*.

Iris reichenbachii Heuffel

Occurs in Transylvania, in the Carpatho-Ukraine, in the region of Moldavia, in Serbia, Bosnia, Herzegovina, Macedonia, and Bulgaria. *I. athoa* Foster, *I. balkana* Janka, *I. bosniaca* Beck, *I. serbica* Pancic, and *I. skorpili* Velenovsky most definitely belong here too.

The scape is cylindric and hollow, 7–10½" (18–27 cm) tall. The leaves grow to 13" (33 cm) long, and are either straight or crescent-shaped, depending on the local form. The blossom color is usually yellow, often a beautiful deep yellow, sometimes with light or dingy-blue shades on the haft, but generally quite variable because of the extensive range. The Banat forms are smaller, those from the south of Romania considerably larger and stronger. *I. reichenbachii* has two yellow blossoms, often with brownish veins in the throat and a large, golden yellow beard. A typical feature of all *I. reichenbachii* are the roundish, sharply ridged spathes, which are clearly distinct from those of *I. chamaeiris*, with which *I. reichenbachii* is often confused. The visible (compared with *I. pumila*) bloomstalk is 2¾–8½" (7.5–22 cm) long.

Purple-brown local forms are often described as *I. bosniaca*. *I. athoa* is a red-violet form from Mount Athos. *I. balkana* also probably belongs here. *I. serbica* Pancic is also a robust *I. reichenbachii* type, about 8½–9" (22–24 cm) tall with light, lemon yellow or greenish yellow blossoms. Distinctly yellow-veined. Spathes have a different form than those of *I. reichenbachii*, but otherwise they are very similar. Leaves relatively large; wide stem leaf. Because of its form, *I. macedonica* Nadji (Charrel) also is affiliated with *I. reichenbachii*.

An iris found in northwestern Turkey is called *I. glockiana* Schwarz, with faint yellow blossoms and a light brownish pattern on the falls. It is uncertain whether its species status is justified. This iris tends toward both *I. reichenbachii* and *I. mellita* (*I. suaveolens* Boiss. et Reuter of *Flora Europaea*).

The yellow form of *I. reichenbachii* is a satisfying garden plant, although it does not have the elegant blossom form with almost floating falls of modern dwarf hybrids. But it has many other advantages: it blooms freely, is a strong grower, and is not tender. It grows well with some clay and lime in the soil, but, of course, no standing water. Its tremendous increase, with rhizome growing over rhizome, makes it necessary to divide and transplant clumps every 3 years. Its robustness makes it a good companion to cushion plants. Blooming period is first half of May. Number of chromosomes 2n=24.

I. reichenbachii Heuff. var. *tenuifolia* Vel. is similar to the lower-growing form in the Banat. The blossoms are yellow, but the falls are partially or completely blueish.

Iris rubromarginata Baker see **Iris mellita**

Iris scariosa Willdenow
Synonym: *I. glaucesens* Bunge

Its range extends from the Urals in the west to Tien Shan in the east; hence it grows in an area—even if sporadically—1,240 mi (2000 km) across. Found in Kazakstan, the Altai region, in Mongolia, in Turkestan. Grows in rocky, steppe soils, often in almost desert-like regions. These sites are always drier than those of *I. pumila*. Also often found in dry salt meadows at the edge of salty steppe lakes.

In form and size, the plant resembles an *I. pumila*. The color of the blossoms is normally red-violet, but there are, though very rarely, yellow blooming specimens. Recently, Soviet botanists found dark

violet, light violet, blue, light blue, and white forms. In the eastern part of their range, the plants are taller, from 7–9" (18–25 cm), occasionally up to 11½" (30 cm). They were formerly known under a special species name (*I. eulefeldii* Regel). The normal type gets only 4–4¾" (10–12 cm) tall. Unlike *I. pumila*, it has thin, papery spathes and two blossoms. It has a distinct scape, again unlike *I. pumila*, and a short perianth tube, which is only 1.5 to 2 times longer than the ovary.

Not really recommended for the garden, it needs a hot, dry location. In cool climates, it is difficult to bring to bloom outdoors. Only for specialists. Possible culture in cold frame with year-round protection from rain, except during its short growing period. Blooms the first 10 days of May. Propagate by seed (from wild plants). Division is not practical due to very slow growth. Number of chromosomes 2n=24.

Iris taurica Loddiges
Native habitat is north of the Caucasus, particularly south of Novorosisk, on dry stony slopes. Some botanists classify it with *I. pumila*, with which it is closely related.

Differs from *I. pumila* mainly in the presence of a visible scape. *I. pumila* has a very long perianth tube, and the ovary practically inserts on the rhizome. *I. taurica* has a scape 3–4" (8–10 cm) long and one blossom that is relatively large. There are specimens with violet and with yellow blossoms. A typical clump is a dense ring.

Attractive iris for the rock garden, but can rarely be obtained. Does not do well in cool, rainy weather; should be planted only in a location that is hot, receiving full sun and with good drainage. Flowers second half of April or the beginning of

May in cooler areas. Number of chromosomes 2n=32 (?).

Iris timofejewii Woronoff

Grows in the Caucasus, especially in Daghestan, on dry, steep slopes of medium-height mountains, only in sites with southern exposure, in both light and clay soils with a large content of loose, limy rock. Forms large, compact colonies.

When not in bloom, the plants resemble Oncocyclus Iris, because of their short, blue-green, crescent-shaped leaves, which are relatively small and about 4–5" (10–14 cm) long. Blossoms are similar to *I. pumila,* and the blossom color is reddish- to blue violet. The blossoms have better substance than *I. pumila.* The closed standards are typical. The falls are fairly narrow, the beard white with a pattern of white streaks on either side. This iris has an obvious scape (unlike *I. pumila*) with 2 blossoms.

Rarely obtainable and extremely tricky to cultivate. Recommended only for dedicated specialists who can meet its requirements; full sun, perfect drainage, loose, rocky soil with lime in it. Only for cultivation in the rain shadow, it is hopeless outdoors in regions with cold, wet summers, but it is just as touchy in the coldhouse in a pot! Decays easily.

In flower the first part of May. Not useful to propagate vegetatively because of slow growth. Propagation by seed also is not easy because the seed often lies dormant for 2 years. According to Rodionenko, more easily crossed with Oncocyclus Iris than with Tall Bearded Iris. Number of chromosomes 2n=24.

Series Iris (Pogon Iris)
Series Elatae

Iris alberti Regel

A plant of the southern Soviet Union; where it occurs in Turkestan, Kazakstan, and Uzbekistan; usually at elevations of 5,600–6,500 ft (1700–2000 m) between or under brush. Was described in 1877 from near the town of Alma-Ata. Unusually vigorous forms can be found on the treeless southern slopes of the Fergana Mountains, where bloomstalks reach a height of 24–28" (60–70 cm). They have a somewhat later blooming period and a cherry red seed capsule. The color disappears after it reaches maturity (*I. alberti* Regel var. *erythrocarpa* Rodionenko).

Normally, the bloomstalk grows to only 15–20" (40–50 cm). The ground color of the flower is a subdued blue-violet with rich olive-yellow to olive-brown stripes on the falls, from the throat up to the tips of the beard. These blend into a shade of violet and spread over more than half the falls. The color does not thin out, but ends rather abruptly. The beard is whitish with yellow tips. Standards are the same color as the falls, the lower third combed with olive-brown veins. The scape has several short branches, which crowd the blossoms together. Flowers have no scent. Leaf tips often are already dried out when the plant blossoms. Yellow-blossomed specimens are recorded. Yellow-blooming *I. albertii* are distinguished from *I. imbricata* by the elongated shape of the falls, compared to the round shape of *I. imbricata.*

The blossoms sound a somewhat discordant note and the plant as a whole is not very decorative, so it is more for collectors and growers. *I. albertii* has two interesting characteristics for hybridizers. It is the earliest blooming Tall Bearded Iris and often reblooms in the fall. *I. albertii* needs a warm, dry location with good drainage, otherwise it is relatively undemanding. More resistant to bacterial diseases than some other species. Annual growth is remarkable. Extremely winter hardy. Blooming period first half of May, often blooms by the end of April, in climatically favorable regions. Fall blossom comes end of September. Number of chromosomes 2n=24.

Iris albicans Lange

In 1860, Lange gave this name to the white iris which he found in the vicinity of Almeria, Spain. The actual homeland of this iris is probably the Arabian Peninsula; it was disseminated, during the wave of Islam expansion over Africa and southwestern Europe, carried along to be planted on graves of fallen Muslim warriors. Grows all over the Near East, in Libya, Tunisia, Algeria, and Morocco. The Spaniards carried it to Mexico. Thus *I. albicans* is also found growing wild all over these countries as a volunteer from gardens. It grows on sunny embankments and slopes. Planted on graves in many Moslem regions.

I. albicans can easily be distinguished from *I. florentina*, the other old, white iris, by its branching habit. While *I. florentina* has good branching, the blossoms of *I. albicans* are held quite close to the stem. *I. albicans* also has no hair at all at the base of the standards, and its spathes are more or less papery at the top when the plant blossoms. It blooms a little later than *I. florentina*. Moreover, *I. albicans* has somewhat wider leaves that tend to twist a bit, giving the plant an unusual appearance. The blossom color is pure white, and the beard is yellow.

Lange called this widespread white form *I. albicans*; a less common form with blue-violet blossoms, found in Yemen, has been called *I. albicans* 'Madonna' or *I. albicans* var. *madonna*. Except for the blossom color, both variants are practically identical.

This iris is for collectors or a welcome souvenir from a vacation. It is very robust in warm regions with good drainage, but acts like a "spoiled brat" in cold areas. More prone to rhizome rot than *I. florentina*. New leaves develop fairly late in the fall, so that either the tips or the whole leaf suffers in cold winters. Blooms freely in the right location. Division is preferable; rarely propagated by seed. Number of chromosomes 2n=44 (Simonet 1932).

Iris aphylla L.

Synonym: *I. nudicaulis* Lam.

An iris species that is native to Germany, particularly Thuringia and the foothills of the Harz Mountains; also Silesia, Moravia, Bohemia, Poland, Hungary, The Piedmont, in European Russia, in Daghestan, and in the eastern Caucasus.

Dies back completely in winter, a conspicuous characteristic. The scape of the typical form grows 9–11½" (25–30 cm) long. Its branching habit, which starts just above the base and is so profuse that, in the case of the lower-growing types, the blossoms almost smother the plant, is another feature.

The pure dark violet blossom colors, which are only occasionally a little off-red, are characteristic of *I. aphylla*. Only *I. aphylla* var. *virescens* has a dingy gray color. It is not clear whether *I. aphylla* var. *coerulea*, with its light ice blue blossoms, is a pure natural form. Since there is no throat veining at all, the blossom colors seem very uniform and vibrant. The substance of the blossoms is, however, less praiseworthy. The hexagonal cross section of the ovary is typical. Green, herbaceous spathes, often tinged with purple-red, are striking; this coloration sometimes extends partly to the bloomstalk and the leaves. The beard is normally white or white tinged with blue.

I. aphylla has several disadvantages as a garden plant. Blossoms are often too crowded on the lower-growing types, and their substance is not exactly ideal. Late frost sometimes threatens leaves and buds. These disadvantages are counterbalanced by a number of positive factors. The abundance of blossoms creates a magnificent spot of color in the garden when they bloom. The iris is completely hardy, and even though good drainage is normal in natural sites, it tolerates, as no other Bearded Iris can, as much moisture as winter can produce. Only the beautiful, upright types should be planted. Scapes of the Rumanian types are often wavy and procumbent! Full sun and a loose, humusy soil is recommended. Plant may remain undivided for many seasons. It does not form a "fairy ring". Blooms in the last part of May, with a possible second bloom in autumn. Propagation by dividing the strong rhizomes is not difficult, nor is seed propagation. Number of chromosomes $2n=48$ (tetraploid!) (Simonet 1934).

Because of its vast range, there are many different local forms and varieties, some taxonomically correct, others not. The status of I. aphylla var. hungarica is probably justified because, unlike many others, it becomes rather tall and hence is better branched—an extremely attractive garden plant. I. aphylla var. polonica and I. aphylla var. bohemica (syn. I. fieberi) are merely local forms and not real varieties. Species status of I. furcata and I. perrieri is justified; these are closely related.

It has to be assumed that I. aphylla was involved in the formation of the I. germanica complex. Tall Bearded Iris and I. aphylla cross freely with one another, the

Table Iris common in the U.S. being one of the results.

Iris babadagica Rzazade et Goln

A dwarf-growing iris from the eastern Caucasus, growing especially on Mount Babadag. Closer to I. furcata than I. alexeenkoi. Unlike I. pumila, it has obvious scapes with two light violet to purple-violet blossoms, one at the tip and another a little way down. Falls have violet-brown veins towards the throat; the beard is whitish, tinged with violet. Spathes are leafy green during the blooming period.

Iris belouinii Boissier et Cornuault

A Bearded Iris from Morocco, little known and uncommon. It grows about 30–47" (80–120 cm) tall. Not of interest to the gardener. Number of chromosomes $2n=48$.

Iris cengialti Ambrosi

This iris occurs in regions of the southern Alps, in Trento, on Lake Garda, Mount Baldo, between Gargnano and Muslone. Classically found in Cengo Alto. Looks very much like a small I. pallida, to which it is closely related, as it is to I. illyrica. The plant gets about 15–20" (40–50 cm) tall. The leaves are greener than the gray-green foliage of I. pallida. Spathes are browner than the latter and papery at blossom time, like the other two iris mentioned. The blossom color is close to lavender.

An extremely useful, charming little iris, which can be planted in a rock garden. Needs a sunny location, soil with lime, and good drainage. Blooming period is end of May to beginning of June. Propagate by rhizome division. Number of chromosomes $2n=24$.

Iris croatica Horvath

Grows in Croatia and only discovered

before World War II. Even less demanding than *I. aphylla*. Grows somewhat taller and blooms very freely. Blossoms are dark violet, the standards somewhat paler than the falls. It has white veining in the throat, unlike *I. aphylla*. The beard is whitish yellow, and the spathes are slightly tinged with red-violet, like those of *I. aphylla*. Much branched.

Free-blooming—but also no beauty. Sunny location; no special requirements; can even make do with heavy soils. Blooming period beginning of May. Hybridized readily with Tall Bearded Iris and is used to produce more resistant varieties. Number of chromosomes 2n=48 (tetraploid).

Iris cypriana Foster et Baker

One of the Near Eastern tetraploid iris, with a precise natural habitat unknown, and species status questionable. It was introduced from Cyprus around the turn of the century by Foster. It was thought that all of these small Near Eastern iris should be part of *I. mesopotamica*. *I. cypriana* has narrow leaves similar to those of *I. mesopotamica*. New foliage is remarkably long in the fall, so frost damage can occur in severe winters. Spathes are very wide and round, and the outer valve is very papery at blossom time. The perianth tube is longer and slimmer than that of *I. mesopotamica*. Blossoms are very large and a nearly pure light blue color with a white beard.

Like the other iris of this group, the rhizomes depend on complete summer maturing and must be protected from summer rain by a pane of glass or piece of foil. If necessary they should be lifted, stored, and planted again in late fall. Recommended for collectors and hybridizers. Number of chromosomes 2n=48.

Iris furcata Marschall von Bieberstein

I. furcata grows in the northern Caucasus and in southwestern Transcaucasia, where it is found on shrub-covered slopes. *I. furcata* apparently replaces *I. aphylla* (with which it is close related) toward the southeast.

Similar to *I. aphylla*, but a great deal smaller overall. The scape of *I. aphylla* branches from the base, whereas with *I. furcata* branching starts only above the mid-point. Hence, the name "Forked Iris". The blossoms of *I. furcata* are smaller than the other *I. aphylla* forms, but have a better structure. The bloomstalk is thinner and the leaves are more elegant than those of *I. aphylla*. The seeds of *I. furcata* are smaller and paler. The blossom is entirely violet.

This species seems to be the most adaptable of all the Bearded Iris species which grow in the Soviet Union. Not easy to obtain. Excellent in rock gardens. Needs a sunny spot and good drainage, but can get along even in slightly shady sites. Blooms in the second part of May. Propagation by division or by seed presents no problems. Passes on its beautiful form to its descendants. Number of chromosomes 2n=24.

Iris illyrica Tommasini

Synonym: *I. germanica* ssp. *illyrica* (Tommasini) Nyman

A native of Istria, the typical form being found near Fiume. Sometimes classified as a variety of *I. cengialti*. *I. illyrica* belongs to the *I. pallida* group, which is noted for its papery spathes. It is probably correct to treat *I. pallida*, *I. cengialti*, and *I. illyrica* as systematic equivalents.

In Vol. V of *Flora Europaea*, this group is subdivided into *I. pallida* ssp. *pallida* and *I. pallida* ssp. *cengialtii* (Ambrosi) Foster. *I. illyrica* is mentioned only as an intermediate form between the two subspecies.

The leaves are dull green and the blossoms have a beautiful satin blue color with a yellow to orange-yellow beard. The spathes are papery. Well suited to sunny rock gardens. A warm, sunny location and soil with lime are important. Blooms in the second part of May. Number of chromosomes 2n=24.

Iris imbricata Lindley
Synonym: *I. sulfurea* Koch. Often incorrectly called *I. flavescens.*

I. imbricata grows in the mountains of eastern Transcaucasia and in Armenia, normally in moist upland meadows and rocky slopes at an elevation of 5,900–6,500 ft (1800–2000 m).

Conspicuous for its sulfur yellow blossoms similar in size to those of *I. alberti,* but easily distinguishable by their roundish shape. The blossoms have no scent. Specimens with bluish blossoms are also found, though rarely. Leaves are a yellowish, spring green and noticeably wide. The distended green spathes are an important feature. During the blooming period they are only papery at the margin (unlike those of *I. flavescens,* the familiar clone of peasant gardens).

This species cannot be compared in beauty to the modern Bearded Iris, but can be recommended for collectors and dedicated iris enthusiasts, since it blooms profusely even in cold regions. Despite its moist natural locations, it is prone to rhizome rot in cool climates, hence requires good drainage and full sun. Blooms at end of May. Number of chromosomes 2n=24.

Iris junonia Schott et Kotschy
Found in the Cilician Taurus Mountains in Turkey.

Has narrow, short leaves growing to about 9–11½" (25–30 cm) long. The scape grows about 24" (60 cm) tall and has a number of side branches bearing lavender-colored blossoms. The standards are pure lavender, falls somewhat bluer with a white beard that is yellow at the tip. The spathes are 1–2" (2.5–5 cm) long; the lower part is leaf green when the plant is in bloom, the upper part papery. This iris loses its leaves in autumn. Probably different from *I. mesopotamica* even though it belongs to the group of the Near Eastern tetraploid species. Number of chromosomes 2n=48.

Iris kashmiriana Baker
Synonym: *I. bartonii* Foster

Iris kashmiriana is native to Kashmir, northwest India, Baluchistan, Afghanistan, also Nepal in the mountains near Khatmandu, on rocky mountain slopes. It can be seen on graves in Moslem regions and in India on the rooftops. The true species has white blossoms as described. Differs from *I. albicans* in its widely spreading, branched scape and from *I. florentina* in its long, green spathes. Its true blossom color is milky white to cream, with delicate green veins. The falls stand out stiffly and do not hang. The broad yellow-green, ribbed leaves are over 20" (50 cm) long. The strong scape, which is mostly oval in cross section, is somewhat shorter than the leaves. The blossom has a strong fragrance. There is also a lavender-colored form, which should not be mistaken for an *I. germanica* form found in Kashmir, which has light violet-blue blossoms with poor substance.

According to Dykes, not easy to grow in cooler climates; recommended only for collectors. Blooms end of May. Number of chromosomes 2n=48 (Dr. Werckmeister, if correct).

Iris lepita Heuffel
Found on bush-covered sandhills in the Banat region of Romania, especially near Grebenac. Botanists classify it either with *I. squalens* or with *I. variegata*. The latter is probably correct. Blossom white, with violet veins from the throat out to the center. *I. leucographa* Kerner is similar.

Iris macrantha hort. (M. Foster)
One of the tetraploid iris from Amasya, Turkey, introduced by Foster. About 28" (70 cm) tall, blossoms have good substance. According to Simonet, a variety of *I. germanica*. Number of chromosomes 2n=48.

Iris mesopotamia Dykes
A Near Eastern tetraploid iris, introduced by Dykes in 1913. Very similar to *I. cypriana*, except that its spathes are longer and narrower, green on the bottom half and papery on the top. The perianth tube is shorter than that of *I. cypriana*. The blossom color is a shade of lavender-blue, similar to that of *I. junonia*. A true species plant of *I. mesopotamica* is almost impossible to purchase. Number of chromosomes 2n=48.

Iris narcissiflora Diels
Native to China, especially Sichuan Province. It is the easternmost Pogon Iris. Very little known about it; probably rare in cultivation. Yellow blossoms in July. Height up to 11½" (30 cm).

Iris pallida Lamarck
Synonyms: *I. glauca* Salisb., *I. odoratissima* Jacq., *I. pallido-coerulea* Pars.

Native to the southern Alps, particularly the southern Tyrol near Bolzano, also on the Istrian Peninsula, in the Crimea, in Dalmatia (Velebit Mts.). Typically found in the environs of the Briccius Chapel on the Nanos, Crimea.

Grows to about 40" (1 m) tall. The broad, sword-shaped leaves are blue-green, with a silvery tinge. The rigid, upright-growing scape is poorly branched with short laterals, in contrast to *I. aphylla* and *I. variegata* with relatively long branches. Spathes are silvery white, even in the budding stage, and papery. Perianth tube very short.

I. cengialti has all these same characteristics, but every part of it is daintier and slimmer, the color of the leaves greener and the papery spathes pale brown and

The use of the new generic name Juno came easily as people had always called them Juno iris.

Upper left: Juno nicolai is a true rarity and practically unobtainable.
Upper right: Juno planifolia is the westernmost species of this genus. Found as far west as the hinterlands of Spain, where it blooms in the first three months of the year, depending on eleva-

tion. Meadows with hundreds of these plants are a stunning sight. They are not sufficiently hardy for Germany. This photograph was taken in the vicinity of Ronda.
Below: Juno × sindpers, one of the few known crosses of the species of this genus made by Van Tubergan, J. sindjarensis × J. persica. With good drainage and some protection from rain and cold weather it can be grown outdoors in Germany.

not silvery white like those of *I. pallida.* Blossoms of *I. pallida* are relatively large, well-formed, very fragrant, light lavender-blue. Now often cultivated in fields around Florence (instead of *I. florentina*) for the rhizomes, which are very fragrant when dried, the orris root of perfumery. Seven or eight blossoms develop on the scape; since the branches are only ⅜–1⅛" (1–3 cm) long, blossoms appear to be growing directly from the stem. Longer branching is rare, but when it occurs, the branches grow parallel to the erect bloomstalk, unlike *I. germanica* types. The falls are about 2¾" (7 cm) long, the standards 2⅝" (6.5 cm); the beard is whitish yellow.

A local form, known as *I. pallida* var. *dalmatica,* differs only insignificantly. Its blossoms are more lilac-blue.

I. pallida is highly recommended for the garden, despite its limited branching; its beautifully-colored, well-shaped, sweet scented blossoms make it worthwhile. The delicate color of its blossoms combines well with other garden flowers. Tolerates extreme dryness and does particularly well on the south side of steep embankments. All it requires is a sunny location and good drainage. Often brought home from vacations in Yugoslavia. Use in the garden with other Tall Bearded Iris species or old hybrids and other old-fashioned plants, such as Common Peonies or Double Columbine.

I. p. 'Variegata', the variegated form, is much more important for the garden. Because of its bicolored leaves it is an ornament throughout the growing season, not just when in bloom. Two different types are listed: the widespread form with gray-green/yellowish white variegation and the rarer, more tender form with gray-green/pure white variegation. Blooming period usually end of May. Number of chromosomes 2n=24.

There is no doubt that *I. pallida* is one of the original parents of our modern Tall Bearded Iris and probably hybrids between *I. pallida* and *I. variegata* existed from the beginning. Where their ranges overlap, hybrids similar to *I. germanica* occur. As the garden strain developed, other species were, of course, also involved.

Iris perrieri Simonet
Occurs in a relatively small region in the French Alps at an elevation of about 5,600–5,900 ft (1700–1800 m). Classically found on Mount d'Archusaz in the Les Bauges group.

Other members of the genus Juno.

Upper left: Juno magnifica (Iris magnifica) is hardy in Germany. It is the largest Juno species that grows in Germany and is an extremely attractive spring bloomer. It must have good drainage. Upper right: Another view of Juno × sindpers. These Juno hybrids can be grown in larger clay pots. Below: Juno bucharica (Iris bucharica) is probably the least tender species of the genus. The garden form with white standards is shown; wild forms are often all yellow. Often referred to as "antler iris" in publications. Blue muscari make ideal companion plants.

It is a medium-tall Bearded Iris of a pure purple-violet color, closely related to *I. aphylla*. The blossoms are very crowded; in the garden, especially south of a stone or mortared retaining wall, where the rhizomes can really bake in full sun, it produces a brilliant splash of violet. Blooms very freely. Good for both collectors and amateurs. Number of chromosomes 2n=24.

Iris reginae Horvath

Native to Macedonia, widely scattered. Often described as a variety of *I. variegata*.

I. reginae grows to about 20–24" (50–60 cm). Its blossom is somewhat larger than that of *I. variegata*, which is closely related. The petals are narrower and longer than those of the latter. The ground color of the blossoms is off-white, and the veins are a beautifully contrasting violet. On closer inspection the standards are also delicately shaded. The leaves are extremely crescent-shaped, and their lengthwise veins stand out even more than *I. variegata*. The standards are somewhat open, and the diameter of the blossom is up to 4" (10 cm).

Has nothing in common with modern Bearded Iris, but I consider this iris species a very suitable garden plant, especially for iris lovers and collectors. Good in natural-type plantings as well as larger rock gardens. Blooms in mid-June. Dies back completely and is winter hardy. The rhizomes do not seem to be particularly affected by moisture. Propagate by division. Number of chromosomes 2n=24.

Iris rudskyi J. et M. Horvath

Native to Macedonia. Sometimes considered a color variation of *I. variegata*. Blooms in June. The falls are silvery lavender with purple-violet veins and the standards are yellow. Unusual color variant in a species. Grows about 11½" (30 cm) tall. Only for collectors.

Iris schachtii Markgraf

Grows in central Turkey in dry fields near Beiram-Ormanie, 30 mi (50 km) southeast of Ankara.

Closely related to *I. imbricata*, but all parts are considerably smaller. The spathes are half herbaceous, half papery during the blossom period and not as distended as those of *I. imbricata*. Blossom light yellow to greenish yellow. Blooming period is May. Grows about 8¾" (23 cm) tall. Not recommended as garden plant; too delicate for the continental climate. Will not bloom outdoors in cooler regions.

Iris subbiflora Brotero

Synonyms: *I. biflora* L., in Hort. Eyst. as *I. portugalica*

I. subbiflora often is classified with *I. aphylla*. They are indeed closely related, but also very different. Classified as a subspecies of *I. lutescens* in the *Flora Europaea*; see under *I. chamaeiris*.

Native to Portugal, southern Spain and Tangiers, where it grows on limestone mountains.

The most common species is the one from Coimbra, with beautiful dark blue blossoms. But there are other color variants, white, gray-blue, purple-red, and strongly striped blue forms. The scape, bearing two blossoms, grows to about 8¾" (23 cm) tall, much taller than the foliage. Botanically this iris is characterized by very atypical spathes, which often are 2⅞" (7.5 cm) long, and by the perianth tube, which is nearly 2" (5 cm) long. Recommended only for collectors, *I. subbiflora* is not completely winter hardy, or at least the Portuguese form is not; the Spanish strain is somewhat hardier. Only for warm, dry, protected locations. Blooming period latter part of May; January/February in the wild.

Iris taochia Woronoff
A little known iris from the Caucasus. Also found in northeastern Turkey. Blossoms in June, 11½–24" (30–60 cm) tall. There are yellow and violet specimens. Only for collectors. According to Erich Pasche, it is probably identical with *I. schachtii.*

Iris trojana Kerner ex Stapf
Found in Troas (vicinity of Troja). One of the first tetraploid species introduced into cultivation, but unknown as a wild plant.

Characterized by strong growth, good branching and large blossoms. The leaves are narrow for such a large plant. The scape is 35" (90 cm) tall and begins branching low on the stalk. Often with 2 blossoms per branch, 5 or 6 blossoms may be open at the same time on each scape. Spathes with slight purple-red cast and papery toward the tip when the first blossom opens. The blossom has rounded standards, which are light blue with shadings of purple-violet. The long, reddish falls contrast with these. The beard is white but yellowish at the tip and entirely yellow toward the throat. Often confused with *I. cypriana.*

A useful garden plant, even though the form of its blossom is rather old-fashioned. Only requirements are a sunny site and good drainage. Backcrosses would be extremely interesting. Number of chromosomes 2n=48.

Iris varbossiana Maly
Pogon Iris from Bosnia; status undetermined. Blooms between May and June. Violet blossoms with darker veining. Grows to 30" (80 cm) tall. Sterile, according to Prodan.

Iris variegata Linne
Found in Austria, Yugoslavia, Rumania, Hungary, and Czechoslovakia. In southern Germany there are also a few strictly protected areas where it is found, e.g. in the vicinity of Munich. Usually on stony slopes covered with brush, in forest clearings, on heaths and rocky outcroppings.

A fairly low-growing species, which like *I. aphylla*, dies back completely in winter (as do all northern Pogon Iris). The spathes are herbaceous and slightly distended. Blossoms are yellow; the falls have blue veins, which sometimes blend into brown spots. Albino forms occur, but very rarely, e.g. *I. variegata* 'Alba' (see also *I. lepita*). The standards are usually lemon yellow to chrome yellow. Because of its large range, *I. variegata* has small variations in many characteristics. The beard is golden yellow.

Height varies from 6–15" (15–40 cm), depending on which type. The blossom is about 2⅝" (6.5 cm) in diameter. *I. variegata* bears 2 blossoms per scape, and the scape is more or less branching, also depending on type. Leaves, too, vary somewhat; they are 6–13" (15–35 cm), with slightly raised, longitudinal veins. Near the rhizome, a purple-violet concentration of pigment can sometimes be found. An attractive rock garden plant, recommended for warm, dry locations. Propagate by division or seed; seeds have a long dormant period. Blooming period lasts an average of 2 weeks, usually starting at the same time as Tall Bearded Iris. Number of chromosomes 2n=24.

There are still other forms, such as *I. variegata* var. *pontica* Prodan from the Dobruja. The standards have a touch of ochre, and the veining on the falls is dense and red-brown to Bordeaux red, sometimes running together to form larger patches. The margin is clear yellow-ochre again. The plant is about 15″ (40 cm) tall. The blossoms are somewhat smaller overall than the type. Diameter of the blossoms about 3″ (3 cm). *I. variegata* 'Alba' has already been mentioned.

A white, violet-veined form is known as *I. amoena* Spach. It should be noted here that iris with white standards and violet or violet-veined falls are today described as amoena meaning flowers with more or less white standards and more or less blue or purple falls.

Old Hybrid Forms of the Elatae

which are commonly listed as species.

Iris bioletii Foster
Found around the Black Sea. It is almost an *I. germanica* type with long, narrow green spathes, herbaceous rather than papery when in flower. The falls are purple-red with brownish veins, with a white background towards the throat. The standards are a little bluer. The crests are opalescent. The leaves have a curious shape, small at the base and widest in the middle. Recommended for historic collections. Number of chromosomes 2n=44 (Simonet).

Iris flavescens De Candolle
This is a clone and not a genuine species; characterized by its vigorous growth and frequently found in old farm gardens. It is thought that this iris comes from the cross *I. pallida* × *I. variegata*. Often mistaken for *I. imbricata* Lindley.

The blossoms are medium-sized, light yellow. The falls have a large bright spot and brownish veins in the throat. Has no requirements except a sunny location. Indestructible, very free-blooming, a yellow highlight in the garden, but not necessarily a beauty. Blooms before Tall Bearded Iris, middle to end of May. Number of chromosomes 2n=24.

Iris florentina Linne, Florentine iris
Synonym: *I. germanica* var. *florentina* (L.) Dykes

An ancient *I. germanica*, a closely related hybrid, or a white variety of same. Arabia often is incorrectly mentioned as its native habitat. It was always confused with *I. albicans* Lange or lumped together with it.

Stem is 18–28″ (45–70 cm) tall, blossoms whitish with the pleasant fragrance of violets. Falls up to 3½″ (9 cm) long, severely recurved, starting at the middle. Standards up to 3¼″ (8.5 cm) long, upright and wavy at the margin. In all aspects very close to *I. germanica*. Differs from *I. albicans* primarily by its strong, well-proportioned branching. The blossoms of *I. albicans* grow close to the main stalk.

A commercially important iris. It is raised in fields in Tuscany and around Verona. The dried rhizomes, which exude a pleasing scent, are sold in drugstores as Rhizoma Iridis or orris. Iris oil is obtained by steam distillation, which, when thinned, has the very pleasant fragrance of violets. For this use *I. florentina* is now being replaced more and more by *I. pallida* var. *dalmatica*. This kind of "iris industry" is not to be underestimated, as it provides jobs for some 10,000 people.

I. florentina is not demanding, needs only a sunny location and porous soil. A very free-blooming white iris, often found in farmyards. In spite of its old-fashioned flower form, it can be used effectively for background plantings. Blooms somewhat before the height of the Tall Bearded Iris season. Propagate only by rhizome division.

206

Iris germanica Linne

An ancient hybrid, probably native to the Mediterranean region. It can be found naturalized and rampant in many countries. Because of its many forms, it has no uniform description. There are two forms in Romania:

1. The typical and rarer form, with a longer, robust scape, somewhat wider, frosted leaves; scape cross section large. Flower with relatively large perianth segments (about 3½" or 90 mm long and ¼" or 6 mm wide). The falls are distinctly different from the standards, which are a darker deep violet color.

2. A form with smaller petals, about 2½–3" (65–70 mm) long and about 1½–1⅝" (35–40 mm) wide. Standards and falls are almost the same color, except that the falls are slightly more reddish. It is the more common and more disease resistant strain (Prodan).

There are many other forms:

I. germanica var. *atropurpurea* (violet self)
I. germanica var. *florentina* (=*I. florentina*)
I. germanica var. *kochii* (=*I. kochii*)
and others.

Recommended only for collectors or for the historic corner of the garden. There are more beautiful iris. Relatively undemanding.

Iris kochii Kerner ex Stapf

An *I. germanica* type, traditionally found around Lake Como. Does not grow quite as tall as other similar types, about 24" (60 cm). The blossoms are uniform dark purple-violet with smooth borders. Similar in form to *I. albicans*. The beard is bluish white with yellow tips. Old, robust garden type.

Iris sambucina Linne, Elder Iris

Synonyms: *I. concolor* Baker, *I. neglecta*

Hornemann

An ancient cultivated plant of dubious origin, most certainly a hybrid, probably a cross of *I. pallida* × *I. variegata*. Often naturalized, in the Swabian Alps, north of the Danube around Regensburg, and in many other places, frequently along castle walls and near ruins. Can also be found on the Iberian Peninsula, in Italy, and on the northern Balkan Peninsula.

Falls lilac-colored or dingy violet, dark veins. The standards are a somewhat paler violet. The sword-shaped leaves are fairly thick. The stalk grows to about 28" (70 cm) and inflorescence attains a length of 8" (20 cm), usually consisting of 5 blossoms. The falls of the blossoms are about 2½" (6 cm) long

A somber rather than bright color combination, suitable only for collectors or for the historic corner of the garden. Very undemanding in porous soil and a warm location. Often grows in the cracks of old castle walls. Blooms very late, often as late as the latter part of June, with the last Bearded Iris.

Iris squalens Linné

Synonyms: *I. lurida* Ker-Gawler, *I. rhaetica* Brügger

Found in Fiori in the southern Tyrol, but there also are places in Germany where it occurs.

Not a true species, but an ancient hybrid that Linnaeus classified as a species. Probably the same parents as *I. sambucina*, *I. pallida* and *I. variegata*.

Thick, stiff leaves about 28" (70 cm) long. Height of the bloomstalk about 24–35" (60–90 cm). The falls are purple-violet with somewhat brownish veins and 2½" (6 cm) long. The violet blade has a yellow-green cast. The standards are 2½" (6 cm) long, a faded brownish or grayish color with a pale violet cast, but never yellowish.

The margins are heavily ruffled. Yellow beard. There are a few color variants.

An undemanding iris, but only for collectors or for the historic corner.

Iris sweertii Lamarck

A medieval iris of hybrid origin. Even compared with its countless modern sisters, it is still an engaging garden plant. Very free-blooming, basic color white covered with violet veins; small but compact blossoms. Generally resistant to disease.

Section Hexapogon
Subsection Regelia

Most species occur in a relatively small region of Central Asia, mainly Turkestan in Buchara and Tadschikistan. But a few species are found far to the west and east. *I. arenaria*, for example (small form of *I. humilis* Georgi), is found close to Vienna and in Moravia. On the other hand, the range of *I. mandschurica* penetrates far into Manchuria, to Korea and northern China.

Regelias grow in more northern regions than Oncocyclus Iris and hence are far hardier. In their native habitat they are found at fairly high elevations, e.g. *I. darwasica* in mountain passes from 9,200–9,800 ft (2800–3000 m). This also accounts for their resistance to frost. Because severe winters occur where they grow naturally, their leaves appear only in spring, unlike Oncocyclus Iris. They share very hot and dry summers. The chief enemy of Regelia Iris, as well as of Oncos, is summer wetness.

Can only be successfully cultivated in extremely sunny and warm sites in the garden. Most important is perfect drainage; standing water is the sure death of these plants. The soil should be as light as possible and not overfertilized. Mix coarse river sand into the soil.

Successful garden culture depends on climate and location. In regions with warm, sunny summers they can often be planted outdoors in a warm, sunny location. During extended periods of rain, the plants should be covered. Blooming period for Regelia Iris is May, about 2 weeks before the height of the Tall Bearded Iris season and the same as Media Iris. The foliage yellows as early as June, and the plants soon die back. Regelia Iris need a summer dormant period of at least 3 months.

People who live in colder and damper climates do not have to go without this pretty iris if they are willing to go to some trouble. One way is to lift plants after the leaves have turned yellow, let the rhizomes dry, then store them in a warm place until fall. They should not be replanted before the end of October or beginning of November. If planted too early, the leaf buds break, producing growth injured in a severe winter. The rhizomes should be planted ¾ to 1⅛" (2 or 3 cm) deep. Another way is to cultivate them in a cold frame. They do not require much care, and all that is needed is some kind of improvised frame. Put on glass sashes in the middle of June, not tightly closed; pieces of lath put between the frame and windows allow for air circulation. In November remove the sashes for a time to allow a few rain showers to come in, thus encouraging the plants to grow again. I replace the sashes again until the beginning of March. From that time on plants can be heavily watered and receive a dressing of complete fertilizer.

Flower standards as well as falls have a "beard" of unicellular hairs. The spathes are ridged; the scapes usually produce multiple blossoms (2 or 3). The seeds have

Natural range of Gynandriris, Oncocylus and Regelia Iris

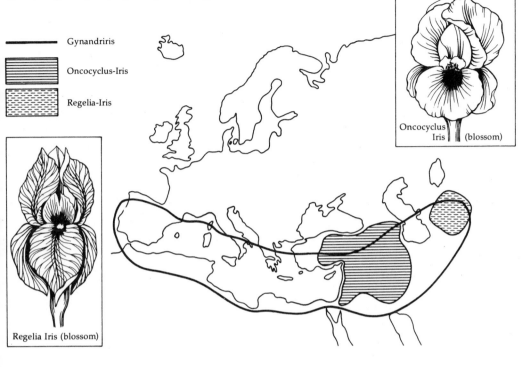

Gynandriris

Oncocyclus-Iris

Regelia-Iris

Oncocyclus Iris (blossom)

Regelia Iris (blossom)

an aril. Propagation usually by division. Regelias form rhizomes with offshoots.

Iris afghanica Wendelbo
Grows in Afghanistan on the north side of the Salang Pass, at the 6,500–9,800 ft (2000–3000 m) elevation. Upright, light green leaves, 9" (25 cm) long. The scape is 7–11½" (18–30 cm) tall and bears 2 blossoms. The blossoms, 4" (10 cm) in diameter, are bi-colored, the falls cream-yellow with reddish brown or dark purple veins, the standards yellow to almost white. Both are fairly pointed. The overall form of this blossom looks like *I. korolkowii*. Both falls and standards have a beard. Blooming period is May-June. Number of chromosomes 2n=22.

Iris bloudowii Bunge (Ledebour)
Found by Ledebour in the Altai Mountains in 1830. But also occurs in other regions of central and east Asia (in Mongolia and in northwestern China). A well known source is in Tien Shan.
I. bloudowii is similar to *I. humilis* (syn. *I. flavissima*) but can be clearly distinguished from it. In its native habitat it does not occur in such extremely sandy soils as *I. humilis*. It grows in meadows, alpine fields or similar places. It is more tolerant of a damp, northern climate, where it blooms and sets seed. The leaves are larger and prominently striped. The dark-brown tips of the emerging leaves in spring, when they are still short, are very striking. This also is characteristic of *I. korolkowii* and *I.*

209

stolonifera, a sign that they belong to the Regelia group Has very pretty, dark yellow blossoms. The scape grows 4–4½" (10–12 cm) tall and bears two terminal blossoms. The spathes are very wide, distended, and ridged. The haft of the falls has brown veins, the blade is bright yellow, the beard golden yellow. The elongated standards are the same color.

This iris is much easier to grow in continental climates than *I. humilis* (syn. *I. flavissima*). If drainage is good, the soil can contain more humus than for *I. humilis.* It is not easy to get *I. bloudowii* to bloom, despite its ability to persist. Although it is completely hardy, it can sometimes only be flowered in a cold frame. Hence recommended only for collectors and iris lovers. Individual blossoms do not last very long in hot weather; blooming period is from end of April to beginning of May. Number of chromosomes 2n=26 (Simonet 1952).

Iris darwasica Regel
Synonym: *I. suwarowii* (Regel)

Native habitat: Bokhara, Central Asia, Darwas, on steep slopes at high elevations, mostly on east side, in limestone or in primary rock. It forms large clumps in somewhat protected places.

The basal foliage is crescent-shaped, but the other leaves are straight. The leaves are 9–11½" (25–30 cm) long and light green. The equally long stems bear 2 blossoms. The predominant color is pale, greenish yellow. Standards and falls are a little more than 2" (5 cm) long and about 1" (2.7 cm) wide. The haft of the falls does not deserve its name, for it is usually wider than the blade and has a sparse beard. The signal spot is dark reddish purple, the blade is heavily spotted and broadly veined in red-purple. The standards have no pattern, except for a purple inner rib, which has a purple beard on it. The stigma is a narrow,

Media iris. The nursery of Goos and Koenemann was world famous around the turn of the century. They developed the first hybrids between tall and lower-growing bearded iris, both in blooming period and height, today called Media iris.

Top left: There are countless cultivars and more are being added every year. Shown here is 'Arctic Mist', a proven variety.
Top right: An older Media iris, recognizable by the shape of its blossom. It does not always have to be the most modern blossom form. Here 'Interim'.
Bottom left: 'June Prom' captivates with its compact growth habit as well as its blossom substance.
Bottom right: 'Blue Asterisk' is another tried and true upright cultivar for cooler climates. Advances in breeding are noticeable especially in this height class.

yellow tongue. This interesting plant cannot, unfortunately, be obtained on the market. In Wisley, England it grows and blooms well. Rodionenko describes blossoms with rounded falls and thinks that it is a variety or a subspecies of *I. korolkowii*.

Iris falcifolia Bunge

Grows primarily in sandy, desertlike regions, from Central Asia almost to the border of Afghanistan, between Mesched and Herat, at elevations above 4,300 ft (1300 m). The soil is sandy loess often eroded by water. Large stretches of ground in its native habitat are under cultivation, planted in wheat and sugar beets. Further expansion of sugar beet fields threatens the existence of this plant (Furse).

I. falcifolia grows in small clumps that never grow very large. Its coarse rhizomes are usually deeply embedded in sand. The leaves are thin, dark green, and wiry, resembling sedges. The stems are about 8½" (22 cm) long and usually bear 2 relatively small blossoms. The falls are narrow, yellowish, spotted with bronze-purple, and heavily veined. The crests are rosy lilac with a white stigma, the filament is white and the anther lavender-blue, when there is no pollen. This iris is very difficult to keep in a garden (even though it thrives in Wisley). Rodionenko feels that *I. falcifolia* Bunge and *I. longiscapa* Ledeb. are one and the same species. Contrary to the above information, he describes it as particularly attractive, with 3–5 blossoms per stem, violet-purple, about 1¼" (3.5 cm) in diameter, and the height of the plant 13–20" (35–50 cm). I assume that Rodionenko is describing *I. longiscapa*, which is quite different from *I. falcifolia*.

Iris heweri Grey-Wilson et Mathew

A native of Afghanistan, usually at elevations of 4,900–6,500 ft (1500–2000 m), growing on open, sunny mountain slopes. Usually grows from 3½–6" (9–15 cm) tall, rarely up to 11¼" (29 cm). Forms small clumps. The rhizomes are thin with fibrous remains of leaf shoots, and send out lateral branches ⅜–2" (1–5 cm) long. The individual leaves are up to 5¾" (14 cm) long (occasionally up to 10½" or 27 cm) and 1/16–3/16" (0.2–0.5 cm) wide; the outer ones are more or less crescent-shaped, green, with a cartilaginous margin.

Iris kaempferi (botanically speaking Iris ensata, according to one recent classification) is for the Japanese what the bearded iris is to the Western gardens. The Japanese have bred them for centuries. Their huge, dish-like blossoms are not invariably attractive, but there are many lovely varieties. What is available changes constantly, but this plate gives a good cross-section of their diversity.

Top left: 'Beni-ohgi', a cultivar from Japan. This would be called a "plicata", to borrow a description from bearded iris.

Top right: A hybrid developed by the German breeder Max Steiger.
Center left: Deep velvety, blue-violet with a strongly contrasting yellow throat pattern.
Center right: Iris kaempferi 'Sorcerer's Triumph' was bred in the U.S.; the delicate veining on the blossom is extremely attractive.
Bottom left: A cultivar similar to that shown in the top left plate, but giving a completely different effect because of the larger violet area.
Bottom right: Iris kaempferi 'Gei-sho-ni', a cultivar from Japan with simple blossoms that give a natural impression.

The scape is 1½–3¾" (4–9 cm) long (occasionally up to 7" or 18 cm) and elongates after flowers fade. It bears 1–2 blossoms. The 2–3 spathes are not uniform in size, are 1¼–2" (3.5–5 cm) long, pointed, partly papery, with a greenish purple hue. The perianth tube is ¾–1" (2–2.5 cm) long, and the blossom segments are dark violet-blue. The beard is white, tinged with purple-violet at the tip. Blooming period May.

Iris hoogiana Dykes
This plant, found in Central Asia up to elevations of 5,900 ft (1800 m) has rhizomes with short branches. The leaves are pale green, about ½–¾" (1.5–2 cm) wide and 20–24" (50–60 cm) long. The stem bears 2–3 blossoms and is about 29" (75 cm) tall. The blossoms have exceptionally fine form. They are lavender-blue with an orange yellow beard. The falls are smaller than the standards, which are attractively waved.

This iris is one of the most beautiful iris species. Dykes named it after the Hoog brothers of the van Tubergen firm in Haarlem, The Netherlands, who had become well-known specialists in rare iris species. It is also a beautiful cut flower. This Regelia Iris does best of all in the open garden. Blooming period is May. It is even more important for the cultivation of tetraploid Regelia hybrids (number of chromosomes of *I. hoogiana* 2n=44) and of Regeliocyclus hybrids.

There are several forms, such as *I. hoogiana* 'Purpurea' with dark purple blossoms, and a white strain. Other named varieties are *I. h.* 'Late Amethyst' and *I. h.* 'Blue Joy'. *I.* 'Bronze Beauty' is a hybrid with *I. stolonifera*.

Iris humilis Georgi, Sand Iris
Synonyms: *I. flavissima* Pall., *I. arenaria* Waldst. et Kit.

According to recent research, the valid name for this iris is *I. humilis*, even though the above synonymous epithets are used in gardening and horticultural circles. Not to be mistaken for *I. humilis* M.B., which is a synonym for *I. pontica*, the Dwarf Spuria.

This iris has—unlike almost any other iris—two widely separated ranges. One lies in the Pontic area of lower Austria, in Moravia, Hungary, Transylvania and in the Moldau region. The second range is Central Asia, specifically the Altai, the Dneiper region, Lake Baikal, Mongolia. The iris found in the west was formerly called *I. arenaria* and the Asiatic type *I. flavissima*. Since the plants are extremely different morphologically, it is questionable whether putting them together into one species was correct, particularly since the entire *I. flavissima-potaninii-bloudowii-manschurica* complex is rather obscure. One form which occurs in the Ukraine is known as *I. pineticola* Klokow.

Usually grows in sparse, isolated stands. The rhizomes begin seasonal growth relatively early. The erect scapes are of different heights, 4" (10 cm) for the western *I. arenaria*, and 8" (20 cm) for the eastern *I. flavissima*. The stems bear 2 blossoms, which vary from light to dark yellow. This iris is xerophilic and is completely hardy. It grows in Siberia, more northerly than any other Bearded Iris. Along the banks of the Lena it occurs as far north as 60 degrees latitude, then southward to Transbaikalia. The leaves are narrow, grasslike. The spathes are rounded and dainty. Unfortunately the blossom is very short-lived and on hot days does not last even a full day; does not open at all if the weather is overcast. Foliage dies back completely in the fall (northern habitat response). Blooming period is end of April-beginning of May. The *I. arenaria* type has falls that are beautifully horizontal.

Not an easy plant in the garden. The description "Sand Iris" refers to the soil in which it grows, which should be sandy or sandy-loam with lime. Requires full sun and perfect drainage. In areas with a high precipitation, it should be planted in almost pure sand in a slight depression. A small amount of well-rotted compost encourages growth. Best time for planting is June. It is difficult to get the plant established. Be very careful when dividing it! Seed should be sown as soon as possible after maturing. It often takes 2 years before they germinate.

Can only be recommended for collectors and iris enthusiasts. Crosses easily with *I. pumila* and *I. chamaeiris* (*I. virescens* in the *Flora Europaea*). Produces attractive but sterile offspring. The carotenes present often give the blossoms very singular color variations.

Older known hybrids are: *I.* 'Tiny Treasure', *I.* 'Promise', *I.* 'Bricky', and *I.* 'Cup and Saucer'. Number of chromosomes 2n=22.

Iris karategina Fedtschenko

The species status of this iris found in Central Asia is questionable. Similar to or identical with *I. lineata*.

Iris korolkowii Regel

A native of Central Asia, this iris does not send out as many lateral branches from its compact rhizomes as, for instance, *I. stolonifera*. The leaves are narrow, light green, and 11½–24" (30–60 cm) long. The scapes bear 2–3 terminal blossoms that are upright with conical standards. The ground of the blossom is white with a greenish gray sheen, over which lies a heavy reddish brown network of veins. Beard and central spot on the falls are red-brown. The standards are a pointed oval shape. This fairly hardy iris is also a delightful cut flower. Blooms in May. Number of chromosomes 2n=44.

There are a number of varieties, which are probably only garden forms: *I. korolkowii* var. *violacea* Fost is more common and has a heavy network of violet veins; *I. korolkowii* var. *concolor* Fost has deeply ridged spathes with a purple cast to them and violet veins; *I. korolkowii* var. *venosa* hort. has particularly heavy veining; *I. korolkowii* var. *leichtliniana*, cream-colored with black veins and a purple-black signal spot. Some of the chromosome counts for these forms are supposedly atypical.

Iris kuschkensis Grey-Wilson et Mathew

Native to Afghanistan at elevations of 5,250 ft (1600 m). A species similar to *I. lineata* and *I. darwasica*, but differing from these mainly by its stout rhizomes. It also differs from *I. lineata* by its wider leaves (3/16–5/16" or 0.6–0.8 cm) and by its rounder perianth segments. It differs from *I. darwasica* by shorter perianth segments (falls 2" or 5 cm long, standards 1½–1¾" or 4–4.4 cm). The seed capsule is 2¼" (5.5 cm) long. Blooming period is April.

Iris lineata Foster

Often lumped together with *I. darwasica*, but is probably an independent species. According to Rodionenko, an earlier name for *I. karategina*. Native to Central Asia. Stolon-like rhizomes. Leaves 4–6" (10–15 cm) long, 3/16" (0.5 cm) wide. Bloomstalk 8–15" (20–40 cm) tall, 2–3 blossoms, usually brownish violet with narrow (¼–½" or 0.8–1.4 cm wide) petals. Not to be confused with *I. lineolata* (Oncocyclus).

Iris longiscapa Ledebour

Rodionenko believes that *I. longiscapa* and *I. falcifolia* are one species, but this may not be accurate, because the description Furse gave for *I. falcifolia* during his travels in

Afghanistan is very different from Rodionenko's. Thus the latter, which appeared
in the 1968 B.I.S. Yearbook, probably
refers to *I. longiscapa*.

The blossoms are not particularly attractive and have no scent; they are violet-
purple, 1⅛–2" (3–5 cm) in diameter. The
plant is about 13–20" (35–50 cm) tall. The
number of blossoms is an important
characteristic for breeders. There are not
the usual 1 or 2 blossoms on each scape,
but 3–5. It grows in sandy desert tracts and
is unaffected by heat. It is practically hopeless to try to cultivate this plant in the
north. But it grows well in warm, dry
climates. Number of chromosomes
2n=18.

Iris mandschurica Meissner
Found in Manchuria, Korea, and the Kazan
region of the Soviet Union. In all important characteristics, including size, this
plant falls between *I. humilis* Georgi (syn. *I.
flavissima* Pallas) and *I. bloudowii*. Unfortunately, this iris is almost impossible to
obtain. Rhizomes do not have stolons. The
scape is 4¼–6¾" (11–17 cm) tall, with
green spathes and bears yellow blossoms.
Number of chromosomes 2n=40.

Iris stolonifera Maximowicz
The slender rhizomes send out stolons
that are up to 8" (20 cm) long. The leaves,
reddish brown as they emerge, are reddish
at the base. The whole plant grows to 15–
24" (40–60 cm). The spathes have a
crimson coloration and are papery at the
tip. Blossoms gape at the top. Standards
and falls are very wavy. The ground color
of the standards is white, with shadings of
light heliotrope, and a broad margin the
color of milk chocolate. The falls also have
a broad milk chocolate margin which
becomes a splendid lilac towards the
center of the blade. The beard is cream-

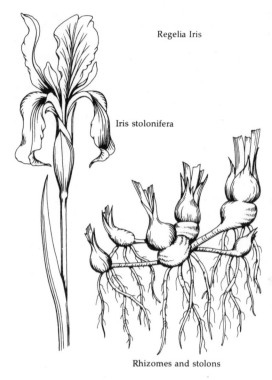

Regelia Iris

Iris stolonifera

Rhizomes and stolons

colored. *I. stolonifera* requires a great deal
of warmth. It and its numerous varieties
make excellent cut flowers. Number of
chromosomes 2n=44 (Tetraploid Regelia
Hybrids).

I. s. var. *leichtlinii* (syn. *I. leichtlinii* Regel).
One of the prettiest of all iris. Its colors are
even more intense than the type species.
The brown color, particularly, stands out.
The tips of the beard hairs are blue, and
sometimes the entire beard is blue.

I. s. 'Zwanenburg Beauty' is a free-
blooming selection with light blue-violet-
bronze blossoms. Nicely ruffled margin.

I. s. 'Vaga Compacta' has brown blossoms shaded with blue and a deep blue
beard. A dwarf of only 11½" (30 cm).

There are other differing clones by the
names *I.* 'Decorated Delight' and *I.* 'Real
Harmony'.

216

Aril Hybrids

Regeliocyclus hybrids

These are relatively well-known iris for warm, sunny locations with perfect drainage. In the beginning the name referred to crosses between *I. korolkowii* and Oncocyclus Iris, but now it is intended for all hybrids between Regelia Iris and Oncocyclus Iris. The basic idea behind the crossbreeding was to get the exotic beauty of many Oncocyclus Iris in a form usable in the garden; Regelia Iris, especially *I. korolkowii,* were easier to grow and hardier. The result of these crosses are attractively curious iris that sometimes inherit the pattern of dots and stripes and sometimes the signal spot of the Oncocyclus Iris as well, even if they do not quite attain the latter's unique quality. Van Tubergen of Haarlem, the world famous Dutch bulb growers, pioneered this hybrid iris breeding.

These distinctive iris hybrids are obviously not plants for everyone. They too require a dry dormant period in the summer. This can be achieved, first by either choosing the correct location or by covering the plant with a piece of glass or plastic from the time it dies back until the fall; or secondly, by lifting the plant with a garden fork after it dies back and storing dry until the end of October or beginning of November, when it is replanted. Experience has shown that the first method is better. The abrupt change from a dry state to having moist soil around it increases the danger of rotting. Regeliocyclus hybrids differ from variety to variety in their sensitivity to moisture.

These iris make very good cut flowers and open nicely in a vase, if cut while in bud. They bloom outdoors somewhat before Tall Bearded Iris. It is only regrettable that they are not more widely available. They are excellent for container culture, in which case their blooming period is advanced. Can easily be transported over long distance in the budding stage.

Varieties often have names from Teutonic, Greek, or Roman mythology, or girl's names. *I.* 'Ancilla', *I.* 'Andromache', *I.* 'Artemis', *I.* 'Barcarole', *I.* 'Bocena', *I.* 'Camilla', *I.* 'Chione', *I.* 'Clara', *I.* 'Clotho', *I.* 'Dardanus', *I.* 'Elvira', *I.* 'Hipermestra', *I.* 'Lucia', *I.* 'Lutetia', *I.* 'Mercurius', *I.* 'Syphide', *I.* 'Teucros', *I.* 'Theseus', *I.* 'Thor', and *I.* 'Vera' are favorites.

These can be referred to as Regeliocyclus or Oncoregelia, depending on whether the mother plant was an Oncocyclus or a Regelia Iris. But since origins are usually obscure, we normally speak only of Regeliocyclus hybrids.

Oncobreds

Both Regelia Iris and Oncocyclus Iris have an aril on their seed, a whitish, fleshy appendage, which surrounded the placental connection to the seed capsule. These Aril Iris have been frequently crossed with Tall and Short Bearded Iris, and enthusiasts of this exotic iris group have joined together in America to form the "International Aril Society". Crosses of Bearded Iris with Regelia or Oncocyclus and vice-versa are known by the collective name "Oncobreds". They bloom about the same time as Tall Bearded Iris. Depending on which groups are combined, they are called Pogoregelia, Pogocyclus, Oncopumila, or Pogoregeliocyclus.

This trend in hybridizing started in 1923, when the breeder William Mohr succeeded in creating a hybrid between a Bearded Iris and an Oncocyclus Iris. It was called *I.* 'William Mohr' after its creator and a whole series of similar hybrids followed.

All have fairly large, roundish blossoms, subdued colors, and a silky sheen. That is the "Onco look". Numerous other Oncobreds were produced, and new ones are being added every year. Details about hybridizing such Oncobreds can be found in this book in the chapter on hybridizing.

Dr. Werckmeister worked for many years with such iris and created, to name only a few, *I.* 'Eulengrund', *I.* 'Kleine Hummel', *I.* 'Zobten' and *I.* 'Natascha'. He even won prizes at the Dwarf Iris Competition in Vienna with these exotic iris, e.g. *I.* 'Nunatakr', *I.* 'Wercilla', and *I.* 'Duftingo'. His triploid, tetraploid, and hexaploid Regeliocyclus hybrids also took honors. Unfortunately we have to admit that all these exotic beauties are very sensitive to summer dampness. Chances are better in regions with hot, rainless summer climates.

The existing Arilbred Hybrids are essentially offspring of the so-called C. G. White hybrids. Because of their origin, they are half Onco and half Tall Bearded Iris, $(10 + 10) + (12 + 12) = 44$ chromosomes. They are not very well suited to the continental climate. Their winter hardiness, which is not adequate for exposed locations, is not the only problem. In moist, cool summers they suffer excessively from rhizome rot and leaf blight; frequently they are a total loss. Besides selecting robust seedlings, Mathes is trying to cross Regeliabreds (hybrids from Regelias and Tall Bearded Iris), which have a similar structure to those of the C. G. White hybrids, $(11 + 11) + (12 + 12) = 46$ chromosomes, in order to improve their resistance. In addition, he thinks it makes sense to change the Eupogon part of the Arilbreds by incorporating 12-chromosome wild species, which have not been used yet. Naturally this is a lengthy process.

At the moment the only hope for cooler climates is that suitable Oncobreds will be produced. But genuine iris lovers will not spare any effort to grow these exotic plants in their gardens, no matter how difficult it is. In regions that are climatically unfavorable, a cold frame is still the best method. They can then be protected from the rain by being covered with a glass sash. But good air circulation has to be provided.

Section Hexapogon
Subsection Pseudoregelia

Pseudoregelia Iris come from the Himalayas and are scattered throughout vast areas of Central Asia. They occur at high elevations, in open, grassy meadows above timberline.

In their native habitat the plants are exposed to considerable temperature fluctuations. From July to September they are bathed in rain and fog. These conditions should not be duplicated in the garden. There the soil should be light but fertile. Good drainage is important, since in the wild they usually grow on gravelly slopes. Pseudoregelias grow fairly slowly in the garden, unlike their growth in nature. In the spring they should receive ample water and in summer they have to be kept fairly dry. It's been observed that after a hot summer, they flower abundantly the following year. No winter protection is necessary, if the leaves have not sprouted in the fall. These iris must remain plants for specialists, however, and cannot really become permanent features in our gardens.

Rhizomes are very short and gnarled, without stolons. Blossoms appear before the linear leaves are fully developed. Beard along the mid-line of the falls. The aril is very small.

Iris goniocarpa Baker

This iris, occurring in Sikkim, southwest China, Tibet, and in the eastern Himalayas, grows at elevations as high as 13,120–16,400 ft (4000–5000 m) in the Chumbi Mountains and in Nepal. It grows in isolated clusters between stunted trees and shrubs and in open birch groves. Within its large range, *I. goniocarpa* is somewhat variable. It is slimmer than *I. kamaonensis* and *I. hookeriana*, has narrower leaves and a somewhat longer scape (about 11½'' or 30 cm tall) that bears only one blossom. In general it is a delicate plant. The blossom is blue-violet to mallow, with dark spots and a white beard. The blossoms seem paler than those of *I. kamaonensis* or *I. hookeriana*. The falls and the standards are both held more horizontally, giving the plant its characteristic appearance. Blooms in May-June. Rarely cultivated.

Iris hookeriana Foster

Native to the northeastern Himalayas, in Tibet and Kashmir up to elevations of 9,800–13,120 ft (3000–4000 m). It grows in large clumps on open mountain slopes. Morphologically it has much in common with *I. kamaonensis*, though the latter grows in eastern regions. *I. hookeriana* has 2 short-stemmed blossoms per stalk and is a strong plant. The blossoms are relatively large. Colors range from pure white, with faintly grayish to lilac markings, to blue-violet and reddish purple. The falls are strikingly speckled in somewhat darker tones. The blossoms have a delightful fragrance. The foliage is not as tall as the blossoms when buds open, but later reaches a height of 11½–13'' (30–35 cm). Seldom cultivated. A few iris enthusiasts in England have grown it successfully. They let the rhizomes mature fully in the summer so that the iris produces its buds late in the spring and thus escapes late frosts. In the wild it blooms in May-June.

Iris kamaonensis Wallich

Wallich named this plant after the Kamao district in the Himalayas, its primary range. It can be considered the eastern counterpart to *I. hookeriana*. At 13,120 ft (4000 m) in Nepal, large areas are covered with this iris. When they are in bloom, the hills are literally colored mallow and lilac. The scapes are only about 2½'' (6 cm) long, so plants appear almost stemless. Scapes bear 1–2 blossoms and the blossoms are 2–2½'' (5–6 cm) in diameter. The perianth tube is longer than that of *I. hookeriana* and marks the difference between the two. When the plant is in bloom, the leaves are about 4–6'' (10–15 cm) long, but later reach a length of 17–20'' (45–50 cm). They die back in mid-summer. Blossoms are mallow-lilac, with dark purple veins and spots; the beard is white. Flowers have a sweet fragrance. The rhizome has a red skin. Plants grow rapidly in the wild, but quite slowly in cultivation. This is an interesting iris, which has frequently been used in hybridizing, but without any great success. Blossoms in May. Number of chromosomes 2n=22.

Iris potaninii Maximowicz

This iris used to belong to the Subsection Regelia. It is very similar to *I. tigridia. I. potaninii* occurs over vast areas, but never in large numbers: Altai, Dahuria, Mongolia, western China, northern and central Tibet. *I. potaninii* is characterized by its strong, yellow blossom color. It has no scent. The scape is only 2–2¾'' (5–7 cm) long and bears only one blossom. It needs dry, warm soil. Unfortunately, it is almost unobtainable.

Iris sikkimensis Dykes

Whether this iris, which is found in Sikkim as its name implies, is a genuine species, is often questioned. It was described and illustrated by Dykes. Some writers suspect that it is a hybrid between *I. kamaonensis* and *I. hookeriana*. The scapes are 4–6" (10–15 cm) long. The leaves are narrower than those of *I. hookeriana* and not as long and strong as those of *I. kamaonensis*. *I. sikkimensis* has 2–3 blossoms, which are violet and have dark spots. The standards are gaping; the beard is white with orange tips. Blooming period is in May.

Iris tigridia Bunge
This species also formerly belonged to the Subsection Regelia. It is not common, but quite widespread: Altai, Dahuria, Manchuria, eastern Siberia. The rhizomes are compact. The blossoms are the same size as *I. pumila*, but are very different in form. The standards are not closed, but are turned outward. The flower is usually various shades of blue, but there are plants with purple and yellow blossoms. The scape is about 1⅛–3" (3–8 cm) tall and bears one blossom. The pigmentation forms small spots on the petals, similar to those of *I. kamaonensis*. The blossoms have a distinctive fragrance. The leaves are heavily ribbed. The plant needs full sun

and good drainage. Unfortunately, it is almost unobtainable.

Section Hexapogon
Subsection Oncocyclus

Regarding nomenclature and systematics, this group is undoubtedly the most complicated of the entire field of iris. As Professor Rodionenko has noted, even Dykes, who was probably among the greatest iris authorities, had difficulties with Onococyclus Iris. There are many reasons for this. The individual species cannot be definitely distinguished in herbariums. Cultivating them in more northern regions is very difficult, making comparisons of growing plants nearly impossible. Besides, only a few species can be obtained, and raising them from seed is an extremely lengthy process. Moreover, ranges of these iris often overlap in the wild, the result being that there is a large number of natural hybrids which were often described as true species by researchers and collectors. It is necessary to mention this, because the following account undoubtedly contains errors and

This plate joins two very different groups, dwarf Spuria and Regelia iris, but both prefer a dry location.

Top left: Iris kerneriana may require a long time to become established. It does not transplant readily; also a patient wait is required during the long period from seedling to first flower. Once established, this, the only yellow dwarf spuria, is a beautiful species and looks good in a spacious rock garden.

Top right: Iris pontica (Iris humilis in gardens), with blossoms similar to the plum-scented iris,

deeply hidden among its foliage. It is more to be appreciated for its decorative foliage in the garden. Blossoms used in small vases are also nothing to scoff at.

Bottom right and left: Iris korolkowii is a regelia iris that is not completely hardy in regions with harsher climates. Dampness in winter rather than the cold is what does the damage. Rhizomes can be lifted in early summer after the plant has died back and then replanted in November. The genuine species (right) with brown coloring is rarer than the violet variety, Iris korolkowii var. violacea (left).

gaps, although it is based on my experience with Oncocyclus Iris, on careful studies of the source material, and, therefore, on most known facts.

The Oncocyclus is native to the Near East, especially the Caucasus region, eastern Turkey, Syria, Lebanon, and Israel to the Negev Desert. In the east it is found in Iraq, Iran, and Afghanistan. *I. acutiloba* var. *lineolata* even penetrates into central Asia. Specific locations are listed under the individual species.

These are difficult to cultivate because of climate. In their native regions, hot summers with little or no precipitation prevail. Autumn and spring are very rainy, and the winter is relatively mild (at least so far as the southern species is concerned), with very little precipitation. This pattern differs slightly for each species, but generally speaking, it fits all Oncocyclus Iris. The northern group from the Caucasus and eastern Turkey is, of course, more unaffected by summer rains than the southern group, as for example, *I. atrofusca* from the Negev Desert. They do not have any particular soil requirements beyond fast drainage. In the wild they often grow in very barren soil, which naturally affects the size of the plant. But typical growing sites always are well drained.

Oncocyclus Iris, with their attractive blossoms, are among the most beautiful plant species. Unfortunately, these beauties are very difficult to grow at our latitudes, but the effort is worth it. The most common species, *I. susiana*, also known as Lady in Mourning, grows satisfactorily in warm, protected locations with good drainage, particularly in the wine producing regions where summers are hot and sunny. But what they need more than anything is protection from summer rains. There are various ways of doing this.

Cultivation in a cold frame is generally recommended. The rhizomes should be planted as late as possible, from the end of October to the beginning of November, depending on the climate. The plant sprouts too vigorously if planted earlier, and the leaves will suffer frost damage. The frame should be covered before any severe frost or heavy snowfall occurs. This protection should be removed at about the beginning of March. At this point Oncocyclus Iris need the same precipitation they receive in their native habitat; if the spring is dry, they should be watered. The plants turn yellow and die back soon after they bloom. The frames are then covered with glass sashes again until late fall, allowing, however, for good ventilation (blocks of wood between frame and sash). In cold climates, put dry peat over the plants in winter, and remove the mulch as growth begins. A cold frame made of

Iris spuria Cultivars.

Top left: The falls of the new cultivars are increasingly wider and more attractive. Shown here 'Thrush Song', a proven cultivar.
Top right: 'Bronce Spur', one of the old cultivars which still has value in the garden. The difference between this and the newer form to the left can be clearly seen.
Below: A late blooming period make spuria iris, also called steppe iris, a valuable garden plant. They love the sun.

The oncocyclus iris takes many forms.

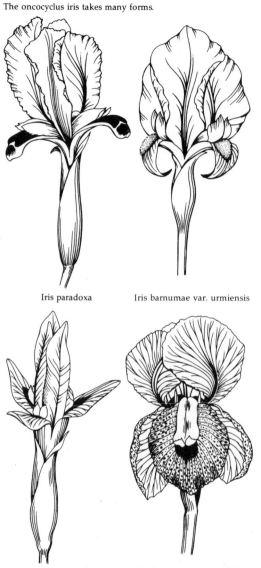

Iris paradoxa   Iris barnumae var. urmiensis

Iris acutiloba var. lineolata   Iris iberica ssp. elegantissima
(syn. Iris ewbankiana)

plexiglass with a honeycomb pattern works well as a substitute for the more expensive glass sash.

The second method is to lift the rhizomes after they die back and subject them to a temperature treatment of 75°F (+23 C) as they do at van Tubergen, the famous specialty nursery. They should be replanted again in late autumn.

The plants should be fertilized occasionally with horn meal or bone meal to keep them growing well. Because of their tuberous, compact rhizomes, they do not establish quickly when divided. Propagation from seed is a very lengthy process, but often the only method available if rhizomes cannot be obtained or are too expensive. Growing plants from seed has advantages. One gets virus-free plants—and Oncocyclus are particularly virus prone. "Lady in Mourning", for instance, can almost never be obtained free of virus. Oncocyclus seed cannot be stimulated by the cutting method. So one has to wait and be patient. Hardly more than 30% germinate in the second or third year. A few seeds germinate every year. I have seen seeds lie dormant for seven years before they decided to sprout. Quicker results can be obtained by embryo culture. The seedlings grow rather quickly and can be transplanted into the seedling bed or deep pots after the fourth leaf appears.

The following method has been tried in England. With some of the more troublesome species from Israel, lift rhizomes from June to October to let them cure sufficiently. Manage the northern species as follows. Construct of brick a raised bed about 24–35" (60–90 cm) high and fill as follows: a layer about 6" (15 cm) deep of coarse drainage material, such as broken brick, small pieces of styrofoam, slag, gravel, etc.; an intermediate layer of ¾–1⅛" (2–3 cm) of dried fern, heather tops, or partially rotted leaf mold; next a layer about 8½–9" (20–25 cm) thick, consisting of loam, well-rotted compost, and well-rotted steer manure all thoroughly mixed. The actual growing medium is a heavy mixture—about 9–11½" (25–30 cm) thick—of 2 parts loam (as sterile as possible) to 2 parts crushed stone about ¼" (6 mm) in diameter. In the south of England a third part of peat is added.

Plant this bed (in October). Finally topdress it 1½" (4 cm) deep with crushed limestone, granite, or gravel. This arrangement prevents quick changes in temperature, helps store warmth during the dormant period, and anchors the rhizomes. Light is important at all times of the year, hence the covering sash must be glazed. Even with this English method, the plants are watered from October onward so that the soil does not dry out during the winter. At the end of March additional watering is stopped and at the end of May the plants are protected with the sash from receiving any moisture at all. When Oncocyclus Iris are planted, care should be taken that the more tender species are planted at the edge of the raised bed, next to the brick framework, since the soil dries more quickly there than in the middle of the bed. Good ventilation is important even when the plants are dormant. The bed should never be tightly covered by sash or polyethylene! Iris should be transplanted every 2 or 3 years. However, the offsets cannot be planted again immediately. The cuts or breaks first have to dry and callus, and perhaps should even be disinfected.

No matter how one proceeds, the two things to bear in mind are: 1) a long, warm summer domancy so the rhizomes can fully cure, and 2) absolutely perfect drainage.

Unlike Regelia Iris, with their sometimes widespreading rhizomes, the rhizomes of Oncocyclus Iris are tuberous-compact, so they are much more difficult to divide. Another common Onco feature is one blossom on every scape. Normally, the falls have a darker zone called the "Onco-spot". Like the other Aril species,

the seeds have an aril. Other features are the round, unridged spathes, and leaves that are usually crescent-shaped. All the Oncocyclus Iris investigated have a chromosome count 2n=20.

Since this subsection is very extensive, in the U.S. it has been subdivided into groups. Some of the species listed, however, do not currently have individual species status, a result of recent research. Since scientists will never all agree about this matter, I shall repeat this division, despite some misgivings.

Acutiloba group: *I. acutiloba* C. A. Meyer, *I. ewbankiana* Foster, *I. grossheimi* Woronow, *I. lineolata* Grossh., *I. schelkownikowii* Fom.

Iberica group: *I. iberica* Hofmann, *I. camillae* Grossh., *I. lycotis* Woronow

Sari group: *I. sari* Schott, *I. maculata* Baker, *I. lupina* Foster

Polakii group: *I. polakii* Stapf, *I. barnumae* Foster et Baker, *I. demavendica* Bornm., *I. mariae* Barb., *I. nigricans* Dinsm., *I. urmiensis* Hoog

Susiana group: *I. susiana* L., *I. basaltica* Dinsm., *I. cedrettii* Dinsm. ex Chaudhary, *I. damascena* Mouterde, *I. hermona* Dinsm., *I. kirkwoodii* Chaudhary, *I. sofarana* Foster, *I. westii* Dinsm., *I. yebrudii* Dinsm. ex Chaudhary

Atropurpurea group: *I. atropurpurea* Baker, *I. antilibonatica* Dinsm., *I. auranitica* Dinsm., *I. bostrensis* Mouterde

Haynei group: *I. haynei* Baker, *I. atrofusca* Baker, *I. jordana* Dinsm.

Species without group classification: *I. bismarckiana* Damm., *I. gatesii* Foster, *I. lortetii* Barb., *I. meda* Stapf, *I. paradoxa* Steven

Iris acutiloba C. A. Meyer

This dwarf iris is found in the Caucasus north of the Kura River and in Dagestan. It is very rarely cultivated. The true species has standards that are always longer than the falls, and the latter have two spots, one in the middle of the blade, another near the tip. Both falls and standards have dark violet veining on a cream-colored to bright violet ground. The falls have a brown beard. In general, the blossoms of this small plant render a somber, batlike effect. This iris has varying descriptions in the literature, probably due in part to the many varieties that exist, some of which are:

I. acutiloba C. A. M. var. *typica* Traut.
I. acutiloba C. A. M. var. *bimaculata* Fomin
I. fomini Woronow
These are all synonyms for various other epithets.

Iris acutiloba C. A. Mey. var. *lineolata* Trautv. Synonyms: *I. ewbankiana* Foster, *I. lineolata* (Trautv.) Grossheim

A very attractive, small plant from Turkmenia with zebra-like stripes, and blossoms the shape of a pointed arch. *I. acutiloba* var. *lineolata* is grown in the Ashkabad Botanical Gardens. Height of the plant 9–11½" (25–30 cm); a clump in the wild produces 5–10 blossoms. In the garden the blossoms have a diameter of almost 4" (10 cm). The background color is white to straw-yellow, with a striking pattern of brownish, forked veins, dots, and lines. There are also forms with reddish and violet veins.

Iris antilibanotica Dinsmore
Found in the Anti Lebanon Mountains above Bludan, where it grows at elevations of 6,500 ft (2000 m). Rarely cultivated. The rhizomes are unusually narrow, the leaves are small and crescent-shaped. The blossom is relatively large for the size of the plant. The standards are violet, the falls much lighter, with warm shading. The Onco-spot just below the yellow beard is narrow and black.

Iris atrofusca Baker
An Oncocyclus Iris from Israel, growing in the Negev Desert and the Judean wilderness. In Judea it is found at elevations of 985–1,640 ft (300–500 m). The soil there is loess, with a high content of lime. It is a considerably larger plant than *I. atropurpurea*, which is also found in Israel, growing to 24" (60 cm) tall with a blossom diameter of 8" (20 cm). The rhizomes are relatively large, the leaves, which stand characteristically erect, are a beautiful bright yellow-green color. The blossoms are extremely variable in the wild. They are usually a beautiful deep brown that looks like polished wood or a freshly peeled horse-chestnut (Kenneth Bastow). Standards and falls are similar. The spot on the falls is black-brown, but there are specimens with a yellow spot.

Iris atropurpurea Baker
Native to Israel, but also pushes into Syria, usually at elevations of 330 ft (100 m). It grows mainly in nutrient poor, sandy loam soil with little lime. Mostly on the coast in the "citrus belt".

Unlike the other Oncocyclus Iris, *I. atropurpurea* often sends out stolons, though they are not as developed as those of *I. nazarena*. There are, however, also plants that do not send out stolons at all, which were described as var. *eggeri* Dinsm.; this variety has broader, more upright foliage, in contrast to the small, crescent-shaped leaves of the typical species.

The varieties of *I. atropurpurea* have blossoms in almost every shade of dark brown, violet, and near-black. Yet in spite of these somber colors, the flowers are strangely appealing, probably because the falls reflect so much light. The diameter of the blossom is 4" (10 cm), the total height of the scape is 28" (70 cm). Plants with yellowish blossoms have also been found. *I. atropurpurea* var. *eggerii*, mentioned above, is slightly brown, but lacks the silky sheen of the typical form; it often has a yellow-green Onco-spot.

Iris auranitica Dinsmore

This iris occurs in only a very limited area, in volcanic lava on Jabal ad Duruz at the edge of the Syrian Desert. This Oncocyclus Iris has large, fragrant, golden yellow blossoms covered with brown dots. The signal spot varies in form and size. Plants from Tell Qouleib are partly reddish. Mouterde called a golden yellow form without any markings *I. auranitica* var. *unicolor*. *I. auranitica* is not easy to grow, its rhizomes being very sensitive to dampness.

Iris barnumae Foster et Baker

This iris was first described from the vicinity of Van, Turkey, where it grows over a large area. It is a dwarf iris with blossoms more reddish violet in color than *I. demavendica*. The blossom is small and fragrant. As with *I. demavendica*, the falls are somewhat darker than the standards; the veins are darker still. The crest is brownish yellow (unlike *I. demavendica*). The beard is a rich yellow, pale yellow, or entirely white, and the hairs are always black tipped. There is a narrow signal spot at the end of the beard. The rhizomes send out more numerous stolons than other Oncos. But here, too, there are forms that do not send out stolons. It has been proposed that *I. barnumae* be considered a variety of the similar *I. polakii* (with a black beard). This question still awaits clarification.

Iris barnumae var. *urmiensis* (Hoog) Dykes Dykes
Synonym: *I. urmiensis* Hoog

This pretty iris was found near the Lake of Urmiah, Iran. Its introduction was purely accidental. It is quite commonly cultivated. The blossom is yellow, the standards somewhat paler than the falls, the signal spot a rich dark yellow. The beard is orange-yellow. The Onco is fragrant. It is often described in the literature as a variety of *I. barnumae* or of *I. polakii*. In 1901 an *I. chrysantha* Baker was described, but since then it has not been grown and is no longer collected. It was probably a large-blossomed *I. barnumae* var. *urmiensis*.

Iris barnumae var. *zenobiae* (Fost. et Bak.) Mouterde
Synonym: *I. zenobiae* Mouterde

A native of Syria, it can be found from Damascus to Palmyra to Aleppo, but also in Tell Chiane. This plant varies greatly in size. The Tell Chiane plants are the largest, the others smaller. The most common color is dark violet with still darker veins. The crests are more bronze-colored than the petals. The beard is yellow with black tips, ending in a yellow line which leads to a round or heart-shaped, shiny black signal spot. The blossoms are fragrant. The plants from around Palmyra send out stolons. The plants from Tell Chiane have stockier rhizomes with many lateral growths. Plants with pinkish white blossoms and yellow blossoms are reported.

Iris bismarckiana (Damman) Regel
Synonyms: *I. hermona* Dinsmore, *I. nazarena* Foster

I. bismarckiana, *I. hermona*, and *I. nazarena* were recently combined into the species *I. bismarckiana*. It was a rather risky undertaking, as they are quite different morphologically.

I. bismarckiana, found in Jordan and in Lebanon, does not send out stolons and is difficult to cultivate. The species known up to now as *I. hermona* comes from Mount

Hermon, where it grows in heavy basaltic soil. The falls are extremely wide and strongly recurved. Their ground color is gray and white with a raised, dark purple spot. Stout scapes, 30–35" (80–90 cm) tall, bear blossoms that may reach a diameter of 8½" (22 cm). The leaves are slender, erect, and bluish green. The rhizomes are crowded. This species readily sets seed. The form known as *I. nazarena* sends out stolons similar to those of Regelia Iris. It grows in Palestine in red clay soil mixed with weathered basalt, at elevations of about 985–1,640 ft. (300–500 m). The single 7" (18 cm) large blossoms have roundish, white standards with blue veins and dots. The falls are strongly recurved and are creamy yellow with brown dots and with an almost black signal spot. Overall height about 20" (50 cm). This form sets seed poorly.

Iris bostrensis Mouterde

Found on Jabalad Duruz, Hamman (Syria), this iris was described and introduced mostly by Pere Mouterde and Dr. Werckmeister. According to their description, the plant is similar to a large *I. barnumae* var. *zenobiae*, but with smaller blossoms, flowers with dark brownish purple veins and markings on a yellow ground. The beard is a magnificent yellow with purple tips. The crests are the same color as the blossoms, but paler. The spathes are wider than those of *I. barnumae* var. *zenobiae*, dotted and more flaring.

Iris camillae Grossheim

Found only in the Soviet Union, in eastern Transcaucasia and Azerbaidzhan. Typically found near the dried up lake of Kanzan-gel. The falls are pale yellow or bluish violet. This color data goes back to the first description of this species and omits the many colors that were later dis-covered. *Flora of the Caucasus*, Part II (1940) mentions 15 different shades of color. Thus there are the forms *lutea*, pale yellow; *coerula*, pale blue; and *sulphurea*, showy golden yellow falls. The form *pallida* has pure white standards and falls heavily sprinkled with brown and a striking, dark violet spot. The form *spectabilis* has cream-colored falls with chocolate brown veins. The falls of the form *speciosissima* are bronze-colored with beautiful dark veins, a splendid yellow beard, and an almost black spot. If this species were to be further researched, the number of colors would undoubtedly increase. In the area of Kazan-gel *I. camillae* grows together with the large *I. iberica,* and the two species cross easily.

Iris cedretti Dinsmore ex Chaudhary

Native habitat is Lebanon. The falls have a white ground, spotted and veined with a delicate maroon or purple-maroon. The signal spot is a glowing dark purple maroon, beard with long pink-purple or brown hairs. The standards are likewise subtly maroon-spotted and -veined on a white base.

Iris damascena Mouterde

This is a local, very low-growing, gray *I. sofarana* type, found in Syria. The falls have grayish white spots and purple-violet veins. The signal spot is dark; the standards have very few dots.

Iris demavendica Bornmuller

Synonym: *I. acutiloba* var. *demavendica*

A dwarf Oncocyclus Iris found in the Elburs, in northern Iran. It has relatively large blossoms of various shades of violet, with veins always the same color but a shade darker. The beard is pale yellow or white and ends in a narrow tongue on the falls which are dotted and recurved. The blossoms have a pleasant fragrance. Plants introduced into English gardens have proven to be strong growers.

Iris elizabethae Siehe
Native to Turkey. Yellow-ground blossoms with violet-brown veins. Purple-red signal spot and yellow beard.

Iris gatesii Foster
The original plant comes from Mardin in northeastern Iraq. This attractive plant is now frequently for sale, so it will undoubtedly become more common in gardens. A well-grown blossom can reach diameters of 8" (20 cm) or more; the stem has a height of 18–24" (45–60 cm). The original plant has a cream-white ground with delicate violet veins and dots and a brownish signal spot. The overall impression is pearl-gray. Dykes called this plant "the prince of iris". *I. gatesii* represents only itself and does not belong to any of the other group of Oncos which often interbreed. It is thought to be a link between the Oncos found in Turkey and Iran and those found in Lebanon, Jordan, and western Syria. Many writers think that *I. basaltica* Dinsmore is a form of *I. gatesii.*

Iris grossheimii Woronow
This plant, which is found in what is today the region of Nakhichevan USSR, has relatively large blossoms, falls 2" (5 cm) long, ¾" (2 cm) wide, with a large black-brown signal spot. The standards are markedly larger. Blossoms are wine-red to dark brown, with dark cinnamon-brown veins. This plant probably has a hybrid origin. In Tiflis, botanist G. N. Matweew crossed *I. lineolata* with *I. lycotis* and produced a hybrid that corresponded in all essential features to *I. grossheimi.*

Iris haynei Baker
Synonym: *I. biggerii* Dinsmore
As Dr. Werckmeister has written, there is a great deal of confusion between *I. haynei, I. atrofusca,* and *I. atropurpurea.* Today only the large-blossomed type from Mt. Gilboa (Israel) can be called *I. haynei.* It is 28" (70 cm) tall when blooming. Pure white specimens also grow where it is found. The plants have large, ruffled, violet blossoms (8" or 20 cm in diameter). They are similar in form to *I. auranitica* and are covered with close veination and small dots. In the wild they grow in red clay soil.

Iris heylandiana Boiss. et Reut.
Synonym: *I. maculata* Baker?
Found in the Kurdish area of southeastern Turkey and in Iraq at elevations of 3,900–9,800 ft. (1200–3000 m). Usually on dry slopes, mostly on limestone rocks. The blossoms have a whitish ground; heavily dotted and veined in a brownish violet color. The signal spot is dark brown. The beard is whitish or yellowish. In *Flora Iranica, I. gatesii* is used as a synonymous description for *I. heylandiana.* I do not agree with this, although they are closely related.

Iris helenae Barbey see Iris mariae

Iris iberica Hoffmann
A very attractive, widespread Oncocyclus Iris. It is found in eastern Turkey, eastern Transcaucasia (environs of Tiflis), Armenia, Iran. It is probably one of the most beautiful iris species. The standards and falls are of equal or almost equal size, in contrast to those of *I. iberica* ssp. *elegantissima.* The standards of the latter are usually smoky yellow, unlike *I. iberica,* which has bluish-veined or pure white standards. The true *I. iberica* grows to 18–24" (45–60 cm).

Because of its wide range, several local

forms obviously occur. For example, *I. iberica* var. *typica* (Gawr.), which is somewhat lower-growing, and *I. iberica* var. *robusta* (Sosn.). See also *I. elegantissima*.

Iris iberica ssp. *elegantissima* (Sosn.) Fedt. et Takht

Synonym: *I. elegantissima* Sosnowsky

This iris was described in 1915 and can be called a more southern variety of *I. iberica*. This plant occurs in the Kars region. North of Erxerum, Turkey, Synge found plants not only with a smoky ground color, as described in the literature, but also some with white standards and still others with heavy veining. The standards of *I. iberica* ssp. *elegantissima* are longer and wider than the falls, unlike those of *I. iberica*, which are about equal. It is not disputed that *I. iberica* ssp. *elegantissima* has a much greater variety of colors than *I. sibirica* (3 are described, 7 found in the wild). The botanist S. G. Tamaenskian, who studied *I. iberica* ssp. *elegantissima* in the area of Erewan, found numerous color variants. The colors of the standards ranged from white to pale blue, cream, pale sulfur yellow to bright lemon yellow. He also found forms with yellow standards, the existence of which several authors had questioned. The form *splendens*, with blossoms of 6½–7″ (17–18 cm), is particularly noteworthy.

I. iberica ssp. *elegantissima* is a rewarding iris, if cultivated according to normal methods. It stays very short, with somewhat elongated, spoon-shaped falls. The standards are dull yellowish white with faint veining. The brown falls are coverd with a finely meshed network of dark veins. The bluish green leaves are extremely crescent-shaped. Height 6″ (15 cm), blossoms at the beginning of June.

Iris iberica ssp. *lycotis* (Woron.) Takht

Synonym: *I. lycotis* Woronow

Grows in the southern Transcaucasian Oncocyclus region. The standards are longer than the falls and stand erect like those of *I. iberica*. The falls are held laterally outwards and are often shaped like pointed ears which is why they are called Wolf's Ears in their native country. Standards and falls are purple-violet, thickly covered with a network of dark veins. Eight color variants of this species have been described, among them a cherry red one and another with an ornamental

Tall Spuria iris. Even the species, not influenced by breeding, makes an ornamental garden plant with stately foliage as a decorative element even outside the blooming period, especially when their main requirements are met: full sun and rich soil.

Top left: Iris spuria var. subbarbata. This is the species which gives the entire group its name. Shown is perhaps the most beautiful variety; not only its elegant growth habit, but its beautiful blue color is striking. It grows natively around Neusiedler Lake.

Top right: Iris crocea comes from Kashmir. It is rare today in the wild, but can always be seen in or near settlements. Its deep yellow blossoms are an asset to the garden. Specimens in nurseries are unfortunately not always genuine.
Bottom left: Iris spuria 'Alba'. The albino form of the species is vigorous and completes the effect by its blossom color.
Bottom right: Iris notha also comes from Kashmir and from the southern Soviet Union. Its habit is not as rigidly erect as similar related plants. The bloomstalks change direction slightly from node to node. The blossom is elegant in form and a beautiful blue color.

reticulum and veins. Size of the falls 2 ×
2½" (5 × 6 cm) of the standards 2½ × 2¾"
(6 × 7 cm). *I. lycotis* can be found at elevations of more than 6,500 ft. (2000 m). The
diameter of a cultivated blossom is 6¼–8"
(16–20 cm). It has been reported from
Tiflis that they have a very long blooming
period (up to 50 days).

Iris jordana Dinsmore
Synonym: *I. hauranensis* Dinsmore

An indefinite species. According to
Dinsmore, it grows in the Jordan Valley
"below sea level". Similar to *I. haynei*. The
rhizomes form dense clumps. Upright
foliage surrounds a scape about 24" (60
cm) tall. The diameter of the blossom is 6"
(15 cm); they are brownish-crimson or
reddish, purple-red signal spot, yellow
beard on a white background. The familiar
type known as *I. hauranensis* has more
purplish blossoms and a light-colored
signal spot, which is striped. The beard is
white with purple tips. The beard of the
genuine *I. jordana* is long and yellow
against a white ground.

Iris kasruwana Dinsmore
Very similar to *I. susiana* f. *sofarana*. Chief
difference is the darker coloring and more
beautiful markings on the blossom. P.
Mouterde described it as a form of *I.
sofarana* (*I. susiana* f. *sofarana*), usually
having a short scape, with standards and
falls the same color and not as two-toned
as *I. susiana* f. *sofarana*.

Iris kirkwoodii Chaudhary
Native to Syria. The falls have a whitish or
pale green ground, with faint, dark purple-
violet veins and dots. The hairs of the
beard are rust or maroon-purple. The
standards are pale light blue, spotted and
veined with blue-violet.

Iris lortetii Barbey
A beautiful Oncocylus Iris. Found at elevations of 985–1,640 ft. (300–500 m) on the
Israel-Lebanon border in upper Galilee.
The overall impression of the blossom is
pink-white. The large standards are always
pure white and covered with thin, violet
veins. The severely recurved falls have a

Moisture loving iris.

**Top left: Iris wilsonii, one of the two yellow Iris
sibirica-related species with 40 chromosomes.
Iris wilsonii has standards that turn outward at an
angle, whereas those of the other, iris forrestii,
stand straight up. They prefer a somewhat moist
soil, but not standing water.**
**Top right: Iris laevigata must stand in water or in
boggy soil, unlike Iris kaempferi, which prefers
water but can also be found in drier places. There
is a whole series of forms, of which Iris laevigata
'Rose Queen' has a particularly attractive color.
Below: White form of Iris laevigata, which has
been somewhat influenced by breeding. Because
it crosses so easily with Iris kaempferi, there are
many intermediate forms. Shown here between
marsh forget-me-nots and marsh marigolds.**

yellow ground and are faintly dotted with crimson; in the center of each is a dark red spot. This Oncocyclus species has one of the largest blossoms (diameter 8" or 20 cm) and blooms the latest. *I. samariae* Dinsm. is a very similar plant with a larger, more crinkled blossom, which looks pinker overall. *I. lortetii* grows to about 28" (70 cm). It is probably extinct in the wild, but is still available in nurseries.

Iris lupina Foster (=*I. sari* on the market) Occurs over a fairly large area of Turkey. It varies greatly in color and form. In general the plant and its blossoms are medium-sized, always having a yellowish ground color and a whitish yellow or yellow beard. The standards are usually more or less rounded, the falls narrower and lanceolate with a blunt tip. The signal spot is always very striking, ranging from green to violet, violet-brown, brown, brown-red to shades of almost black. The entire blossom is covered with delicate violet dots and gaudy veins and spots, giving the blossom a generally bizarre appearance. Standards and falls usually have an exceptionally wavy margin; the falls are recurved to the signal spot. The crests are also very striking. Many forms have a fragrant honey-like scent.

Iris manissadijanii Freyn
This iris is found in Turkey and is probably identical to *I. lupina.*

Iris mariae Barbey
Synonym: *I. helenae* Barbey
This is the southernmost iris, growing in sandy soils, sometimes mixed with loess, in the desert regions of the Negev between Egypt and Palestine and on the Sinai Peninsula. Average elevation about 330 ft. (100 m). It is one of the most dwarf-like species of the Oncocyclus Iris. The rhi-

zomes are surprisingly large; the scanty foliage is crescent-shaped. The blossoms vary from pink to lilac and violet. The falls have a black-violet signal spot in the center of the dotted background. The standards are significantly larger than the falls; the beard is deep purple. *I. mariae* grows and blooms much earlier than many other Oncocyclus Iris and correspondingly longer. In cultivation, it reaches a height of up to 20" (50 cm) with a blossom diameter of 6" (15 cm)

Iris meda Stapf
Found in Iran and Iraq. A violet or yellow dwarf-like iris with a yellow beard. The narrow petals, the thick, almost linear yellow beard, and the combination of striking, parallel veins running to the middle of the standards are characteristic of *I. meda.* The dark signal spot is very conspicuous. The standards stand more or less erect; the falls are slightly recurved. Plant collectors have recently discovered somewhat different forms. Usually found in soils with a high clay content.

Iris medwedewii Fomin
Probably a synonym of *I. paradoxa* var. *coshab.* For details see under the latter.

Iris nigricans Dinsmore
It grows in red clay soils on the east bank of the Dead Sea in Jordan between the desert and agricultural lands. Appears difficult to grow and dies off easily. Slender rhizomes and narrow, gray-green, crescent-shaped foliage. The color of the blossom varies, but the pure black forms that gave the plant its name are very rare. The beard is purple-black on a white base. It grows to 8–11½" (20–30 cm); the diameter of the blossom is 4½–6¼" (12–16 cm).

Iris paradoxa Steven

An easily identifiable dwarf Oncocyclus Iris, found in southern and eastern Transcaucasia, Armenia, and Iran. Its chief characteristic is the unusual difference in size between standards and falls. The shortened, dark purple falls, held horizontally, are always covered with a dense, black beard. They are more than ½" (1.3 cm) wide and have a very good substance, in contrast to the large, delicate standards. The standards of the typical form found in southern and eastern Transcaucasia always have a violet sheen, but vary in size and shape.

There are different forms, such as *I.p. atrata, I.p. mirabilis,* and others. *I. paradoxa* var. *coshab* occurs over a wide range in southeastern Turkey and northwestern Iran. It is more common in gardens than the original form. It was first found near Coshab in Turkey, after which it is named. The Russian form, which is not very different in appearance from the southern plants, was described as *I. medwedewii.* This form always has pure white standards ornamentally adorned with heavy blue-violet veins and an elongated signal spot. A form with unveined, white standards and a narrow, butter-colored spot at the tip of the haft is listed. It is supposed to be found, though it rarely is, among clusters of *I. paradoxa* var. *coshab.*

Iris petrana Dinsmore

Even more rarely cultivated than *I. nigricans,* which it strongly resembles. Its range lies further south than *I. nigricans.* It is smaller than the latter and has smaller, fragrant blossoms. Found in rather dry areas, especially near Petra in Jordan.

Iris polakii Stapf

This is a small plant that grows in Iranian Kurdistan. It has violet blossoms of varying shades. As with *I. barnumae,* the crests are a different color than the standards and falls. The latter have unusual overtones of bronze and orange. The beard is black. The typical form has an oval, black signal spot at each side of the end of the beard. This form, however, is probably not now in cultivation. Forms without signal spots or with only one are more common. Three main forms with overlapping ranges are listed. The form found mainly in the northern region around Khoi is bronze-red-purple, 8–9¼" (20–26 cm) tall, with spherical blossoms over 2½–3" (5–7.9 cm) in diameter. A smaller, dark violet form tinted with bronze, can be found at the northern corner of Lake Rezaieh. The more southern form, found near Hamadan, is slimmer and paler violet. It hybridizes in many parts of Kurdistan with *I. meda.*

Iris samariae Dinsmore

Differs only slightly from *I. lortetii.* Grows in Samaria in red clay soils. But it blossoms much more freely than the true *I. lortetii.*

Iris sari Schott ex Baker

This violet-blossomed iris is not cultivated and can no longer be found in its native habitat. All plants sold or under cultivation under the name *I. sari* are probably *I. lupina* Foster (for details see under the latter).

Iris schelkownikowii Fomin

I. schelkownikowii is found in a narrow band midway between Baku and Tiflis on the left bank of the Kura River. With its dotted tips, it is similar to the *I. lineolata* type. Several color forms, 3 of which are illustrated in the book from the Florence Symposium, are recorded. This iris has a delicate fragrance, which is unusual for

Oncocyclus Iris. The shape of the blossom is very elegant and larger than that of *I. acutiloba*. The beard is yellow.

Iris sprengeri Siehe
Native to Turkey. The falls have a yellow ground, dotted and veined in a purple-red hue. The signal spot is the same color. The veins on the standards are silver-white, purple-red, or almost black.

Iris susiana Linné
Synonym: *Iris basaltica* Dinsmore

This is probably the best known Oncocyclus Iris, commonly called Lady in Mourning; also probably one of the oldest species of all in cultivation. Although it always suffers from virus, it grows vigorously and blossoms early. It is more inexpensive than other Oncos, and anyone who wants to grow them should start with this one. It can be grown outdoors in warm, dry, protected spots. The base color of the almost circular blossoms is cream-white, dotted and veined in brown-purple. The standards are somewhat lighter than the falls; the crests are reddish black; and the beard brown-black. The iris known as *I. basaltica* Dinsmore is basically identical with *I. susiana*, except that the latter always has more reddish crests. It, therefore, has to be considered a form.

There are several forms of this iris:

Iris susiana f. *sofarana* (Foster)
Synonym: *Iris sofarana* Foster
I. calcarea Dinsmore
This Oncocylcus Iris is native to and is found also near Damascus. It is very similar to *I. susiana*. The blossom is smaller and more attractively colored with dark purple dots on a cream-white ground. The large crests are dark purple. Compared with *I. susiana*, *I. susiana* f. *sofarana* is much more precisely and subtly veined. The standards and falls are narrower and slimmer, the form of the blossom is more conical than rounded. The standards are normally lighter than the falls. The relatively low plant blooms very early.

Iris susiana f. *westii* (Dinsmore)
Synonym: *I. westii* Dinsmore
The tall stems of this plant bear blossoms with standards normally very pale, and with sparse dots and veins. The falls are dark purple. A form with yellow blossoms has also been found. *I. susiana* f. *westii* and *I. kasruwana* can always be found in larger colonies of *I. susiana* f. *sofarana*, and vice-versa. Now only found on Jabal Nina in southern Lebanon at about the 3,900 ft. (1200 m) level.

Iris yebrudii Dinsmore ex Chaud
Found in Syria. The falls have delicate violet-purple or brown-purple dots and veins on a whitish yellow ground. The signal spot is dark purple-violet, and the standards have dark purple-violet dots on a white base.

One subspecies is recorded: *I. yebrudii* ssp. *edgecombii* Chaudhary. It is also native to Syria. The pale yellow or pale green ground of the falls is covered with red-purple specks and veins. The signal spot is maroon-purple, the beard dark purple with yellowish tips. The standards are white or pale yellow, with maroon-purple veins and dots.

Unfortunately there are many synonyms, which does not exactly simplify the whole Oncocyclus complex. The Species Group of the B.I.S. has published the following list of these synonyms:
basaltica Dinsm. = *susiana* L.
benjaminii? = *bismarckiana* Damman
biggeri Dinsmore = *haynei* (Bak.) Mallett
calcarea Dinsmore? = *susiana* L. f. *sofarana*
eggeri Dinsmore = *atropurpurea* Bak. var.

eggeri Dinsmore

elegantissima Sosnowsky = *iberica* Hoffm. subsp. *elegantissima* (Sos.) Fed. et Takht

ewbankiana Foster = *acutiloba* C. A. Meyer var. *lineolata* Trautr.

fibrosa Freyn = *meda* Stapf

fomini Woronow = *acutiloba* C. A. Meyer

hauranensis Dinsmore = *jordana* Dinsmore

helena (K. Koch) K. Koch = *acutiloba* C. A. Mey. var. *lineolata* Trautv.

helenae Barbey ex Boiss. = *mariae* Barbey

hermona Dinsmore = *bismarckiana* Damman

lineolata (Trautv.) Grossheim = *acutiloba* C. A. Mey. var. *lineolata* Tautv.

lycotis Woronow = *iberica* Hoffm. ssp. *lycotis* (Woron.) Takht

maculata Bak. = *heylandiana* Boiss. et Reut. ex. Boiss.

medwedewii Fomin = *paradoxa* Stev. var. *coshab* Hoog

nazarena Foster = *bismarckiana* Damman

quasioumensis (nomen nudum)

sofarana Foster = *susiana* L. f. *sofarana* (Fost.)

urmiensis Hoog = *barnumae* var. *urmiensis* (Hoog) Dykes

westii Dinsmore = *susiana* Linn. f. *westii* (Dinsm.)

zenobiae Mouterde = *barnumae* var. *zenobiae* (Mounterde)

Natural Hybrids

As I have mentioned, all Oncocyclus Iris have the same number of chromosomes, n=20. Many Oncycyclus Iris ranges overlap in the wild, allowing natural hybrids to occur. These hybrid plants are responsible for the nomenclatural puzzle of the entire Oncocyclus group. Some well-known natural hybrids should be mentioned in passing:

I. meda Stapf × *I. barnumae* Baker et Foster f. *protonyma* (Stapf) Mathew et Wendelbo. Grows in Iran in the northwestern range of *I. meda*. These hybrid specimens are similar to *I. meda*. However, many have a beard with long, yellowish hairs; others have velvety, short, dark violet to black-purple hairs similar to those of *I. barnumae* f. *protonyma*, but they are even denser and shorter than those of the named form.

Another hybrid is *I. barnumae* Baker et Foster × *I. acutiloba* C. A. Mey. ssp. *lineolata* (Trautv.) Mathew et Wendelbo. Also found in Iran, 16 mi. (26 km) southeast of Tabriz. It resembles its second parent species more, yet the hybrid has few veins, the standards are rounder, and the beard is not dense and dark purple.

Many natural hybrids, that were not immediately recognized as such, were given species names. Among them are *I. annae* Grossheim, *I. kazachensis* Grossheim ex Gawrilenko, *I. koenigii* Sosnowsky, *I. sinistra* Sosnowsky, *I. tatianae* Grossheim, *I. zurandicus* Grossheim ex Gawrilenko, and others.

Genus Xiphium

The species of this genus grow in a relatively limited region extending from southern France and the Pyrenees to Portugal and eastern and southern Spain. In North Africa it includes the regions of Morocco, Algeria, and Tunisia. *Xiphium* species probably were introduced into Sicily where they naturalized.

Because of their origin, these iris need a typical Mediterranean climate: mild winters with some precipitation and hot, dry summers; hence, most of these species are not suitable for colder climates.

In their native habitat all the species

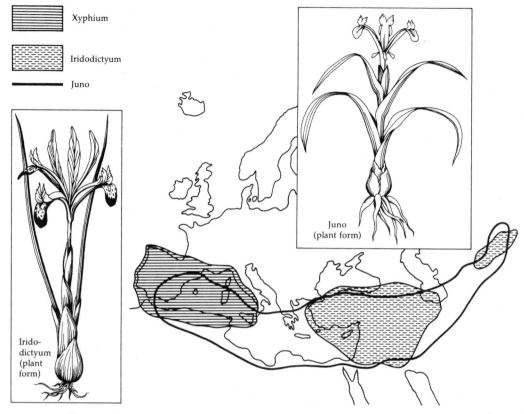

Xyphium

Iridodictyum

Juno

Juno
(plant form)

Irido-
dictyum
(plant
form)

grow on dry, rocky, usually heavy soils. One species is a non-conformist: *Xiphium latifolium*. It grows in the more marshy, moist soils of the Pyrenees, which are often saturated with water from melting snow.

Only *Xiphium vulgare* and *Xiphium latifolium* are suitable for growing outdoors; the other species are not winter hardy or only partially so. In contrast to its habitat in nature, *X. vulgare* grows best in the garden in light porous soil in areas with much summer precipitation. These "Spanish Iris" are difficult to combine in natural plantings. They are better grown as cut flowers in a special bed for that purpose. *X. latifolium,* the English Iris, has garden soil requirements similar to condi-

tions in its wild habitat, that is, moist, humus-rich loam. It will grow and prosper in such soil. Unfortunately, it is often planted in a location that is too dry. But the fact that it requires soil moisture does not mean that it should be planted in a shady spot. Full sun is also a prerequisite for good growth. The rest of the species of this genus need good winter protection or have to be cultivated free from frost (coldhouse). A weak solution of a complete soluble fertilizer once or twice a year is sufficient fertilization. The bulbs should be planted 3–4" (8–10 cm) deep. Cultivation of "Dutch Iris" is treated in a separate section.

This genus has much larger bulbs, taller growth habit, and later blooming period

(May–June) than the other Bulbous Iris in the genus *Iridodictyum*.

Xiphium boissieri (Henriques) Rodion
Synonyms: *I. boissieri, I. diversifolia*

A fairly rare species with a small range in the Sierra de Gerez, a mountainous region in northern Portugal, close to the Spanish border. Found at elevations of 2,600–3,280 ft. (800–1000 m). The plant has a scape 11½–15" (30–40 cm) tall with one or two blossoms, 2¾" (7 cm) in diameter. The flower is purple-blue with purple-red veins; falls have a yellow central stripe that does not go quite to the tip. This unique hairy yellow stripe is the main difference between this iris and others in the genus *Xiphium*. It is an attractive plant, but since it is not easily cultivated, it is not often seen. Cannot be purchased on the market. If obtainable, it should be grown in pots in the greenhouse, where it can easily bloom from the end of July to October. In its native habitat it flowers in June. Number of chromosomes 2n=36.

Xiphium filifolium (Boissier) Klatt
Synonym: *I. filifolia*

A striking species with vibrant purple-red blossoms, native to southern Spain and northwestern Africa. The falls have a decorative orange spot and an irregular dark blue band on the margin. The scape grows to about 17½" (45 cm) and produces 1 or 2 blossoms. The perianth tube is elongated. The leaves are narrow-linear, but not as narrow as its name suggests. Blooms end of May, beginning of June. It is hardy enough for southwestern England, but is a victim of winter in colder climates. Thus it has to be cultivated in a coldhouse or a cold frame filled with dry peat during the winter. It deserves to be more intensively propagated. Number of chromosomes 2n=32.

Xiphium fontanesii (syn. *I. fontanesii*) see *Xiphium tingitanum*

Xiphium junceum (Poiret) Klatt
Synonyms: *I. juncea, I. imberbis*

In North Africa from Tunesia to Tangier, also in Sicily, but probably introduced there. Named after its rush-like leaves. The blossoms are golden yellow, but there are quite a number of color variants (some with brown veins), some of which go by local names. It is a fairly rare species. Similar to a Spanish Iris, but more beautifully colored. The slender scape grows about 11½" (30 cm) tall, bearing 1 or 2 blossoms. The falls point vertically downwards and the blade is practically round. The bulb is rounded, with a thick outer skin, bristly on top. Blooms in June. Exudes a nice fragrance. Needs to be well protected, is seldom cultivated and not obtainable on the market. Number of chromosomes 2n=32.

The following varieties exist:
var. *mermieri,* a sulfur yellow variety
var. *numidicum,* a variety from North Africa with lemon yellow blossoms
var. *pallidum,* has large, light canary yellow blossoms

Xiphium latifolium (Miller)
Synonyms: *I. xiphioides, I. anglica*

The well-known English Iris that is not native to England, but was brought to Britain by English seamen from northern Spanish ports and was described there by Clusius. Native habitat is marshy or at least moist meadows in the Pyrenees and in Andorra. In the wild, *X. latifolium* almost always has deep blue blossoms, only occasionally white. There are no yellow forms. Blooming period is end of June, beginning of July. The scape grows to about 24" (60 cm) and bears 2 or 3 large blossoms that open sequentially. Blossom diameter of 4¼–4⅝'' (12–13 cm); dark blue with a striking, gold spot. A special characteristic of *X. latifolium* is that leaves emerge in early spring, unlike other species which initiate growth in the fall. The leaves are blue-green, rigid, and grooved. The bulbs are fairly large with a dark brown, thin outer skin. They should be planted as soon as received, at a depth of 4–6'' (10–15 cm). Beautiful cut flowers. Number of chromosomes 2n=42.

Some beautiful color varieties can be purchased under the names

X.l. 'Alona', standards violet-blue, falls delicate blue, large blossoms.

X.l. 'Blue Giant', dark blue, purple and dark blue spotting, falls dark blue with a white spot. Blossom very large.

X.l. 'Delft Blue', dark blue on a bluish white ground. Variable.

X.l. 'King of the Blues', dark blue with darker spotting.

X.l. 'La Nuit', dark reddish purple with darker and whitish dots.

X.l. 'Mirabeau', in various deep shades of blue, white zones on the falls. Vigorous grower.

X.l. 'Montblanc', pure white, very beautiful, large.

X.l. 'Prince Albert', beautiful, silver-blue color.

X.l. 'Queen of the Blues', in several shades of blue, large blossoms.

X.l. 'The Giant', dark blue, large blossoms.

Xiphium lusitanicum (syn. *I. lusitanica*) see *X. vulgare*

Xiphium serotinum (Willkomm)
Synonym: *I. serotina*

An independent species and not a form of *X. vulgare* according to Brian Mathew. Blooms in August in its native habitat of Spain, whereas *X. vulgare* blooms in June. This plant has grasslike leaves; the blossom is mauve with a flat, yellow comb on the falls. Its overall appearance is similar to *X. vulgare,* except for the standards which have been reduced to small bristlelike vestiges, like those of *I. setosa.* Height 15–24'' (40–60 cm). After it blossoms and the bulb matures, it goes dormant until late fall, when root activity begins again. An interesting, but not very ornamental plant.

Xiphium taitii (syn. *I. taitii*) see *X. vulgare*

Xiphium tingitanum (Boiss. et Reut.) Baker
Synonyms: *I. tingitana, I. fontanesii*

Typical plant from Morocco. Normally not hardy in cold climates. It can be grown

Aquatic and moisture-loving iris. With their upright, reed-like foliage, iris belong alongside lily ponds and pools. They act as the vertical counterbalance to the horizontal water-lilies.

Top left: There are several color types of Iris versicolor. The normal violet form tolerates more dryness than the white, pink and crimson (var. kermesina) forms. White cultivars often have attractive bluish veining. Iris versicolor also tolerates a small amount of standing water at its base.

Top right: Occidental gardeners sometimes have a hard time relating to the often overburdened-looking Japanese cultivars, with their gigantic, double blossoms. The single, pure white Iris kaempferi 'Unschuld', on the other hand, has a natural charm about it.

Below left: Iris pseudacorus 'Flore Pleno', the double form of our native yellow flag, which most people find more strange than beautiful. Collectors of various cultivars, however, will not want to be without this one.

Below right: The variegated cultivar of Iris pseudacorus is much prettier; particularly in the early stages of growth the contrast of yellow and green is striking. This beautiful specimen was photographed in the Rock Garden of the Edinburgh Botanical Gardens.

outdoors only in a very favorable location, otherwise it would be as treasured in gardens as much as it is in the coldhouse. It is relatd to *X. vulgare,* but has a longer perianth tube and narrower, pointed standards. *X. tingitanum* also blooms earlier (in April). It can easily be forced earlier, thus it is good for cultivating in a greenhouse. Scape about 15–24″ (40–60 cm) tall, with 2–3 large blossoms. Color is flat bluish purple. The falls have a light blue central stripe and a yellow spot on the haft and the blade. Grows in somewhat fertile soil even in the wild. Leaves emerge in the fall. One of the parents of the Dutch Iris. Number of chromosomes 2n=42. (Simonet 1932, as *I. tingitana* hort. Vilm.); 2n=28, R. and R. 1954).

There are two known varieties:

X.t. var. *fontanesii,* a somewhat more slender plant, later blooming and with darker violet-blue blossoms

X.t. var. *mellori* (described as a variety of *I. fontanesii*), a very robust variety, growing to 40″ (1 m) tall, with beautiful purple-violet blossoms with a round patch on the falls.

Xiphium vulgare (Miller), Spanish Iris
Synonym: *I. xiphium*

Native to Portugal, Spain, southwestern France, and northwest Africa. The soil must dry completely in summer for the bulbs to mature properly.

There are a number of local forms with very different flower sizes and blooming periods. The lower its habitat, the larger the blossom and the earlier the blooming period. Normally, *X. vulgare* blossoms two weeks before *X. latifolium.*

The scape is 24″ (60 cm) tall and bears 1 or 2 blossoms about 4¼″ (12 cm) in diameter. The wild form is usually pale or dark purple. The central stripe on the falls is a stunning dark yellow, reaching almost to the tip and varying in contour. The color of the standards is usually somewhat darker than the falls. The perianth tube is either very short or completely absent. The blade of the falls is roundish and held on a long haft. There is no narrowing between blade and haft. The leaves are bluish green and emerge in the fall. With some winter protection plants tend to be perennial.

Pogoregelia and Pogocyclus iris. Aril iris attempt to combine the exotic beauty of Oncocyclus and Regelia iris with the vigorousness and resistance of tall bearded iris. It would be wrong to say that this has been completely successful. But from all the attempts at crossbreeding have come a whole series of extremely valuable garden iris.

Top left: Iris × autosyndetica, first achieved by Simonet by crossing regelia iris having 44 chromosomes with tetraploid bearded iris. These seedlings are very resistant in cold climates. But their flower substance could be better. The brown

of the regelias comes out in this form.
Top right: 'Lady Mohr' from the "Mohr family" caused a sensation at the time of its introduction because of its large blossoms, which all the Mohr varieties have.
Lower left: In the early years Iris susiana × Iris lutescens hybrids also belonged to the aril iris collection. They include cultivars that can still be planted today, modern selections being prettier than older ones.
Lower right: Iris × autosyndetica. Another cultivar from this cross (by Dr. Peter Werckmeister).

The following varieties are known:

X.v. var. *praecox,* a very early blooming form (end of April, middle of May)

X.v. var. *lusitanicum* (syn. *I. lusitanica*), a yellow-blooming variety common to Spain and Portugal

X.v. var. *xiphium,* blue, mauve, or violet blossoms

X.v. var. *battandieri* (syn. *I. battandieri*), white with orange margin on the falls. From Morocco and Algeria.

X.v. var. *taitii* (syn. *I. taitii*), blooms in the latter part of May. Known in gardens in a pale to bright blue form.

Selections from wild forms and hybrids have resulted in the large palette of the "Spanish Iris" (Iris Hispanica Hybrids). Up to about the mid-50's, they were important cut iris, but were later supplanted by Dutch Iris. Spanish Iris are still rewarding garden plants, especially as cut flowers. The following varieties are recommended:

X. 'Blue Angel', bright cornflower blue with a yellow spot.

X. 'Cajanus', vibrant, medium yellow, tall stem.

X. 'Frederika', good cut flower, ivory-white, large blossoms with a yellow spot.

X. 'Hercules', blue-violet bronze shade, with a large orange spot on the falls.

X. 'King of the Blues', dark blue with a small yellow spot.

X. 'King of the Whites', beautiful, pure white variety.

X. 'Queen Wilhelmina', white with a small yellow spot, early blooming, outstanding.

X. 'Prince Heinrich', standards purple-brown, falls bronze-brown with a large yellow spot. Very distinctive.

X. 'Reconnaissance', standards purple, falls bronze with an orange spot.

X. latifolium is unique because it does not cross with the other *Xiphium* species. Among the others, the following crosses exist: *X. boissieri* × *X. junceum, X. boissieri* × *X. tingitanum, X.junceum* × *X. filifolium, X. fontanesii* (=form of *X. tingitanum*) × *X. vulgare* var. *praecox, X. vulgare* × *X. filifolium, X. vulgare* × *X. tingitanum;* moreover, back-crosses of Dutch Iris (Iris Hispanica Hybrids) with species exist. In areas where the botanical merges with the horticultural, the name "Iris" must be retained. Names like "Dutch Xiphium" or "Xiphium-Hispanicum Hybrids" are not likely to find acceptance.

Iris Hollandica Hybrids, Dutch Iris

Also known by the synonym *I.* × *hollandica* Tub. The most commercially successful iris of all. It is cultivated and forced in enormous numbers and sold in nurseries all year ("Year-round Iris"). The Dutch bulb firm of van Tubergen in Haarlem pioneered their cultivation and participated significantly in their further development. Dutch Iris are crosses between various *Xiphium* species. Although the genesis of these hybrids does not go back very far, there are several accounts of how they actually began. Some say they came from crosses between *X. tingitanum, X. vulgare* var. *praecox* and *X. boissieri;* others that *X. vulgare* var. *praecox* was first crossed with *X. vulgare* var. *lusitanicum.* In addition, *X. filifolium* was also used. Newer hybrids, of course, make use of existing varieties, but certain varieties were back-crossed with wild species.

The assortment is enormous; every year new cultivars are added and older ones culled out, despite the fact that a few of the older cultivars are still top sellers. Major growing areas are Holland, southern France, Israel and California. Because of different parentage, the individual cultivars vary in color, form, and size of blossom, number of buds per stem, blooming period, production of offsets, and suitability for forcing.

Most Important Cultivars

Cultivars marked with an asterisk (*) are particularly important for year-round cultivation. (These all are referred to as Iris.)

I. 'Blue Triumphator', standards bluebell blue with a touch of violet, falls blue with a yellow spot.

I. 'Bronze Queen', standards bluish bronze, falls bronze with an orange spot.

I. 'Golden Harvest', one of the best dark yellow varieties. Good for forcing, but not as good for retarding. Blossoms hold well after cutting. Long stem that could be more rigid. Blooms outdoors 2–3 weeks after the blue I. 'Wedgewood'.

I. *'H. C. van Vliet', falls light blue with a small orange spot, standards somewhat darker. Good strong, long scape. Suited for both forcing and retarding. Normally blooms 2–3 weeks after I. 'Wedgewood'. Somewhat more frost sensitive outdoors than others.

I. *'Ideal', mutant of I. 'Wedgewood', with dark blue blossoms, particularly good for forcing.

I. 'Imperator', medium dark blue. Ideal cultivar for coldhouse forcing. Very long lasting as a cut flower, opens reliably. Also suitable for retarding. Outdoors blooms 3 weeks later than I. 'Wedgewood'.

I. 'King Mauve', uniform mallow blue blossoms on very long scapes. Late bloomer.

I. 'Marquette', cream-white standards, yellow falls with orange spot.

I. 'Prinzessin Irene', standards white, falls dark orange, one of the best cultivars.

I. *'Professor Blaauw', ultramarine-gentian blue with very large blossoms. Good for cold forcing. The scape is somewhat shorter than other cultivars. As cut flower, cannot be kept as long as others. Should not be cut in bud. Vigorous grower; also good for retarding.

I. 'Purple Sensation', very beautiful color combination. The blossom is dark purple-violet; every fall has a yellow marking with a gentian blue rim.

I. *'Royal Yellow', standards buttercup yellow, falls sunflower yellow.

I. *'Wedgewood', most important cultivar of the entire group. Most widely grown and sold. Very early bloomer. Ideal for forcing and retarding. Blossoms sky blue with a yellow spot on the falls.

I. 'White Excelsior', pure white with very small yellow dots. Early bloomer, ideal for forcing and retarding. Keeps well as cut flower. Buds open easily. Blooms two weeks after I. 'Wedgewood' outdoors.

I. 'White Perfection', the best pure white cultivar, with large blossoms on tall stems. Good for forcing and retarding. Keeps well as cut flower if not cut as buds.

I. 'White Superior', an improvement over I. 'White Excelsior', with larger blossoms.

I. 'Yellow Queen', golden yellow; one of the best cultivars for forcing, but not for retarding. Very vigorous. Frost sensitive outdoors, blooms two weeks after I. 'Wedgewood'.

Also important for the commercial nurseryman are:

Blue: I. 'Blue Champion', I. 'Blue Giant', I. 'Dominator'.

Yellow: I. 'Covent Garden', I. 'Golden Emperor', I. 'Lemon Queen'.

I. 'Pride of Holland', I. 'Sunshine'.

White: I. 'Angels Wings', I. 'White van Vliet'

Cultivating Dutch Iris

Successful cultivation depends on light to medium heavy soils. A groundwater level of 20–28" (50–70 cm), as often found in The Netherlands, is ideal. Some cultivars have special requirements; I. 'Wedgewood', for example, requires somewhat more humus. Fertilize with a chlorine-free complete soluble fertilizer.

Propagate by bulblets. 4–7 form on every bulb. Some of these small bulbs will blossom in the second year and definitely by the third. Cultivation is not worthwhile in cold climates because conditions in other areas are more suitable. Producing cut flowers and, specifically, forcing them is far more important in the northerly, latitudes.

Forcing and Retarding Dutch Iris Bulbs for the Cut-flower Market

Several treatments have led to today's "Year-round Iris". At any time of the year cut iris can be bought in florist shops. To achieve this, both forcing and retarding growth are necessary. Cooled bulbs must be used to produce blossoms for the end of December to the end of February. The choice of varieties available for this purpose is limited mainly to I. 'Wedgewood', I. 'Ideal', and I. 'Dominator'.

For flowers in March–April, uncooled bulbs are necessary; here the choice of varieties is larger. In addition to the above, there are I. 'White Excelsior', I. 'H. C. van Vliet', I. 'Golden Harvest', I. 'Imperator', and I. 'Professor Blaauw'. These uncooled bulbs have to be kept frost-free until the middle of January, then the temperature is maintained at 60°F (15 C) until they bloom. To produce flowers from the end of April to the beginning of June (when iris growing outdoors can be cut), bulbs undergo a relatively early forcing. During this mid-to-early forcing, the plants are grown in cold greenhouses or in frost free frames. Almost all cultivars can be used for this process, but it is important that a temperature of 54–56°F (12–13 C) not be exceeded. The outdoor harvest can be extended by staggered plantings. For flowers from September to the beginning of December, so-called retarded bulbs are used. This is done using bulbs that were lifted late and storing them immediately at 85°F (30 C). This gives them an additional "summer rest period" when all growing ceases. Six weeks of cooling are then necessary before bulbs can be planted for forcing.

A large amount of light is necessary for the forcing process, so only very bright greenhouses can be used. Flats measuring 13 × 15" (35 × 40 cm) and 4¼–6" (12–15 cm) deep usually are used, especially for very early forcing. The bulbs are planted so that their tips just show above the soil line. It is important to plant them vertically. When planting in beds, use 100 4" (10 cm)-size to 170 2¾" (7 cm)-size bulbs per 11 sq. ft. (square meter). Planting depth differs for individual varieties: tips just showing above ground for I. 'Wedgewood', I. 'Ideal', and I. 'Dominator'; all the others should be covered by ¾" (2 cm) of soil. Retarded bulbs should be planted with more space: 80–120 per 11 sq. ft. (square meter) outdoors, covered by ¾" (2 cm) of soil; under glass, 1½–2" (4–5 cm) of soil. A hot water heating system is ideal for forcing bulbs, as hot air ventilation can cause damage, such as irregular blossoms. Do not fertilize before planting; if the leaves look pale, apply a nitrogen fertilizer after planting. 8–12 weeks is the normal period of cultivation, planting to cutting.

Harvesting Dutch Iris

Should be cut when budding. As indicated in the description of individual cul-

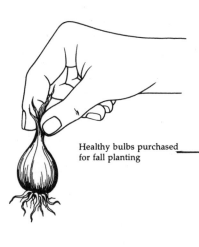

Cycle of small bulbous iris from the genus Iridodictyum (Iris danfordiae) that develop numerous offset bulblets

Healthy bulbs purchased for fall planting

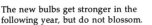

These are exhausted after the early spring growing period and begin to develop bulblets, which are in turn removed and re-planted.

The new bulbs get stronger in the following year, but do not blossom.

Another year, and they are fully developed and ready to bloom.

tivars, there are some that should not be cut too early. Differences in the cultivars should be observed. Stalks can be cut just above the ground or pulled out of the bulb. In any case, the white portion at the bottom of the stem should be trimmed because it interferes with water intake. The budding flowers can be held for 4 or 5 days at low temperatures (35–40°F or 2–5°C) if wrapped in paper, and another 5 or 6 days if they are then put in water.

Pests and Diseases of Dutch Iris

It's not surprising that plants grown in such masses are subject to a host of diseases and pests.

Eelworm (Nematode) disease (Ditylenchus destructor). Poorly developed shoots with stunted branches, extremely delayed flower formation. Brownish rot present in the bulb. Destroy affected plants. Take preventive measures when bulbs are dormant by disinfecting with hot water.

Spray individual plants in otherwise healthy stands with Metasystox.

Fusarium rot (Fusarium oxysporum f. gladioli). Shoots are twisted and yellowed; the roots, the bottom of the bulbs and skin rot, causing the entire plant to die. Remove damaged plants at once. Prevent by disinfecting with mercury where legal. Protect bulbs from injury!

Penicillium bulb rot (Penicillium corymbiferum). Gray-brown spots on bulbs, which spread and can quickly cover the entire surface. Usually leads to soft rot inside the bulb. Sort out affected bulbs, discard bulbs with lesions!

Sclerotinia disease (Sclerotium tuliparum). Base of leaves and bulbs rot, the entire plant withers and dies. There is often a white mycelium on the bad spot, and the interior of the bulb is gray with dry rot. Disinfect bulbs as preventive measure and plant in an absolutely clean growing medium.

Botrytis disease (Botrytis spp.). Brownish wet spots on leaves and blossoms, affected parts rot, with ultimate death of the plant. Destroy diseased plants. Repeated use of Dexon, Botran, etc.

In spite of the range of cultivars, there are still some features hybridizers would like to see. For example, the year-round availability of an "I. 'Wedgewood' " type in some of the other color groups. Also some of the colors could be improved.

Genus Iridodictyum

As a result of Prof. Rodionenko's reclassification of the genus *Iris* and related genera in 1961, Bulbous Iris of the Reticulata group were separated and set up as an independent genus, *Iridodictyum*.

Native habitat: northern and eastern Turkey, Lebanon, Syria, Israel, Iraq, Soviet regions south of the Caucasus, Iran; and several hundred kilometers away from it in Turkestan—*Iridodictyum kolpakowskianum.*

Since all the species grow at higher elevations, they are entirely winter hardy in cooler climates, despite their more southerly origins. Only *Iridodictyum vartanii* from Israel and varieties of *I. histrio* are exceptions to this.

The soil in their native habitats is usually rather heavy. I found *I. histrio* in the mountains of Lebanon in reddish clay mixed with fractured limestone, albeit on slopes. These soil conditions should not be replicated in the garden, where summer rains have to be taken into account.

Although most species of the genus *Iridodictyum* are hardy, they should be planted in a sheltered place in the garden. They are among the first flowers to bloom, and in a favorable site they will blossom earlier still. Plant in full sun. Unlike their natural site, the soil should be porous and have additional drainage. Sandy loam with crushed lime has proven successful. Care should be taken that the bulbs not be planted deeper than 3" (8 cm) and a depth of 2½" (5 cm) is ideal. If heavy rainfall occurs in the summer, they should be covered by a sheet of glass. Lifting them every year after they die back and planting them again in the fall is probably too much trouble, considering the cost of new bulbs. In addition to growing well outdoors, these early bloomers also take to pot culture. At least 5 bulbs in a 4 inch pot are necessary to get a good effect. Good drainage is necessary. Pots should not be placed in too warm a location. Bulbs are unfortunately subject to black spot (see section on "Protecting your Iris in the Garden"); diseased bulbs should be destroyed at once.

Plants of the genus *Iridodictyum* have some unique characteristics which distinguish them from *Xiphium* species, the other group of early Bulbous Iris. When dry, the bulbs have a reticulated skin. The leaves are rushlike and have 4–8 ribs. Usually only one blossom on a short scape. The bulbs are much smaller than those of *Xiphium* species.

Classification into Groups

Rodionenko subdivides the genus *Iridodictyum* into two sections. The section *Iridodictyum* includes:

I. *winogradowii*
I. *reticulatum*
I. *vartanii*
I. *histrioides*
I. *histrio*
I. *danfordiae*
I. *pamphylicum*
I. *bakerianum*
I. *hyrcanum*

The section *Monolepis* includes:
  I. kolpakowskianum
  I. winkleri

Section *Iridodictyum*

Iridodictyum bakerianum (Foster) Rodion.
Synonym: *Iris bakeriana*
  Native to eastern Turkey, Armenia, Kurdistan, Syria, and northern Iran. It is a very attractive plant; chief features are leaves with 8 ribs and a blackish spot on the oval curve of the falls. Grows 4½–8" (12–20 cm) tall. The standards are dull purple-violet; falls are held horizontally all the way to the tip. *Iridodictyum bakerianum* is variable. On some days the blossoms give off a scent of violets. Main blooming period is February and March. This species is unfortunately not as vigorous as other species; bulbs have to be replaced every 2 or 3 years. But it is worthwhile growing because of its beauty. It should be planted in a more protected spot than other species. It will live somewhat longer if grown in a pot in the coldhouse. The beautiful hybrid *I.* 'Clairette' resulted from a cross between *I. bakerianum* and *I. reticulatum*. Number of chromosomes 2n=20.

Iridodictyum danfordia (Baker) Nothdurft.
Synonyms: *Iris bornmuelleri, Iris danfordiae*
  Found primarily in eastern Turkey. The yellow blossoms of this species are especially valuable in the garden. The haft of the falls is covered with black dots; the lip is speckled green. The standards are hardly noticeable, almost bristle-like. This early spring bloomer seldom exceeds a height of 4" (10 cm) when in bloom; the blossom has a diameter of 2" (5 cm). The quadrangular leaves are not as tall as the fragrant blossoms when the plant flowers; later they elongate to a height of 11½–15" (30–40 cm). The bulbs are an elongated oval-shape. Highly recommended for the garden in spite of some disadvantages, primarily the disturbing effect of the long foliage after the plant blooms. Also, after the growing period the bulb separates into many bulblets that require several years before they bloom again. But this is offset by their very low purchase price, so new bulbs can be planted every year. Blooming period is February and March, somewhat behind that of *Iris histrioides* 'Major'. Number of chromosomes 2n=28.

Iridodictyum histrio (Rchb. f.) Rodion.
Synonym: *Iris histrio*
  Widely distributed over a large area: Turkey, Lebanon, Syria, Armenia. This species seems to be closely related to *Iris histrioides* and varies in color from a vibrant blue to purple-violet, with beautiful white spots. Flowering plant height 4–6" (10–15 cm); the blossoms have a diameter of 2½–2¾" (6–7 cm). This is a shorter and a more graceful species than *I. reticulatum*. A white stripe, sometimes with shades of gold in it, runs down the center of the haft to the tip. The standards are slim and about the same length as the falls. The blossom has no scent. The quadrangular leaves are somewhat higher than the blossom when the plant is in bloom. Unfortunately this species is not as hardy in the garden as *Iris histrioides*. However, it blooms earlier and is indeed the earliest blooming Bulbous Iris (end of January to end of February). It may be more desirable to grow it in a coldhouse. I have found it in the latter part of February on slopes in the Lebanese mountains near Sofar, between thorny thickets, dry thistles, and the last receding snows. The blossoms were a vibrant royal blue. Number of chromosomes 2n=20.

There are a few varieties of this species. *I. histrio* var. *aintabiensis,* which grow a little better in the garden and increase more rapidly. The leaves are about the same height as the blossom when the plant is in bloom. The blossom color is sky blue to medium blue, and the falls are gayly spotted (hence the name "histrio" = actor). The spotting is particularly thick around the yellow signal spot. In addition, the falls are narrower than those of the species. Grows in volcanic soil in the Turkish province of Aintab. *I. histrio* var. *atropurpurea* is a uniform dark purple without a signal spot.

Iridodictyum histrioides (G. F. Wils) Nothdurft
Synonym: *Iris histrioides*

Occurs from northern Asia Minor to northwestern Iran; the var. *I.h. major* near Amasia in the hill country (Armenia). Perhaps the most beautiful, and for gardeners the most useful, species of this genus. The magnificent blue blossoms are much larger than those of *I. reticulatum.*

And yet it is only 2–3" (5–8 cm) tall. The leaves at blooming time are either not visible or are just beginning to emerge from the ground. Blossoms are a bright royal blue, the base of the falls has a white center and a gold rib. The blade is almost circular. The standards are large (as large as the falls) and stand upright. The sturdy buds often show above ground by January, yet they bloom after *Iridodictyum histrio* var. *aintabensis.* Bulbs increase quite rapidly and seed from the capsules, partly submerged in the ground, also grow well. Cannot be recommended too highly for the garden, especially *I. histrioides* var. *major.* Can be maintained for many years in a rock garden in fertile soil. It is extremely hardy. The blossom may be frozen stiff by a sudden frost, but after an hour's sunshine it looks as if nothing had happened. The plant is, unfortunately, a magnet for snails, especially the buds. Number of chromosomes 2n=16.

Forms hybrids with *I. reticulatum,* an example of which is the beautiful *I.* 'Harmony'. *I. histrioides* var. *sopheriensis* is a

Californica iris. Enchanting shapes from the iris kingdom, though their hardiness leaves something to be desired. Their requirements are all different, depending on the individual species and its origin. Of those from the Pacific Coast of the U.S., the species growing in Oregon and Washington are less tender than those from California.

Top left: Iris tenax grows furthest north of all the Californicas. Yet it is still not the most willing

grower in German gardens. Lime is especially detrimental to it.
Top right: Iris tenuissima is attractive, but can only be kept in a coldframe in areas where the climate is unsuitable. Makes beautiful cut flowers.
Below: Iris innominata cultivar. Crosses between I. innominata and I. douglasiana produce the loveliest and least tender Californica iris. Hybrids and their cultivars are also known as Pacific Coast iris.

smaller form that is often classified with *I. histrio*. The blossoms are a duller blue and the standards and falls are narrower; the stigma is dull sea green. Rarely cultivated. Two further types were selected in England: *I.h.* 'G. P. Baker' with Moorish blue blossoms and *I.h.* 'Lady Beatrix Stanley' with a similar color.

Iridodictyum hyrcanum (Woronow ex Grossheim) Rodion
Synonym: *Iris hyrcana*

Found in mountainous regions southwest of the Caspian Sea. It was first described from the area of the Talysk Range. An elegant, small iris only about 4" (10 cm) tall. It is bright blue with an orange spot on the falls. Blooms at the same time as *I. reticulatum*, but has smaller blossoms. Characterized by forming many offsets, just as do *I. danfordiae* and *I. histrioides*. In *Flora Iranica*, Mathew and Wendelbo consider *I. hyrcanum* as a subspecies of *I. reticulatum*.

Iridodictyum pamphylicum (Hedge)
Synonymn: *Iris pamphylica*

A species from the Taurus mountains of southern Turkey that was discovered very late, but is available (bulbs still very expensive). Graceful, slender blossoms. The ground color of the standards is violet with shades of olive green or brown. The falls are dark purple with shades of olive green and a light yellow spot. The styles stand clearly above the falls, which give the blossom an elegant appearance. Blooming period middle to end of April. Height 3–4" (8–10 cm).

Iridodictyum reticulatum (Marschall von Bieberstein) Rodion
Synonym: *Iris reticulata*

Its habitat is centered around the Caucasus and Transcaucasia; from there this species radiates into Turkey and northern Iran. The name comes from the strongly reticulate pattern on the dry bulbs. Scapes are about 6–8" (15–20 cm)

Beardless iris species (Apogon). Species that grow in very diverse climates. Forms of Iris setosa occur in northern Canada and northeastern Siberia, where the lower layers of soil do not thaw even in summer, while some Louisiana iris grow in the humid climate of the Mississippi delta.

Top left: Iris giganticaerulea is unfortunately not hardy. The only chance of growing it is in a tub, in a spot protected from winter frosts.
Top right: Iris brevicaulis and I. 'Dorothea K. Williamson'. Iris brevicaulis is the only truly hardy species of this section that will thrive in regions with cold winters. It, too, prefers a somewhat damper soil. It becomes somewhat rank in a favorable location. The violet 'Dorothea K. Williamson' is one of the few cultivars suitable for the climate in Germany. It is an old garden plant with few requirements, except space.

Middle left: Again Iris 'Dorothea K. Williamson', the most robust of all the Louisiana iris group. Its blossoms grow horizontally from the leaf axil. They make excellent cut flowers.
Middle right: Iris fulva has a unique color among iris species. It has made a fundamental contribution to the large color spectrum of Louisiana iris cultivars. In European wine country these will easily grow outdoors. An interesting note: in their native habitat flowers are pollinated by hummingbirds.
Bottom left: Iris setosa var. tricuspis. A whole series of forms and varieties of this species exist due to its enormous range. All of them are extremely useful in natural garden plantings.
Bottom right: Iris setosa 'Dwarf Form' is an Arctic dwarf form, which can be used for plantings in troughs. An attractive dwarf which cannot, however, tolerate too much dryness and prefers an acid soil. Can be easily grown from seed.

tall, with foliage sometimes higher than the blossoms when the plant is in bloom. The graceful blossoms, smelling strongly of violets, are dark violet-blue with a gold central stripe and white streaks on the falls. The blossom is 2" (5 cm) tall and 2½" (6 cm) wide. Strangely enough, the cultivated dark blue-violet form has never been found in the wild and is perhaps a hybrid. The wild forms are reddish purple resembling *I.r.* var. *krelagei*. An inexpensive and highly recommended garden plant, even though what I have said about *I. danfordiae* also applies here, namely long leaves (up to 13" or 35 cm) and bulbs which separate into numerous offsets after blooming. Should be planted about 3" (8 cm) deep in porous soil with a slight lime content. Blooming period in cool climates usually March. Beautiful with *Crocus chrysanthus* cultivars.

Iridodictyum vartanii (Foster) Rodion.
Synonym: *Iris vartanii*

Found in Israel; particularly abundant around Nazareth. It is very delicate, dwarf species that blossoms in December. The flower is pure white to dull blue, with a light yellow central stripe on the haft of the falls. *I. vartanii* 'Alba' is available. Not a strong grower and usually dies after blooming; not hardy in cold climates; grow it outdoors only in an exceptionally sheltered, warm location. It should be grown in the coldhouse or indoors. In a warm room it emits a strong scent of almonds. Strictly protected in its natural habitat. Number of chromosomes 2n=20.

Iridodictyum winogradowii (Fomin) Rodion.
Synonym: *Iris winogradowii*

Grows in mountain meadows in the Caucasus. Though it has not been in cultivation for a long time, it is among the most attractive species of this genus. Unfortunately, it is very expensive. Hardy and grows well in soil with ample lime and good drainage. Blossoms February to mid-March. An ideal companion to *I. histrioides* 'Major'. Dwarf plant; dull lemon-yellow blossom with an orange central stripe on the falls and small dark streaks; falls are about ¾" (2 cm) wide. Leaves somewhat ridged, dull green and only attain their full length after the plant blooms. Bulbs have a light brown outer skin. Differs from *I. danfordiae* in its relatively large, lanceolate standards, which are 2" (5 cm) long. Blossoms have a delicate scent of elder. Increases well with large offsets. Best to lift the plant every other year and replant the offsets individually. For forcing, increase heat only by mid-January when root formation is mostly complete. Number of chromosomes 2n=16.

Section Monolepis

Iridodictyum kolpakowskianum (Regel) Rodion.
Synonym: *Iris kolpakowskiana*

Named after General Kolpolowskian, a district governor in Turkestan. Its native habitat is Tien Shan and the environs of Alma Ata. Characterized by the fibrous, dark brown outer skin on the bulb and its linear, crocus-like leaves, with a ridged central rib and somewhat thicker edge. It is a dwarf species to (4" or 10 cm tall). Blossom without stem, perianth tube 2" (5 cm) long; falls greenish yellow on the underside, cream-white with an orange-yellow central stripe above with a long tip on the blade streaked with vibrant purple. Stigma and standards are dull purple-violet. Leaves do not reach the height of the blossom, but later grow to 9–11½" (25–30 cm). Difficult to grow but worth trying; occasionally is available, but rather expensive. Possible to grow from seed, but takes about three years till it blossoms. Blooms in March–April. Requires ample calcium and magnesium in the form of crushed dolomitic limestone.

Iridodictyum winkleri (Regel) Rodion.
Synonym: *Iris winkleri*
    Grows in Tien Shan above 9,800 ft. (3000 m). Closely related to *I. kolpakowskianum*. Not in cultivation.

Small Bulbous Iris Hybrids

Several of the above-mentioned species have been used for crossbreeding in The Netherlands and in England. Van Tubergen, in Haarlem, has been very active in this field. As a result we now have a whole series of early spring bulbous iris for the garden. Their culture is the same as for the genus *Iridodictyum*. The following cultivars are available on the market:

I. 'Cantab', an older, proven variety that is very perennial. The blossom is pale blue with an orange spot on each fall. Very pretty in rock gardens, bowls, and pots.
I. 'Clairette', standards sky blue, falls dark blue with a white pattern and a narrow stripe on the haft. Gives an elegant impression.
I. 'Harmony', should be in every garden. Beautiful cross between *I. histrioides* 'Major' and *I. reticulatum*. Compact blossoms. Uniform dark sky blue with a yellow midstripe on the blade of the falls. Multiplies in the garden. Also very good for pot culture because the foliage is very short when the plant is in bloom.
I. 'Jeannine', a recent attractive variety of a bright purple-violet color with a striking orange spot on the falls. It has a delicate fragrance and is highly recommended.

I. 'Joyce', sky blue, orange comb on the blade of the falls. Similar to I. 'Harmony'.
I. 'J. S. Dijt', a hybrid with reddish purple, fragrant blossoms. A significant improvement over the old cultivar I. 'Hercules'. Multiplies freely.
I. 'Katherine Hodgkin', a recent hybrid from England that is still very expensive. E. B. Anderson succeeded in crossing *I. histrioides* 'Major' with *I. danfordiae* for the first time. Large, rounded blossoms, slightly yellowish white with a wash of light yellow and azure. Blooms February to March—January when forced in the greenhouse. 2¾–4" (7–10 cm) tall.
I. 'Pauline', purple-violet with a white spot. Newer cultivar.
I. 'Royal Blue', dark blue blossoms with particularly large falls and a yellow spot.
I. 'Springtime', standards medium blue, falls dark blue with a white pattern. A cross between *I. reticulatum* and *I. bakerianum*. A very early bloomer. Much more perennial than *I. bakerianum*.
I. 'Violet Beauty', standards violet, falls somewhat darker with an orange comb. A free-blooming perennial cultivar and a good multiplier.
I. 'Wentworth', vibrant purple-blue blossoms. A significant improvement over *I. reticulatum*.
    Where parentage is not given, cultivars are selections of *I. reticulatum*.
    Aside from the above-mentioned cultivars, which are readily available, there are those which are less frequently seen in the catalogues:
I. 'Angels Tears', a smaller, lower-growing hybrid in dark blue-violet. Sets seed exceptionally well.
I. 'Blue Veil', has medium blue flowers; petals somewhat wider than those of other cultivars. Sterile.

I. 'Hercules', similar to the older cultivar I. 'J. S. Dijt'.

In The Netherlands, W. P. van Eden has bred other very beautiful cultivars: I. 'Edward', I. 'George', I. 'Gordon', I. 'Ida', I. 'Michael' and I. 'Natascha'. It is hoped that they will soon be marketed. In England, I found two other types. I. 'Lady Beatrix Stanley' was discovered in an *I. histrioides* group. I. G. P. Baker comes from an *I. histrioides* collection in Turkey.

Genus *Hermodactylus*

Hermodactylus tuberosus Salisbury
Synonym: *Iris tuberosa* Linné
Called Snake's Head Iris.

Found in southern Europe, abundant in Sicily and Greece. It is a distinctive, spring blooming Iris, usually on rocky mountain slopes among grasses and orchids.

Hermodactylus tuberosus is not completely winter hardy in cooler climates. Yet it will grow as long as it has a sunny location and peat mulch for winter protection, though its ability to blossom suffers. It must have good drainage. Pot culture in a frost-free container or in the coldhouse is better in cold regions. It's important that the temperature not exceed 54° F (12 C). In a warm site it blooms at the same time as snowdrops and various bulbous iris species.

Distinguished from the genus *Iris* by its one-celled ovary (3-celled in *Iris*). The tuber is branched like fingers (Hermodactylus = finger of Hermes, the Greek messenger of the gods). Leaves are linear, narrow, lanceolate. The weak stem grows to 6" (30 cm). Blossoms have a diameter of about 2" (5 cm); falls are blackish purple and the standards pale yellowish green. Hardly differs in form from a Bulbous Iris blossom (*Iridodictyum*).

Genus *Gynandriris*

Gynandriris sisyrinchium (Linné) Parl.
Synonym: *Iris sisyrinchium* Linné. In the 11th ed. of Zander, this plant was again called *Iris sisyrinchium.*

This little iris-like plant is widely distributed throughout the entire region of the Mediterranean, in Asia Minor, from Saudi Arabia to Syria, Iran, and Afghanistan. Abundant in coastal areas. It has iris-like blossoms, but growth habit similar to *Moraea*. Unfortunately, not hardy in central and northern Europe, where it has to be grown in pots, in frost-free frames, or in the coldhouse. Growing medium should contain lime. In its natural habitat *Gynandriris sisyrinchium* grows in masses, so that some areas are blanketed with millions of blue blossoms. Usually grows in heavy loam soils with ample lime. The more the soil sun bakes in summer, the better this species thrives. Any vacationer who tries to dig one up knows how deeply the tuber is imbedded in the soil.

Small, lilac blue blossoms with golden yellow and white areas. Seldom gets taller than 8" (20 cm). Each blossom lasts only one day and then only from 11:00 a.m. to 6:00 p.m. Rootstock is in the form of a bulb, the outer skin reticulated. Leaves are narrow and thread-like. Number of chromosomes 2n=24. Recommended only for serious amateurs, collectors, or as a souvenir from a vacation.

Gynandriris maricoides Regel
Less known and rarely cultivated. Found chiefly in Central Asia, Tedzhikistan, the mountainous regions of Turkmenistan.

Genus Juno

Professor Rodionenko removed the plants known as Juno Iris or Scorpiris from the genus *Iris* and made them into the independent genus *Juno*. Since gardeners had always used the term "Juno", this adaptation did not present any problem.

Junos are distributed over a very large area, in which some species are scattered far and wide, while others are locally endemic. *Juno alata* (*Juno planifolia*) is found farthest west: in Sicily, Spain, and North Africa. From there it spreads east into Turkey, all of Asia Minor, and Afghanistan. Its occurrence is more northerly in the Soviet Union, where it begins in the Caucasus and spreads from there into Central Asia. The *Flora of the U.S.S.R.* alone lists 27 species, according to Komarov.

Junos grow almost exclusively in stony, lime-rich soil, usually scattered on gentle slopes, where rain quickly drains off.

Unfortunately, most of these attractive plants are not winter hardy. Only *Juno bucharica, Juno magnifica,* and *Juno graeberiana* have been grown successfully outdoors—and with reservations, *Juno orchioides, Juno warleyensis,* and *Juno willmottiae* 'Alba' (they need winter protection). The aforementioned do much better in loam than in sandy soil, provided the site is very sunny and hard baked in the summer. In such a location they increase well by offsets although, generally speaking, they increase minimally. Propagation by seed sown following cold stratification is not difficult, but 4 or 5 years growth is needed before seedlings bloom. Bulbs taken from the wild usually flower well the first year, but soon weaken. Junos tolerate complete summer drought; however, their characteristically fleshy roots must not be allowed to dry out completely. They must have ample moisture and nutrients during the growing period and a sunny location. Gardeners with coldhouses have a better chance of growing rare Junos in containers, provided there is no danger of frost. And there they will bloom starting in February.

More delicate species can be grown in a cold frame. English iris lovers plant these in frames on a bank-bed of 6" (15 cm) of cinders, but the same kind of drainage layer can be created with fired clay pellets or volcanic slag. Use growing soil of pH 8. From the time the leaves die back until October, the box should be covered. During October the sash is removed, then replaced again when heavy frost threatens until March or April, depending on the weather, at which time it is again removed. Fertilize plants in spring with bone meal, horn meal, and potassium sulfate.

Junos can also be grown in a coldhouse in beds which can be covered with glass to keep water out, or plant them in sinks, tubs, or large pots. Water from October on, even during the winter as soon as the soil begins to dry out. In March and April they should be heavily watered. I have had good luck planting only the fleshy roots in soil and surrounding the bulbs with fine lava rock, fired clay pellets, or similar material.

Propagation is usually by division. The brittle fleshy roots need to be handled with care, but if one of them does break off, it should not be thrown away but planted in sandy soil. With luck it will produce a new bulb.

Basically, the typical structure of the plant is like that of a miniature corn plant, with blossoms nestled in the leaf axils, and sometimes also terminal. It grows from a bulb, relatively large in the case of most species, with tough, fleshy roots (care should be taken in transporting them; they should not be damaged). During the growing period, slender lateral roots, the actual organs for the intake of nourishment, sprout from the tuberous roots. Leaves are deeply furrowed or ridged and clasp the stem. It is characteristic of the blossom that the standards are very small and point laterally or downwards.

Juno aitchisonii (Baker) Klatt
Synonym: *Iris aitchisonii*

This species, which is found in the northern border regions of Pakistan, in parts of Afghanistan, and around Rawalpindi, is very rare and seldom cultivated. An early-blooming species, with a stem about 24" (60 cm) tall. The blossom is lilac-purple with a yellow-white central stripe on the falls; the blade dark purple. A yellow and bronze form is listed.

Juno albo-marginata (Foster)
Synonyms: *Iris albo-marginata, Iris coerulea*

Native to Tien Shan in Central Asia. There is considerable confusion surrounding this species. Many plants that went by the synonym *Iris coerulea* apparently had to be reclassified under *Juno magnifica.*

The typical plant has a very short stem that is said to be only 2" (5 cm) tall in the wild. The blossom is quite small and bluish purple-violet. The *Iris coerulea* described by Dykes in *The Genus Iris*, is now considered to be a *Juno vicaria*.

Juno almaatensis (N. Paplov)
Synonym: *Iris almaatensis*

Aside from being mentioned in Rodionenko's iris book, there are no other accounts of this species.

Juno atropatana (Grossheim)
Synonym: *Iris atropatana*

A species from Transcaucasia which has only recently been described. Yellow-blooming dwarf, very similar to *Juno caucasia*.

Juno aucheri (Baker) Klatt
Synonyms: *Iris aucheri, Iris fumosa, Iris sindjarensis*

Native to Iran, Turkey, Jordan, Syria, and Iraq. Available on the market. This species grow to about 9" (25 cm); leaves about 13" (35 cm) long. The stem bears up to 6 blossoms about 2½" (6 cm) in diameter, light blue with prominent darker veins; the small central stripe is yellow; the haft of the falls is prominently winged and has darker veins; standards are relatively large for a Juno and recurved. Blossoms with violet-like scent. Blooms in February–March. In the wild this attractive plant grows in lowlands, in contrast to other Junos. *J. aucheri* is recommended for outdoor planting only in very mild climates, and even then it must be given winter protection. Grow it under glass or in an alpine greenhouse. This beautiful Juno is, unfortunately, not entirely perennial. It must cure completely in order to produce good blossoms the following year. A delicate white form is listed.

Juno baldshuanica (B. Fedtschenko)
Synonyms: *Iris baldschuanica, Iris rosenbachiana* var. *baldschuanica*

A miniature Juno from Pamir, Altai, in Central Asia. Very rare and seldom cultivated. The blossom varies from dull lilac to dark purple. The falls have an orange border. There is apparently also a yellowish form with purple veins. In habit and behavior it strongly resembles *J. rosenbachiana*, but is later blooming (beginning of March).

Juno bucharica (Foster)
Synonym: *Iris bucharica*

This is probably the best known species of this genus in gardening circles; commonly known among gardeners as the Horned Iris. Native to eastern Bukhara, where *bucharica* grows at elevations of up to 4,900 ft. (1500 m). In nutrient-rich loam it will grow to 20" (50 cm). Leaves are fairly long and broad, glossy green, grooved, with a white, horny margin. Fragrant blossoms grow from the leaf axils and have a diameter of 2" (5 cm). Standards are white, small and project horizontally; the falls are cream-white, with a rich, dark yellow color on the wide blade. Blooming period is end of April–beginning of May. It makes a nice companion to *Muscari armeniacum* or other blue bulbs blooming at this time. *J. bucharica* is completely winter hardy, if the bulbs have fully cured. In a sunny, favorable location it forms large clumps. Take care when transplanting or dividing not to break the brittle extra-long, fleshy, roots. The *J. orchioides* grown in gardens could be a pure yellow form of *J. bucharica*.

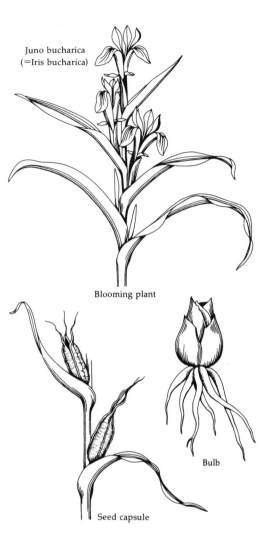

Juno bucharica
(=Iris bucharica)

Blooming plant

Bulb

Seed capsule

Juno cabulica (Gilli)

Synonym: *Iris cabulica*

A species found in Afghanistan and named after its capital Kabul. Grows particularly on western slopes in scree at elevations of 5,900–6,500 ft. (1800–2000 m). Seldom cultivated.

Usually with 4 leaves, more rarely 3, which are grooved and crescent-shaped; they are about 4–4½" (10–12 cm) long and ¾" (2 cm) wide. The stem grows only 1⅛" (3 cm) tall. The plant produces 2–4 blossoms. The spathes are 2⅞–3¼" (7.5–8.5 cm) long, slender and papery; they are longer than the perianth tube. The blossoms have a somewhat unpleasant scent. The falls of the robust blossoms are light lilac covered with violet veins, which are lighter toward the margin and darker toward the center; a yellow line down the center ends in a spot on the blade. Seeds

have a white aril. Blooms in the wild in March–April.

Juno carterorum (Mathew et Wendelbo)

Synonym: *Iris carterorum*

A species from Afghanistan that has only recently been discovered. Produces 4 leaves that are well developed by the time the plant blossoms. The lower ones about 5¾" (14 cm) long and 1" (2.4 cm) broad (at the widest point); the upper ones are narrower, of a gray-green color with a

259

narrow white margin. The stem is about 2¾" high (7 cm) and bears 2 blossoms. The spathes are green and 2–2⅛" (5–5.5 cm) long. The perianth tube is yellow-green, with deep black-purple spots on the lower parts; falls are deep yellow and the standards are yellow. It blooms in the wild in April–May.

Juno caucasica (Hoffmann)
Synonym: *Iris caucasica*

Native to the Caucasus, northeastern Turkey, and northern Iran. A miniature species with pale yellow, almost transparent blossoms. The stem is rather short and produces 1–4 blossoms. The standards are very small and turned downwards. The leaves are fan-shaped, blue-green beneath, with a horny margin. They are well developed when the plant is in bloom.

Two varieties are described in the leterature: *J.c.* var. *major,* larger than the original species, with up to 5 leaves per stem. Also called *J.c.* var. *turkestanica.* Has also been classified as *Juno orchioides. J.c.* var. *kharput* has been collected in central and eastern Turkey. The stem grows about 11½" (30 cm) tall and bears up to 5 greenish yellow blossoms with orange combs on the falls. Has a stiffer growth habit than the type species. Can be purchased. Appears to be hardy, but still probably more successfully grown in a coldhouse or in pots. A productive plant has to have good drainage and must cure completely in summer.

Juno cycloglossa (Wendelbo)
Synonym: *Iris cycloglossa*

Collected southwest of Herat in Afghanistan. Grows up to elevations of 4,900 ft. (1500 m). It differs distinctly from the other Junos. While the bulb with its long, fleshy storage roots is typical, its habitat of damp, grassy sites is unusual for a Juno. The branched stems reach a height of 17½–29" (45–75 cm) with only a few narrow stem leaves. In cultivation the plant blossoms very late, May–June. It produces quite large blossoms (larger than *Xiphium vulgare*), which are bright medium blue with a white and yellow spot on the circular blade (1⅛–1½" or 3–4 cm wide) of the falls; the standards are not curved inwards like those of other Junos, but are large, semi-upright, and almost spoon-shaped. Spathes papery. A very attractive Juno that resembles a blue *Xiphium vulgare* when it is in bloom.

Dwarf iris cultivars. New varieties are introduced every year and the possibilities are far from exhausted.

Top left: 'Lady'. This cultivar could not have been better named. Its blossoms have a particularly elegant shape.
Top right: 'Three Smokes' is less effective at a distance and is a plant for specialists. The "three columns of smoke" can only be seen at close range.

Center left: 'Toskaner Prinz'. A prize winning hybrid by Eckard Berlin from Biberach. A proven variety, even in cold regions.
Center right: 'Pink Amber'. A pink color was achieved much later than with the tall bearded iris. A significant enrichment of the palette.
Bottom left: 'Bembes', another cultivar by Eckard Berlin, outstanding for its vigorousness and unique color.
Bottom right: 'Parinita'. A whole series of good varieties with yellow/brown combinations is available. This is one of the most reliable.

Juno doabensis (Mathew)
Synonym: *Iris doabesis*

Grows in the Doab district of the Hindu Kush range in Afghanistan and was found only a few years ago. It resembles *J. nicolae*, grows very compactly, so that the stem is somewhat visible only when the seed is mature. Otherwise, the overlapping, wide, glossy green leaves form a sort of spathe valve, out of which dark yellow blossoms appear one after the other, with a long perianth tube, 2¾–3" (7–8 cm), which holds the blossom well above the foliage; falls curve downwards, claw-like; standards are narrow and held at right angles to the receptacle. The yellow blossoms have an orange comb and several green veins on the falls. Slightly pineapple-scented. Roots are similar to *J. rosenbachiana*, relatively fleshy, almost carrot-like. Suitable for the coldhouse.

Juno drepanophylla (Aitchison et Baker)
Synonym: *Iris drepanophylla*

Native habitat Herat in southwestern Afghanistan, 3,900 ft (1200 m) level; mountainous regions of Turkmenia. The seeds have a white aril like *Juno rosenbachiana* and *Juno linifolia*. From 2–12 blossoms, pale yellow or greenish, falls darker, brownish veins. Only traces of standards remain. Height 6¼–12½" (16–32 cm).

Very thick, fleshy roots.

Two subspecies are listed: *Juno drepanophylla* ssp. *drepanophylla* grows in dry locations at elevations of 1,970–5,600 ft. (600–1700 m). Yellow blossoms in April. *Juno drepanophylla* ssp. *chlorotica* grows on grassy slopes at elevations of 2,300–4,600 ft. (700–1400 m). The blossoms are greenish with a pale yellow comb on the outer falls. Flowers in April.

Juno edomensis (Sealy)
Synonym: *Iris edomensis*

A rare species from Jordan. 1–2 blossoms on a very short stem. Whitish, with many purple-violet spots. Similar in form to *J. persica* and *J. albo-marginata*.

Juno eleonorae (Holmboe)
Synonym: *Iris eleonorae*

Found in Iran. Some writers think that it is a synonym of *J. persica* var. *purpurea*. A dark purple-blue dwarf with very long crests.

Juno fosteriana (Aitchison et Baker)
Synonyms: *Iris fosteriana, Iris caucasica* var. *bicolor*

Native to Central Asia, particularly the mountains of Turkmenistan, also Transcaspia, and northwestern Afghanistan, where it grows at elevations up to 3,900 ft.

Nothing demonstrates the change in blossom form produced by hybridizing than the juxtaposition of these two varieties. It has followed the same pattern as in the tall bearded iris.

Top: 'Dale Dennis' represents the older forms with downward curved falls. But the elegant plicata pattern still makes the flower attractive. Bottom: 'Lady' has the modern shape with falls that almost seem to be floating. Seen from above, it creates a much more intense splash of color.

263

(1200 m). Also other locations, but always in dry mountainous sites. The outer skin of the bulb is dark olive-gree. The plant grows about 11½" (30 cm) tall. Leaves are long and fan-shaped. The plants produce 1 or 2 blossoms. The falls are dull cream-yellow with darker blade, ruffled margin and purple stripes; standards are horizontal or silghtly down curved, vibrant purple-violet, broad, 1" (2.5 cm) long and ¾" (2 cm) wide. *J. fosteriana* is fairly rare, can be grown only in a coldhouse. The bulbs are not large and the roots, in contrast to other Junos, are not as developed or fleshy. Botanists think this species may be a link between the genus *Juno* and the genus *Xiphium*. Blooms in March.

Juno graeberiana (Sealy)
Synonym: *Iris graeberiana*

Turkestan is the home of this plant, which grows to 8–15" (20–40 cm), depending on its location, and bears 4–6 blossoms. The spreading, upright leaves are 5–6½" (13–17 cm) long. Blossoms are about 2½" (6 cm) in diameter, light silvery blue; blade of the falls is methylene blue with a lighter center and blue veins. Blooming period is end of April, beginning of May. This species, available commercially, is perennial in a warm, sunny location and is very free-blooming. In regions with much summer rain, lift them in August and replant them again in November. (Do not let the fleshy roots dry out) According to English accounts, this is the only tetraploid species of this genus.

Juno hymenospatha (Mathew et Wendelbo)
Synonym: *Iris hymenospatha*

A recently described species from Iran. Has much in common with *Juno persica*, but clearly differs from it in its drooping, papery spathes and the color of its blos-

soms. Differs from *Juno caucasica*, which it also resembles, in its longer perianth tube; *Juno caucasica* also has herbaceous spathes.

Juno hymenospatha grows to 2¾–4¼" (7–12 cm). The roots are slender, not very fleshy. Leaves (3–4 or even 5) are fairly short when the plant is in bloom (1½–4" or 4–10 cm long and ⅛–⅝" or 0.4–1.6 cm wide); as flowers fade they elongate and broaden. The stem is very short, bearing only 1 blossom. Rarely a plant may produce 2 or 3 blossoms. The white, papery spathes are 2½" (6 cm) long. The overall impression of the blossom color is whitish; the outer perianth tube is covered with blue-violet veins and about 2¾" (7 cm) long; falls white with a yellow central line, daubed and streaked on either side with dark violet; blade with a yellowish comb surrounded by a zone of violet. Blooming period February–May.

Two subspecies are listed: *J. hymnenospatha* subsp. *hymenospatha* (syn. *I. persica* var. *issacsonii*). On rocky, limestone slopes among shrubs, but in the open, at elevations of 4,900–6,500 ft. (1500–2000 m). Blossoms appear at the end of January. Very narrow leaves, more or less upright when the plant is in bloom, covered with multiple silvery white veins. *J. hymenospatha* subsp. *leptoneura*. On dry slopes at elevations of 3,900–7,400 ft. (1200–2250 m). Blooms somewhat later, beginning in February. The leaves are relatively broad, crescent-shaped, semi-upright when the plant is in bloom, and with indistinct veins at the base.

Juno kopetdaghensis Vvedensky
Synonym: *Iris kopetdaghensis*

Rare species from Central Asia, particularly the mountains of Turkmenistan, in the eastern interior of Iran and into Afghanistan; 2–10 pale greenish blossoms. The blade of the falls has a yellow spot; standards reduced to the merest vestige. 6¼–12½" (16–32 cm) tall.

Juno kuschakewiczii (B. Fedtschenko)
Synonym: *Iris kuschakewiczii*

Found in Turkestan, in Tien Shan and a few other parts of Soviet Central Asia. Grows to only 3–4½" (8–12 cm) when in bloom, but gets somewhat taller later. Lower stem leaves about 4½" (12 cm) long, fairly thick at the base; glossy gray-green with wavy, horn-like margins. Upper leaves proportionately smaller. A short stem bears typically 3–4 blossoms. The terminal blossom is scarcely 1½" (4 cm) wide, the axillary blossoms correspondingly smaller. Flower ground color is usually pale violet, but this may be more intense; tips of the crests and the horizontally borne standards are darker violet; the falls are slightly wavy with a deep maroon signal spot, from which several dark violet lines radiate into the haft. The brown bulb measures ½–¾" (1.3–2 cm) in diameter, with several fleshy roots. This species is very difficult to obtain.

Juno leptorrhiza Vvedensky
Synonym: *Iris leptorrhiza*

Pamir Altai in Central Asia. Not attractive! Has only one greenish violet blossom. Roots only thread-like, rather than thick/fleshy like other Junose. Practically no stem.

Juno linifolia (O. Fedtschenko)
Synonyms: *Iris linifolia, Iris caucasica* var. *linifolia*

Central Asia: Kirghiz, eastern Afghanistan, northern Bukhara, Turkestan. A little known species, probably not cultivated. It has a short stem, to 6" (15 cm). Falls are greenish white with a yellow zone on the blade; standards are narrow, but broader at

the base. The leaves are linear. Characterized by a 2-lobed stigma and the white aril on the seed. Probably difficult to grow.

Juno magnifica (Vvedensky)
Synonyms: *Iris magnifica, Iris vicaria, Iris caucasica* var. *major*

One of the most splendid Juno species found in Turkestan. It is usually available commercially. The stem may rise to 24" (60 cm) and bear up to 7 blossoms. They are light lavender-blue, but may also be whitish. The blade of the falls has a yellow zone. Blooming period is end of April. This robust species grows even in colder climates without any protection. It sets seed well and often seeds itself. Several Junos that were sometimes called *Iris coerulea* should probably be classified with this species. *Juno magnifica* var. *alba* is a pure white form.

Juno maracandica Vvedensky
Synonym: *Iris maracandica*

A rare species from around Samarkand. 1–4 blossoms, pale yellow; falls with dark yellow crests. Grows about 7" (18 cm) tall.

Juno microglossa (Wendelbo)
Synonym: *Iris microglossa*

A very characteristic species, found in Afghanistan; fairly isolated. Grows on dry slopes at elevations of 5,600–6,900 ft. (1700–2100 m), often together with juniper.

It is often described as being shorter, but according to *Flora Iranica* this species grows to 4½–15" (12–40 cm). The bulbs are dark brown, occasionally gray-brown, and the roots are rather thick. The 4–6 leaves are fully developed as the plant comes into bloom, the lower ones being 8" (20 cm) long and ½" (1.5 cm) wide at the base. They are 9" (25 cm) long and 1" (2.7 cm) wide when the plant is mature, but narrower toward the top of the stem. They are bluish gray-green above, paler gray-green beneath. The stem is 2½–6¼″ (6–16 cm) long when the plant is in bloom and up to 13″ (35 cm) as the capsules ripen. 1–4 blossoms. The spathes are 2¼–2⅝″ (5.5–6.5 cm) long, gray-green with bristly margins. The perianth tube is 1⅛–1⅝″ (3–4.5 cm) long. Blossoms are whitish to pale mauve. The falls have a broad, winged haft. The blade is recurved, lanceolate.

Juno narbuti (O. Fedtschenko)
Synonym: *Iris narbuti*
Found in Central Asia, but questionable whether its a separate species or belongs with *J. fosteriana*.

Has greenish yellow or pale violet blossoms with a velvety violet signal spot surrounded by a zone of pale yellow on either side of the white comb. Stem to 1½″ (4 cm); 1–2 blossoms.

Juno narynensis (O. Fedtschenko)
Synonym: *Iris narynensis*
Native to Tien Shan. 1–2 dark violet blossoms. The falls have a somewhat lighter edge, the crests are white, the stem is up to 4¼″ (11 cm) tall.

Juno nicolai Vvedensky
Synonym: *Iris nicolai*
Occurs in Central Asia in the Pamir Mountains. Related to *J. rosenbachiana*, but blossoms earlier and has narrower flowers. 1–2 blossoms; falls pale pink-violet with a dark purple-violet signal spot and dots, and with golden yellow crests; haft whitish. About 7″ (18 cm) tall.

Juno nusairiensis (Mouterde)
Synonym: *Iris nusairiensis*
This Juno was discovered in Syria in only 1953 growing on stony soil at elevations up to 4,900 ft. (1500 m) and first described by Pater Mouterde. The bulb

diameter is about ½″ (1.5 cm), oval and with a blackish husk. The stem is only 2¾–4″ tall with two papery leaf sheaths at the base. Leaves are opposite, crescent-shaped and slightly twisted, ½″ (1.5 cm) wide. The uppermost pair of leaves has an elongated leaf sheath (the chief characteristic of this species). The color of the 3–6 blossoms is a beautiful shade of blue; standards lanceolate and more flaring than recurved; falls not contracted but rounded at the tip, with yellow central strip. Is about as winter hardy as *J. aucheri*, hence coldhouse culture is recommended. Needs summer dryness from July to October. More beautiful than *J. aucheri!*

Juno odontostyla (Mathew et Wendelbo)
Synonym: *Iris odontostyla*
A recently named species from Afghanistan, which grows on stony slopes and rocky ledges at around 4,900 ft. (1500 m). It is similar to *J. stocksii* and *J. platyptera*. It differs from *J. stocksii* in the circular spot on the falls, which is grayish violet rather than reddish violet; also by toothed lobes on the crests, and longer standards. It differs from *J. platyptera* in that its roots are not tuberous, and by green spathes, and by the large, round spot on the falls.

Grows about 5″ (13 cm) tall. The hard roots are long and not swollen. Its 4–5 leaves are well formed when the plant is in bloom, about 7″ (18 cm) long and ½″ (1.5 cm) wide at the base, slightly crescent-shaped, glossy dark green above and paler below, covered with a narrow but striking white margin, prominently veined toward the top. A very short stem, enclosed by leaves. One blossom. Spathes differ only slightly, 2¼″ (5.5 cm) long, green with a narrow, papery margin. Perianth tube 1½″ (4 cm) long, gray-violet. Falls with an orange-yellow comb ringed by an almost white zone.

Juno orchioides (Carr.)

Synonym: *Iris orchioides, Iris caucasica* var. *oculata*

Turkestan, in the Tien Shan mountains at elevations up to 6,500 ft. (2000 m). The stem is about 11½" (30 cm) tall with broad, opposite leaves with horny margins. The plant produces 3–6 blossoms, 2–3" (5–8 cm) in diameter, yellow merging into shades of blue. The stripe is orange, the stigma large and light yellow. Lilac specimens have also been found. The bulbs are fairly large and oval. This beautiful plant, somewhat reminiscent of *J. bucharica,* is recommended only for protected locations. The form cultivated in gardens under the name *J. orchioides* is actually a pure yellow *J. bucharica.*

Juno palaestina (Klatt)

Synonym: *Iris palaestina*

Closely related to *J. planifolia (I. alata).* Native to the Lebanon mountains near Saida; also at Jaffa, Gaza, Hebron. In full bloom in February south of the Beirut airport. It is smaller than *J. planifolia.* The 1- or 2-blossomed plant almost seems stemless. The leaves emerge from the soil. Plants with 3 blossoms occasionally occur. In a garden, however, *J. palaestina* can grow to 17½" (45 cm) tall, with one terminal and two axillary blossoms. In Beirut gardens the leaves are 13½" (35 cm) long and 1" (2.6 cm) wide and the plant bears three large blossoms. The blossoms themselves are white with a yellow central groove. According to Gideon Schulz, there are new but similar species with various chromosome counts.

Juno parvula Vvedensky

Synonym: *Iris parvula*

Native to Pamir Altai in Central Asia.

Blossoms are greenish yellow with darker green veins. About 4" (10 cm) tall.

Juno persica (Linne)

Synonym: *Iris persica*

Widely distributed from Turkey to Iran, but never present in masses. It was described by Parkinson as early as 1697 and illustrated in the Botanical Magazine in 1787. This Juno species has been popular among plant lovers, even though hard to grow. It now is commercially available. It is not easy to make it a long-term guest in your garden. Many varieties of this Juno are listed. The typical form is 6–8" (15–20 cm) tall, sometimes shorter, with one or two pale greenish blue blossoms, about 2¾" (7 cm) in diameter, on each stem. The falls have a dark purple zone on the lower lobe and a golden yellow, black-spotted center groove. The standards are small, held horizontally. The narrow leaves are ribbed. Bulbs are oval with a dark parchment-colored outer skin (deeply buried in its native habitat). Blooming period in the wild is January/March; in cool climates usually April. Requires protection from frost; the ideal place for it is the coldhouse. Should be well watered during the growing period and kept quite dry in summer. Seems to grow better in heavy loam than in sandy soils. Number of chromosomes 2n=26.

Most varieties are fragrant. Following are some better known sorts:

J.p. var. *bolleana,* light yellow with a violet to purple spot on the falls. In the southeastern Taurus mountains up to 2,300 ft. (700 m).

J.p. var. *galatica,* dull, pale gray, sometimes with a tinge of purple, light brown, or yellow. Purple dots on the falls. Found especially in northern Cappadocia.

J.p. var. *isaacsonii,* cream white blossoms with a cast of green, dark violet veins, but no spots. Southern Iran. (Now *J. hymenospatha* ssp. *hymenospatha*.)

J.p. var. *issica*, pure straw yellow except for a few black dots on the orange border. From southeastern Turkey.

J.p. var. *mardinensis,* pale greenish blue with a dark, purple-violet spot. North Syrian variety.

J.p. var. *purpurea,* reddish purple blossoms, orange central groove on the falls and a dark purple spot on the lobe.

J.p. var. *sieheana,* reddish purple on a silver-gray or greenish yellow ground. Native to Turkey.

J.p. var. *stenophylla,* dull gray-blue blossom and a blue-black blade. Border of stigma unusually large. Region of Taurus mountains.

J.p. var. *tauri,* dark violet blossom, falls have white veins. Center groove orange with purple dots. According to Dykes, among the easiest species to grow.

Juno planifolia ([Miller] Ascherson et Graebner)

Synonyms: *Iris alata, Iris planifolia*

Probably the most widespread Juno species. Portugal, Spain, Sardinia, Sicily, Algeria, Lybia. As a result there are many forms; for example, Sicilian form bears only pale blue flowers.

Blossoms in its various locations from winter to early spring. *J. planifolia* grows about 9" (25 cm) tall. The blossom is various shades of blue, depending on the location, very rarely white. Soon after the blooming period, the foliage starts to yellow and elongated seed capsules develop. The plant is dormant from April until fall. When precipitation begins again in the Mediterranean region, *J. planifolia* starts to emerge.

Tourists like to take these plants home with them, which is not a recommended practice. This Juno species is unfor-

tunately not hardy enough for cool climates where it must be grown in pots or in a greenhouse. The bulbs, with their thick, fleshy roots, should be potted in August–September. After being well watered, new roots start to grow and the stem begins to emerge. Long, cornstalk-like leaves develop, and the first blossoms appear already in November or December. They are very fragrant. After the plant dies back, the pot should be kept dry. Bunches of *J. planifolia* are sold in all the North African port towns at Christmas time. Since every stalk produces three blossoms, with diameters of 3½" (9 cm) it makes a very respectable winter bloomer. Unfortunately, this Juno cannot be maintained over any length of time in continental climates.

J.p. var. *alba* has pure white blossoms; *J.p.* var. *marginata,* dark blue falls with a white margin.

Juno platyptera (Mathew et Wendelbo)

Synonym: *Iris platyptera*

A recently introduced species from Afghanistan and Pakistan, where it grows on dry, rocky slopes at elevations of 5,900–8,850 ft. (1800–2700 m).

Grows about 3–5¾" (8–14 cm) tall. The roots below the bulbs are short and stocky. The bulb is chestnut brown, with a well-formed neck. The 4–6 leaves are up to 7" (18 cm) long and ⅜–1⅛" wide, usually very crescent-shaped with a definite white margin. Short stem surrounded by leaves bears 2, rarely 3, completely developed blossoms during the blooming period. Spathes 2–2⅝" (5–6.5 cm) long, papery. The periath tube is 1½" (4 cm) long; blossoms are violet-brown, with a yellow comb on the falls. There are also pale violet individuals. Blooming period March to April.

Juno popovii Vvedensky
Synonym: *Iris popovii*

A Central Asian Juno. Grows at high elevations (above 12,000 ft. or 3600 m), usually in loam soil. Has 2–4 light violet to blue blossoms. Blade of the falls with yellowish veins. Grows about 4¼" (12 cm) tall.

Juno porphyrochrysa (Wendelbo)
Synonym: *Iris porphyrochrysa*

Native to Afghanistan: Parvan, Shibar Pass. Grows at elevations of 8,850–9,800 ft. (2700–3000 m) on dry slopes among *Acantholimon, Cousinia,* and *Astragalus.*

Only 4–4⅝" (10–12 cm) tall. Roots of the bulb are long and thick. The 4 leaves (3, 5 and 6 are also possible), fully developed when the plant flowers are 4–6¾" (10–17 cm) long and ¼–½" (0.6–1.1 cm) wide, crescent-shaped, grooved, gray-green with a narrow but striking white margin and prominent central vein on the lower half. The short stem enclosed by the leaves bears 1–3 blossoms. Spathes are 2–2⅝" (5–6.5 cm) long, the outer valve being shorter than the inner one, gray-green, and rather papery. The perianth tube is 1¼–1½" (3.5–4 cm) long and purple-brown on the upper part. The falls are brown-purple; the blade is dark yellow with orange comb ⅜" (1 cm) long, and toothed. The standards are purple-brown and horizontal.

Juno postii (Mouterde)
Synonym: *Iris postii*

Found in Iraq and Syria (Palmyra). Was formerly described as *Iris palaestina* (Bak.) Boiss. var. *coerulea* Post, but is not like *Juno palaestina.* Unlike other Junos, this one has slender, tangled roots. The bulb neck is long and papery (buried in nature). Leaves are about 6⅜" (16 cm) long and up to ⅜" (1 cm) wide, somewhat broader at the base, grayish-green on the underside. The plant grows 4–8" (10–20 cm) tall when in bloom, the stem hidden among the dense foliage; only during the fruiting period are some parts of it visible. The 1–3 blossoms are spotted and veined, violet or brownish violet on a pale lilac ground; falls are 1⅛–1½" (3–4 cm) long; the narrower, horizontal standards ½–⅝" (1.2–1.8 cm); the short perianth tube (1–1¾" or 2.5–4.5 cm long) distinguishes this species from *J. persica.* Distantly related to *J. persica.*

This species is difficult to maintain. It is adapted to cold, dry winters and a short growing period with burning hot summers.

Juno pseudocaucasica (Grossheim)
Synonym: *Iris pseudocaucasica*

Native to the Caucasus and Transcaucasia at elevations of up to 3,280 ft. (1000 m). The blossoms are blue to pale violet, but there are also specimens with a yellowish luster. Flower falls with yellow groove. Very closely related to *J. caucasica,* but with a different blossom color. Dwarfish species, 4¼–4⅝" (12–13 cm) tall, blooms end of April.

Juno rosenbachiana (Regel)
Synonym: *Iris rosenbachiana*

A very attractive miniature species from the mountains of Turkestan and Bukhara, usually at elevations of 5,900–8,850 ft. (1800–2700 m). The stem is very short, barely 6" (15 cm) tall when the plant is in bloom. Each stalk bears 1 or 3 blossoms, each with a diameter of 2½" (6 cm) and a perianth tube 2¾" (7 cm) long. Blossoms vary greatly in color, but are frequently light purple-violet; falls are dark purple with a dark yellow or orange groove and irregular, white dots; stigma is pale lilac with a large border, yellow above. The standards are small, horizontal to pendulous. The slightly crescent-shaped, dark-green leaves are short during the blooming period. In cultivation, blooms fron January to March. It could be completely hardy, but it is safer to grow it in a coldhouse in cool climates. Dykes was able to produce white seedlings. The seeds of *J. rosenbachiana* have a white aril.

Juno schischkinii (Grossheim)
Synonym: *Iris schischkinii*

Native to Transcaucasia at elevations of 6,900 ft. (2100 m). Grows about 8–11½" (20–30 cm) tall, and normally has 3–6 blossoms, or very occasionally 8–10. Blossom yellowish.

Juno stocksii (Boissier)
Synonym: *Iris stocksii*

Similar to *J. caucasica*, but with purple blossoms. Found in Afghanistan at elevations up to 9,800 ft. (3000 m), and is found on the northwestern border of India. It is a fairly inconspicuous plant that grows 6⅜–8½" (16–22 cm) tall, with 1–3 spindly, reddish mauve blossoms with a broad, yellow central stripe. The leaves have a prominent, silvery margin.

Juno subdecolorata (Vvedensky)
Synonym: *Iris subdecolorata*

Rare Central Asian species found in Tashkent. 1–3 pale, dull greenish or violet blossoms. Very short. Stem little more than 1⅛" (3 cm) long.

Juno tadshikorum (Vvedensky)
Synonym: *Iris tadshikorum*

Very little known Central Asian species from Pamir Altai. 2–4 pale violet blossoms, stem 2–2½" (5–6 cm) long.

Juno tubergeniana (Foster)
Synonym: *Iris tubergeniana*

Central Asia, in the loam hills of Tashkent. Also similar to *J. caucasica*, but with clearly striped blue-gray leaves. It is a dwarfish species with dark yellow blossoms. The falls are 2" (5 cm) long, with a gold margin; stigmas large, greenish yellow, with well defined margins; standards are very small. Blooms very early in January–March with *Iridodictyum reticulatum*. Very rare and not in cultivation at the present time, but should be.

Juno vicaria (Vvedensky)
Synonym: *Iris vicaria, Iris orchiodes* var. *coerulea*

Central Asia, on stony slopes in Turkestan. Very closely related to *J. magnifica*. The stalk is well-developed. The blossoms are blue-violet, with dark yellow spots on the falls. Little known and probably not cultivated.

Iris sibirica cultivars with 28 and 40 chromosomes.

Top left: 'Berliner Riesen'. Tall, robust hybrid from Dr. Tamberg of Berlin. A hybrid with 40 chromosomes, and amazing vitality, since "grass iris" usually grow very slowly.
Top right: Iris sibirica 'Alba'. There are several natural albino varieties of this iris, not to mention white cultivars. These small-flowered, free-blooming varieties please some enthusiasts and have a place in the garden.

Bottom left: Iris × chrysofor. Various hybrid types having different shapes and colors have resulted from crossings of Iris chrysographes × Iris forrestii. Some of the color combinations are more strange than beautiful.
Bottom right: Iris sibirica. Older varieties are often more robust than modern cultivars and tolerate more dryness as well. Shown here, a type very close to the wild species. These typical Sibericas mix well in the typical perennial border and in naturalized plantings.

270

Juno vvedenski (Nevski)
Synonym: *Iris vvedenskyi*

Found in Transcaspia in Turkestan. 1–2 blossoms, pale yellow with darker falls and orange crests. Dwarfish, stalk only 2–2½″ (5–6 cm) long.

Juno warleyensis (Foster)
Synonym: *Iris warleyensis*

Native to Central Asia, Kukkara, western Samarkand. It is a taller-growing Juno. The plant grows 9–17½″ (25–45 cm) tall, with 3–5 blossoms, occasionally more. The blossom color is dark violet to pale mauve. Haft of the falls has dark violet veins on a light violet ground; blade has a dark violet zone and a lobe rimmed with white, the margin a vibrant orange. Some variations in color are noted. The leaves have a horny margin. Blooms in March and is hardy. Thrives in gardens in sandy soil. Unfortunately rarely cultivated.

Juno wendelboi (Grey Wilson et Mathew)
Synonym: *Iris wendelboi*

Native to Afghanistan. Has 1–2 dark violet-blue blossoms. Golden yellow crests on the falls, erect standards. The plant is 3⅜–4¼″ (9–12 cm) tall.

Juno willmottiana (Foster)
Synonym: *Iris willmottiana*

Native to Central Asia, from the mountains of eastern Turkestan, where it is found at high elevations. Strongly resembles *J. caucasica*. The stem is short, with 4–6 blossoms that vary in color, but are usually lavender-blue or whitish with shades of lavender-blue. The leaves have a thickened, horny margin. The bulb is very round. Blooming period is earlier than *J. caucasica*.

A white-blooming strain or hybrid, *J. willmottiana* var. *alba*, collected from its native habitat, can be purchased. It is very pretty and recommended.

There are, unfortunately, very few hybrids among the Junos, and much should be done in this area. Van Tubergen in Haarlem has produced a few beautiful hybrids, intending to increase winter hardiness. *J.* × *sindjareichii* (*J. sindjarensis* × *J. persica* var. *heldreichii*), a dark-blue, early

---

Iris rarities sensitive to frost.

Top left: Iris cretensis from the island of Crete is one of the winter iris. It is the hardiest of the three species from sub-tropical climates, yet can stand only mild winters in Germany and is best kept in a coldhouse in colder regions.
Top right: Iris grant-duffii. This iris grows in eastern Turkey, Syria and Lebanon and is probably the link between rhizomatous and bulbous iris because of its unusual, bristly rootstock. Can be grown in a coldhouse, but care must be taken during summer dormancy.
Below: Iris unguicularis comes from the Algerian oak forests. Hence this winter iris can only be recommended for the coldhouse. But during its blooming period from November to February it will also blossom at a basement window.

spring iris and *J. × sindpur,* which Karl Foerster called Purple Iris, are unfortunately no longer cultivated. But two attractive hybrids are marketed:

J. × sindpers, a cross between *J. sindjarensis* and *J. persica.* This dwarf, which Karl Foerster called Porcelain Iris, grows about 2¾″ (7 cm) tall and blooms in March–April. The color is a bright procelain blue with sea green and orange. A treasure for protected locations in the rock garden or for pot culture in the coldhouse.

Another hybrid is *J. × warlsind (J. warleyensis × J. sindjarensis),* which is quite winter hardy and free-blooming even outdoors. The standards are dark blue, the falls yellow with a blue margin. This is a unique color combination for Junos. Blooming period is March–April. Grows about 11½″ (30 cm) tall, considerably taller than the aforementioned cross.

Juno xanthoclora (Wendelbo)
Synonym: *Iris xanthochlora*

Native to Afghanistan. Stem is about 3″ (8 cm) tall, with 1–3 yellow-green blossoms. The crescent-shaped dark green leaves are fully formed when the plant blossoms, the margins are whitish and horny. Probably close to *J. linifolia,* but differs from it by the claw-like outer parts of the petals.

Juno zaprjagajewii (U. V. Abranov)
Synonym: *Iris zaprjagajewii*

This Juno grows in Central Asia in the Pamir region at elevations up to 7,550 ft. (2300 m), where winters are very severe and the summers hot and dry. Should be quite hardy in cool climates. It is closely related to *J. rosenbachiana* and *J. doabensis.* They all have the same carrot-like roots and stocky appearance, with broad leaves that form a thick sheath at the base.

Grayish-white blossoms with long perianth tubes, and with a yellow comb on the falls, appear in March–April, while the leaves are still short. The falls are claw-like, pendulous. Very rare.

If seeds or bulbs can be obtained, it is rewarding to grow. The smooth bulb has short, cylindrical roots that absolutely must be protected from damage when being planted. Best suited to the coldhouse, where it can be grown in larger pots or containers. Its main requirements are full sun and good drainage. During the growing period, the plant requires ample water (simulating spring runoff from the glaciers and snowfields of the Pamirs). Blooming period is quite short. In intense sunlight, the blossoms last only 3–4 days, longer, of course, outdoors. Blossoms on the upper parts of the plant wither promptly as the last flower fades. During its long dormancy, the plant should be kept as dry as possible. Soil needed for cultivation: rich, sandy loam, no compost. Give some winter protection outdoors.

Iris Hybridization

by Dr. Peter Werckmeister

No garden flower has awakened the imagination more than the iris. At first the eye may be so overwhelmed by its beauty that it gets lost in details of the veining or in the nuances of color gradation. Then suddenly it sees something quite different, namely the flower's ingenious system for pollination. Fingers reach for the stamens and dust the pollen grains onto the stigma. That is the moment when the gardener is hooked. He has discovered that there is something very special he can do himself and now he wants to try it. Instead of sowing seed provided by nature, as he always did before, he has discovered that he can create something for himself by combining whatever characteristics he wants. That he has to try!

It is a good thing to realize that two completely different stimuli have turned our unbiased gardener into a hybridizer. First, the surprise and pleasure which accompany the sudden realization of the possibilities hybridizing offers turns the observer into a doer. This transformation will require considerable future research and dedication. Second, to pure sensory impressions is added a new perspective. The ex-gardener turned hybridizer will notice right away that he is no longer comfortable conversing with someone who sees flowers only as pretty objects in the garden or in a vase.

If we are going to talk about hybridizing iris, we have to realize from the outset that everyone's goals and methods are not the same and should be kept clearly separated. Without this understanding, an individual's results might be in jeopardy. We cannot describe, outline, or establish hybridizing goals without taking aesthetic considerations into account. And there cannot be aesthetics without judgment. If we end up arguing about goals in hybridizing, it is usually about what is more and what is less beautiful. But this should never preclude or interfere with open discussions about methods of hybridizing.

The method depends on what nature will allow us to do, and only on that! It is not a question of what we should or should not do, but what we can and cannot do. This requires scientific thinking and experimentation. It has nothing to do with aesthetics. The poor beginner who confuses these two aspects will not get very far.

He may, for instance, be stymied by some kind of veining. But it will not dawn on him to ask himself if a particular pattern he observes is inheritable, and then if and how he can find out. He will make random experiments, grow hundreds of seedlings, that will all end up on the compost heap, and he will not have learned a thing from it.

Maybe he has a bit of luck! Chance drops a seedling in his path that has something unexpectedly new about it. Too many hybridizers rely all too heavily on this kind of luck. He then pursues this new characteristic but without applying the thought processes necessary for scientific experimentation. Nothing is learned about the methodology; he has no idea where the new character arose or how to duplicate it. Maybe some valuable piece of information from the seed bed will not even be noticed. Then there are all the things to look up and learn about. If these steps in the scientific method are ignored, process will be slowed unnecessarily.

First, therefore, our aesthetic goals and our objective methodology must be clearly separated from each other, without minimizing either.

Style Characteristics

If we think our present-day irises are more beautiful than anything before, we can expect similar progress in the future. This is encouraging to the hybridizer. Yet the question still remains whether these future possibilities can be addressed more precisely.

The point of hybridizing is first and foremost to heighten the effect of the blossom, which usually means larger flowers and more vibrant colors. Yet iris blossoms have something special about them. From the moment the bud begins to unfold, they are constantly changing. *An iris blossom is not an object; it is an event!* In order to follow this event, every single stage of blossoming will be evaluated.

Consider the old cultivar *I.* 'Rheingauperle', which Goos and Koenemann introduced in 1927. Its then new purplish-pink color is still attractive today, but its petals look crestfallen, even when it is in full bloom. This was true of many older cultivars. These "crestfallen" flowers remind us right away that they are soon going to wilt and "die". There's no other flower that contains this antithesis, this obvious life-and-death symbolism, as the iris blossom does. Thus a primary goal of hybridizers was to create sturdier petals. In this way, attention was drawn to other features that hinged *only* on our concept of style and were not favored by nature at all.

This concept of style demands that the three inner perianth segments, the standards (petals), incline towards each other and remain closed, while the three outer segments, the falls or wings (sepals), flare out from the receptacle at an angle and not appear pendulous. If these two features coincide, it creates an immediate impression of sturdiness. And yet none of this is necessarily intended by nature. For a time Goos and Koenemann were trying to create long, wide, vertically inclined falls (e.g. I. 'Norräna'). This was called "hands on the trouser seams" and made perfect sense because, when viewed from a distance, the greatest possible surface was visible and therefore did, indeed, heighten the effect of the blossom.

Along with an increase in sturdiness, and in "substance", came the introduction of ruffles and waves. Alexander Steffen noted quite early that these characteristics served to support our notions of sturdiness because they reminded us of corrugated iron, which, compared to a flat sheet, is stiffer. Using a term such as "corrugated iron" in connection with a blossom may be shocking at first, but it is indisputably the *mot just*.

The word "substance" has a real meaning here and refers to mesophyll, the tissue between the two epidermal layers, which shows an increase in the number of cells in many garden flowers. Petals containing more mesophyll do, in fact, have greater sturdiness and therefore durability. This substance is so great in the standards of some modern varieties that their tips are too stiff to bow together and gape slightly. Because the eye makes up for this by really noticing the substance, such a cultivar will seldom be downgraded in competition.

In the case of large-blossomed plants, those with a compact growth habit—that grow in clumps—should always be selected. Spreading plants, which otherwise

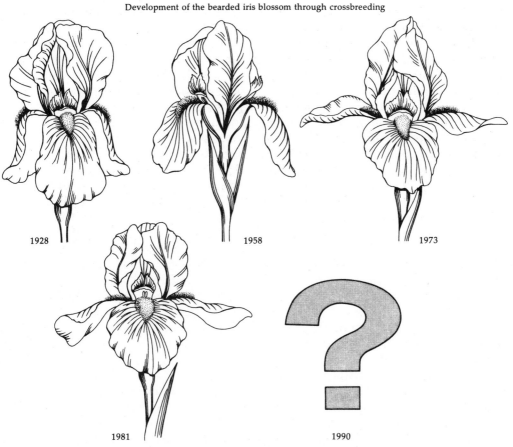

1928   1958   1973

1981   1990

play such an important role in the land-scape, never attain the individuality of a solitary plant that opens its blossoms high above the foliage. So where large-blossomed plants are involved, plants with compact growth should be selected. Runners of plants which produce them are "bred out". This means that single, free-running rhizomes are undesirable in iris. Ideally a rhizome should develop many side-shoots which must stay short. But this leads to overcrowding of the clump with leaf shoots that then have to be pains-takingly thinned by hand. In a stand of wild iris such a dense crowding would lead to depletion of soil nutrients under the clump, deterioration of that colony.

Hence this sort of breeding is done for purely practical reasons. It has nothing to do with our conception of style and little to do with aesthetics.

Many of the modern iris varieties, which were cultivated for blossom size, form, and color, sometimes have only 5 buds per bloomstalk. This poor inflores-cence is a regression, although these make attractive foreground plantings in small gardens. In their efforts to increase the blossoming effect, hybridizers created beautiful and prolific branching on all the clump iris. We should mention here what is called in the U.S. and Canada "candel-abra branching", which was first seen on the old cultivar *I.* 'Blue Rhythm'. This is not

277

just simple branching. The lateral branches are themselves branched, which considerably increases the number of buds. Nine buds per inflorescence should be the minimum number for any given cultivar of Tall Bearded Iris.

As the luxuriance and proliferation of blossoms increased, along with substance and ruffles, the size and breadth of the standards also grew so they eventually overlapped each other at the throat. This was a highly desirable characteristic. Moreover, as with many other plants (such as cyclamen) fast growing segment margins developed crinkled or laced edges, a trait only recently isolated to become a valuable asset to plant fanciers. This characteristic, however, is not always assessed more favorably in official judging.

In 1884, Heinrich discerned a certain characteristic in the descendants of his *Iris pallida*, which he called "petaloid overextension". He noticed that the lower tip of the beard was detached from the blade of the sepal, or fall, and projected out over it. In certain cases, the tip of the beard could broaden out, allowing the appendages thus formed to enlarge like standards. The beginnings of this phenomenon appeared again in the 20's in a few Cayeux cultivars. In the past few decades, Lloyd Austin has introduced various clones of this type in the U.S., called "horned", "spooned", or "flounced", depending on the shape of the appendage. Our concept of style can accept this feature inasmuch as heraldic floral emblems were based on the iris blossom, although they actually derived from the Oriental horns of David. Protuberances like this were also observed in these derivational heraldic symbols and could be considered comparable formations.

The amount of attention devoted to one characteristic, especially a new charac-teristic, depends on the intensity of interest. As early as 1921 a succession of iris experts from the U.S., England, and France gathered in Paris under the auspices of the French Horticultural Society. About this time separate iris societies were also founded in those countries. Without these societies the rapid advances and increased interest in hybridizing—up to the current high level—would not have been possible. Because of this active participation, prizes and awards, as well as rankings and lists of evaluations, were established. The most important trophy for hybridizers is the Dykes Medal, named after the famous authority on iris, William Rickatson Dykes. In the beginning it was awarded in France, England, and the U.S. Merit rankings were later established, with the Popularity Poll and the Judges' Choice in the U.S. setting the trend. The competition in Florence for the Premio Firenze, important because it is entered anonymously, and the Dwarf Iris and Aril Iris competitions in Vienna have also spurred international competition.

In the course of this development, style characteristics obviously became established. Whereas a kind of standardization results in the trade simply by supply and demand, the members of this society formed—in their minds, so to speak—a whole set of additional rules. The American Iris Society soon formalized the rank of iris judge, and all were given a special booklet of rules for judging. An existing standard was thereby solidified, and the flexibility of value judgments limited.

In every respect the standard of today's garden iris has moved drastically away from the wild flower, and it is possible that, because of this, a number of other style and form characteristics have been ignored. On the other hand, we notice how many elements of style have been introduced that do not occur in the wild form.

Throat veination is one characteristic of the wild flower that has disappeared in modern garden varieties—was "bred out"—and is now of particular interest. The famous iris hybridizer from New Zealand, Jean Stevens, who has been working very successfully since 1920, writes: "In those (beginning) days, prominent veining in the throat was not only accepted as an essential part of iris coloration, but hybridizers tried to outdo one another in their precise descriptions of different colored markings in the throat of their seedlings and to discuss their merits. Apparently we made a virtue of something we had not or could not get rid of yet. We convinced ourselves that throat veining was a special attraction of the iris blossom!"

It is obvious that throat veining detracts from the unified effect of the blossom color of an iris, indeed that it generally increases the gray value of a color, especially from a distance. In the future it would become the rule to suppress this veining as much as possible. This signified a tendency in itself, a departure from the natural type of the wildflower. The history of the value placed on throat veining in the garden iris is a good example of how much the development of a garden flower means a departure from the prototype of the wildflower, and this expresses our own ideas of style.

The opposite can also be shown by the Oncocyclus blossom. This largest and most beautiful iris blossom is first and foremost a wild species. As wild species, these iris have so far successfully resisted being introduced into garden culture because of their very special ecological requirements. Take *Iris lortetii, I. gatesii, I. auranitica,* and *I. iberica* as the most beautiful representatives of this group; their prototype is still *Iris susiana,* because for

centuries it was the only one that would grow in southern regions. Its blossom is large and round, i.e. the outer perianth segments (falls) are curved—and the entire blossom is veined. Not excluding the large, usually black signal spot, which is the unique feature of the Oncocyclus Iris, we have the essential style characteristics of a new type of iris blossom, that are obviously worth breeding for. But, the prototype is a *wildflower!* And all the hybridizers who work with these species, rather than trying to get away from the wild form, work directly toward incorporating their wild features into an easily grown garden flower.

The problem of prototypes in hybridizing is shown here in all its peculiarity. Are all our notions of style in breeding based on comparison? Indeed, it would probably be difficult to find a hybridizer doing anything other than combining features that he has seen someplace else before. Can the imagination devise an entirely new breeding goal without some kind of model? Whether or not this is so, nature has to allow us to reach this breeding goal methodically.

Taking only the enormous number of variations in Oncocylcus and Regelia Iris, the prototypes and style characteristics are practically inexhaustible. We have to be prepared for the completely unexpected. In fact we actually have to "plan the unexpected"! As much as we could have foreseen a shell pink iris, that is how much as we are able to foresee what will happen with the Arils. Reflecting on the experiences that determine our methodology shows that an important goal—aside from any aesthetic considerations—is to set up fertile families. We can only hope to meet the unexpected in later departures from parent stock, if a line is fertile. That skeptical question about whether imagination alone can create original breeding goals remains unanswered. But in every instance, the goals have to be something that nature allows us to do.

Similarly, the question of bigger and bigger blossoms also has to remain unanswered for now. Thanks to the work of hybridizers, blossoms now exist, the size of which could not have been imagined at the beginning. Varieties from the "Mohr family" in particular surpassed everything we had known up to that time about tetraploid true Pogon Iris. Their original size was only later attained again. In spite of this, attempts to find a size that can be achieved only through breeding "accidents" still lie within the realm of possibility.

The greater the impact of the blossom itself, i.e. the more importance placed on size in overall effect of the blossom, the more some hybridizers will work in the opposite direction, that is, work toward achieving the smallest, but nonetheless exquisite style characteristics. Space allows us to mention only the Dwarf Iris, later called "Miniatures", developed by Paul Cook and Walter Welch, cultivars such as *I.* 'Cherry Spot', *I.* 'Veri Gay', and *I.* Hearts Content', that are extremely special stylistically and can no longer be compared to the wild *I. pumila*. The possibility of having many different sizes is being rather obscured right now for the other taller "classes" because of the stan-dardizing effect of height restrictions. Style characteristics in all the smaller size classifications are being influenced by tall garden iris, but there's no reason why that has to remain so.

Colors

The goddess of the rainbow gave our plant its name so we assume it should represent all the colors of the rainbow. But it does not. On the contrary, many colors are not represented, but the history of hybridizing has shown that completely new colors, colors that could not have been dreamed of, appeared unexpectedly. This proves to the hybridizer that it pays to hybridize.

First of all it is important to be as precise as possible about color. A color chart, displaying the various shades side by side, is the most accessible tool. Granted, this comparison of colors is not ideal. There are physical methods of determining color that are far more precise. But we have to stick with what we can do. It will not take us long to determine that the exact color of the blossom we are holding in our hand does not appear in the color chart. So we have to learn to interpolate. The color spectrum is arranged in a circle—well actually more like a triangle. When interpolating, we may say a red value is a little bluer or a little oranger than the next red value on the chart. This gives us a working

Iris sintenisii. **A truly rewarding dwarf spuria for the rock garden with many pluses. The blossom is an appealing blue color, it is not so buried in the foliage as those of related species are, and it blossoms relatively late, about two weeks after the other dwarf spurias.**

approximation. If we decide that our color is a little brighter than the comparable hue in the color chart, then this means it is more saturated, as defined by Helmholz. But in general, this treats a petal as though it were a piece of cloth, which is too imprecise and does not take into consideration that what we are seeing is the cell sap in the upper epidermis. This tissue can sometimes appear as though it had its own light, especially when the sun shines on it and its papillae produce a velvety sheen. So we have to compromise.

With iris, we have the additional problem of numerous intermediate shades. In this respect Ostwald's system is, if not perfectly satisfactory, at least easier to use. According to it, colors are composed of hue, plus parts of black and white. Clarifications with white are usually easy to interpolate. By means of the color chart one can indicate: bluer than . . . paler (whiter) than. . . . This is for hues mixed with white. But this is very hard to do with hues mixed with black because it is impossible to determine what the base color is. Since iris have numerous brown hues (frequently called "red"), we should use a color chart that has a wide range of browns. The best one I know of is Baumann's New Color Chart. The best way to explain the differences in gradations between Ostwald's system and Helmholz's is that Ostwald's instrument for composing colors was a color gyroscope, while Helmholz's was a color-light mixing mechanism.

Sometimes the only thing to do is to compare the specimen at hand with a known standard variety. Errors are frequently made because of careless color descriptions. *I.* 'Flavescens' and *I.* 'Elsa Sass', for example, are both described as "pale yellow", though their colors have nothing in common. *I.* 'Flavescens' is a medium yellow lightened with white, whereas *I.* 'Elsa Sass' is a vibrant, pure spectrum yellow, closer to greenish yellow in the chart. But we call both "pale". This imprecision is especially disturbing in this case because the two hues are genetically somewhat different. It is even more disturbing where the blues are concerned. We never describe a lavender color in iris as blue, if for no other reason than it is a formidable task to hybridize a "true blue" ("gentian blue", "spectrum blue"). A velvety sheen, which some highly praised blue varieties do not have, is what really matters here.

There are also difficulties with the numerous shades of gray. "Blue-grays" were frequently present in older cultivars, and hybridizers were anxious to "breed them out" in the interests of purer colors. This we will take up when we discuss co-pigments. The cultivar *I.* 'Floridor' (Cayeux, 1929) demonstrates that specific gray tones can be discussed and acknowledged. It was described as "dove gray" or "slate". But its color stands out among other turbid blues. Moreover, it has a new anthocyanine, floridorine, which also stands out among reds because of its

This form of Iris laevigata was even depicted in Dykes' famous masograph *The Genus Iris* under the name Iris laevigata var. albopurpurea. It is now called Iris laevigata 'Albopurpurea'. It does best in marshes or shallow water. The blossom looks as if it were sprayed with Russian ink.

murkier color. Nonetheless, this by itself does not explain why the color is different. Co-pigments, which make the color turbid, probably come into play too and not just the floridorine. It cannot be explained simply by correlations.

The few negative comments that have been made here on the subject of color are meant only to emphasize how important it is, in the field of plant breeding, to be able to describe colors and spot them again in the seedling bed. Thus it is very advantageous to school the eye in interpolating and to gain familiarity with the color charts.

Iris Blossom Pigments

Can we expect more new iris colors? The answer to this question concerns not only iris breeders but anyone who thrills to their colors as the new varieties come out each year. The great popularity of the flamingo pink iris goes to show how much more important a new color is than any other advance in breeding.

New colors are possible if, at some future time, a new or as yet unknown pigment shows up in the genus *Iris*. But can we expect really new pigments? And does it follow that completely new colors will appear? One should not get too carried away with such speculations. After all, we are not in the business of producing lifeless wallpaper flowers. First of all, we have to learn from all the other garden flowers just which conditions and which pigments lead to their great color variety. Then we have to find out which pigments are present in iris and which ones are not. And finally we should know how pigments that are not present in iris, but are needed to produce new colors, show up as mutations in other flowers. This is the only

way we can reasonably predict what will happen.

In the past, new colors appeared unexpectedly, and then it took all the skill hybridizers had to combine this advantage with other characteristics to create superior garden varieties. One of the first examples of such an unexpected inherited mutation were the scarlet sweetpeas. Chemically speaking, the mutation was one step from the pigment cyanidine towards pelargonidine. Today our considerable knowledge of blossom pigments lets us predict what can be expected with iris and shows us how these expectations can become reality. The following sections cover what we currently know about this field.

The Presence of Pigments

When an iris petal is dissected and examined under a microscope, it is amazing to see that the pigment is usually concentrated only in the thin epidermal layer. The parenchyma cells that lie just under it do not show color in daylight; but under ultraviolet light fluorescent pigments can be seen. These should not be disregarded because, as co-pigments, they alter the appearance of the visible pigments. It is astounding that nature produces such saturated colors in such an extremely thin epidermal layer. Here the papilla-shape of the epidermal cells plays an important role. All surfaces with papillae have what is called a *velvet sheen.* This is absent on surfaces where the cells are flat or even rounded. Velvety, dark violet pansies, for example, have such papillae, but a dull black variety like *V.* 'Wotan' has only round cells that do not protrude. Such blossoms are really black, as black as the foot of a microscope, and demonstrate clearly that this is a physical and not a chemical phenomenon. This

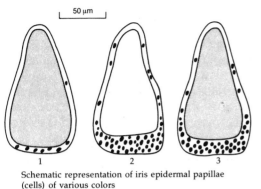

Schematic representation of iris epidermal papillae (cells) of various colors
1. violet blossom with colored cell sap
2. yellow blossom with colorless cell sap and yellow plastids
3. brown falls of a variegata with violet colored cell sap and yellow plastids

black is based on the fact that all the light falling on its surface is absorbed. With papilla-shaped cells, all the incoming light is also captured due to their shape. But when it is refracted back again, it is saturated with color. This can be very easily and convincingly demonstrated by taking a petal with velvet sheen and slowly turning it in direct light: It shows pure color at every angle. You never see white light reflected, but only that which comes out of the petal itself.

Velvet sheen and a highly concentrated pigmentation create the effect of dark violet iris. This effect is especially beautiful in the signal spot of *Iris susiana* and other Oncocyclus species. The colors of iris are always more vivid in the presence of velvet sheen. This phenomenon is less important with the whites and yellows, but the old breeders definitely saw and praised velvet sheen in yellow and white cultivars, e.g. *I.* 'Spungold'. When the pigmented epidermal cells of iris blossoms are observed under the microscope, two different classes of pigment can be seen in different parts of the cell.

We can differentiate between *plasmachrome*, pigments such as the fat-soluble carotenoids, (carotene, lycopine, etc.) localized in the plastid bodies, and the *chymochrome* pigments, above all the anthocyanidines, which are found in cell sap in an aqueous solution. Both are found in adjacent parts of the same cell in gray, brown, and sometimes in purple-red blossoms.

Flamingo and Shell Pinks

The color of the petals and sepals (standards and falls) of the new pink iris is determined by the reappearance of the carotenoid called lycopine. This is the pigment in red tomatoes. It occurs in plastids and concentrates particularly in the "tangerine-colored" beards of these varieties. Thus the beautiful shell pink is actually tomato red lightened by white. Its presence in plastids explains why this pigment can be combined with all the various shades of cell sap pigments. Each of the pigments is found in various carriers of the epidermal cells. However, it is difficult to recognize pink if it occurs together with a yellow plastid pigment.

This is important in plant breeding. We cannot tell whether or not lycopine is present if the beard is orange. But this can be determined by a simple test, since lycopine is not soluble in alcohol (methanol). Thus, when orange beards are placed in methanol, all their yellow carotinoids are dissolved—except lycopine. If a beard contains lycopine when alcohol leached, it will turn pink; if none is present, it turns white. A seedling population can easily be examined this way, and any plants containing lycopine that might be genetically valuable can be identified by this test.

Colors from Red to Blue Created by Anthocyanine

Cell sap pigments are primarily the carriers of colors in the red to blue part of the spectrum. These are the anthocyanins and their co-pigments, various flavone compounds. The most important iris anthocyanin is *violanin*. Lately this pigment has been called delphinin (the English use this term too), but I shall stay with the term violanin because that name has been in use since the researches of Willstaetters (1917) and Karrers, who identified the pigment in *Viola*. *Viola* and *Iris* have so many color factors in common that do not exist between *Iris* and *Delphinium* so the latter relationship cannot be justified. Violanin has recently been carefully researched by Hayashi, Takeda, and their students, using the latest methods. There can no longer by any doubt as to its composition. It is a p-cumaroyl-triglucoside of *delphinidin* and always occurs together with delphinidin-3.5-diglucoside (delphinin). It is extremely common, if not the rule, to find in blossoms a higher molecular anthocyanin with a similar, simple glycoside. We have recently discovered another delphinidin-glycoside in the cultiver *I*. 'Floridor' (Cayeux, 1929), the floridorin (delphinidin-3-glucose-rhamnose-p-coumaric acid) that occurs with tulipanin (delphinidin-3-glucose-rhamose). So far these are the most important iris delphinidin-glucosides, but others may be discovered. Hayashi and his colleagues found a malvidin-glucoside in *Iris ensata* Thunberg (syn. *I. kaempferi* Siebold) called ensatin which seems to be peculiar to Apogon Iris. Malvidine-glycoside with delphinidin-glucosides were also found in *I. chrysographes, I. fulva,* and even in Oncocyclus Iris. It seems we should pay special attention to this in plant breeding.

Every anthocyanin is a glucoside (glycoside, in some literature) of a sugar-free framework, i.e. of an anthocyanidin. This chemical structure is interesting because even the smallest molecular change can produce a change in color. Eight different anthocyanidins have currently been identified in garden flowers. Since mutants originate from genetic damage, it follows that some molecules are reduced. For our purposes, this change into a simpler molecule structure actually means a step toward a color closer to red. It is important for the breeder to realize that he has to be able to recognize this step with the naked eye, when and if it occurs in his seedling bed. If he has any suspicions, he should keep working until he is absolutely sure that he is dealing with such a color mutation.

Paper Chromatography of Anthocyanins
Anthocyanins and their so-called co-pigments can be identified by simple paper chromatography. The exact method can be found in texts dealing with this subject. But since many iris breeders like to experiment, we will deal briefly with this interesting procedure. A tall canning jar will be needed, as well as stiff chromatography paper, made into a cylinder, and simple solvent mixtures such as 2%, or 15% acetic acid, preferably with butanol or isopropanol as the solvent. Put the paper cylinder into a small amount of the solvent mixture at the bottom of the jar, so that the mixture can slowly rise (by capillary action) and spread the substances of the blossom pigment solutions, which have been dripping down at intervals, over the entire surface of the paper. The anthocyanins are now visible. Other substances can only be seen under UV light or by using chemical reactions.

Evidence of malvidin pigments together with delphinidin in iris such as Apogons or Oncocyclus is of particular interest. It is not necessary to separate the sugar from the anthocyanidins beforehand by hydrolysis, i.e. boiling them in diluted acids, because delphinidin pigments and malvidin pigments can be differentiated by a very characteristic color reaction. This is fortunate because the stains of both glucosides of these anthocyanidines are usually so close together that they cannot be clearly separated and do not stand out. Since the point is really to identify malvadin, I call it the malvadine test.

Using an atomizer, spray the chromatogram with a solution of aluminum-subacetate (basic aluminum acetate). It is important that the entire chromatogram stay weekly acidic when sprayed (not strongly acidic), since all anthocyanins turn red in mineral acid; but not neutral to alkaline because another color—usually blue—develops in an alkaline solution. The chromatogram (paper cylinder) can be sprayed again with a standard acetate solution (pH 4.62) just to be certain of getting the exact color of the aluminum chelate reaction with the anthocyanins. To be absolutely sure, a delphinidin glycoside should always be present with its unmistakable genitian blue aluminum chelate color. After the reaction takes place, one always obtains the delphinidin-glucoside "gentian blue" ("true blue"), the malvedin-glucoside crimson and the cyanidin-glucoside purple-violet. Even if this chromatographic separation is not very sharp, the colors are easy to differentiate. Only petunidin and delphinidin are indistinguishable. However, what is important is the cyanidin can also be clearly distinguished, which is an important piece of evidence if a cyanidin mutation has taken place. This can all be established in one operation and avoids producing anthocyanidine by hydrolysis.

The Role of External Conditions in Anthocyanin Color Changes

From the time anthocyanin research began, it has been known that they turn red in the presence of an acid and blue in the presence of an alkali. They also frequently turn green when mixed with an alkali. This is caused by the presence of co-pigments (flavone compounds), which go from colorless to yellow in the process. Willstaetter found the same cyanin in red roses and blue cornflowers and therefore thought that the color was due to the pH factor. We now know that the pigment of blue cornflowers differs in the size of its molecules. The red pigment passes through a dialysing membrane, the blue does not.

In any case the pH of cell sap varies only within a very limited range. So a large difference in color caused by the pH-factor is unlikely. Moreover, precise measurements of pH values in living cell sap are somewhat questionable. Nonetheless, the cell sap pH effect on bluing of cyanin cannot be discounted altogether. The way many garden plants turn blue when they wilt gives a clue. There is every reason to believe that this has something to do with the cell sap becoming more alkaline. The behavior of the aurons, the cell sap pigments of many yellow blossoms, is another indication. If alkali is added to an extract of yellow *Oenothera* blossoms, it becomes reddish. This same reddish color can be observed in evening primroses (*Oenothera* sp.) as they wither. It is highly unlikely that the same principle, in this case that cell sap gets more alkaline as blossoms wither, would manifest itself in such different plants if it did not have the same source.

In the previous paragraph we referred to the meaning of a change in the anthocyanidin molecule, i.e. in sugar-free

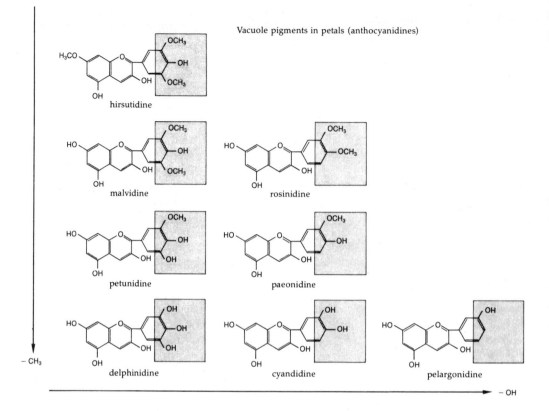

Vacuole pigments in petals (anthocyanidines)

hirsutidine

malvidine

rosinidine

petunidine

paeonidine

delphinidine

cyandidine

pelargonidine

– CH$_3$

– OH

aglycon. It would be helpful in this respect to compare the colors of other garden flowers. What strikes one is that the most complicated anthocyanidins occur in wild-flowers, for example, hirsutidin in *Primula hirsuta* and rosinidin in *Primula rosea.* The molecule becomes simpler with color changes in garden varieties. We can assume that this is always the case. The chemical formulas illustrated above are arranged to show this change from a more complex to a simpler molecule (note arrow).

All gentian blue blossoms contain delphinidin-glucoside, with the exception of blue cornflowers and perhaps a few other composites that contain cyanidin. Delphinidin is the primary anthocyanidin in garden iris, and the anthocyanins that

come from it differ mainly in the amount of sugar and organic acids.

The colors of the anthocyanidins on the acid chromatogram demonstrates largely what can be expected of them in the red color range. More acid will not produce a redder color. The anthocyanidins form three color groups, according to their molecular structure.

Delphinidin, petunidin, malvidin, and hirsutidin are purple; cyandidin, peonidin, and rosinidin are crimson; pelargonidin is scarlet. The anthocyanidins were prepared from the anthocyanins by boiling them with a strong hydrochloric acid. After being dried, they were developed two-dimensionally with a butanol agent and with Forestal solvent.

The fuchsia is a good example of color

modification in blossoms as a function of anthocyanidins. The crimson-colored calyx has peonidin, the purple crown, malvidin.

The most progress delphinidin has made toward red has been in wildflowers, namely in the red flax *Linum grandiflorum* 'Rubrum'. It is also found in red strains of *Primula obconica.* It would be correct to assume that we cannot get any redder than this in breeding irises. No further progression is possible even with the malvidin-glucoside ensatin used by Hayashi in *Iris ensata* Thunberg (syn. *I. kaempferi* Siebold). If we want redder reds, we will have to wait for a mutation that goes toward cyanidin or pelargonidin. Such mutations are probably most likely to occur in Beardless Iris and in Oncocyclus, where malvidin and delphinidin are already together in the same cells.

Scott-Moncrieff showed that changes in the glucoside level can also cause color changes. In the case of *Primula sinensis,* diglucosides have resulted in bluer colors than monoglucosides. It remains to be seen just how much we can generalize about this. The blue-gray color of *Iris* 'Floridor' (Cayeux) is probably caused less by the anthocyanin than by other chemical entities in the cell sap.

The following factors might be more important. We will simply summarize them because they cannot be so clearly separated from each other as when they were first described. These are the so-called co-pigment factor, the chelate factor, the colloid factor, and the dilution factor. The word co-pigment is a collective term for several different chemical components in the cell sap, of which the most important are flavone compounds. One is the fluorescent orange mangiferin, and there are other important ones like the glycosides of irigenin, principally iridin.

Many of these flavones show up as fluorescent stains on newly made chromatograms. These stains are far more numerous on the chromatograms of blue varieties than those of red varieties. So even the chromatogram demonstrates the impact of co-pigments on color changes to blue.

These co-enzymes are sometimes capable, along with other molecules of their type or with anthocyanins, of combining into larger colloid molecules. Sometimes it may be nothing more than an absorption into other materials, in which case even pectins can be involved. But sometimes they can combine with a so-called chelate under bond of a metal ion. It may not be important for us just now to pay so much attention to these possibilities. It is probably sufficient to realize that the formation of larger colloid particles favors color changes toward blue. A color change between red and blue does not, however, mean the formation of true blue. We will take this up later.

The dilution factor I have observed can also be attributed to the colloidal state in freshly prepared, but not in pure (i.e. crystalloid) anthocyanins. If a pycnometer (a bottle with a very narrow neck) is filled with flower extract (or else diluted in distilled water), the solution in the neck of the bottle (as well as the diluted solution) is not only paler, but also visibly bluer than in the flask. This shows that a kind of Tyndall effect, that has nothing to do with a chemical change, is involved. This effect is of interest because it can also occur in living cells and can fool us in the seedling bed. Paler standards look bluer only because of this effect, and we can overlook a cyanidin mutant because we expect a redder color. Moreover, there is not a single variety of iris whose standards are paler than its falls, in which the standards are not also somewhat bluer. This, too, shows that the effect is a natural one.

The Question of a True Blue Iris

We know quite a lot about true blue flowers today. Hayashi, Takeda and their students isolated commelinin, cyanocentaurin (protocyanin), cinerarin, and other polymolecular crystalline anthocyanins from highly purified solutions. It is safe to conclude that these very pure anthocyanins involve obvious stoichometric compounds. Commelinin is a compound of the anthocyanin awobanin with flavocommelinin and an atom of magnesium. This compound was successfully separated and then reconstituted without using any additional agent. What was surprising was that this compound could even be synthesized using another bivalent atom such as cobalt, instead of magnesium, and the resultant compound would be only slightly different. Moreover, this altered compound could also be crystallized.

This plays a significant role in the physiology of metabolism because a wide spectrum of metabolic compounds, which are the waste products of plasma, are generally found in cell sap. This is normal and unmistakable in murky blue cell sap, where much accumulates, even pectins. But this does not seem to be the case with true blue cell sap, which apparently has to be manufactured as a single molecule and only from a few components so that it can combine unhampered with other uniform, large molecules.

If this hypothesis is correct, then breeding true blue flowers means nothing more than breeding very pure cell sap which produce the described results without upsetting normal cellular metabolism.

Patterns

Patterns occur when pigmentation is not evenly distributed over the entire surface of the petal. This is primarily true of the carotenoids, though these yellow pigments are not very attractive and thus not so interesting to hybridizers. On the other hand, great contrasts are sometimes created if less anthocyanin is present. If this distribution forms a pattern, the pattern is given a special name, usually as it is first observed. One of the oldest recognized iris patterns is the *plicata*. It was illustrated as far back as 1647 in a watercolor by Johannes Walther, one of Dürer's students, which now hangs in the collection of the Botanical Institute in Florence. The plicata pattern occurs on the margins of petals and follows the course of the outermost extremity of the vascular system. Since there are some very similar, major pigmentation patterns on other flowers as well, one must be aware that the

Iris milesii. The Chinese also call it the water-bird iris. It is a crested iris (Evansia), which will grow outdoors in a favorable location. It is important that the leaves are not damaged during the winter, otherwise it will not bloom the following spring. Will also grow in containers. It prefers an acid soil and somewhat more moisture during the growing period.

plicata pattern should not be casually interchanged with the term "picotee", which forms on the margin of the petal in quite another way. The plicata pattern is characteristic of Tall Garden Iris and has always been highly desirable. It is constantly used in breeding and has frequently been genetically researched.

To form anthocyanin, pigment first has to form in the epidermal cells, specifically in the vacuoles. Simply put, the vacuole is the cell's waste receptacle and is separated from the working plasma by tonoplast, an extremely thin molecular membrane. Metabolic by-products of all sorts are emptied into the vacuole. These, however, can react with each other chemically to form larger—sometimes extremely large—molecules. Thus, anthocyanins result from the combining of such components.

On the other hand, anthocyanins can combine with related pigment precursor and pigment compounds, usually flavone compounds, forming large colloidal particles too large to pass through a differentally permeable membrane.

We can conclude from all of this that it is the components of anthocyanin that move across membranes and not the anthocyanins themselves. The latter occur as final compounds only in the intact cell. But the patterns can now tell us about the type of movement, and if we can identify anything about the way they move, the patterns will give us clues. The plicatas are of particular interest because anthocyanin precursors usually are transferred with the vascular system, where the molecules are small at first, containing anthocyanin only at their ends. But note that it is the epidermal cells above the vascular system, not the cells of the veins themselves, which are colored. From this we can conclude that there is a specific component carried by the vascular system that is not found in adjacent, colorless cells.

It should be added that the plicata pattern in irises is attributed to a specific gene locus. It is recessive, which means that in a cross between a solid color and a plicata, the pattern disappears in the first generation, but true to Mendel's law appears again in typical numbers if self-pollinated, in sib crosses, or if it is backcrossed.

The following three factors can be reliably correlated:
1. the direct impression of the pattern on the senses,
2. the shortening of an anthocyanin component that occurs in metabolism because of the vascular system,
3. the appropriate "instruction" for this physiological process anchored in a chromosome-linked locus.

Iris variegata var. pontica. This botanical name should not be confused with Iris pontica (Iris humilis), the small dwarf spuria. This is a color variant of Iris variegata; the brown veining on the falls fuses to form pools of color. An old garden iris, common in old American gardens.

This clear correlation serves as a good model for us in plant breeding, one which we should always try to recognize in other contexts.

Since working with the plicata pattern was so easy, it was attributed long ago to a recessive gene identified as pl. With diploid varieties, only the genetically double-recessive pl pl types are a plicata and the others, Pl pl and Pl Pl, are solids, or at least not plicatas.

In principle it's possible to conceive of several genes having one and the same locus. These genes are called *multiple alleles*. This concept was applied to the plicata and the idea took root, especially in the U.S. Based on the physiological context described, I cannot agree with this concept. A multiple allele can indeed alter the intensity of a given feature, but not its physiological character.

At one time something other than the multiple allele was associated with the plicata pattern, namely the "all white" specimen (e.g. *I.* 'Matterhorn'). The supposed all-white allele is therefore written pla. But a careful look at the all-white plants show that they do not form any anthocyanin at all in the area of the perianth, not in a single cell. The plicata pattern, however, always has at least a few colored cells at the base of the blossom (on the hafts). It is highly unlikely that two different physiological principles would have the same locus.

It is characteristic for all-white plants to form anthocyanin everywhere but in the area of the perianth. The bases of the leaf shoots of *I.* 'Matterhorn' are obviously covered with an epidermis containing anthocyanin, and these even contain a cyanidin glucoside not found in the area of the blossom in iris. A physiological explanation for "all white" is that the *separating tissue,* which separates the

perianth from the ovary, completely eliminates any anthocyanidin components from crossing over. The separating tissue is a "closed" border!

One pattern that is being sold in the U.S. as a multiple allele to plicata is called *luminata.* I first published the principle of this pattern as illustrated in Theodor Schwarz's *I.* 'Havelberg', which was discovered long before the war, but I would like to use the term *luminata* because comparing this patterning principle to "manuscript illuminations" is such a good one. The blade looks as though it had been lightly sprayed with color. There is no comparison to a solid colored blossom. The blossom usually has no color at its base and no veining. In very intensely colored luminata cultivars such as *I.* 'Salem Lass' by Olson (U.S.A.), this is so strongly pronounced that they could be mistaken for solid-colored cultivars. Following the concept of a multiple allele in plicata, this pattern is genetically indicated in the U.S. as pllu, though it is probably correct to attribute it to its own locus. The concept of a multiple allele is fostered when two patterns appear simultaneously in one blossom. But compared with plicata that is quite different.

The method of seeing a pattern in the distribution or supply of pigment components, which is somewhat limited, generally allows the appearance of partly or completely white blossoms to be classified. In each case, it can be assumed that the supply of some component is missing. However, two things are possible. An anthocyanidin molecule is a complicated chemical compound. If the molecule's chemical formation can be interrupted at one or more specific points, it will not become an anthocyanidin molecule. Each interruption, no matter where it is made, will appear by itself as a deficiency mutant, hence is caused by a recessive locus. So all of these will be found to be "recessive whites", even though they are all different and attributed to different loci. Some are already familiar Tall Garden Iris. Their F_1 hybrids will by nature be colored by anthocyanin, reassorting again only in the F_2 generation which identifies the recessive gene.

The other possibility is that the necessary components for forming anthocyanin are present, but that physiological conditions in the individual cell prevent the formation of anthocyanin. These conditions may also be recessive, if the absence of this condition can be ascribed to a deficiency mutant, although nothing like this has ever been observed. On the contrary, another condition has become very familiar. In this case the formation of anthocyanin is suppressed, but the anthocyanin is present as a colorless pseudo-base. Color develops immediately when the precursor is put in mineral acid, so this can be used as a test for the pseudo-base. Cultivars frequently called 'dominant white" are characterized by this pseudo-base. Before dominant heredity has been definitely established, the term should not be used. The pseudo-base is commonly identified in species hybrids.

We should also mention *variegata, neglecta,* and *amoena,* three patterns that originally were primarily used as species names. Since then, these terms have been applied to the distribution of pigmentation in garden cultivars, indicating color patterns. Other features are barely taken into account any more. Consequently a variegata cultivar is one in which the standards are yellow and the falls brown. In this case, as with similar cultivars, the way the colors are distributed over the surface is identified. Neglecta specimens have pale standards, with falls deeply colored by anthocyanin; with amoenas the standards are pure white and the falls deeply colored by anthocyanin. The later two are thus pure anthocyanin colors with no yellow.

The physiological correlation between the three color patterns mentioned above is in the way the blossoms open during anthesis. This can be easily observed in the two diploid cultivars *I.* 'Folkwang' and *I.* 'Rheintochter' by Goos and Koenemann. The blossoms of these two cultivars open very irregularly during anthesis. They often have disproportionate standards and falls, for which they partly compensate. Individual perianth parts, then, correspond only to the standards or only to the falls. Parts that correspond to the standards always have very little anthocyanin coloring, while those that correspond to the falls are strongly colored by anthocyanin, as required by the amoena specimen. Coloring always depends on geotropic induction. Pigmentation caused by the way a blossom opens corresponds, as already genetically dictated, to particular upward or downward movements.

This dependency of pigmentation on geotropism is characteristic of various garden flowers, for example, the signal spot on gladiolas and English geraniums.

A pigmentation was recently introduced in Tall Garden Iris by Paul Cook and since then these plants have been known as Paul Cook bicolors. He crossed a wild tetraploid species, perhaps an *Iris reichenbachii,* with Tall Garden Iris and obtained a short, but fertile seedling, which he called *I.* "progenitor", with yellow-white and violet-blue pigmentation like one of the amoenas. Further work with this seedling showed that he had something really different, because its pigmentation consistently showed up immediately in the first generation and then remained. In the U.S.

this pigmentation is usually termed dominant. *I.* 'Whole Cloth', one of its descendants, won the Dykes Medal. A very different form, with an almost white blossom with lightly anthocyanin-colored margins, split off from this bicolor. This *I.* 'Emma Cook' type could not be considered a plicata, as its color was very evenly distributed along the margins. The way pigmentation follows the course of the vascular system in plicatas was completely absent. The historical term "picotee" might best be used in this case.

Variegata, neglecta, and amoena specimens are usually characterized by a particular border pattern, that is a pale to almost white border, with very little anthocyanin, against an intensely colored blade. We have to consider this feature as being linked to the gene locus, although it is hardly mentioned in the literature. In the future, it is to be hoped that presently overlooked characteristics will be adequately described.

It seems too early to go into all the patterns of the wild species of Oncocyclus and Regelia species and their hybrids.

The Effects of Chromosomal Relationships on Hybridizing

Within the large, ideal disorder of the inanimate world, the principle of order in the animate world is inheritance. This principle of order is not absolute; it provides for change and has allowed organisms to pass these adaptation changes in their environment to their descendants throughout the course of time.

The carriers of this principle of order are the chromosomes. When they were first discovered under the microscope, they were named "color bodies" not because they were so colorful, but because they could be so beautifully stained in the laboratory, making them visible. They were easy to identify among other cellular components by this ability to accept color. It was difficult to ignore the fact that the number of chromosomes was always the same in a given organism. It may give iris enthusiasts a particular pleasure to know that among the first chromosome counts was that of the twelve haploid chromosomes of *Iris pallida* made by Strasburger in 1882.

Thus the number of chromosomes a plant had could be indicated as a characteristic, and so in the following years an army of cell researchers—cytologists—busied themselves counting the number of chromosomes in all the plants available for study. An important result of these endeavors were the indispensable reference works on plant chromosome counts by Tischler and Darlington. Lists of chromosome counts from current writings appeared regularly in the collection *Regnum Vegetabile* under the title *Index to Chromosome Numbers in Plants.*

By using information from the chromosomes, nature itself can get specific jobs done in an ordered fashion inside the living plant, as though by code. Among the most important new discoveries was that the chromosome was the carrier of such a code. It carries the genes, the inheritance factors, which present the information needed by the organism to maintain its physiological processes. We imagine that a specific gene controls a specific enzyme reaction. Of course, it is not absolutely certain that the existence of a gene is a real thing. All we can prove is the presence of an "entity" in a specific location on the chromosome, the locus—and this is the accurate term, even though we are used to the word "gene". According to the old definition of Johannsen, a gene is "an indefinite something with very definite effects". The latest D.N.A., R.N.A., and gene-splicing research is furnishing more facts about these "control" sites.

According to recent thinking, a gene seems to be a real thing, namely a sequence of the recently elucidated nucleic acid molecule. We cannot identify the gene under the microscope because it is too small, but we know from its "very definite effects" that it is the smallest working unit in the principle of order contained in the chromosome. However, the chromosome of a higher plant is itself a complex structure, made up of many DNA filaments, and simply cannot be equated with the simple DNA filaments in a bacteriophage.

The code has to be communicated to every living cell in an organism and must be available at all times in the same way to every living cell of a plant. Thus, division of the nucleus and the chromosome precedes every cell division. The chromosomes are "copied", so to speak, in the process, and the two identical chromosomes coming from this division are equally divided between the two daughter cells. This cell division is reserved for certain youthful, "meristematic" cells, which only function to divide and to provide all the cells of the developing plant body. To observe and count chromosomes, therefore, we have to look for these cells in the young plant tissues—the meristem—at the tips of roots and leaf shoots. They will no longer exist as discrete entities in cells of mature, green leaves and elsewhere.

In addition to this vegetative nuclear division (mitosis) in root and leaf tips, there is another important type of division called reduction division (meiosis). It occurs only periodically in the life cycle of the plant, as the flower begins to form. As

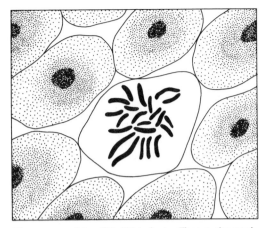

Chromosomes: Iris pallida × Iris iberica. The two elongated chromosomes of I. iberica can be seen at the lower left.

gardeners, we are accustomed to seeing this life cycle start with the germinating seed, but we have to revise this notion and bear in mind that every seed already contains an embryo that even at this early stage represents the entire plant. It has the potential for all the capabilities and morphological qualities of the later, fully developed plant. And like the later plant, every cell in the embryo already has a complete set of chromosomes and genes. When the plant prepares to blossom, it develops reproductive organs, which are the reason why the plant blossoms, as this process serves to preserve the species (rather than the individual plant, which maintains itself by vegetative reproduction). The decisive turning-points in the life of a species take place here in the blossom, not in the seed. And here too, the reduction division (or meiosis) has to be triggered before sperm cells in the pollen or egg cells in the ovules can form. Its more important function is to reduce the number of chromosomes to the simple or haploid set of chromosomes.

Thanks to today's simplified methods, investigating chromosomal relationships both at the tips of roots and leaf shoots to determine the number and form of vegetative chromosomes in the diploid stage, as well as examining behavior during reduction division in the stamens of very young buds, can now be done by amateur botanists who know how to use a microscope. For this there is hardly a better subject than the iris, especially if someone wants to learn about the reasons for his findings when hybridizing. It cannot be stated clearly enough, just how much this microscopic picture can increase one's knowledge—and this is especially true of iris—particularly if one is working with species crosses and other such fascinating projects.

The plant parts are "fixed" in a mixture of alcohol and glacial acetic acid (3:1), then put into carmine acetic acid (a red stain specific for chromosomes) (45% solution, boiled ca. ½ hour in a reflux condenser, then filtered) and later mounted on a slide in this staining solution. One gets better at this with experience. A little practice is necessary since crushed preparation and boiled preparation, as the steps are called, do not mean that the plant parts should be arbitrarily crushed or boiled under the glass cover. Simply stirring them with a regular dissecting needle will do (not stainless steel!). This will release a small amount of iron into the carmine, which will only improve the stain. Once the stain is deep enough, I usually stir in a small drop of syrup, made by mixing 7 parts chloralhydrate with 4 parts fructose, dissolved in a little bit of warm water. The syrup prevents the preparation from drying too soon and improves the quality of the slide. But it cannot be kept very long. We will not go into this carmine acetic acid process more thoroughly here, especially since numerous variations in the technique have recently been published.

Since we wish to observe chromosomes, our interest lies in the middle stage of meiosis, specifically diakinesis and the stages of metaphase, where chromosomes can be easily identified individually. The chromosomes are easy to count in the midpoint of meiosis, and irregularities can be identified that may later cause sterility. The chromosomes are usually arranged in pairs. This is called conjugation and presupposes that the two chromosomes of each pair are identical in all or in most parts. That is, that they match, that they are "homologous". But even homologues are sometimes partly heteromorphic. The appearance of chromosomes in the various stages of meiosis can vary a great deal temporarily because their screwing and unscrewing motions change their shapes. This makes it difficult to identify them repeatedly for purposes of comparison.

In this respect, it is easier to reliably identify individual chromosomes during mitosis, where nuclear divisions are arranged in a special way. In mitosis the chromosomes are flattened out so that they can all be seen lying next to each other. They then can be drawn or photographed this way, and each one identified according to size and form, such as the type branching, especially those with long, excentric extensions: the metacentric (uniform) and the acrocentric (excentric), which acts like one arm. This is called karyotype analysis.

Counting Iris Chromosomes

Over the years, cytologists have determined not only the chromosome counts of pure *Iris* species, but also those of many garden hybrids and complicated species crosses. If one were to make a list of all these counts, there would be so many thousands of them, the poor beginner would be totally confused. In order to explain what it all means, we have to try to interpret them right from the start.

Take the main species of Pogon Iris for openers. By using Stasburger's count $2n = 24$ for *I. pallida*, we will see right away that the basic, single Pogon Iris set is $n = 12$, that is, there are 12 different chromosomes. This is a common count for many species, for instance *I. illyrica*, *I. mellita*, and *I. reichenbachii*. So we can take $X = 12$ as a basic unit for many Pogon Iris.

This count is also frequently found in garden varieties except that we also find $2n = 23, 24, 25$ and 26 in various individuals. This means that during reduction division the homologous bond was not always strong enough to distribute the pairs evenly to the daughter cells. This results in "univalent" chromosomes that are either transmitted to the pollen or the egg cells as extras, or which get lost. They are then either present in the descendants as an extra or are completely lacking; this does not happen very often. This indicates the great value of the $n = 12$ set as an integral unit. Any further increase or loss seems to be less well tolerated, so that the highest counts we ever see are $2n = 24\pm2$.

But shortly after the first iris species were studied, some were found with particularly large sets. When the cytologists studied these plants, they discovered that they often had $2n = 48$ chromosomes (e.g. *I. macrantha*, *I. cypriana*, *I. mesopotamica*). It was natural to assume that the basic set had quadrupled, so they were written $2n = 4X = 48$ chromosomes. But even these usually used the reduced number of chromosomes to form pollen and egg cells, which contained $n = 2X = 24$ chromosomes. They were called tetraploid to distinguish them from their diploid ancestors. This phenomenon of species with lower chromosome counts producing, in the course of phylogenesis, species with higher counts, can be observed in many plant genera and is called polyploidism.

It was understandable for hybridizers to use these larger iris because they were both taller and larger-blossomed. Increasing the blossoming effect naturally centered on making the blossoms larger. But despite larger blossoms, intense colors were lacking, so crosses were made with colorful, small-blossomed cultivars—especially in the beginning when the knowledge of cytology could not be taken for granted. The expected outcome of such crossings were plants with $2n = 2X + 1X = 3X = 36$ chromosomes. They were called triploids and many of these cultivars were developed in the past (*I.* 'Ballerina', *I.* 'Isoline', etc.). If one considers the processes during reduction in such triploid plants, one would assume right from the start that it would be severely interrupted because a complete set of chromosomes for conjugation is lacking. The result is a high rate of sterility. But the patience and persistence of breeders overcame this lack. Their successes suggest that they should be doing it occasionally today. Sometimes reduction did not occur at all. Then by a stroke of luck the problem resolved itself. Seedlings developed that got $2X = 24$ chromosomes from both diploid and tetraploid parents, thus they immediately had $2n = 4X = 48$ chromosomes. Some famous examples are *I.* 'Snow Flurry' (*I.* 'Thais' $\times$ *I.* 'Purissima') and Alexander Steffen's *I.* 'Elfenlied' (*I.* 'Athanael' $\times$ *I.* 'Rheingauperle'). From the standpoint of aesthetics, one should screw up one's courage and confidence and try these crossings all over again from the beginning.

The work of amateurs, armed only with intuition and lacking the knowledge we have today, should not be underrated. The iris blossom, in particular, seems to have inspired attempts at the impossible. And thanks to its durability, this apparently useless hybrid was still around years later when men were ready to start examining it seriously. We can take a lesson from this by calculating which crosses are worth repeating. But to insist, for the sake of botanical purism, on blossoms "free from aesthetic considerations"—and I have often heard this opinion expressed—would simply be a regression.

Chromosome Counts in Species Crosses

Examinations of Pogon Iris chromosomes soon showed that they had yet another base number, namely $X = 8$. This is represented by *I. attica* with $2n = (2X) = 16$ and *I. pumila*, with $2n = 4X = 32$ chromosomes. Cytological investigations using hybrids from this group of Pogons and those of the previous group showed that conjugation between the $X = 8$ set and the $X = 12$ set took place only on a very small scale. This meant that such hybrids were sterile.

But Simonet's investigations turned up something new and surprising. The Mediterranean species, *I. chamaeiris*, which grows from Italy and southern France to Spain (variously known as *I. italica, I. olbiensis,* and *I. portugalica*) had $2n = 40$ chromosomes. Simonet discovered that this number represented a doubling of the 8 and 12 sets. If this is written out according to the method indicated above, *I. chamaeiris* has $2n = 2(X = 8) + 2(X = 12) = 16 + 24 = 40$ chromosomes. Hence both sets are duplicated and both are present in this species as diploids. This was called amphidiploid (amphi = both, diplous = doubled). But the plant is also tetraploid, only in this case two different sets are doubled. It behaves in breeding like a diploid. The case of an autotetraploid plant described above is much different that this, because here the only set, $X = 12$, is quadrupled, thus $2n = 4X = 48$.

Even before they knew about such things, hybridizers tried to breed early Dwarf Iris using *I. chamaeiris* $\times$ *I. pumila*. Thus in all the old catalogues, almost all the early Dwarf Iris were listed under *I. pumila,* which was of course incorrect. But just look what came of it! *Chamaeiris* $\times$ *pumila* got $2n = 20 + 16$ chromosomes— and was sterile! This is obvious when we see that this plant contained $X = 8$ three times and $X = 12$ only once! Thus no practical conjugation was possible during meiosis. *I. pumila* 'Coerulea', a clone of this plant, was widely distributed and was depicted in Dykes' famous work, *The Genus Iris,* in the *I. pumila* plate—he was still unaware of developments in 1913.

Now we must think a bit further. What do we have to do to breed early Dwarf Iris?

Iris tectorum. Called the roof iris in China (and in America) because it supposedly grows there spontaneously on the damp thatched roofs. It is the hardiest and most vigorous species of the tall crested iris (Evansia) which occur in areas of Central Europe with cold winters. Best combined with its white albino form, large rock gardens are ideal, but it looks good in many other situations.

What should be the result? Plants with chromosomes similar to those of *I. chamaeiris*, of course. We can arrive at this if we cross two autotetraploid plants with base figures of $\times = 8$ and $\times = 12$. This was done and resulted in the dwarf strain we now call "Lilliputs". There were, however, obstacles because the plants were often taller than the hoped-for miiniature size and often branched, which was not desirable. Here, too, one has to be selective.

That meant falling back on the incomparable and unjustifiably ignored Central European *I. pumila*, which graces the feathergrass steppe from Bohemia, Moravia, and the Hainburger Mountains to Europe's only desert, the Deliblatski Pesak in Serbia. Admittedly it is short-lived as a garden plant and has a brief blooming period, but to make up for this it has more features than any other species of *Iris*. It always catches the eye of collectors. The other parent for this cross was, of course, the Tall Garden Iris with its $2n = 4\times = 48$ chromosomes. This was not to be the easiest project, as the Tall Garden Iris introduced branching, a taller growth habit, and other negative characteristics. But as far as variety was concerned, especially color variety, this breeding type was practically inexhaustible. Even sterile clones from backcrosses with *I. pumila* could be tried again.

Iris Germanica and Iris Florentina

Goos and Koenemann introduced a class called Interregna, in an effort to bridge the blooming gap, the interregnum, between Dwarf Iris and Tall Bearded Iris. They used many of their own varieties in this project, as did Caperne with his *I.* 'Ivorine'. The latter was, moreover, the only variety that had transmitted its entire set of chromosomes, $2n = 44$, through the pollen to the hybrid (*I. stolonifera* $\times$ *I.* 'Ivorine', $2n = 66$). The fact that these newer foundlings came from ancient hybrids of unknown ancestry which existed since prerecorded times and must have survived through some of the most trying periods of history should not be overlooked. But no "German" flag, as Linnaeus called it, or "Florentine" flag was ever involved. One might just as well say they originated in India or southern Arabia. Their present geographic distribution stretches far beyond that of a Pogon Iris.

Cytologists said the German Iris must be a hybrid. Its combined chromosome count was $2n = 20 + 24 = 44$, which indicates a cross between *I. chamaeiris* and a tall Pogon Iris, but this can't be proved. Without the benefit of cytology, many of these iris were named and described as true species. Today we must content ourselves with the knowledge that there are plant hybrids much older than we can imagine. Did the old Arabs develop them?

Iris variegata. A native European bearded iris, though there are only few left in their native habitat. Only in the vicinity of Munich are there still a few wild stands. There is no question that it took part in the breeding of our tall bearded iris, even if throat veining, which came from this iris, has been bred out in the new varieties. It belongs in the rock garden because of its size. Blooms at the same time as tall bearded iris.

Or an even more ancient people? In any case, it should never cease to amaze us that iris hybrids survived among their fellow plants on the rubble of decaying settlements, were transplanted from there into the gardens of newly erected settlements, and eventually established themselves along the walls of medieval German castles, where they were given the name *Iris germanica*. There they survived for centuries (perhaps millenia) not by seed reproduction, but only by vegetative propagation as clones—a perennialness matched by very few garden plants.

Chromosome Counts in Section Crosses

One of the peculiarities of the genus *Iris* is that species from the sections Pogon Iris, Oncocyclus, and Regelia will cross with each other. (Related Falcifolia groups, Psammiris, Arenaria, and Pseudoregelia are not covered, as they are rarely used in crossbreeding.) For all intents and purposes, all the species of these three groups can be crossed with each other.

All species hybrids that can be developed are by no means fertile. Recent cytological studies of species hybrids, most of which were hybridized by amateurs, showed that fertility and sterility were basically caused by chromosomal relationships. In what follows, therefore, the knowledge gained from Pogon Iris can be applied to setting up a consistent hybridizing program.

Unlike the Pogons, Oncocyclus and Regelia Iris have a white aril surrounding the micropyle, the area from which the primary root emerges during germination. This aril has given its name to the entire group, including the hybrids. We speak of Arils, Aril iris, or Arilbreds. Further subdivisons based on the extraordinarily different appearance of these hybrids have also been given names. The original name Oncobreds refers almost exclusively to direct crosses between diploid Pogon Iris and Oncocyclus species, which are mostly sterile. Generally the compound terms Regeliocyclus (Oncoregelia), Pogocyclus, Pogoregelia, and Pogoregeliocyclus are used, as indeed they should be, since they identify the parent genera of a hybrid.

Aside from the fact that there are several physiological reasons for sterility, experience tells us that fertility depends on the presence of two homologous sets of chromosomes during meiosis that allow the chromosomes to pair up without interruption. This has some surprising consequences in a breeding program, which have still only barely been understood and therefore hardly been put to use.

So let us start again with the sets of chromosomes we came to know from the Pogon Iris, $X = 8$ and $X = 12$. To these we can now add $X = 10$ for the Oncocyclus and $X = 11$ for the Regelias. Having learned that $X = 8$ and $X = 12$ cannot be successfully paired, we can assume something similar for the others too, that is, for all the four sets used in breeding Arils.

But right away there is a big exception, that is still not understood. When an Oncocyclus species is crossed with the diploid Regelia species *Iris korolkowii*, it usually produces a fertile hybrid. This means that the $X = 10$ of the Oncocyclus and the $X = 11$ of the Regelia should be able to enter into a bond with each other similar to conjugation. But based on our current knowledge, this cannot be true, less because of the difference in the numbers of chromosomes than because of their shapes, which are so very different. Yet the undeniable fact is that the diploid Regeliocyclus hybrids introduced by van Tubergen at the end of the last century

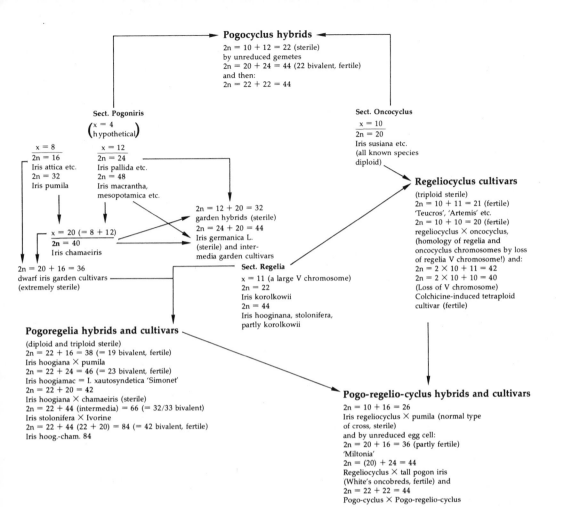

Pogocyclus hybrids
2n = 10 + 12 = 22 (sterile)
by unreduced gemetes
2n = 20 + 24 = 44 (22 bivalent, fertile)
and then:
2n = 22 + 22 = 44

Sect. Pogoniris
(x = 4 hypothetical)

Sect. Oncocyclus
x = 10
2n = 20
Iris susiana etc.
(all known species diploid)

x = 8
2n = 16
Iris attica etc.
2n = 32
Iris pumila

x = 12
2n = 24
Iris pallida etc.
2n = 48
Iris macrantha, mesopotamica etc.

2n = 12 + 20 = 32
garden hybrids (sterile)
2n = 24 + 20 = 44
Iris germanica L.
(sterile) and inter-media garden cultivars

Regeliocyclus cultivars
(triploid sterile)
2n = 10 + 11 = 21 (fertile)
'Teucros', 'Artemis' etc.
2n = 10 + 10 = 20 (fertile)
regeliocyclus × oncocyclus,
(homology of regelia and oncocyclus chromosomes by loss of regelia V chromosome!) and:
2n = 2 × 10 + 11 = 42
2n = 2 × 10 + 10 = 40
(Loss of V chromosome)
Colchicine-induced tetraploid cultivar (fertile)

x = 20 (= 8 + 12)
2n = 40
Iris chamaeiris

2n = 20 + 16 = 36
dwarf iris garden cultivars
(extremely sterile)

Sect. Regelia
x = 11 (a large V chromosome)
2n = 22
Iris korolkowii
2n = 44
Iris hooginana, stolonifera, partly korolkowii

Pogoregelia hybrids and cultivars
(diploid and triploid sterile)
2n = 22 + 16 = 38 (= 19 bivalent, fertile)
Iris hoogiana × pumila
2n = 22 + 24 = 46 (= 23 bivalent, fertile)
Iris hoogiamac = I. xautosyndetica 'Simonet'
2n = 22 + 20 = 42
Iris hoogiana × chamaeiris (sterile)
2n = 22 + 44 (intermedia) = 66 (= 32/33 bivalent)
Iris stolonifera × Ivorine
2n = 22 + 44 (22 + 20) = 84 (= 42 bivalent, fertile)
Iris hoog.-cham. 84

Pogo-regelio-cyclus hybrids and cultivars
2n = 10 + 16 = 26
Iris regeliocyclus × pumila (normal type of cross, sterile)
and by unreduced egg cell:
2n = 20 + 16 = 36 (partly fertile)
'Miltonia'
2n = (20) + 24 = 44
Regeliocyclus × tall pogon iris
(White's oncobreds, fertile) and
2n = 22 + 22 = 44
Pogo-cyclus × Pogo-regelio-cyclus

were extremely fertile. I. 'Teucros', for example, was one of the best seed-bearers. Even with the true Oncocyclus species *Iris susiana* it gave abundant, well-developed seeds. Why this happens, nobody knows. One would have to reproduce the original hybrids from known parents, then grow their progeny, and examine them minutely.

Even without the benefit of total knowledge, we can assume that I. 'Teucros' × I. *susiana* will produce hundred of normal seeds and the seedlings will end up looking much more like Oncocyclus than the original Regeliocyclus. But their chromosomal relationships, which for the time being we only know from root tip counts, are by far the most interesting aspect. They all have either 2n=20 or 2n=21. When this data was published, Simonet was sure I had made a mistake; my plants must have been true Oncocyclus and not Regeliocyclus hybrids, because they had only 20 chromosomes and did not have the characteristic metacentric Regelia chromosome. I was able to say that the pod parent had indeed been the Regeliocyclus, so no mistake could have been made. Since that time we have learned that it is the characteristic metacentric Regelia chromosome that "becomes lost" during meiosis. Moreover, I made chromosome duplicating tests at the time with colchicine in embryo culture. I obtained a few plants with 2n=40 and 2n=42 chromosomes, which also confirmed my findings.

In order to clarify this behavior during meiosis in future reports and papers, I proposed a new way of writing it, which I would like to use here. By arranging chromosome sets one above the other, the individual sets can immediately be identified, whether they are paired or not. Starting again with Pogon Iris,

$$2n = \frac{8}{12} = 20$$

we can easily see that they hybrid *I. attica* × *I. mellita* will be sterile, whereas a plant with

$$2n = \frac{8\ 12}{8\ 12} = 40$$

is very likely to be fertile, whether it's an *I. chamaeiris* or a Lilliput.

If this is applied to our Aril hybrids, it is clear that an (Oncobred Pogocyclus)

$$2n = \frac{10}{12} = 22$$

will be sterile. Hence the sets have to be duplicated, as they are in the section hybrid 'Ib-mac',

$$2n = \frac{10\ 12}{10\ 12} = 44$$

if there is to be any hope of fertility.

The most interesting exceptions are the Regeliocyclus hybrids, which have

$$2n = \frac{10}{(11)} = 20 \text{ and } 2n = \frac{10}{(11)} = 21$$

chromosomes.

These can be backcrossed to *Iris susiana* and will usually produce fertile hybrids, which can be used in turn to develop fertile populations for crossbreeding. Fertility is clearly one of the most impor-tant prerequisites for any successful breeding program. Once we realize this, it becomes obvious that this knowledge will, in a suitable climate, lead most quickly to obtaining garden plants similar to the Oncocyclus Iris so sought after.

Simonet made the important discovery that this behavior of Oncocyclus and Regeliocyclus chromosomes was true for tetraploids as well as diploids. This meant that these tetraploid types were so fertile that—regardless of the lost Regelia chromosomes—the American Clarence G. White was able to develop a Pogo-regeliocyclus family, which today bears his name, even though he did not know about such chromosomal relationships yet. These Clarence G. White hybrids, CGW's for short, thus have

$$2n = \frac{10\ 12}{(10)\ 12} = 44 \text{ chromosomes.}$$

Their prototype was I. 'Joppa Parrot'. Through sib mating they have now been developed into large numbers of seedlings in order to expand their variety. *I.* 'Imaret' by Theodore Wilkes, a yellow with a large onco spot, was a great success. However, pairing between such morphologically different Oncocyclus and Regelia chromosomes is still inexplicable, and their behavior during meiosis is a subject for further research.

The most notable Regelias available on the market are the tetraploids *I. hoogiana* and *I. stolonifera*, and *I. korolkowii*, which is usually a diploid. These species can be used to great advantage in every aspect of breeding. The first two have

$$2n = 4X = \frac{11\ 11}{11\ 11} = 44$$

and the third has

$$2n = 2X = \frac{11}{11} = 22.$$

The two tetraploids have extremely different blossoms and therefore offer promise of a colorful Mendelian series of recombinations. *I. korolkowii* has been used primarily for direct crossings with Oncocyclus species and for expanding diploid Regeliocyclus hybrids.

The development of Pogoregeliocyclus hybrids is primarily limited to tetraploids because at this level they produce very fertile amphidiploid hybrids which resemble a new synthetic species. First developed by Simonet from *I. hoogiana* × *I. macrantha* (hoogia-mac), he called it *I. autosyndetica*.

Yet in all these scientifically important findings, we should not lose sight of aesthetics! The large number of variations we see in today's garden iris and the number of variations still to come (e.g. blue with yellow margins) from the 4n-Regelia cross already mentioned, will produce an enormous number of variations in ornamental cultivars that are very vigorous and even have new growth habits. We have to remember that Pogocyclus and Pogoregelia Iris will cross at the tetraploid level, as Simonet already explained, which means we can expect completely new types from the standpoint of aesthetics. As far as chromosomes are concerned, this cross appears as

$$2n = \frac{12\ 11}{12\ 11} = 46 \text{ for Pogoregelias}$$

and

$$2n = \frac{12\ 10}{12\ 10} = 44 \text{ for the Pogocyclus,}$$

which become a Pogoregeliocyclus, stabilized at

$$2n = \frac{12\ 10}{12\ (10)} = 44$$

when the two are crossed. CGW's came from this development.

Tall Polyploids and Irregularities

We have already shown that it is worth crossing diploid and tetraploid Pogon Iris,

because with luck, tetraploids can sometimes be immediately obtained, as was the case with *I.* 'Snow Flurry' and *I.* 'Elfenlied', when reduction division does not take place. This can also happen with hybrids, in which case fertilization with an unreduced gamete can lead to higher polyploids. Thus Simonet attained the pentaploid level during the breeding of his *I.* 'Koriantha', by using his triploid (sterile) *I.* 'Koris' and normal *I. autosyndetica* pollen. I arrived at the hexaploid level

$$2n = 22 + 44 \frac{11\ 12\quad 8}{11\ 12\ 12} = 66$$

by crossing *I. stolonifera* with Caperne's *I. intermedia* 'Ivorine'. The three 'Stolorines' from this cross were fertile; the pollen transmitted 33 chromosomes to its various progeny, which was later explained by the even distribution of univalents during meiosis, but not by any normal distribution of bivalents, which the above formula also rules out.

A few successful attempts to reach higher polyploid levels were made using colchicine. The hybrid *I. hoogiana* × *I. chamaeiris*

$$2n = \frac{11\quad 8}{11\ 12} = 42$$

(*I.* 'Spotless') was, as expected, sterile. If the theory of duplication developed thus far is correct, repeated duplication of the sets should result in fertility. This did occur using colchicine in embryo culture. The resultant hoog-cham 84 chromosomes with

$$2n = \frac{11\ 11\quad 8\ 12}{11\ 11\quad 8\ 12} = 84 \text{ was fertile.}$$

This hybrid was not larger than the earlier plant. It had the highest chromosome count of any fertile Pogon Iris. I grew a number of hexaploid seedlings from it, using *I. hoogiana* as a pod parent. But they all looked the same. At this point the question arises whether it makes any sense to go on creating such high polyploids for crossbreeding. The abundance of hereditary material and individual characteristics accumulated in the cells of these plants may no longer allow any one desirable characteristic to dominate sufficiently to produce a garden variety that is at all different.

The Mohr Hybrids
It is indeed a phenomenon that the multitude of iris we have today is the result of random experimentation and crossbreeding. The Mohr hybrids, among others, were developed without any knowledge of cytology or genetics. Shortly before his death, William Mohr crossed the old diploid plicata *I.* 'Parisiana' with the Oncocyclus Iris *I. gatesii,* and his friend Prof. Essig later put these extraordinarily large seedlings on the market as *I.* 'William Mohr'. Their size inspired many breeders to cross these normally sterile plants with tetraploid Tall Bearded Iris. But luck being a factor, by chance a very few seeds were actually obtained, among them *I.* 'Capitola' ('William Mohr' × *I.* ib-mac), a significant hybrid that produced a plant with 44 chromosomes from an unreduced *I.* 'William Mohr' egg cell; it later became an important fertile parent. These advances in improving ornamental iris hybrids were achieved by "hybridizers" ignorant of the work of their trade. If they had had the cytological knowledge we have today, perhaps this iris would never have existed because they would know that the crosses could not work!

Crosses with tetraploid Tall Bearded Iris were made quite unscientifically and with the least amount of success. Nevertheless, two famous cultivars were obtained in this manner: *I.* 'Elmohr', which won the Dykes Medal, and *I.* 'Lady Mohr', which is still admired for its unique beauty and distinction as a garden ornamental. If the guidelines regarding fertile families, which we have suggested, had been established at that time, these exceptional flowers would not have existed. But they did not sell well, probably due to cultural difficulties, and were dropped from the catalogues. They are functionally sterile and it serves no purpose to attempt to crossbreed with them today. But since they can be propagated vegetatively, it is always interesting to try such unlikely crosses to see if something particularly attractive comes out of them. The cross

$$2n = 22 + 24 = \frac{10\ 12}{12\ 12} = 46,$$

which corresponds to this type, would never be acceptable on paper. However, one should always be prepared to break with convention if one has a hunch about something. A good example of this would be the Regelias crossed with Pogon Iris, which hardly anyone thought would be successful.

Dwarf Aril Iris
Since there are not only small Pogons, but also small Oncocyclus, small Arils would not be difficult to breed. We can presume that the hybrids would be very different, almost different classes, because the parent species are so different. But it is too early to anticipate something that does not yet exist. Even the name Arilmedians, invented by Americans, seems inappropriate. It is also suggested that measurement in centimeters alone, in the face of such anticipated wide variation, can be no criterion and, indeed, leaves out aesthetics altogether.

Nonetheless, mulling over the idea of Dwarf Arils is not unproductive; the reason was *Iris pumila*. In addition to Tall Garden Iris, autotetraploid *I. pumila* could also be crossed with tetraploid Regelias, to form highly fertile families with

$$2n = \frac{8\ 11}{8\ 11} = 38 \text{ chromosomes.}$$

Given the tremendous range of variation in the parents, progeny could be developed in all sorts of colors and would be an addition to the host of spring bloomers. In crossing Regeliocyclus with *I. pumila,* there is a chance that the reduction division will not occur. This happened with my cross *I.* 'Miltonia' and resulted in fertile progeny, like the tall iris from the cross between (*I. hoogiana* $\times$ *I. pumila*) $\times$ *I.* Regeliocyclus, once again validating the still mysterious equation between Oncocyclus and Regelia chromosome sets.

The fertility of "hoog-pums" also demonstrates that *I. pumila* behaves like a true autotetraploid. All the $\times=8$ sets have the same value. Under the microscope, hundred of meiosis metaphase slides will show a striking similarity and not a single anomaly. This contradicts Randolph and Mitra's hypothesis that *I. pumila* is an amphidiploid from *I. attica* $\times$ *I. pseudopumila.*

Clones and Lines

Based on his horticultural experience, the breeder will be drawn into clone selection, especially through discussions with his colleagues. He selects his most beautiful seedling and tries by vegetative means to make something permanent out of it that can be entered in competition or sold. He selects a clone. This he considers the prototype of a new cultivar to be named.

It is not quite so easy to think in terms of breeding lines and then later, in terms of fertile families. Fixing individual plants is accepted practice, where crossing individuals with very different forms leads to sterile hybrids. The visual image defines the outer appearance; mental reflection, with egg and sperm cells waiting in the background to be combined and with imbalanced hereditary traits to be disposed of in later generations, is unusual.

Studying several consecutive generations and observing the way characteristics from the original parents recombine has become in this century the domain of genetics. Masses of literature are written in this field, and it should certainly be consulted. It is no longer possible to go into iris genetics thoroughly in a general book about iris, although until recently it was tried. Nevertheless, we will mention a few things here, which will help the reader to better understand examples from the work of iris breeding, since didactic presentations in textbooks usually approach this introductory material quite differently.

Years ago I worked rather intensively with Alexander Steffen's cultivar *I.* 'Zephir' because of its particularly pure, pale purplish pink color. One could see right away, with the breeder's eye, that it was a descendant of *I.* 'Rheingauperle' (G. & K.), although mentally there were problems: *I.* 'Rheingauperle' is a diploid, *I.* 'Zephir' a tetraploid. I wanted to know whether the color corresponded to a locus that could be fixed by heredity and whether this could be discovered by cross-breeding, this being the only cultivar of this type. The all-white, recessive homozygote *I.* 'Matterhorn' was used as a breeding partner. The F_1 of this pair, consisting of only a few plants, showed all-white and "blue" in a 1 : 1 presumable ratio. At first this finding could lead to only *one* conclusion: at least one of the parents was a heterozygote. Otherwise the F_1 would all have looked alike; yet they were far from uniform. Then the following theories occurred to me that had to be worked out by a breeding experiment in later generations. *I.* 'Zephir' must have had the locus for all-white as a *recessive* heterozygote, and therefore invisible because of the formation of anthocyanine, otherwise these all-white seedlings with *I.* 'Matterhorn' could not have been homozygotes. *I.* 'Matterhorn' could not have had the allele for purple-pink, otherwise the other plants would have looked purple-pink, not "blue". That meant that the plants of the F_1 generation had to be backcrossed with *I.* 'Zephir' as a recessive parent. There would be only a few purple-pink plants in the next generation if my theory was correct. In fact, such a plant did occur in the relatively small number of progeny. That was the proof. But let us not fool ourselves; it was a stroke of luck. The number of progeny was too small to offer any validity. Had there been no purple-pink plant, nothing at all could have been proved! It might not have shown up at all because there were so few progeny. In such cases not only the theoretical random figures have to be taken into account, but also the theoretical minimum number of progeny.

An expected theoretical number is always compared with a given, empirical figure, and then the quality of the agreement is determined by the quality of the expectation. If I expected a ratio of 3 : 1 seedlings and perhaps get a split of 7 : 1, then 7 : 1 should be compared with 6 : 2. Since $7 - 6 = 1$ and $2 - 1 = 1$ and 1 is the least possible number of plants, 7 : 1 is not a bad outcome, although it seems like it at first. The easiest theoretical ratio to verify is 1 : 1. "Backcrossing with the recessive parent" should be incorporated into one's planning as often as possible. But this is done mainly to confirm necessary findings and not for aesthetic reasons.

By their very nature iris allow us to keep a "copy" of these progeny for years, carefully labeled, of course. This special opportunity afforded by iris should always be taken advantage of.

Cayeux's *I.* 'Floridor' is diploid; the backcross (*I. plicata* $\times$ *I.* 'Floridor') $\times$ *I.* 'Floridor' had enough numbers (43 : 45 individuals) to guarantee a 1 : 1 split, so identifying floridorin as a recessive mutant vis-a-vis violin, the original iris anthocyanin, was no longer any problem. But we have greater difficulties with today's garden iris because they are tetraploid, so much more complicated recombinations can be expected. These tetraploid recombinations are covered in more recent books on iris, but I would rather refer the reader to specific treatises. No matter what, I would strongly advise every hybridizer dealing with tetraploid recombinations to take paper and pencil and, on a long winter night, work out the frequencies he expects. Only then will he under-

Iris pseudacorus. Our yellow flag has defended itself best of all the iris at one time native to Germany. It still can be frequently seen. No doubt this is due to its adaptability, for though it is basically a swamp plant, it can also get along in dry soils. Shown is a seedling from the cultivar 'Golden Queen', which no longer has the brown pattern of the species.

stand how to manipulate these calculations. This is much more useful than poring over books.

It is not an easy procedure, even with letter indexing. For example, the lovely shell-pink blossom color that stems from the tomato pigment, lycopin, has been genetically related to a recessive locus t (tangerin). Small t indicates immediately that it is recessive. Its dominent allele is identified as capital T, but we do not know what it will do as a dominant allele. It is reasonable not to insist on ascribing a particular characteristic to a dominant allele. In any case, it has no effect whatsoever on the presence of lycopin and the color characteristic tangerine. It is well just to ignore a dominant allele. In this instance, we have to show that every locus has to be present four times, hence that there are many more heterozygotes than there are in diploids. To simplify this, we abbreviate the letter formulas a bit. So now they look like this: the heterozygotes and homozygotes would be: TTTT, TTTt, TTtt, Tttt and tttt. If we add the dominant and recessive alleles together, this is abbreviated: T_4t_0, T_3t_1, T_2t_2, T_1t_3 and T_0t_4. If we eliminate the dominant ones as being less important, it is reduced to t_0, t_1, t_2, t_3 and t_4. One eventually gets used to this indexing after a while and is able to understand what is meant by w_4t_4. It is understood that t_3 probably contains only a small amount of lycopin and that only t_4 shows enough lycopin to determine color. If we work out the frequencies of all the heterozygotes, the worst that can be expected would be a frequency of 35 : 1 for t_4. That is extremely low when compared with 3 : 1 for diploids.

I was interested at one time in whether two different characteristics could be recombined in tetraploid garden iris. If we take w4 as an arbitrary (in this case all-white) recessive white, our task would be to breed a w_4t_4 plant. If we use the same unfavorable ratio as a basis, the expected frequency for the homozygote w_4t_4 plant would be $(35 : 1) \cdot (35 : 1) = 1225 : 35 : 35 : 1$. That would be only one plant in more than a thousand. Any iris breeder, considering the chances for his garden, would simply shrug his shoulders and give up. But breeders do not give up a possible objective lightly.

The question arose, what would happen if a small amount of lycopin that was invisible next to all the orange could be identified by using a test. This can be done by extracting pigment from the beards with methanol. Only the insoluble lycopin that is left behind stays pink and stands out against the beards, which turn white. Suppose these few plants that stay pink were t_3 plants? Then their expected frequency would be much higher than the t_4 plants. Exactly *how* much higher can be worked out. As I said, these are calculations for a long winter evening.

From 70 "yellow" progeny, selected carefully, I was finally able to get 3 plants

This is a blossom of an Iris sibirica hybrid cultivar with 40 chromosomes. The species of this group cross with each other readily. In this case Iris bulleyana and Iris delavayi are probable ancestors. Variations appear in seedling populations from self-pollinated species, but few will be as beautiful as hybridized offspring.

with only a little lycopin, though it took me several years. The anticipated F_2 results were postponed by a few generations. The rest was just work. I now have the w_4t_4 line I was looking for as a pure line. This did not have any aesthetic purpose to it, but did confirm our expectations. It was worthwhile working out this kind of recombination and then seeing it to its conclusions.

Amphidiploid species crosses, whether Lilliputs, Pogoregelias, CGW's, or other Aril types, behave, according to Mendel's law, like diploids. We should not get discouraged by theoreticians who point to missing recombinations between various species and forecast recombinations that will not take place in later generations. And then they do recombine! But above all, there are gaps in manifestation (genetic gaps?) where rare characteristics can be isolated. The many plicatas, luminatas, and tangerines that have come from these dwarf iris since then, cannot be otherwise explained. On the other hand, we should not be led to the false conclusion that possibilities for recombination among the numerous species characteristics of fertile amphidiploid species crosses are inexhaustible.

But the limits of Anderson's so-called recombination spindle oppose this. The principle, which we will go into further, states that a profusion of very different genes are always combined on single chromosomes in single linkage groups and cannot combine freely. But since we cannot work with so many characteristics at once, we will follow these trains of thought quantitatively with perhaps two groups of characteristics.

Although a great number of these studies involve iris, specifically Louisiana Iris, I tried to find something in my own garden that would be easier to work with,

and selected a cross between native *Dianthus superbus* and a Chinese or Rainbow Pink, purchased from a nursery. One only needs a few F_1 plants that do not look very characteristic, and then it is surprising how various and colorful the F_2 generation is, especially if they are grown in larger stands. At first you actually think, everything is here! One works through a certain group of characteristics, say the colors between reddish purple and bluish purple, limiting oneself to easily visible differences. The same is done with the *D. superbus* recombining and this is indicated on graph paper. If every single plant is registered like this with a dot in a square, corresponding to horizontal and vertical categories, the result is not an evenly filled out sheet, as might be expected, but an accumulation of dots along a kind of spindle, following one of the diagonals. So in fact every combination in infinite numbers is not the result.

This picture also illustrates how a mistake frequently made in combination breeding can be avoided. Taking the pinks as an example—if we want to breed for a "blue pink", we should not always select crosses that come from the collection of types similar to the parents. The picture demonstrates that one always comes close to the "backcross with the recessive parent" and always stays near the F_1 cross, without locating the recombination. On the other hand it is much more difficult to look for "sib pairings". Rebreeding requires that heterozygotes combine to further stimulate segregation. To retain the arrangement of the recombination spindle, one moves within the center of the spindle or in another, shorter, diagonal.

Patient, persistent segregation of very large combinations of characteristics very often leads not so much to the rare as to the unexpected. Aril hybridizers will be familiar with *I.* 'Some Love', a small sterile hybrid that has nothing of the familiar wild iris about it, but always reminds us, with its pattern like that of a rare bird's egg, that in breeding Arils everything unexpected is still "inside".

We have already referred to the problems of multiple alleles. Their specialty is developing unusual, distinct levels of intensity of one and the same physiological characteristic. It is often wrongly thought that characteristics that are able to manifest themselves next to each other, but are physiologically very different, are multiple alleles. Various levels of intensity in a characteristic can also be caused in polyploids when characteristics accumulate. This dosage effect is not easy to analyze.

One other thing: clones from determinate recombinations should be kept for years, carefully labelled of course and with their paperwork for future reference! Another recommendation: always carry a small notebook when visiting any of the large modern collections. Note not so much what is new, as what is not there! Make careful comparisons based on what is *not* seen. You have no idea how useful and stimulating this kind of information is later in one's own hybridizing work.

Sterility

If we cannot obtain well developed seed from a garden iris cultivar, this cultivar is infertile, or sterile. If the plant does not set seed, but demonstrates other characteristics that only partially reduce fertility, the variety is said to be semi-sterile. Semi-sterility is quite common in garden iris cultivars. *I.* 'Snow Flurry' is famous for its *pollen sterility*. But with pollen from other varieties it produces such abundant seed that it was often used as a seed bearer. It is

even used to test the fertility of questionable pollen.

There are numerous signs of sterility which have to be learned by observation. First of all, iris can be *self-sterile,* especially Tall Garden Iris. It is unlikely that seeds could be obtained from such a plant by selfing. But this is not true for all iris, particularly not for *Iris spuria* and other Apogon Iris. Self-sterile means that a cultivar or clone—an individual—will not set seed when pollinated with its own pollen. Yet it is by no means true that every clone will set seed with the pollen of any other clone. What happens is that individual A will not produce seed with individual B, but will with individual C. With some very specific individuals, therefore, there is an *intersterility*. The conditions of this intersterility in iris have not been researched nearly enough because of their generational variations. But it can be a very disruptive factor if one wants to develop specific lines, because inbreeding cannot then be easily done. This forces the breeder to develop several genetically different lines and try to reach his goal by crosses between these. The two latter forms of sterility do not manifest any exterior signs.

Between pollination and fertilization lie all the physiological barriers that hinder final seed production. At the least, either the ovules or the pollen grains may be sterile. Both of these can be seen under a microscope, but often they can be seen with the naked eye; when the ovary is cut open or split, one can see that the seeds are irregularly arranged on the placenta and are of different sizes and stages of development. If the seeds are all the same size and are arranged like a string of pearls on the placenta, one can be pretty sure that they are normal and well developed. The pollen grains, too, may be different sizes if many are sterile. If they are all the same size, they can usually be evenly brushed off and are also abundant in the anthers. But this can all be seen more easily under a microscope. Granted, there is no guarantee that large, round, perfect-looking grains that develop uniformly are sure to be fertile. The percent of their stainability is often taken as proof of their viability, but the most reliable test is to let them germinate on the stigmatic lip and then examine the quality of the pollen tubes.

Iris offer a particularly good opportunity to observe this process. If dry pollen is placed on the stigmatic lip in the evening and allowed to germinate overnight, it can be easily observed in the morning. The crests are separated from the stigma; the pollen on the stigmas is carefully scraped together with tweezers and after that, removed. Entire beards of pollen sacs can sometimes be stripped off, in which case it is certain that the pollen is well-germinated. This is the easiest way of checking.

Pollen sacs can be easily stained with a heavily diluted solution of methylviolet or Janus green B. This staining is extremely useful for following the pollen tubes from the style canal and the placenta in the ovary to the micropyles of the ovules. They can even be traced into the ovule.

Often, even with poorly developed pollen, there will be some good seeds that came from the few functional pollen grains. This is particularly important for those working with species hybrids and difficult polyploids. So semi-sterility is no reason to give up on a cross or some other experiment too early.

All these different ways of checking are helpful when looking for more details about the causes of sterility. More than anything, it prevents us from treating all appearances of sterility alike.

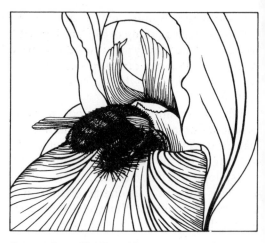

Carpenter bee pollinating an iris

Pollination

The illustration of the carpenter bee shows how pollen is transferred to the stigma. In the background is the stamen from which it takes pollen when it flies to the next blossom in its search for nectar. To duplicate this process artificially, it is best to hold the stamen with curved tweezers, so that it can be used confidently and safely in any situation.

Pollen grains burst open in water, and are otherwise very sensitive to moisture of any kind. This should be kept in mind when pollinating; make sure that the pollen placed on the stigmatic lip is always dry. But pollen from a newly opened stamen is not completely dry yet. If several pollinations are planned for one day, it is best to gather a supply of just opened stamens in small containers (labeled!). It is easiest just to keep them on the desk until they are to be used, but in any case they should never be put in direct sunlight. They should not be used then before the late morning.

Hand pollination of iris

1. Removal of mature anther with tweezers

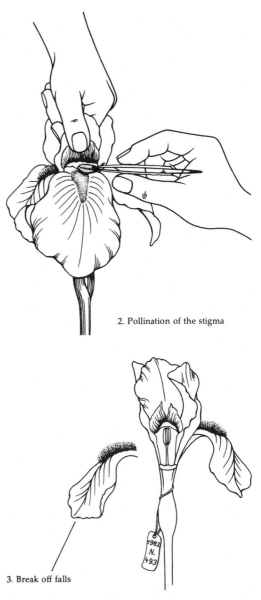

2. Pollination of the stigma

3. Break off falls

Doing the pollinating oneself and noting the type of pollination ensures that the right pollen gets to the right stigma. Insects cannot be allowed to "trespass". The simplest way of preventing this is to break off the falls of the target buds early in the morning when they first open. Then one has the whole day to do one's work without worrying about beating the bees to the blossoms.

Gathering the pollen ahead of time has the further advantage of being able to use it over a longer period of time, e.g. the pollen of early *Iris pumila* can be used on later garden iris varieties, and can even be shipped or exchanged. In areas where early summers are warm, no additional precautions are necessary. But to store pollen over a long period of time, a desiccator (a tightly closed container that contains a dehydrating agent at the bottom, such as silica gel, calcium nitrate for desiccators, or concentrated sulfuric acid) is needed. But the pollen should always be air dried at room temperature before being put in the container. At lower temperatures it might keep for more than a year. This is the way difficult species crosses are possible, even continents away.

I have personally made crosses with pollen shipped from the U.S.

Observing germinating pollen is useful in another way. If one sees that the pollen germinates profusely, the pollen tubes will compete with each other just like seedlings in a seedling bed. So only a small amount should be used for pollinating, to give the pollen tubes that are not as far along in their development a chance.

If carefully pollinated fruits drop prematurely, it is not the fault of the pollination, but the ovary's growth regulating mechanism. The usual cause is the separating tissue below the ovary. To prevent premature dropping, the style can be cut off a couple of days after the blossom has been pollinated and the exposed surface covered with a growth hormone.

Fertilization

After the pollen has germinated on the stigma, the path of the pollen tubes from the stigma and style canals to the micropyle of the ovule represents the period between pollination and fertilization.

What counts from now on is what happens in the ovule's embryo sac. The pollen tube breaks open and releases two sperm nuclei that developed when the generative pollen cell divided as the pollen tube elongated. Incidentally, this division of the sperm nucleus is easy to see in iris, using nucleus staining methods, if the pollen tubes are removed after the first night and stained as described. This can be helpful if the number of chromosomes transferred by the nuclei cannot be predicted.

The two sperm nuclei have fulfilled their function when one unites with the egg cell (fertilization) and the other fuses with the secondary embryo sac nucleus. In the case of the first union, two haploids (sperm and egg) produce a diploid (zygote) nucleus, which will, through cell division, develop into the embryo of the new plant. The second, the embryo sac nucleus, is already diploid because it developed from the union of two polar nuclei. If we add to this the second sperm nucleus, the result is the triploid endosperm nucleus. It is well to remember later in the seed's development, that both these nuclei are already different, that physiological tensions can arise if the metabolism of the two do not synchronize. Anomalous seed presumably starts developing this way.

But there is another concept here that may be harder to accept. It has become customary to refer to the fertilized egg from this point on as the embryo. But all we know about this initial situation is what we see under the microscope. It is questionable whether that is sufficient. What strikes us is that for days the fertilized egg "does nothing", whereas the endosperm nucleus has already burst into a series of divisions. Does this dormancy mean inactivity? Or is something basic happening here which we simply cannot perceive?

It is a large step from the fertilized egg to the embryo, a bigger step than we perhaps realize. First of all, only two nuclei have united, and from here on their two sets of genetic information have to work in concert. But this nucleus first has to acquire an *identity*. A new "being with organization" has to emerge that not only has the capacity, but also the tendency, to realize its inherited traits. Only when the fertilized egg (zygote) has acquired this new individuality, can we speak of an embryo.

If we were to describe and classify all the various structures in anomalous seeds, we would see that many of them are not embryos at all, though they may have developed from fertilized eggs. They are at best calluses. A callus is not even a tissue, but a heterogeneous mass of cells that has no organization and not individuality. It has the rudiments of many different types of tissue, but no organization. Destroying

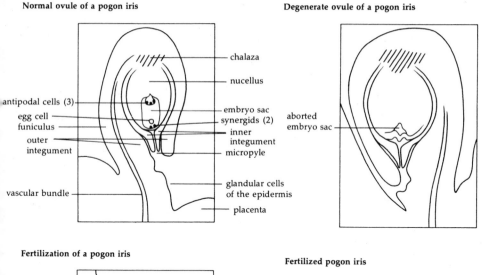

Normal ovule of a pogon iris

- chalaza
- nucellus
- antipodal cells (3)
- egg cell
- funiculus
- embryo sac
- synergids (2)
- inner integument
- micropyle
- outer integument
- vascular bundle
- glandular cells of the epidermis
- placenta

Degenerate ovule of a pogon iris

- aborted embryo sac

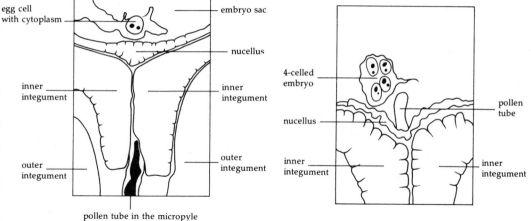

Fertilization of a pogon iris

- egg cell with cytoplasm
- embryo sac
- nucellus
- inner integument
- inner integument
- outer integument
- outer integument

pollen tube in the micropyle

Fertilized pogon iris

- 4-celled embryo
- pollen tube
- nucellus
- inner integument
- inner integument

the organization in tissue culture with 2,4-dichloro-phenoxyacetic acid makes comparison possible, but the difference is that the anomalies in these anomalous seeds have been caused by hybridization, not by the chemical composition of the culture medium.

The abstract concept of individuality has not played a role in the field of physiology for some time because chemical-physiological thinking has dominated the interpretation of this phenomenon. It stemmed from the discovery in the last century that all living things were made up of cells, and therefore cells must be the smallest individuality. The discussion had already taken place between Julius Sachs from Schleiden and Alexander Braun and was apparently abandoned in the discussions concerning vitalism. But this whole way of thinking was again given credence when Julius Sachs said, "The cell has to give up its own individuality for the good of the individuality of the total organism,"

319

i.e. for the good of a hierarchical structure composed of various levels, such as cell, tissue, organ, organism, and the regulation between them. These ideas are hampered by the fact that we do not know what the qualifications for an embryo should be that is a fertilized egg but is not quite an embryo. However, studies in embryo culture and tissue culture admit the possibility that a single or isolated cell might possess multiple individualities, either its own or those of a higher organism, without it being obvious to us.

One of the peculiarities of the embryo sac is that everything in it is fed *glandularly* by its antipodial organ. Along all the other walls with organs and tissues of the mother plant, the wall structure excludes any exchange of nutrients or other substances. This is only possible in the embryo sac because of the antipodial organ, and this glandular release of substances differs fundamentally from the exchange of substances between cells, which goes on in all the adjacent tissue.

It can be said with good reason that "the embryo sac is the only place in a plant where an individuality can be nourished, that is separate from the individuality of the mother plant". In addition, embryonic growth as a special embryonic phase of growth is limited to the embryo sac.

Embryonic growth produces only cells that are rich in plasma and still do not have vacuoles. Growth that creates a regulating system between the embryonic and vacuolising phases of growth out of what till now had been exclusively embryonic growth only begins at germination. Continuing embryonic growth produces the vacuole-free cells of the vegetative cones and continues the embryonic phase in them, enabling it to *persist* (Strasburger). The vacuolizing phase produces the various vegetative cells of the young plant. Regulation inside the embryo sac, however, provides only for embryonic growth.

If, however, the supposed hormonal regulation of growth between the individuality of the mother plant and the individuality of the embryo is interrupted at all, the results will strongly resemble what happens in tissue culture after treatment with 2,4-D. Usually seeds will develop that are sterile and do not have a firm endosperm. They will shrink and finally rot when put in the ground.

The results of these first findings led directly to embryo culture. The methods of sterile technique were well known. If a viable embryo were found in a seed that was functionally sterile and unable to germinate, it became obvious that such techniques could be used to grow it artificially.

Iris carthaliniae. There is an extensive series of species and forms of tall spuria iris from the Soviet Union. Iris cartheliniae is a beautiful shade of blue and grows stiffly upright. It has the widest leaves of this group. It will only bloom in a warm site.

Embryo Culture

Numerous persons, mostly amateurs, learned these new methods. Since that time, the methodology has acquired other uses, mostly in making difficult crosses, primarily Aril crosses. They were simply too valuable to trust to the normal practice of sowing in earth. This new methodology enabled them to be observed right from the start.

Experience with abnormally formed seed could be applied here, as well as experience with *delayed germination.* Seeds from all three sections have a very annoying delay in germinating, which is probably useful in maintaining the species, but severely hampers orderly cultivation in the garden. The dormant seeds often had to be written off as lost. In many cases delayed germination could be attributed only to the embryo's hermetic seal. It would start germinating at once if the micropyle was opened to expose the radicle. A Pogon Iris embryo from an opened seed will immediately germinate, no matter what the time of year and even after being dry for several years. An Oncocyclus seed, slightly opened at the micropyle, is much slower to germinate. Thus the reason for a delay in germination can be sought in the endosperm and attributed to an inhibitor. Regelia embryos are the only exception, because they carry the principle of inhibiting germination right inside themselves. Exposed embryos from Regelias continue their embryonic growth on agar without ever germinating. This continuation of embryonic growth outside the seed is peculiar to the Regelia section and distinguishes it from all other *Iris* sections. The embryo continues growing until it is many times the size of the lumen of the original seed. Primary root and leaf bud (radicle and plumule) are not involved in this embryonic growth in delayed germination. Regeliocyclus embryos also demonstrate this behavior to a certain extent, but not Pogoregelias.

To get these embryos to germinate in flasks, we have learned by experimentation that putting them in a normal refrigerator for about 2 months will overcome delayed germination. The flasks should be removed one by one as the embryos show signs of germinating. This refrigeration method is also recommended for other dormant aril seeds, although a scientific study of the effects of cooling during this "quiet" period still remains to be done. Intact seeds do not have to be treated in a sterile medium, so living sphagnum moss can be used and is recommended. A peculiar type of seed which has previously resisted embryo culture can be made to germinate on this substrate. These seeds, which have only recently been observed, are small, long, and narrow. They rarely have endosperms, but when they do, these are also

Iris halophila. A tall spuria iris, of questionable species status. A robust garden iris, which can also self-sow. It varies in color somewhat from yellowish to bluish shades.

tiny, spherical proembryos. They could not be made to germinate on agar. But they will readily germinate on sphagnum moss when left undisturbed for several months under refrigeration. Their proembryonic development is thus allowed to continue until it reaches the germinating capability of normal seeds.

Embryo culture has developed in every way into a methodology that goes far beyond its original application for anomalous hybrid embryos. New ideas are being added to it all the time from the field of tissue culture, to which amateur breeders have contributed enormously. Its most important element is still *germ-free, aseptic culture,* without which breeding on artificial substrates is not possible. Working with sterile instruments has to be learned. This can be done, sometimes with very simple means, as success the world over has shown. It is amazing to see what has been accomplished outside of scientific laboratories in the last two decades.

Working in a sterile environment is easier the more the initial procedure, i.e., harvesting the fruit, is already adapted to it. If, for instance, one originally planned that a capsule should fully ripen on the scape, experience with already opened fruits will soon show that it is preferable not to wait that long. The first fruits that show signs of ripening are often laterally constricted, indicating that most of their seeds are not very sizable, which means that they may be likely candidates for embryo culture. It is advisable to prepare them as soon as possible. The smooth and round capsules should be removed as they begin to mature; ripeness must be closely followed. If a capsule is allowed to mature outdoors, the seeds will usually be molded or shriveled and are no longer suitable for embryo culture work. Even capsules matured to full ripeness indoors are prone to infection. The more we know about harvesting seed, the more we realize they should be harvested quickly. You gradually get to know when they have just the right brown sheen and are, therefore, mature. At this point, the lightly-colored seeds should be carefully separated so the air can circulate around them and they can dry better. This way one can count on getting evenly-sized, light brown seeds.

This is also the point at which the embryo reaches the maximum size allotted to it by the lumen and endosperm. What comes next is anabiosis, or more properly in this case, anhydrobiosis. This is the maximum amount of water the seed can lose as it dries and still remain viable. Now the "quiet period" of germination begins, the seed's continuation as a "latent life". If the embryo and endosperm have dried sufficiently, they can survive for years with minimal metabolism, mainly respiration. The embryo is as hard as glass in this condition, without its seed case, and will crack just like glass. If it is put in water, it will swell up momentarily and then die. Experiments have shown that being covered with water is what kills it. The only way to rehydrate it, is to let it slowly swell again in a very humid room. This does not happen by imbibition. Here again we are getting to know a purely physical concept, that of wetting and wetability, which has a decisive influence on life processes and is not chemically induced.

In this way the limits of embryo culture are defined. If a seed in this state of "quiet germination" is to be treated, it has to be softened. Even if it looks healthy, it should be treated in a germ-killing wash, such as much diluted chlorinated lime solution (calciumhypochlorite, such as B-K, used by dairymen) and then rinsed quickly in boiled water. From softening to treatment takes about three days and can be done at

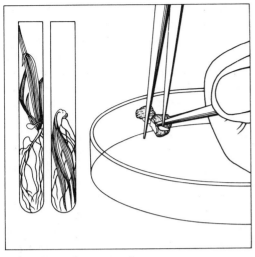

Embryo tissue culture preparation

any time of year. But with this method of harvesting, good seed is always available. To grow these without infection, the following method is recommended. Use dry, milled sphagnum; soak some in a solution of 10 g of potassium pyrosulfite (1 tablet for wine deacidification) in 5 quarts of water, kneading it in until the peat is thoroughly damp, but not dripping. Mix this with an equal amount of clean beach sand (river sand must be sterilized with a hypochlorite solution and leached repeatedly with boiled water) and use it as a growing medium in pots or bowls. Sink the pots outdoors in the ground and expose to winter weather. When repotting in spring, care should be taken to see that the seed leaves (cotyledons), which have grown quite long and which determine the position of the embryo, do not break off and take the attached embryos with them. If this happens, the embryos usually have to be given up for lost.

Depending on its density, 7–10 g of agar and 20 g of sucrose (cane sugar) should be used per liter of water as a substrate for embryo culture. This will then be put into test tubes or flasks. Nutrient salts, trace elements, organic nutrients, active ingredients, and growth hormones should also be added. There are so many formulas now that it would be difficult just to list the most important ones. We use a formula derived from the old Burgeff EG1 recipe, but using less calcium, as a mineral salt base for iris agar. The advantage of this formula is that calcium does not precipitate out during sterilization. The iris substrate contains:

0.1 g Ca $(NO_3)_2$ = calcium nitrate
0.5 g KNO_3 = potassium nitrate
0.25 g $(NH_4)_2SO_4$ = ammonium sulfate
0.25 g $MgSo_4$ = magnesium sulfate (Epsom Salts)
0.25 g KH_2PO_4 = monobasic potassium phosphate
0.25 g K_2HPO_4 = dibasic potassium phosphate
0.02 g $FeSO_4$ = ferrous (iron) sulfate

The biggest problem in making up the substrate involves the amount of trace elements and active ingredients to be used. I recommend making up a reserve solution, so that a small amount can be added to the culture broth at any time. The most important trace elements are boron, manganese, zinc, molybdenum, copper, cobalt, and potassium iodide. 30 mg of glycine per liter serves as a protein base. The most familiar vitamin ingredients included in the formulas are ascorbic acid, thiamin, pyridoxin, niacinamide, calcium pantothenate, inosite, p-aminobenzoic acid, folic acid, adenine, riboflavin, and biotin. The significance and value of trace elements and vitamins were mostly learned from empirical studies of other plants, and these substances were then added to the nutrient media. Whether they are necessary to iris has not yet been specifically proven. Today many culture media can be purchased ready-made, although most of them have been made for microbiological purposes. Liquid fertilizer for flowers, which can be purchased almost anywhere, would also be something to consider.

Just pointing out the fact that substrates were originally developed for microbiology is an implied criticism. We should be aware that the gelatinous surface of agar was geared for culturing bacteria and fungi. It is questionable whether this is ideal for higher plants, where we are trying to duplicate "natural soil" which is, on the other hand, difficult to properly enrich and sterilize. One experiment warrants this criticism. If one gram of animal charcoal (carbo animalis) is added to a liter of agar solution, a black, opaque substrate results, which can be useful if living embryos turn brown and suggest a morbid development of polyphenols. Charcoal agar was able to reverse this process successfully in many cases. But it has to be shaken just before the agar sets, so the charcoal does not settle, which is inconvenient. Charcoal agar produces unexpected results with *Cymbidium* meristems. The explants quickly develop ground roots, and tall leafy shoots soon suppress growth of the embryonic meristem. This can be interpreted as the effects of light polarity. So both this characteristic and, above all, its capacity to adsorb should be taken into consideration when using animal charcoal. But we can probably expect growth adjustments for iris in the future that will make it advisable to try other substrates besides agar.

The bipolarity of the embryo itself provides another reference point. This is set up to absorb inorganic nutrients through the root and organic nutrients (from the endosperm) through the cotyledon. My own investigations into "bipolar feeding" in the "test tube endosperm" prove this. Although these tests could not be concluded, they showed that the cotyledon almost adhered to the agar in the narrow test tube and that it can tolerate up to a 15% sugar solution, permitting the leaf bud to grow much faster. The endosperm had attached itself so firmly in the flask that I could not go any farther with my tests, but bipolarity was proven. This indicates that the metabolic activity of the cotyledon effects the regulation of bipolar growth.

The tendency of agar to dry out on the surface, especially after months of culture, also is not a plus. When the medium is dessicated, the relatively tender embryos have to be transplanted a second time. If this is done, they have to be cleaned, which entails finding space on the small work bench for embroidery scissors in addition to hooked tweezers, tweezers, and fingernail clippers. If the embryos are large enough to be potted in sandy soil, they should be separated from any embryonic tissue, particularly from cotyledon tissue. The latter is extremely prone to all kinds of decay. They should also begin their growth in soil when they have adventitious roots if possible. Plantlets should be at a stage where the primary root cannot be removed as transplanting into soil proceeds.

Tissue Culture

Tissue culture is done in well equipped laboratories. Most of the work is theoretical, but practical applications were soon drawn from it. One of these is vegetative propagation in laboratories. Formerly plants had to be painstakingly separated as clones, whereas now propagation in culture flasks allows rapid increase of tissue.

The most famous subject is the carrot. A liquid culture, containing a trace of 2,4-dichoro-phenoxyacetic acid, tempered and rotated under lights, separates tissue into component cells. The cells are removed from the liquid and put in a nutrient medium without 2,4-D, where each cell develops into a normal embryo. Thus the vegetative cells produce embryos comparable to fertilized eggs in the embryo sac. Embryoids have even been produced from iris tissue. Where this extreme form of growing young plants does not work, at least isolating young meristem tissues in the culture medium yields abundant young plants. The cloning of valuable asparagus plants, for instance, was done in this way.

The ability to separate plant tissue into individual cells and grow them in a liquid culture has led to further experimentation. Separation into single cells could be done with pectin-soluble enzymes. In addition, cell walls could be dissolved with cellulose-soluble enzymes and the resultant naked protoplasts grown. Naked protoplasts may, under certain circumstances, make crosses beyond the limits of genus and species possible. Instead of crossing plants, cells, even perhaps nuclei, could be fused in test tubes. Of course, there are limits to speculation, despite the amazing results that have been achieved. We can get all the genetic material of two plants in one cell. To transmit the red of a gladiolus to an iris, for instance, or the other way around, the blue of an iris to a gladiolus, only a few genes would be necessary. However, we have hopes that taxanomic walls will be breached, which cannot be done by classical methods.

Tables of Iris and Other Useful References

Assortments for Every Purpose

Flowering Sequence in the Home Garden (Mid-North Temperate Zone)

"15 inches of blooming iris in the garden, from Mardi Gras to the last robin's song in July." Foerster

Iris specialists can lengthen the blooming period even more. The following summary is based on normal garden soil conditions.

A. Bulbous Iris (Genera *Iridodictyum* and *Juno*)
1. End of February to Middle of March
   Iridodictyum (Iris) histrio var. *aintabensis*
   Iridodictyum (Iris) histrioides 'Major'
   Iridodictyum (Iris) bakerianum
   Iridodictyum (Iris) danfordiae
2. Middle of March to Beginning of April
   Named Varieties of Small Bulbous Iris, especially 'Harmony'
   Iridodictyum (Iris) reticulatum
   Juno sindjarensis
3. From About the Beginning to the Middle of April
   Juno (Iris) bucharica
   Juno (Iris) graeberiana
   Juno (Iris) magnifica
4. End of May to Beginning of June
   Xiphium (Iris)-Hispanicum Hybrids
   Xiphium (Iris)-Hollandica Hybrids
5. June to July
   Xiphium (Iris) latifolium

B. Rhizomatous Iris
1. End of April to about the Middle of May
   Iris pumila
   Iris attica
   Iris reichenbachii
   Iris chamaeiris
   Dwarf iris Hybrids (MDB) = Miniature Dwarf Bearded
   Small Iris Hybrids (STB) = Standard Dwarf Bearded
2. About Middle of May
   Media Iris
   Iris florentina
   Border Iris
3. Last Two Weeks of May to Middle of June
   Tall Bearded Iris Hybrids
   Iris variegata
   Iris missouriensis
4. Up to Middle of June
   Iris sibirica hybrids
   Iris sanguinea 'Snow Queen'
   Iris pseudacorus
   Iris graminea
   Iris sibirica (with 40 chromosomes)

329

5. Last Two Weeks of June
    Iris laevigata
    Iris orientalis (*I. ochroleuca* 'Gigan-
      tea')
    Iris spuria
    Iris spuria hybrids
6. First Two Weeks of July
    Iris crocea
    Iris kaempferi hybrids (now *I. ensata*
    Thunberg)

In cooler weather regions, blooming times will be delayed. Blooming periods of individual varieties can also vary according to microclimatic conditions.

Iris for Confined Plantings, Such as in Troughs, Barrels, and Bowls

Iris arenaria
Iris pumila
Iris chamaeiris (only the smallest types)
Iris mellita
Iris lacustris
Iris setosa 'Dwarf Form'
Iris attica

Small bulbous Iris Species and Varieties
  (*Iridodictyum*). All Dwarf Iris Hybrids
  (MDB-Miniature Dwarf Bearded)

Juno for Planting in the Open

Juno (Iris) bucharica
Juno (Iris) graeberiana
Juno (Iris) magnifica
With Some Protection
Juno caucasica

Juno willmottiana
Juno orchioides
Juno sindjarensis
Juno × *sindpers*
Juno × *warlsind*

Iris reginae. An iris from the Balkans, which is closely related to Iris variegata. This is more of a quiet beauty than an attention getting garden plant, but one which collectors should grow as a significant species.

Iris for Water Gardens and Artificial Bogs

In the Water:
Iris pseudacorus and varieties
Iris laevigata

In the Water, Summer Only:
Iris kaempferi (*Iris ensata* Thunb.)

Boggy Places:
Iris versicolor
Iris fulva
Iris nelsonii
Iris giganticaerulea
Iris brevicaulis

Prefer Moist Location:
Iris sibirica
Iris sanguinea
Iris wilsonii
Iris forrestii
Iris delavayi
Iris chrysographes
Iris clarkei
Iris setosa

Dwarf Iris Selections
The following list of dwarf iris was compiled by Countess Helene von Stein-Zeppelin. All the varieties named have been tested in Laufen. Those marked MDB are Miniature Dwarf Bearded Iris; the others are all Standard Dwarf Bearded Iris.

White	'Bright White'	(Welch 1960)MDB
	'Cotton Blossom'	(B. Jones 1970)
Plicata	'Circlette'	(Goett 1962)
	'Pepper Mill'	(Hager 1977)
Amoena	'Boo'	(Markham 1971)
	'Sky and Snow'	(Warburton 1972)
Light Blue without Spot	'Blue Denim'	(Warburton 1959)
	'Biberach'	(Berlin 1978)
	'Key Haven'	(Taylor 1971)
Light Blue with Spot	'April Ballet'	(Palmer 1973)MDB
	'Ornament'	(Hager 1971)
	'Pepita'	(Schreiner 1965)
Dark Blue and Violet	'Blautopf'	(Berlin 1978)
	'Double Lament	(Taylor 1969)
	'Myra's Child'	(Greenlee 1971)
	'Royal Fairy'	(Brown 1967)
	'Silkie'	(Hager 1969)

Iris ensata. An iris from the Himalayas; the old name, Iris ensata, was removed by botanists in order to place it with Iris kaempferi. For the time being we are staying with the description as presented in this volume. Not an intoxicating beauty, but one with few requirements.

Black-red	'Demon'	(Hager 1972)
	'Temno'	(Blazek 1969)MDB
Violet, Two-toned	'Regards'	(Hager 1967)
Lilac-pink	'Fairy Ballet'	(Sarro 1968)
Purple-red	'French Wine'	(Roberts 1967)MDB
	'Fuchsia Gem'	(Jones 1968)MDB
	'Ripe Raspberry'	(Dunbar-Sindt 1972)
Brown-red	'Little Buccaneer'	(Schreiner 1974)
	'Ruby Contrast'	(Brown 1971)
	'Tomingo'	(Roberts 1969)
Bronze and Tobacco	'Gingerbread Man'	(Jones 1968)
Cream-yellow	'Soft Air'	(Warburton 1973)
Lemon yellow	'Lemon Puff'	(Dunbar 1969)MDB
	'Spring Bells'	(Jones 1972)
Light Yellow	'Laced Lemonade'	(Warburton 1970)
	'Stockholm'	(Warburton 1972)
Medium and Golden	'April Accent'	(Brown 1966)MDB
Yellow	'Golden Fair'	(Warburton 1960)
Orange-yellow	'Orange Caper'	(Warburton 1964)
Variegata	'Curio'	(Hager 1972)MDB
	'Pagan Butterfly'	(Roberts 1969)
	'Watercolor'	(Roberts 1968)

Collector's Varieties in Intermediate Shades (S = Standards, F = Falls)

'Emerald Rays'	(Dunbar 1971)	medium yellow, olive veins on F
'Kentucky Blue Grass'	(Jones 1971)	green-yellow with vibrant blue beard
'Indian Pow-Wow'	(Brown 1972)	S olive, F brown
'Love Note'	(Brown 1972)	S olive-cream, F olive, vibrant blue beard
'Meadow Moss'	(Jones 1969)	S olive, F greenish, blue beard
'Mrs. Nate Rudolph'	(Briscoe 1975)	bronze-green, blue beard, small-blossomed, branching
'Olive Accent'	(Braun 1972)	olive-green, light blue beard
'Parchment Plum'	(Sindt 1968)	S smokey lilac, F with wine-red spot
'Sea Change'	(Warburton 1973)	lavender-gray with greenish center
'Vim'	(Schreiner 1973)	carmine-pink, wine-red spot

IB, BB and MTB Selections (Proposed by Countess Helene von Stein-Zeppelin)

Iris Intermedia Group (IB)

White	'Astralite'	(Roberts 1960)
	'Cheers'	(Hager 1975)
	'Cutie'	(Schreiner 1962)
Light Blue	'June Prom'	(Brown 1967)
	'Sea Patrol'	(Palmer 1969)
Dark Blue and Violet	'Adrienne Taylor'	(GB Taylor 1963)
	'Annikins'	(Warburton 1967)
Plicata	'Arctic Fancy'	(Brown 1964)
	'Swizzle'	(Hager 1972)
Pink	'Sweetie'	(Warburton 1971)
Brown	'Apache Warrior'	(Brown 1972)
	'Light Cavalry'	(Jones 1967)
Light Yellow	'Frosted Cream'	(Brown 1968)
	'Trio'	(Hager 1971)
Medium Yellow	'Interim'	(Salman 1962)
Dark Yellow	'Alaskan Gold'	(Mahood 1959)
Wine Red	'Vamp'	(Gatty 1972)
Unclassified color	'Overtone'	(Du Bose 1971)

Border Iris (BB)

Light Blue	'Blue Warbler'	(Tucker 1971)
Plicata	'Embroidery'	(Keppel 1971)
Light Yellow	'Ellen'	(Peck 1965)
	'Miss Petite'	(Wright 1972)
Yellow	'Tulare'	(Hamblen 1961)
Wine Red	'Frenchi'	(Jones 1959)
	'Raspberry Sundae'	(Nieswonger 1972)

Miniature Tall Bearded Iris (MTB)

White	'Pee Wee'	(Williamson 1934)
White-blue	'Bit o'Afton'	(Guild 1967)
Plicata	'Mockingbird'	(Roberts 1962)
Violet	'Tom Tit'	(GB Bliss 1919)
Yellow	'Topsy Turvy'	(Welch 1964)

* = Varieties that we know and think are attractive, but whose vigorousness we have not tested over a period of time.

White	'Cup Race'	(Buttrick 1963)
	'Wedding Vow'*	(Ghio 1972)
	'Winter Olympics'	(Brown 1963)
White with Yellow	'Brides Halo'*	(Mohr 1973)
	'Christmas Angel'	(DeForest 1960)
	'Tinsel Town'	(Tompkins 1967)
White with Red Beard	'Christmas Time'	(Schreiner 1965)
Plicata Blue	'Blue Petticoats'	(Schreiner 1965)
	'Going my Way'*	(Gibson 1972)
	'Loop the Loop'*	(Schreiner 1975)
	'Stepping Out'	(Schreiner 1964)
Plicata Pink and Blue	'Crinoline'	(Schreiner 1965)
	'High Life'	(Schreiner 1964)
	'Mod Mode'	(Gibson 1970)
	'Rondo'	(Schreiner 1973)
Plicata Brown	'Kilt Lilt'	(Gibson 1970)
	'Radiant Apogee'	(Gibson 1966)
	'Spreckles'	(Schreiner 1972)
Amoena Blue	'Margarita'	(Schreiner 1968)
	'Miss Indiana'	(Cook 1961)
	'Snow Mound'*	(Schreiner 1976)
Amoena Yellow	'Glacier Gold'	(Wills 1963)
Amoena Red and Brown	'Bold Hour'*	(Schreiner 1974)
	'Breaking Dawn'	(Schreiner 1971)
	'Repartee'	(Smith 1968)
Light Blue	'Azure Apogee'	(Durrance 1967)
	'Babbling Brook'	(Keppel 1966)
	'Blue Reflection'*	(Schreiner 1974)
	'Sapphire Hills'	(Schreiner 1971)
	'Sky Watch'	(Benson 1964)
	'Victoria Falls'*	(Schreiner 1977)
Medium Blue	'Big League'	(Schreiner 1969)
	'Blue Lustre'*	(Brown 1973)
	'Bristol Gem'	(Leavitt 1965)
	'Shipshape'	(Babson 1969)
	'Tyrolean Blue'	(Schreiner 1963)

Medium Blue, Two-toned	'Dream Lover'*	(Tams 1971)
	'Lord Baltimore'	(Nearpass 1969)
	'Mystique'*	(Ghio 1975)
	'Out Yonder'	(Wickersham 1969)
Dark Blue	'Matinata'	(Schreiner 1968)
	'Navy Strut'*	(Schreiner 1974)
	'Royal Touch'	(Schreiner 1967)
Black-blue and Violet	'Dusky Dancer'	(Luihn 1967)
	'Night Owl'	(Schreiner 1970)
	'Storm Flurry'*	(Schreiner 1975)
	'Tuxedo'	(Schreiner 1965)
Blue with Subdued Gray	'Dusky Evening	(Schreiner 1971)
Lilac	'Dream Time'	(Schreiner 1967)
	'Pearl Chiffon'*	(Varner 1972)
Medium Violet	'George Specht'	(GB Fletcher 1964)
	'Prince Indigo'	(Schreiner 1964)
Violet, with Brownish Shades	'Pagan'	(Dunn 1973)
Flamingo Pink	'One Desire'	(Shoop 1960)
	'Pink Angel'*	(Rudolph 1973)
	'Pink Fringe'	(Rudolph 1967)
	'Symphonette'	(Noyd 1969)
	'Tahiti Sunrise'	(Ernst 1963)
	'Vanity'	(Hager 1975)
Lilac-pink	'Loudon Lassie'*	(Crossman 1972)
	'Priceless Pearl'	(Schreiner 1972)
Medium Pink, Two-toned	'Camelot Rose'	(Tompkins 1965)
	'Latin Lover'	(Shoop 1969)
Purple-red	'Grape Festival'	(Gaulther 1969)
	'Jewel Tone'*	(Schreiner 1966)
	'Mulberry Wine'	(Moldovan 1966)
	'Raspberry Ripples'	(Nieswonger 1969)
Brown-red	'Royal Trumpter'	(Raynold 1971)
	'Spartan'	(Schreiner 1973)
	'Sultans Palace'*	(Schreiner 1977)
	'Vitafire'	(Schreiner 1968)
Copper	'Candalaria'	(Schreiner 1968)
	'Rusticana'	(Schreiner 1961)
Bronze and Tobacco	'Neon Rainbow'*	(Schreiner 1971)
Light Brown	'Olympic Torch'	(Schreiner 1958)
Cream-yellow	'Soft Moonbeam'	(Schreiner 1973)
	'Southern Comfort'	(Hinkle 1965)

Lemon Yellow	'Green Quest'	(Brown 1960)
	'Launching Pad'	(Knopf 1969)
	'Lime Fizz'	(Hall 1963)
	'New Moon'*	(Sexton 1968)
Golden Yellow	'Carolina Gold'*	(Powell 1970)
	'Golden Promenade'	(Schreiner 1975)
	'Sun Worshipper'	(Hager 1972)
	'Warm Gold'*	(Schreiner 1972)
Apricot Shades	'Glaced Orange'	(Schreiner 1969)
	'Minnesota Glitters'	(Bakke-Messer 1967)
Two Colors	'Ballihoo'	(Keppel 1970)
(Variegata)	'Caramba'*	(Keppel 1975)
	'Gala Madrid'	(Peterson 1968)
	'Loud Music'	(Muhlestein 1971)

Laufen/Baden Iris Spuria Selection (Suggested by Countess Helene von Stein-Zeppelin)

'Archie Owen'	(Hager 1970)	golden yellow
'Cherokee Chief'	(Nies 1949)	brown
'Contradiction'	(Ferguson 1963)	mahogany red
'Dutch Defiance'	(Nies 1943)	light blue
'Eagle'	(Hager 1971)	golden yellow
'Elixir'	(Hager 1963)	yellow
'Fireplace'	Ferguson 1967)	red-brown
'Golden Lady'	(Combs 1957)	light yellow
'Lydia Jane'	(Walker 1965)	ivory
'Marilyn Holloway'	(Hager 1970)	lavender-blue
'Neophyte'	(Hager 1964)	blue
'Protege'	(Hager 1966)	blue
'Sarong'	(Hager 1974)	brown-purple
'Wakerobin'	(Ferguson 1958)	white
'Woodwind'	(Hager 1967)	bronze-brown

Badenweiler Iris Spuria Selection (Compiled by Bruno Muller, Frankfurt/Main, Palmengarten)

The following varieties have done well in Badenweiler and have proved to be relatively fungus resistant.

'Archie Owen'	'Fireplace'	'Marilyn Holloway'!!
'Belise'!	'Fluted Buttercup'	'Moon by Day'
'Cambridge Blue'!	'Fort Ridge'	'Port of Call'
'Connoisseur'	'Golden Lady'	'Premier'!
'Crow Wing'	'Good Nature'!	'Purple Knight'
'Dawn Candle'	'Highline Bluebird'	'Red Oak'
'Driftwood'	'Highline Lavender'!	'Sunny Day'!
'Eagle'	'Landscape Blue'	

The following crosses with a wild species were particularly exciting, but were unfortunately prone to disease in Badenweiler.

'Essay'
'Neophyte'
'Protege'
'Suspense'

Older, Free-flowering Spuria Iris
for regions with harsher climates (observed by the author in eastern Upper Franconia).

'Cambridge'	'Trush Song'
'Premier'	'Zeppelin Sämling'
'Cherokee Chief'	

Japanese Iris (*Iris kaempferi* in the garden, *Iris ensata* Thunb.)

Good selection available on the market in Germany. The original varieties from Japan have Japanese names.

'Agaki'	dark pink
'Amazone'	(Neuheit Wachter), medium-early, purple-violet, not tender, long blossom period
'Aoigata'	very early, beautiful dark violet, free-flowering, blossom diameter 4¾'' (12 cm)
'Ashi No Ukifune'	white with dark violet veins and dark violet standards
'Bambino'	late, white, striking violet veins, small blossomed
'Basho'	blue violet
'Benibotan'	dark purple-pink
'Biedermeierzeit'	mid-season, velvety dark violet, double
'Blaudom'	late, light blue, pale veining, double, slightly wavy
'Blaue Plicata'	late, light porcelain blue, veined, blossom diameter 6½'' (16 cm)
'Blaue Stunde'	mid-season, rich blue-lilac, double
'Blauer Berg'	medium-late, vibrant light blue, free-flowering, blossom diameter 6½'' (16 cm)
'Blue Pompon'	late, blue self, compact blossom
'Chidori'	late, white with delicate blue pattern, large, full blossoms
'Chiyodayo'	falls white-violet, standards violet
'Embossed'	mid-season, white ground, violet veins, large, full blossoms
'Emotion'	very delicate lilac, double, free-flowering
'Ezonishiki'	falls violet-white, standards violet
'Fujikosoda'	medium-early, pure pink, very pendulous petals
'Gefullte Orchidee'	late, pink, lower-growing variety
'Gekko No Nano'	late, violet, low-growing
'Geisha Dance'	late, lilac-pink marbelized on light blue, large-blossomed
'Gei Sho Ne'	medium-late, violet, very low-growing
'Good Omen'	early, reddish-violet blossom, doubled petals, free-flowering, vigorous
'Hakubotan'	pure white
'Hanagasa'	purple-red violet with white veining
'Hito Jakii'	late, marine blue with purple sheen, erect petals, free-flowering
'Innocense'	pure white, single blossom
'Kagurajishi'	dark purple-violet red
'Kokuryuden'	purple-red
'Lustige Witwe'	mid-season, white with lilac veins, double
'Mainhime'	medium-late, white background bordered with red
'Mai Ohgi'	late, pure white, yellow mid-stripe
'Mikohagura'	late, light reddish-violet, strongly veined, very large blossoms
'Minako'	falls lavender-blue violet with fine, white veins, standards white with definite narrow margin the color of the falls

'Miya No Shiruyiku'	white, yellow sap mark
'Montblanc'	early, pure white, free-flowering, blossom diameter 5⅛" (13 cm), very good
'Nagasaki'	blossoms small in unusual shade of lilac-pink, falls with darker zone and yellow sap mark
'Onarumi'	violet-red with white veins
'Over the Waves'	early, reddish-violet with large, pendulous petals
'Pink Frost'	medium-early, delicate pink, slightly wavy margin, vigorous and free-flowering
'Raspberry Rimmed'	(McEwen 1979) tetraploid *Iris kaempferi*, falls white with raspberry-colored margin, standards white
'Renaku'	white, yellow sap mark
'Royal Pageant'	late, whitish-gray ground, red-violet veins, large blossoms, very beautiful
'Ruby King'	wine red
'Sea Titan'	medium-late, sea blue, slightly lilac toward the margin, blossom has distinct yellow mid-stripe
'Seemann'	medium-late, violet-blue, reddish waves on margins of petals
'Shihoden'	dark violet
'Shio-O-Tacki'	late, whitish-gray background with bluish sheen
'Shisi-No-Ikari'	medium-early, reddish purple, lighter toward the margin, strongly veined, small blossoms and tall-growing
'Shushi-No Homare'	falls pink with white, standards white
'Summer Storm'	late, reddish-violet with blue veins, very attractive petals, blossom diameter 7¼" (18 cm), very good
'Taiheiraku'	lavender-blue
'Taiko'	violet with white
'Tamo-Shirga'	late, marine blue with purple sheen, almost erect petals
'Tan Yu'	violet-blue with white margin
'Tinted Cloud'	very late, warm light blue, double
'Toryumon'	blossom pink, white at the base
'Tropennacht'	violet double, yellow sap mark
'Unschuld'	early, pure white, slightly wavy petals, petals more thickly formed
'U Shu'	early, violet-blue, 5 falls held almost horizontal, free-flowering
'Variegata'	mid-season, violet, striped whitish yellow
'Warai Hotel'	falls light blue, standard dark blue
'Weisse Taube'	mid-season, white, single
'Wella'	early, pure pink, blossom diameter 6⅛" (15 cm)
'Windjammer'	mid-season, dark lilac, very vibrant double

Results of Iris sibirica Rating

Compiled by Prof. Ehsen, Pflanzenprüfgarten FH,Osnabrück Fb. Lp. (1979 standing)

+++ = very qualified ++ = qualified + = conditionally qualified

1. Selection for Natural Plantings and Care

Color	Name & rating	Height in cm	Growth	Blos. per stem	Blos. diam. in cm	Flowering
light blue	'Blue Celeste'+++	100–120	strong	4–5	8	vg-g
	'Perrys Blue'++	110–120	strong	4	9	g
	'Thelma Perry'++	110–120	strong	3–4	9	vg
	'Papillon'+	110–120	strong	4–5	8	g
bluish red	'Elfe'+++	100–130	strong	4–5	9	vg
pale pink lilac	'Mrs. Rowe'+++	100–110	medium-strong	4	8	vg
white	'Snow Crest'+++	90–100	strong	2	9	g
	'Alba'+	80–100	medium	6	6	s

2. Selection for Garden-type Plantings and Care

Color	Name & rating	Height in cm	Growth	Blos. per stem	Blos. diam. in cm	Flowering
light blue	'Cambridge'++	75–95	medium-strong	2–3	11–12	s-g
clear blue	'Sea Shadows'+++	80–110	strong	3–4	12–13	g
	'Mountain Lake'++	70–80	medium-strong	3	11–12	s-g
2-tone lt-dk blue	'Blue Moon'++	90–110	strong	3	12–13	m
reddish blue	'Dreaming Spire'+++	80–90	strong	2	12	g
dark violet	'Caesars Brother'+ (true type)	100–130	medium-strong	2	11	m
white	'White Swirl'+++	80–100	strong	2–3	11	g
	'Weisser	60–85	medium-	3	10	g

	Orient'++		strong			
white	'Dreaming	75–95	medium-	2–3	11–12	g
yellowish	Yellow'+++		strong			

vg = very good g = good s = satisfactory m = moderate

3. Nonessential Varieties

'Blue Brilliant'   'Helen Astor'   'Snow Queen'
'Blue Cape'   'Mountain Pool'   'Snowy Egret'
'Blue Mere'   'Möwe'   'Strandperle'
'Dabash'   'My Love'   'Superba'
'Eric the Red'   'Purple Mere'

Iris sibirica and Related Species

Results of plant ratings. New hybrids are not included in this rating, but it gives a good idea of the garden value of older varieties.

***highest garden value **higher garden value *high garden value w = wild plant

'Caesar'	dark violet-blue	***
'Blue Moon'	violet-blue	*
'Mountain Lake'	blue	**
'Mrs. Rove'	silvery pink	*
'My Love'	light blue	**
'Perrys Blue'	light blue	*
Iris sanguinea 'Snow Queen'		**
Iris chrysographes		w
Iris forrestii		w
Iris sanguinea		w
Iris wilsonii		w

Modern Iris sibirica Varieties with High Garden Value (1980 standing)
Compiled by Dr. Thomas Tamberg, Berlin

'Cambridge'   'Ego'   'Dreaming Yellow'   'Lilienthal'
'Dreaming Spires'   'Apfelblüte'   'Kobaltblau'   'Lichterfelde'
'Sea Shadows'   'Ewen'   'Cambrita'

Iris Competition Winners

We are grateful to the Iris Interest Group of the Gesellschaft der Stadenfreunde under the leadership of E. Wörfel.

S = Standards F = Falls

Prizewinners of Iris Competition in the Palmengarten, Frankfurt

F = Winner of Karl Foerster Medal
Z = Winner of Countess Zeppelin Cup

1973	F	'Lime Fizz'	Schreiners 1968
	Z	'Alstersegel'	Dendewitz 1968
1974	F	'Alstersegel'	Denkewitz 1968
	Z	'Latin Lover'	Shoop	1969
1975	F	'Kilt Lilt'	Gibson	1969
	Z	'Leopold Grossmann'	Heimann	1975
1976	F	'Spartan'	Schreiners 1972
	Z	'Berliner Nacht'	Heimann	1975
1977	F	'Blue Ambition'	Heimann	1976
	Z	'Hanau'	Haslinger 1977
1978	F	'Sehnsucht'	Denkewitz 1978
1979	F	'Sehnsucht'	Denkewitz 1978
	Z	'Sempronio'	Wörfel	1976

Prizewinners of the Premio Firenze

1957	'Rehobeth'	DeForest, 1953	pale blue self
1958	'Swan Ballet'	Muhlestein, 1953	white self, beard white
1959	'La Negra Flor'	Crosby, 1956	dark purple
1960	'Allaglow'	Tompkins, 1958	rich copper yellow
1961	'Whole Cloth'	P. Cook, 1956	S pure white, F lt. violet
1962	'Indiglow'	Schortman, 1957	violet-blue self, beard blue-orange
1963	'Dancer's Veil'	Hutchison, 1959	purp.-blue plicata on white ground
1964	'Midnight Waltz'	Burbridge, 1959	S purple-blue, F black-blue
1965	'Lorna Lee'	Gibson, 1965	orange-pink self
1967	'Christie Anne'	Gaulter, 1963	orange-pink with white
1968	'Bewitching'	Lyon, 1965	lilac-pink self
1969	'Irish Charm'	Pickard, 1965	S clear pink, F white with pink
1970	'Launching Pad'	Knopf, 1966	S sulfur-yellow, F white with yellow margin
1971	'Foggy Dew'	Keppel, 1968	S cream-gray lavender, F pale violet on white

1973	'Rosso Fiorentino'	Specht, 1973	red-brown
1974	'Sunset Sky'	Roe, 1968	S yellow, purple, shoulders and beard yellow
1975	'Queen of Florence'	R. Mallory, 1975	S lt. yellow, F light yellowish violet
1976	'Dialogue'	J. Ghio, 1970	S lt. blue, F dark blue-violet
1977	'Chamber Music'	B. Williamson, 1972	S brown, F violet with brown margin

Winners of Britain's Dykes Medal

1927	'Margot Holmes'	Perry, 1927	*I. chrysographes* × *douglasiana*
1929	'Jovance'	K. Dykes, 1929	
1920	'G. B. Baker	Perry, 1930	
1931	'Gudrun'	K. Dykes, 1930	
1934	'Golden Hind'	Chadburn, 1931	'Gold Imperial' × 'W. R. Dykes'
1935	'Sahara'	Pilkington, 1934	'Bruno' × 'W. R. Dykes'
1940	'White City'	Murell, 1937	'Pageant' × 'Pervaneh'
1941	'Mabel Chadburn'	Chadburn, 1939	'Golden Hind' × 'Sämling'
1948	'Mrs. J. L. Gibson'	Gibson, 1930	
1949	'Blue Ensign'	H. R. Meyer, 1937	
1952	'Seathwaite'	Randall, 1951	'Helen McGregor' × 'Cahokia', pale blue
1953	'Arabi Pasha'	Anley, 1951	cornflower blue
1955	'Benton Cordelia'	Morris, 1953	pale mallow, orange-red beard
1957	'Golden Alps'	Brummit, 1952	cream-white/deep yellow bi-tone
1958	'Tarn Hows'	Randall, 1951	tobacco-brown self
1959	'Headlines'	Brummit, 1953	S pure white, F almost black
1960	'Kanchenjunga'	Miller, 1955	white self
1961	'Patterdale'	Randall, 1955	pale blue self
1962	'Acardy'	Fothergill, 1959	S pale blue, F with darker center
1963	'Dancers Veil'	Hutchinson, 1959	purple-blue plicata with white background
1964	'Primrose Drift'	Brummit, 1960	primrose yellow self, yellow beard
1965	'Mary Todd'	Randall, 1960	rich tobacco brown self
1966	'Ancient Egypt'	Fothergill, 1962	S gold-orange, F red-orange
1967	'Blue-Eyed Brunette'	C. C. Hall, 1962	brown, blue mirror
1969	'Golden Forest'	Hutchison, 1958	brownish gold, F lighter, shoulders darker
1970	'Constance West'	Howe, 1967	purple lilac
1971	'Cambridge' (sib.)	M. Brummit, 1964	turkish blue, F with yellow-white pattern
1972	'Shepherds Delight'	Fothergill, 1969	pure pink base of F yellowish
1973	'Muriel Nevill'	Fothergill, 1963	carmine-pink bi-tone
1975	'Tyrian Robe'	C. Hall, 1968	violet-purple self

1976	'No Name' (Pac.Coast)	Brummit, 1968	S lt. yellow, F yellow
1977	'Annabel Jane'	Dodsworth, 1973	S lt. lilac, F lilac
1978	'Cotsgold'	Taylor, 1974	deep yellow

Winners of American Dykes Medal

1927	'San Francisco'	Mohr, 1927	'Conquistador' × 'Parisiana'
1929	'Dauntless'	Connell, 1929	'Cardinal' × 'Rose Madler'
1932	'Rameses'	H. Sass, 1928	
1933	'Coralie'	Ayres, 1932	(Slg) × (Loute × mesopotamica) × Dauntless
1935	'Sierra Blue'	Essig, 1932	'Souv. de Mmme. Gaudichau' × 'Sta. Barbara'
1936	'Mary Geddes'	Stahlmann, 1931	
1937	'Missouri'	Grinter, 1933	'Blue Ribbon' × 'Sensation'
1938	'Copper Lustre'	Kirkland, 1934	
1939	'Rosy Wings'	Gage, 1935	'Dauntless' × pollen mixture
1940	'Wabash'	Williamson, 1936	'Dorothy Dietz' × 'Cantabile'
1941	'The Red Douglas'	J. Sass, 1937	
1942	'Great Lakes'	Cousins, 1938	('Dominion' × . . .) × ('Conquistador' × . . .)
1943	'Prairie Sunset'	H. Sass, 1939	
1944	'Spun Gold'	Glutzbeck, 1940	
1945	'Elmohr'	Loomis, 1942	'William Mohr' × R. seedling
1947	'Chivalry'	Wills, 1943	'Missouri' × 'Great Lakes'
1948	'Ola Kala'	J. Sass, 1942	('Prairie Sunset × . . .) × ('Golden Age' × . . .)
1950	'Blue Rhythm'	Whiting, 1945	'Annabel' × 'Blue Zenith'
1951	'Cherie'	Hall, 1945	'Casa Morena' × 'Tobacco Road'
1952	'Argus Pheasant'	DeForest, 1947	'Rameses' × 'Far West'
1953	'Truly Yours'	Fay, 1949	
1954	'Mary Randall'	Fay, 1950	Bengal pink with red beard
1955	'Sable Night'	P. Cook, 1950	black-purple self
1956	'First Violet'	DeForest, 1951	manganese violet self
1957	'Violet Harmony'	Lowry, 1948	'Snow Flurry' × 'Cloud Castle'
1958	'Blue Sapphire'	B. Schreiner, 1953	blue self, slightly silvery
1959	'Swan Ballet'	Muhlestein, 1953	white self, white beard
1961	'Eleanor's Pride'	Watkins, 1952	lt. & med. blue self
1962	'Whole Cloth'	P. Cook, 1956	S pure white, F lt. violet (amoena)
1963	'Amethyst Flame'	R. Schreiner, 1957	amethyst violet self
1964	'Allegiance'	P. Cook, 1957	violet-ultramarine, beard med. blue; med. yellow
1965	'Pacific Panorama'	Sexton, 1960	lt.-med. blue self
1966	'Rippling Waters'	Fay, 1961	pale lilac-blue, red-orange beard

1967	'Winter Olympics'	O. Brown, 1961	white
1968	'Stepping Out'	Schreiners, 1964	blue-purple-violet plicata against white
1970	'Skywatch'	Benson, 1963	lavender-pink self
1971	'Debby Rairdon'	Kuntz, 1964	yellow-white to pearl-white, reverse side white
1972	'Babbling Brook'	Keppel, 1965	light blue
1973	'New Moon'	Sexton, 1968	dark lemon yellow, yellow beard
1974	'Shipshape'	Babson, 1969	light blue self
1975	'Pink Taffeta'	Rudolph, 1965	carnation pink
1976	'Kilt Lilt'	Gibson, 1969	S brown on gold, F maroon on gold
1977	'Dream Lover'	E. Tams, 1970	S white-ice blue, F purple-blue
1978	'Bride's Halo'	H. Mohr, 1971	white with yellow-ocher margins

Dwarf Iris Competition in Vienna
Compiled by Prof. Franz Kurzmann, Baden bei Wien

Prizewinners

1. Zwergiris (Miniature Dwarfs = MDB)

1967 1. 'Claire' (Brown), 2. 'Violet Imp' (Taylor), 3. 'Vari Bright' (Mahood)

1968 1.'Lemon Doll' (Warburton), 2. 'Himmelsauge' (van Nes), 3. 'Hula Doll' (Brown)

1969 1. 'Gay Dreamer' (Kavan), 2. 'April Accent' (Brown)

1970 1. 'Allotria' (Berlin), 2. 'Temno' (Blazek), 3. 'Golden Dart' (Kavan), 4. 'Navy Flirt' (Tutmark), 5. 'Golding' (Taylor)

1971 1. 'Red Pixie' (Brown), 2. 'Marsh Imp' (Taylor), 3. 'Lemon Puff' (Dunbar), 4. 'Buttercup Charm' (Brown)

1972 1. 'Fuzzy' (Westfall), 2. 'Cherry Halo' (Mahood), 3. 'Blue Beret' (Roberts)

1973 1. 'Raisin Eyes' (Dunbar), 2. 'Canary Caper' (Roberts)

1974 Keine Preise

1975 1. Nummernsorte von Schreiner, 2. 'Oliver' (Nichols)

1976 1. 'Inca Toy' (Roberts), 2. 'Scribe' (Taylor)

1977 1. 'Small Gem' (Hamblen), 2. 'Dewberry' (Williams), 3. 'Magic Dot' (Schreiner), 4. 'Nuggets' (Sindl), 5. 'Dunlin' (Taylor), 6. 'Music Capers' (Roberts)

1978 1. 'April Ballet' (Cleo Palmer), 2. Nr. SA 25 (Ger. Storey)

1979 1. 'Brass Tacks' (Keppel)

1980 1. 'Zipper' (Sindt), 2. 'Penny Candy' (Hamblen), 3. 'Gizmo' (Hager)

1981 1. Nicht besetzt, 2. 'Quip' (Sindt), 3. 'Jo-Jo' (Cleo Palmer), 4. 'Pixie Pink' (Boushay)

2. Kleiniris (Standard Dwarfs = SDB)

1967 1. 'Carilla' (Taylor), 2. 'Ziep' (Goett), 3. 'Green Meteor' (Motsch)

1968 1. 'Forest Glow' (Taylor), 2. 'Lilli Bambi' (Steiger), 3. 'Blueberry Muffins' (Warburton)

1969 1. 'Ruby Rock' (Street), 2. 'Pink Amber' (Roberts), 3. 'Merry and Gay' (Kavan)

1970 1. 'Frisky' (Schreiner), 2. 'Meadow Moss' (Jones), 3. 'Dark Spark' (Sindt), 4. 'Sonnenprinz' (Ziepke), 5. 'Blue Space' (Motsch)

1971 1. 'Cotton Blossom' (Jones), 2. 'Bonbonniere' (Berlin), 3. 'Double Lament' (Taylor), 4. 'Blazon Day' (Taylor), 5. 'Sun Clipper' (Dunbar), 6. 'Furnaceman' (Taylor)

1972 1. 'Tomingo' (Roberts), 2. 'Royal Fairy' (Brown), 3. 'Shanrock Fan' (Mahood, ist aber MDB), 4. 'Troll' (Schreiner), 5. 'Ruffled Sprite' (Brown)

1973 1. 'Saltwood' (Taylor), 2. 'Pixie Princess' (Schreiner), 3. 'Hallo' (Berlin), 4. 'Morning Dew' (Brown), 5. 'Mandarin Jewel' (Roberts), 6. 'Lady' (Warburton), 7. 'Bembes' (Berlin), 8. 'Irish Sea' (Roberts)

1974 1. 'Melon Honey' (Roberts), 2. 'Ouverture' (Hald), 3. 'Anne Elizabeth' (Taylor), 4. 'Ripe Raspberry' (Sindt), 5. 'Blauburgund' (Berlin), 6. 'Orange Riot' (Brown)

1975 1. 'Bibury' (Taylor), 2. 'Candy Apple' (Hamblen), 3. 'Alsterquelle' (Denkewitz), 4. Nummernsorte (Schreiner), 5. 'Amazon Princess' (Nichols), 6. 'Scherborne' (Taylor)

1976 1. 'Karin' (Denkewitz), 2. 'Soft Air' (Warburton), 3. 'Starry Eyed' (J. Gatty)

1977 1. 'Myra's Child' (Greenlee), 2. 'Little Miss Muffet' (Hamblen), 3. 'Nanny' (Schreiner), 4. 'Wine Pixie' (Foster) 5. 'Purple Mini' (Kuesel), 6. 'Butterscotch Frills' (Hamblen)

1978 1. 'Winer Traumnacht' (E. Zelina), 2. R. 28/2 (Taylor), 3. N-74-1 (Denkewitz), 4. 'Byword' (Boushay)

1979 1. 'Clap Hands' (Hager), 2. 'Clun' (Taylor), 3. 'Karamell' (Denkewitz), 4. 'Lianne' (Delany), 5. 'Bromyard' (Taylor)

1980 1. 'Royal Elf' (Brown), 2. 'Jan Reagen' (Shaver), 3. 'Erlkönig' (Denkewitz)

1981 1. 'Michael Paul' (William Jones), 2. 'Bright Gold' (Palmer), 3. 'Blauracke' (Kummert), 4. 'Sarah Taylor' (John Taylor), 5. 'Vanille Eis' (Denkewitz)

3. Media-, Border- und Table-Iris (JB, BB, MTB)

1967 1. 'Adrienne Taylor' (Taylor), 2. 'Gletscherspalte' (van Nes), 3. 'Libellula' (Werckmeister)

1968 1. 'Tamino' (Schreiner), 2. 'Annikins' (Warburton), 3. 'Curlew' (Taylor)

1969 1. 'Dilly Dilly' (Warburton), 2. 'Elfin Silver' (Roberts), 3. 'June Prom' (Brown)

1970 1. 'Jolly Elf' (Schreiner), 2. 'Intermezzo' (Hald), 3. 'Valeska' (Berlin), 4. 'Devilry' (Taylor)

1971 1. 'Wow' (Brown), 2. 'Keyhaven' (Taylor), 3. 'Tiger Blaze' (Sindt), 4. 'Crown' (Warburton), 5. 'Happy Mood' (Brown), 6. 'Ottonel' (Berlin)

1972 1. 'Pink Reverie' (Brown), 2. 'Laced Lemonade' (Warburton), 3. 'Three Smoks' (Warburton), 4. 'Watercolor' (Roberts), 5. 'Bany' (Taylor), 6. 'Paricutin' (Taylor)

1973 1. 'Isle of Dreams' (Brown), 2. 'Solo' (Schreiner), 3. 'Snow Fiddler' (Dunbar), 4. 'Burford' (Taylor), 5. 'Dinger' (Schreiner)

1974 1. 'Cotsgold' (Taylor-Britische Dykesmed. 1978), 2. 'Lemon Tart' (Roberts), 3. 'Coral Eyes' (Roberts)

1975 1. 'Dandelion' (Warburton), 2. 'Frechdachs' (Denkewitz), 3. 'Ruby Rose' (Warburton)

1976 1. 'Overtone' (Du Bose), 2. 'Swizzle' (Ben Hager), 3. 'Kolksee' (Denkewitz), 4. 'Donauweise' (Kurzmann)

1977 1. 'Foxcote' (Taylor), 2. 'Snappie' (Warburton), 3. 'Azure Echo' (Durrance), 4. 'Rainbow Music' (Willot), 5. Nr. 7043 (Schreiner), 6. 'Appleblossom Pink' (Bushay)

1978 1. 'Angelic Blue' (Cleo Palmer), 2. 'Radiant Love' (Roberts), 3. 'Teeny Bikini' (Storey)

1979 1. 'Morgendämmerung' (Ziepke), 2. 'Party Finery' (Roberts), 3. 'Pot Luck' (Hager), 4. 'Wenlock' (Taylor), 5. 'Snow Festival' (Palmer)

1980 1. 'Bold Print' (Gatty), 2. 'Vorfreude' (Heimann), 3. 'Scouts Honor' (Gatty), 4. 'Lieslkind' (Kurzmann)

1981 1. 'Azap' (Ensminger), 2. 'Looking Good' (Ben Hager), 3. 'Fashion Drama' (Delany), 4. 'Confederate Soldier' (Nichols), 5. 'Impelling' (Jack Boushay)

4. Arilbreds

1967 no prize

1968 1.'Plusia' (Werckmeister), 2. 'Nunatakr' (Werckmeister), 3. 'Saletta' (Street)

1969 1. 'Saletta' (Street), 2. 'Wercilla' (Werckmeister)

1970 1. 'Border Queen' (Valette), 2. 'Duftingo' (Werckmeister)

1971 tetraploid Regeliocyclus (Werckmeister)

1972 no prize

1973 1. 'Mint Parfait' (Foster), 2. 'Hidden Violets' (Foster), 3. 'Fairy Goblin' (Foster)

1974 no prize

1975 no prize

1976 1. tetraploid (Werckmeister), 2. hexaploid (Werckmeister)

1977 no prize

1978 no prize

1979 1. 'Steppenwolf' (Ramisch)

1980 1. 'Hummelflug' (Ramisch), 2. 'Lady Bernstein' (Mathes), 3. 'Himmel und Erde' (Mathes)

1981 1. 'Klein Esther' (Kummert), 2. 'Vistagold' (Doris Foster), 3. 'Eispalast' (Mathes)

National Prizewinners

1967 'Arctic Fancy' (Brown—Media iris)

1968 'Cherry Garden' (Jones—Standard Dwarf)

1969 'Pamela Ann' (Goett—Standard Dwarf)

1970 no prize

1971 'Curlew' (Taylor—Media iris)

1972 'Cotton Blossom' (Jones—Standard Dwarf)

1973 'Laced Lemonade' (Warburton—Media iris)

1974 'Hallo' (Berlin—Standard Dwarf)

1975 no prize

1976 'Orange Riot' (Alta Brown—Media iris)

1977 'Starry Eyed' (Gatty—Standard Dwarf)

1978 no prize

1979 'Foxcote' (Taylor—Media iris)

1980 'Snow Festival' (Palmer—Media iris)

1981 'Sapphire Jewel' (Melba Hamblen—Standard Dwarf)

Special Award of the Gesellschaft der Staudenfreunde
(Previously DIG) for Advances in Breeding
1967 no prize
1968 no prize
1969 'Lenna M' (Roberts—Standard Dwarf)
1970 'Gingerbread Man' (Jones—Standard Dwarf)
1971 'Sky Bolt' (Jones—Standard Dwarf)
1972 'Pagan Butterfly' (Brown—Standard Dwarf)
1973 'Vim' (Schreiner—Standard Dwarf)
1974 no prize
1975 no prize
1976 'Demon' (Ben Hager—Standard Dwarf), 'Angel's Kiss' (Willot—Standard Dwarf)
1977 'Galleon Gold' (Schreiner—Standard Dwarf), 'Angel's Kiss' (Willot—Standard Dwarf)
1978 'Cherub Tears' (Boushay—Standard Dwarf)
1979 'Cheers' (Hager—Media iris)
1980 1. 'Spitzbube' (Heimann), 2. Liebling' (Gatty)
1981 'Tivoli' (Kummert—Media iris)

The iris are listed here in the classes in which they were judged. Because of different height restrictions, some of these may be classified differently in the U.S.

Horticultural Societies

There are the following special interest groups in the AIS:

West Germany
Gesellschaft der Staudenfreude e. V., Präsident: Hermann Hald, Justinus-Kerner-Str. 11, 7250 Leonberg

Fachgruppe Iris der Gesellschaft der Staudenfreunde, Koordinator: Erhard Wörfel, Meisenweg 1, 6234 Hattersheim 3

Switzerland
Schweizer Iris- und Lilienfreunde, Guggenbuhlstr. 24, Postfach 89, CH 8304 Wallisellen/Zürich, Schweiz

Great Britain
The British Iris Society (BIS), President: B. L. C. Dodsworth, Treasurer and Membership Secretary: Miss E. M. Sharland, Broad View, Farnborough Common, Farnborough, Kent BR 6 7Bu

The Alpine Garden Society, Lye End Link, St. John's, Woking GU21, 1SW Surrey

The Scottish Rock Garden Club, Secretary: D. J. Donald Esq. Morea, Main Road, Balbeggie, Perth PH2 6EZ

Denmark
The Danish Iris Society, H. Ingemann-Peterson, 6950 Ringkobing, Danmark

Belgium
Belgische Iris-Gesellschaft, E. Ponsaerts, 8 Ave. de Exposition Universelle, Box 13, 1080 Brüssel, Belgien

France
Societe Francaise des Iris et Plantes Bulbeuses, c/o Mme. Helene Muzard, 6 Rue Villaret de Joyeuse, 75017 Paris, France

Italy
Societa Italiana dell'Iris, The Secretary, Palazzo Strozzi, Fierenze (Florenz), Italia

South Africa
Iris Society of Southern Africa, Hon. Treasurer/Secretary, P. O. Box 82, Bedfordview, Transvaal, S. Africa

USA
The American Iris Society (AIS), President: Leon C. Wolford, 7530 Forney Road, Dallas, TX 75227 Membership Secretary: Ronald Mullin, Route 3, Pawnee, OK 74058

The AIS has the following sections:
1. Median Iris Society
2. The Society for Sibirican Irises
3. Spuria Iris Society
4. Society for Japanese Irises
5. Reblooming Iris Society
6. American Aril Society
7. Society for Pacific Coast Native Iris
8. Species Iris Group of North America
9. Louisiana Iris Society of America

American Rock Garden Society, Secretary: Donald Peach, Box 185, Halls Corner, Wisconsin 53130, USA

Canada
Canadian Iris Society, Mrs. Alberta Richardson, R. R. 2 Hannon, Ontario, Canada

Australia
The Iris Society of Australia, c/o Robert Raabe, P.O. Box 22, Entworthville, New South Wales 2145, Australia

Japan
The Japan Iris Society, 17 Kitamomodani, Minami-Ku, Osaka City, Japan

New Zealand
The New Zealand Iris Society, Secretary: Mrs. H. E. Collins, R. D. 1 Cambridge Road, Tauranga, New Zealand

Unfortunately the addresses of some horticultural groups change frequently, but the above were still valid as of 1980.

Suppliers

There are iris everywhere, but it can often be very difficult to procure a particular species. The following suppliers are known by the author, but their selection may be incomplete. Also, almost all nurseries have a more-or-less large selection of iris for sale, so it is best to go first to the nursery one has been dealing with in the past. It goes without saying that not everyone has kept pace with the latest developments in iris breeding, so some selections will no longer reflect recent advances.

Those who are looking for something special will find it from the suppliers listed below. Having iris shipped from abroad is easier than with most other plants, hence we have also listed foreign firms, although one has to put up with health certificates and customs regulations.

If requesting a catalogue, enclose at least the equivalent ($2 or £2) of its value or a bit more; this usually ensures a response. It can't be expected that these firms will send catalogues out free, with only the minimum expectation of an order.

West Germany

Gärtnerischer Pflanzenbau Dr. Hans Simon, Georg-Mayr-Str. 70, 8772 Marktheidenfeld (lovely assortment, species too)

Gräfin von Zeppelin, Staudengärtnerei in Laufen/Baden, 7811 Sulzburg 2 (large selection of Iris)

Gewiehs Heinrich, Blumenzwiebelimport, Postfach 446, 213 Rotenburg (Wümme) (Iris-Hollandica hybrids and other bulbous iris, also Regeliocyclus Iris—representative of van Tubergen, Haarlem, Holland)

H. Hagemann, Staudengärtnerei, 3001 Krähenwinkel bei Hannover

Albrecht Hoch, Pflanzenimporteur aus aller Welt, Karl-Marx-Str. 58, Postfach 110, 1000 Berlin 44, (Tall Bearded Iris—representative of Cooley's Gardens, Silverton, Oregon 97381)

Kayser und Seibert, Odenwälder Pflanzenkulturen, 6101 Roßdorf bei Darmstadt (selections of various Iris, also botanical species)

Heinz Klose, Staudengärtnerei, Rosenstr. 10, 3503 Lohfelden bei Kassel, (selections of various Iris, particularly *Iris sibirica*)

Schöppinger Gemeinschaftskatalog der Gärten: Aalburg, Berlin, Gerke, Reinermann, Stobberg, Dr. Tamberg und Zelina. Adresse Werner Reinermann, Bürgerweg 8, 4431 Schöppingen

Albert Treppens u. Co., Stresemannstr. 52, 1000 Berlin 61, (bulbous Iris)

Karl Wachter KG., Stauden- und Wasserpflanzengärtnerei, 2081 Appen b. Pinneberg (specializing in aquatic Iris)

Switzerland

Château de Vūllierens, CH 8461 Wildensbuch, Schweiz (Miniature Dwarfs, Tall Bearded Iris, and new Swiss hybrids, Iris species)

Great Britain

Walter Blom and Son Ltd., Leavesden, Watford, Herefordshire, England (bulbous Iris)

C. G. Hollet, Greenbank Nursery, Sedbergh Combria LA 10 5AG, England (special species and proven Miniature Dwarfs)

V. H. Humphrey, 8 Howbeck Road, Arnold, Nottingham NG5 8AD, England (Miniature Dwarfs, Media Iris, Tall Bearded Iris, Table Iris, Spuria, Louisiana, Japanese, Sibirica, Pacific Coast Iris)

W. E. Th. Ingwersen Ltd., Birch Farm Nursery, Gravetye, East Grinstead, Sussex RH19 4LE, England (specializing in species)

Kelway's Irises, Kelway's Nurseries, Langport, Somerset TA10 9SL, England

Sidney Linnegar, 6 Oban Gardens, Woodley, nr. Reading, Berks RG5 3RG, England (Californica, Louisiana, Sibirica, Spuria, Pogon, Arilbred, Oncocyclus, Regelia Iris)

Norton Hall Nurseries, 115 Kynaston Road, Panfield nr. Braintree/Essex, England (Bearded Iris, Sibirica, Pacific Coast, Louisiana Iris, Iris species)

The Orpington Nurseries, Rocky Lane, Gatton Park, Reigate, Surrey RH2 OTA, England

Perry's Hardy Plant Farm, Enfield Middlesex EN2 9BG, England (specializing in *Iris laevigata*)

The plantsmen, Buckshaw Gardens, Holwell, Sherborne Dorset (Oncocyclus, Regelia and Regeliocyclus Iris)

Sunningdale Nurseries, Windlesham, Surrey, England (Bearded Iris)

The Netherlands

Gartenbaubetrieb van Tubergen, 86 Koninginnenweg, Haarlem, Niederlande (Iridodictyum, Iris-Hollandica hybrids, Spanish Iris, English Iris, Juno, Oncocyclus, Regelia, Regeliocyclus Iris. Wholesale only!)

France

J. Cayeux s. a., Poilly-Lez-Gien, 45500 Gien (Loiret), France (specializing in Tall Bearded Iris)

Iris en Provence, Pierre Anfosso, 83260 La Crau, C. C. P. 819 89 Marseille, France (Tall Bearded Iris, Median, Spuria Iris)

Israel

Tira Nurseries, Tirat Tsvi Doar Na, Emek Bet Shean 10815 Israel (specializing in Oncocyclus Iris and Oncobreds)

USA

Bay View Gardens, 1201 Bay Street, Santa Cruz, California 95060, U.S.A (Tall Bearded Iris, Pacific Coast, Louisiana, Spuria, Siberica Iris)

Cordon Bleu Farms, 418 Buena Creek Road, San Marcos, California 92069, U.S.A. (Tall Bearded Iris, Median, Sibirica, Spuria, Louisiana Iris)

Dr. and Mrs. Currier McEwen, South Harpswell, Maine 04079, U.S.A. (specializing in Sibirica Iris and *I. kaempferi* hybrids)

Walker Ferguson, 1160 North Broadway, Escondido 92025, U.S.A. (Spuria Iris)

Garden of Dr. William G. and Ester C. McGarvey, 1-Etwilla Lane RD3, Oswego, New York 13126, U.S.A. (latest Sibirica Iris)

Illini-Iris, S. Steve Varner, N. State Street Road, Monticello, Ill. 61856, U.S.A. (Sibirica Iris)

Iris Test Gardens, Austin and Ione Morgan, 1010 Highland Park Drive, College Place, Wa. 99324, U.S.A.

Keiht Keppel, P.O. Box 8173, Stockton, California 95208, U.S.A. (Tall Bearded Iris, Miniature Dwarfs, Median, Border Iris)

Louisiana Nursery, Ken and Belle Durio, RT. 1, Box 43, Opelousas, LA 70570, U.S.A. (Louisiana Iris)

Melrose Gardens, 309 Best Road South, Stockton, California 95205, U.S.A. (Tall Bearded Iris, Reblooming Bearded Iris, Arilmeds, Arilbreds, Miniature Dwarfs, Standard Dwarfs, Median, Border, Table [Miniature Tall Bearded], Louisiana, Sibirica Iris, *Iris kaempferi*)

Mission Bell Gardens, Jim and Melba Hamblen, 2778 West 5600 South Roy, Utah 85067, U.S.A. (Tall Bearded Iris, Border Iris, Miniature Dwarfs)

Richland Iris, Richland Center Wisconsin 53581, One Route Three, U.S.A. (Sibirica Iris)

Riverdale Iris Gardens, Glenn and Zula Hanson, 7124 Riverdale Road, Minneapolis, Minnesota 55430, U.S.A. (Tall Bearded Iris, Median, Border, "Miniature Tall Bearded" = Table Iris, Arilmeds, Pogon species)

Schreiner's Gardens, 3625 Quinaby Rd. N. E. Salem, Oregon 97303, U.S.A. (Tall

Bearded, Sibirica, Spuria Iris, Miniature Dwarfs)

Tranquil Lake Nursery, 45 River Street, Rehoboth, Mass. 02769, U.S.A. (Sibirica, Japanese Iris)

Gilbert H. Wild and Son Inc., Sarcoxie, Missouri 64862, U.S.A. (specializing in Tall Bearded Iris)

Please keep in mind that addresses occasionally change!

Bibliography

An Alphabetical Table and Cultivation Guide to the Species of the Genus Iris. British Iris Society, 1974.

Anley, C.: Irises, their Culture and Selection. W. H. and L. Collingridge, London 1946.
Atti del Simposio internazionale dell'Iris. Societa Italiana dell'Iris. Tipografia Giuntina, Florenz 1963.

Baker, G.: Irideae, Reprint von 1892, J. Cramer, Lehre.

Bowley, M. E. A.: Publications of the Species Group, British Iris Society, Brook Orchard, Graffam nr. Petworth, Sussex, England.

Cave, N. L.: The Iris. Faber and Faber, London 1959.

Cohen, V. A.: A Guide to the Pacific Coast Irises. British Iris Society 1967.

Dykes, W. R.: A Handbook of Garden Irises. Martin Hopkinson and Co., London 1924.

Dykes, W. R.: The Genus Iris. Reprint von 1913. Dover Publications Inc., New York 1974.

The Eupogon Iris Species. Prodan. The Median Iris Society, a Section of the American Iris Society. Mis Press-

Hudson Printers, Westborough, Massachusetts, USA 1970.

Flora Republicii Socialiste Romania. Academia Republicii Socialiste Romania. Editure Academici Republicii Socialiste Romania, 1966.

Foster, Michael: Bulbous Irises (Printed for the Royal Horticultural Society), London 1882.

Grunert, Ch.: Das große Blumenzwiebelbuch. VEB Deutscher Landwirtschaftsverlag, Berlin 1978, 3. Auflage (Lizenzausgabe für die Bundesrepublik Deutschland: Verlag Eugen Ulmer, Stuttgart).

Ingemann-Petersen, H.: Iris Regenbuens Blomst., Aarhus 1970.

Yearbooks and other publications of the Deutsche Iris- and Liliengesellschaft (now Gesellschaft der Staudenfreunde), Justinus-Kerner-Str. 11, 7250 Leonberg bei Stuttgart.

Jelitto, L., und Schacht, W. (Hrsg.): Die Freilandschmuckstauden, Band 1 und Band 2. Verlag Eugen Ulmer, Stuttgart 1966.

Köhlein, F.: Pflanzen vermehren. Verlag Eugen Ulmer, Stuttgart 1980, 5. Auflage.

Lynch, R. I.: The Book of the Iris. John Lane: The Bodley Head, London and New York 1903.

Mathew, B.: Dwarf Bulbs. B. T. Batsford Ltd. in association with The Royal Horticultural Society, London 1973.- Members of the American Iris Society: The Iris an ideal hardy Perennial. Nashville, Tenn. USA 1947.

van Nes, H.: Iris im Garten. BLV, München 1967.

Price, M.: The Iris Book. Constable and Company Ltd., London 1966.

Publications Committee, the Median Iris Society and Warburton, B. A.: The Median Bearded Irises. Introduction and Varietal Listing. The Median Iris

Society, a Section of the American Iris Society. Mis Press-Hudson Printers, Westborough, Massachusetts, USA 1972.

Randall, H.: Irises, B. T. Batsford Ltd., London 1969.

Rechinger, K. H.: Iridaceae in: Flora des Iranischen Hochlandes und der umrahmenden , Gebirge. Akademische Druck- und Verlagsanstalt, Graz 1975.

Schacht, W.: Blumenzwiebel für Heim und Garten. Verlag Eugen Ulmer, Stuttgart 1955.

Schubert, R., und Wagner, G.: Pflanzennamen und botanische Fachwörter. Neumann Verlag, Radebeul I DDR 1975, 6. Auflage.

Singh, G., and Kachroo, P.: Forest Flora of Srinagar, Bishen Singh Mahendra Pal Singh 23-A, Dehra Dun, India.

Spender, R. E. S., and Pesel, L. F.: Iris Culture for Amateurs. Country Life Ltd., London 1937.

"Staudengarten", quarterly journal of the Gesellschaft der Staudenfreunde. Justinus-Kerner-Str. 11, 7250 Leonberg bei Stuttgart.

Synge, M.: Gartenfreude durch Blumenzwiebeln. Verlag J. Neumann-Neudamm, Melsungen 1966.

Warburton, B. A., and Gantz, Ch. O.: The Eupogon Iris Species in Cultivation. The Median Iris Society, a Section of the American Iris Society, Mis Press-Hudson Printers, Westborough, Massachusetts, USA 1970.

Warburton, B. A., and Hamblen, M.: The World of Irises. The American Iris Society/Wichita, Kansas, Publisher's Press, Salt Lake City, Utah, USA 1978

Wendelbo, Per: Tulips and Irisis of Iran. Botanical Institute of Iran, Botanischer Garten Teheran, Iran 1977.

Werckmeister, P.: Catalogus Iridis (names and synonyms of the genus *Iris*), yearbook II. Part of the Deutsche Iris- und Liliengesellschaft e. V., Leonberg/Stuttgart (published privately). Now Gesellschaft der Staudenfreunde.

The Iris Yearbooks and other publications of the British Iris Society.

Zander, Handwörterbuch der Pflanzennamen. Neubearbeitet von F. Encke, G. Buchheim und S. Seybold. Verlag Eugen Ulmer, Stuttgart 1980, 12. Auflage.

von Zeppelin, Gräfin: Kataloge der Staudengärrtnerei.

Glossary

People who love iris, especially those who have become real experts, often have to use specialized botanical terms. Those who want to go deeper into the subject should familiarize themselves with some of the more important of these terms and definitions. They don't all appear in the text of this book, but they are listed here in the interest of offering a more complete picture. A great many of them come from English.

Allele = Matching genes from two sets of chromosomes are called alleles (Gegengene). They are localized in precisely corresponding places of homologous chromosomes in a diploid set. With respect to this pair of alleles, if they are identical, the organism is a homozygote; if they are different, it is a heterozygote.

Amoena = Iris having white or nearly white standards, with falls of a contrasting color, usually blue, purple, or brown, and in some cases with a narrow, white margin.

Amphidiploidism = A fusion of diploid sets of chromosomes from both parents by crossing two different species.

Anabiosis = State of latent life; surviving unfavorable circumstances (e.g. drying, freezing); reduction of viability to a minimum. Revival when circumstances are favorable again.

Anhydrobiosis = Dry state; seed dries until it reaches the minimum point at which it can still sustain life.

Anthers = Part of the stamen that contains pollen in blooming plants.

Anthesis = Developmental phase of flower from end of budding stage until it begins to wither.

Aril = Cream-white, collar-shaped growth on the micropyle of the seed of various iris.

Arils = Regelia and Oncocyclus Iris and their hybrids that have an aril on the seed.

Autotetraploid plants = Tetraploid plants in which each of the 4 sets of chromosomes is equivalent to the other. Opposite of allotetraploid plants, in which all 4 sets are different. If 2 and 2 are alike, we speak of plants as amphidiploids.

Beard = Typical feature of Pogon Iris (Bearded Iris). Usually a strikingly colored tongue of short hair on the falls.

Bicolor = Standards and falls are different colors, the falls usually being darker.

Bipolarity = In this special instance, an embryo is adapted to feed from the substrate of inorganic nutrients with its root and from its own endosperm with its cotyledon.

Bitone = Standards and falls have different shades of the same color.

Blade, Leaf blade, Lamina = The broad, usually flat part of the leaf.

Blend = All the undefinable color mixtures from yellow and violet pigments that are otherwise difficult to classify.

Bract = Leaf in whose axil a lateral shoot or blossom develops.

C. G. W. = Abbreviation for C. G. White Arilbred.

Callus = Tissue excrescence at site of incursion, very prone to develop on cambium (e.g. callous tissue on cuttings).

Chromosomes = Highly stainable structures ("nuclear loops") in the cell nucleus of plants, animals, and humans. They are the carriers of hereditary material.

Clone = Plants propagated by vegetative means, to obtain the typical characteristics of the original plant without any changes.

Crests = Arms of triple-forked style, usually broadened out like petals. Often paler or darker or differently colored than the falls, resulting in attractive color combinations. Also called stigma branches or stalks.

Delayed germination = Late germination caused by inability of seed coat to swell properly or by unfavorable germinating conditions; also "endogenic" caused by inhibitors.

Diakinesis = End of the prophase in meiosis. Spiralization of paired chromosomes completed (occurrence of fibrous spindle).

Diploid (Diploidism) = A doubled (i.e. complete) set of hereditary material is present in cell nucleus, one from the maternal side and one from the paternal side. Most, but not all wild iris are diploids. The old, small-blossomed Bearded Iris still seen in many gardens are, for example, diploid.

Diploid phase = Phase within the generation cycle from fertilized egg (zygote with two sets of chromosomes) to reduction division (meiosis).

Disc = Outer, round, oval, or oblong-ovate part of the falls, also known as blade.

Dome = Formed from the three inner perigone leaves (standards), usually upright and compact, but also often short, stunted, and curved outward.

Embryo culture = The embryo from the embryo axis, radical, and cotyledons is separated from the surrounding endosperm, and cultivation continues on an artificial culture medium.

Endemic = Occurrence of a species in a specific, narrowly defined area.

Endosperm = Nourishment for the embryo in the embryo sac of blooming plants.

Epidermis = Upper layer of skin; outer, usually unicellular layer of tissue.

Eupogon = True Bearded Iris.

Falls = The three outer perigone leaves of iris blossoms. This designation shouldn't be taken literally, as the falls often stand out horizontally, especially those of modern hybrids. Landing pad for insects.

Flaring = Projection of the outer perigone leaves (falls).

Fol. var. = Plant with variegated leaves. More recent way of writing it = variegata, especially in the case of hybrids. Botanically correct: var. foliis variegatis.

Forma (f) = Form in the botanical (taxonomic) sense.

Frilled = Delicately waved, said of the margins of petals, especially of modern Tall Bearded Iris hybrids.

Gametes = Male and female germ cells with haploid (simple) sets of chromosomes, which join to form a zygote at fertilization.

Generative reproduction = Propagation by sexual means.

Genes = Hereditary factors or hereditary traits.

Genus = Group of species, which share many characteristics. Plant systematics is still very much in flux. Based on new information about existing systematic groups, split-offs have been made and new independent units have been formed (e.g., Prof. Rodionenko split Juno, Iridodictyum and Xyphium from the genus *Iris* to form their own genera).

Haft = Inner part of the falls, next to the dome, usually quite narrow. Also known as the base of the falls.

Haploid (haploidism) = A simple set of hereditary traits is present in the nucleus of the cell.

Heterozygous = Designation for individuals with recessive genes for characteristics.

Homozygous = Individuals having two identical genes for characteristics.

Induction = Initiation of any developmental process in an organism.

Inflorescence = In the development of flowers, the state of blossoming of the part of the stem for that purpose, separated from the vegetative part of the plant by variant foliation.

Inner perigone leaves = Standards.

Intermedia = Former term for hybrids whose size and blooming period falls between Dwarf and Tall Bearded Iris. Official name = Iris Barbata Media.

Intersterility = Sterility in a cross or of a group. Infertility between varieties despite normal formation of the germ cells.

Lilliput = Small Bearded Iris up to a height of 25 cm. Technically, Lilliputs are only crosses between *Iris pumila* and Tall bearded Iris. But the term is being used more and more for all dwarfs.

Local form = Local modification. Variations from the type caused by external circumstances, in part hereditary, and sometimes lasting only as long as the external circumstances exist. Here we are only interested in types with hereditary variations.

Lumen = Space inside the cell.

Meiosis = Maturation division or reduction division. The doubled (diploid) set of chromosomes is reduced to the single (haploid) set of chromosomes in two sequential nuclear divisions. Four haploid daughter cells develop from a diploid cell.

Mesophyll = Basic tissue or parenchyma of the leaf.

Metaphase = Second phase of nuclear and cell division (mitosis), during which the chromosomes in the middle of the cell (central spindle) arrange themselves along the equatorial plate.

Micropyle = Small entrance to the inner part of the ovule, through which the pollen grains can make their way to the nucleus of the ovule (nucellus).

Mirror = White or off-white zone found on the falls of various varieties.

Mitosis = Nuclear and cell division, in which the mother cell splits into two daughter cells, whose nuclei each contain the same set of chromosomes as the mother cell.

Mutation = Spontaneous appearance of inherited variation of individual characteristics.

Natural hybrid = Result of cross between two different species in the wild.

Neglecta = Special name for Tall Bearded Iris hybrids, in which the standards are light blue and the falls darker blue.

Onco = Common abbreviation for Oncocyclus Iris.

Oncobred = Term used to designate crosses between Tall Bearded Iris and Oncocyclus Iris.

Onco spot = Typical sap mark on the falls

below the beard on Oncocyclus Iris.

Oncopumila = Crosses between *Iris pumila* and Oncocyclus Iris.

Oncoregelia = Same as Regeliocyclus (also Regeliacyclus). Crosses between Oncocylus and Regelia Iris. As is the case with all of these combined terms, the pod parent precedes the pollen parent.

Outer perigone leaves = Falls.

Papillae = Short, conical protrusions of the epidermal cells.

Parenchyma = Essential or packing tissue. Parenchyma consists mostly of isodiametric (isolation and storage tissue), barely differentiated cells.

Perianth tube = Tube-shaped lower part of the blossom. Also often called the perigone tube.

Perigone = Floral envelope, whose members are fundamentally identical, hence not jointed in the throat and crown. The floral envelope of Iris is a perigone.

Perigone tube = See perianth tube.

pH value = Indicates the concentration of hydrogen ions in an aqueous solution. The scale runs from 0 to 14. Seven is neutral, lower is acid, higher basic (alkaline). In gardening, it often depends on what is known as the soil reaction.

Plastids = Plasma organelles in plant cells, which normally form fat-soluble pigments. Among them are chloroplasts, chromoplasts, and leukoplasts, which carry out such important functions such as photosynthesis, pigmentation, and storage of starch.

Plicata = Bearded Iris varieties, the interior of whose petals are light colored. Dark-colored dots and dashes appear toward the exterior, condensing at the margins and following the vascular system (more detailed explanation in the text).

Pogocyclus = Crosses between Tall Bearded Iris and Oncocyclus Iris.

Pogoregelis = Crosses between Tall Bearded Iris and Regelia Iris.

Pogoregeliocyclus = Crosses between Tall Bearded Iris and Regeliocyclus Iris.

Pollination = In crossbreeding, application of pollen to the stigmas of the same or another blossom.

Polyploidism = Multiplication of chromosomes in a cell. Most cultivated plants are polyploids. Polyploiding is artificial, e.g. by means of colchicine treatment, Kaltestrahlen, x-rays, etc.

Regeliocyclus = Crosses between Regelia and Oncocyclus Iris.

Sap mark = Striking, usually darker-colored spot on the falls. Lure for insects. Called Onco spot on Oncocyclus Iris.

Spathe valves = The leaves enclosing the bud. The most important diagnostic tool for differentiating iris species. During the blooming period the spathes can be either partially or completely herbaceous or papery. One of the two iris spathes can be larger than the other or have a different shape.

Species = Some iris enthusiasts incorrectly call all Iris hybrids (except Pogon Iris) species.

Spot = Eye or area of contrasting color on the falls. In the case of *Iris pumila,* often seen in natural forms and transmitted to many of its hybrids.

Stem leaves = Leaves on the stem, as opposed to basal leaves.

Sterile = Infertile; germ-free.

Sterility = Infertility (in plants).

Stigma stalks = See crests.

Stolons = Runners, e.g. found on Regelia Iris.

Substance = Important characteristic of modern hybrids. Indicates the firmness and strength of the petals. Good substance is important for blossom durability, expecially in rain or inclement weather.

Synonym = Another botanical name (secondary name) for a plant aside from the officially recognized one.

Tepals = The identical petals of a perigone.

Terminal = Apical, borne at the tip.

Tetraploid = Plants or animals with four sets of chromosomes. Iris which, by nature or through special treatment by breeders, have four sets of chromosomes instead of two. All our modern Tall Bearded Iris are tetraploid. They developed from interbreeding between Near Eastern tetraploid species. Tetraploid Iris have larger blossoms and usually better substance. The other parts of the plant are usually stronger too.

Tonoplast = Inner layer of plasma, which separates the protoplasts from the vacuoles.

Triploid = Organisms containing triple set of chromosomes of the haploid germ cell. Their gametes have three; i.e., more than two, sets of chromosomes, which partly accounts for sterile pollen.

Vacuoles = Spaces in cell sap.

Variegata = A Tall bearded Iris with yellow standards and brown, reddish, or purple falls.

Variegated = Leaves have two or more colors (e.g., with irregular yellowish- or cream-colored stripes).

Varietas (var.) = Variety in the botanical (taxonomic) sense.

Vegetative propagation = Asexual reproduction.

Picture sources

Franz Kurzmann, Baden bei Wien: p. 18 lower right.

Erich Pasche, Jr., Velbert: p. 144 upper right, p. 180 lower right, p. 268 upper right.

Sebastian Seidl, Botanischer Garten München: p. 18 upper and lower left, p. 35 above, p. 89 upper left and right, center left, lower left, p. 107 below, p. 144 below, p. 161 all three, p. 162 all three, p. 180 lower left, p. 197 upper left and below, p. 198 below, p. 208 center left, lower left, p. 218 upper left, p. 237 upper right, p. 247 below, p. 267 lower right, p. 269 below.

The colored pictures on pages 277, 278, 287, 288, 298, 307, 308, 317, 318, 327, and 328 were made available to us by the CILAG AG, Schaffhausen. Photographs by U. Leibacher, Lohningen, from the author's garden.

The other 105 colored photographs belong to the author, including the photograph on the jacket, depicting the Spuria hybrid 'Premier'—bred as early as 1899, but still modern looking.

Drawings by Marlene Gemke after the author's sketches, based partly on depictions from older publications.

Index to Plant Names

An asterisk (*) after a page number
indicates photo or illustration.